FROM RECLAMATION
TO SUSTAINABILITY

FROM RECLAMATION
TO SUSTAINABILITY

WATER, AGRICULTURE, AND THE
ENVIRONMENT IN THE AMERICAN WEST

LAWRENCE J. MACDONNELL

IN COOPERATION WITH
THE NATURAL RESOURCES LAW CENTER

UNIVERSITY PRESS OF COLORADO

Copyright © 1999 by Lawrence J. MacDonnell
International Standard Book Number 0-87081-533-4

Published by the University Press of Colorado
P.O. Box 849
Niwot, Colorado 80544

The University Press of Colorado is a cooperative publishing enterprise
supported, in part, by Adams State College, Colorado State University, Fort
Lewis College, Mesa State College, Metropolitan State College of Denver,
University of Colorado, University of Northern Colorado, University of
Southern Colorado, and Western State College of Colorado.

The paper used in this publication meets the minimum requirements of the
American National Standard for Information Sciences–Permanence of
Paper for Printed Library Materials. ANSI Z39.48-1984.

Library of Congress Cataloging-in-Publication Data

MacDonnell, Lawrence J.
    From reclamation to sustainability : water, agriculture, and the
environment in the American West / Lawrence J. MacDonnell.
        p.   cm.
    "In cooperation with the Natural Resources Law Center."
    Includes bibliographical references and index.
    ISBN 0-87081-533-4 (hc. : alk. paper)
    1. Water-supply–Economic aspects–West (U.S.)–History.
2. Reclamation of land–West (U.S.)–History. 3. Irrigation–
Environmental aspects–West (U.S.)–History. 4. Sustainable
agriculture–West (U.S.)–History. I. University of Colorado.
Boulder. Natural Resources Law Center. II. Title.
HD1695.W4M33 19999
333.91'00978–dc21   99-21012
                                                                    CIP

08 07 06 05 04 03 02 01 00 99   10 9 8 7 6 5 4 3 2 1

Contents

List of Figures   vii

Preface   ix

Introduction: Living in a Land of Limited Water   1

Part 1. The Lower Arkansas Valley: After the Water is Gone   11

    Chapter 1. Colorado's Arkansas River   13

    Chapter 2. Watering and Cultivating the Prairie   23

    Chapter 3. Stretching a Limited Water Supply   35

    Chapter 4. Irrigation Water for Sale?   51

    Chapter 5. A Hostile Takeover?   61

    Chapter 6. Looking Ahead   75

Part 2. The Grand Valley, Colorado: Where Fruit, Fish,   87
    and Growth Collide

    Chapter 7. Growing Peaches in an Arid Mountain Valley   89

    Chapter 8. The Problem of Salt   109

    Chapter 9. Competition From Across the Divide and   115
    Closer to Home

    Chapter 10. Water for Native Fish   119

    Chapter 11. The Promise—and Problems—of Water   127
    Conservation

Part 3. The Truckee and Carson Basins: Sharing Water   135
    in a Desert

    Chapter 12. Life in a Land in Between   137

    Chapter 13. Redeeming the "Irredeemable"   143

    Chapter 14. An Environmental Reckoning   153

    Chapter 15. The Ongoing Search for Redemption   159

    Chapter 16. What Happens to Irrigation?   167

    Chapter 17. What Next?   171

Part 4. The Yakima Basin, Washington: Making the 179
    "Old West" Work

    Chapter 18. The Place   181
    Chapter 19. The First People   185
    Chapter 20. Reclamation in the Yakima   189
    Chapter 21. A Tale of Two Irrigation Districts   199
    Chapter 22. Adjudicating Water Rights   205
    Chapter 23. The Salmon   209
    Chapter 24. Taking Stock   219

Part 5. From Reclamation to Sustainability   229

    Chapter 25. From Reclamation to Sustainability   231
    Chapter 26. Reducing the Gap Between Diversion   239
        and Consumption
    Chapter 27. Allowing Our Rivers to Function Like Rivers   247
    Chapter 28. Water That Changes Use to Meet Demand   257
    Chapter 29. Getting There   265

Epilogue: A Faustian Bargain?   287
Notes   295
Index   367

Figures

1.1	The Arkansas River Basin, Colorado	12
1.2	Site of the Sand Creek Massacre	21
2.1	Colorado irrigation canals started by T. C. Henry, 1883–1892	28
2.2	Typical Twin Lakes Land and Water Company Advertisement	33
3.1	John Martin Dam and Reservoir	39
3.2	Carl Genova setting gated pipe	46
3.3	Retention pond for return water	47
3.4	Extension Service Agent Jim Valliant explaining surge irrigation demonstration project	48
4.1	Downtown Ordway	57
4.2	Side oats–a native grass	58
5.1	Saline soils in the Lower Arkansas Valley	68
6.1	Frank Milenski at the Catlin Canal Diversion Dam	79
6.2	Sunset at Nee Noshe Reservoir	84
7.1	The Grand Valley, Colorado	90
7.2	The Grand Valley Region	91
7.3	Book Cliffs as seen from Orchard Mesa	92
7.4	View of Grand Valley lands prior to the Grand Valley Project	96
7.5	Waiting for project water in the Grand Valley, 1913	97
7.6	The Roller Dam on the Colorado River	98
7.7	Irrigating oats with water from the Grand Valley Project, 1917	100
7.8	Talbott Farms on Orchard Mesa	104
7.9	Packing peaches at Talbott's Plant	105
9.1	The Colorado River Basin	114
10.1	A Colorado pikeminnow caught in the Yampa River, 1935	120
11.1	May 1947: Kenneth Matchett uses siphons to irrigate on his farm near Grand Junction, Colorado	128

12.1 Truckee-Carson Basin   138
12.2 Pyramid Lake   139
13.1 Homesteading along the Carson River, 1908   145
13.2 The Carson Desert prior to irrigation, 1911   146
13.3 Building the Truckee Canal to carry water to the Carson 146
     Watershed, 1905
13.4 The dedication of Derby Dam, 1905   147
13.5 Lahontan Dam, 1912   148
13.6 Truckee Canal emptying into Lahontan Reservoir   149
13.7 Flood irrigating alfalfa, 1908   150
14.1 Historical Pyramid Lake Levels   155
15.1 Measuring cui-uis at Marble Bluff Dam   161
18.1 Yakima River Basin   180
18.2 Espresso stand in Ellensburg   182
19.1 Tribal fishing platforms in the Yakima River   186
20.1 Yakima Project Map   193
20.2 Building the Tieton Dam, 1915   194
20.3 Building the Tieton Canal to carry water to the Naches   195
     Watershed, 1916
20.4 Camp at Keechelus Dam Site, 1913   196
20.5 Pulling stumps to build dam at Keechelus near head-   197
     waters of the Yakima River, 1913
20.6 Cle Elum Reservoir in the headwaters of the Yakima   198
     River
21.1 The Sunnyside Canal   200
23.1 Chinook salmon life cycle   210
23.2 Fish passageway at Roza Diversion Dam   212
24.1 Yakima Project office   220
31.1 Orchard Mesa Check Dam   324

Preface

Like many in the West today, I am a transplanted easterner. I moved to Denver from Michigan in 1967, courtesy of the U.S. Air Force. What kept me in Colorado after the Air Force was the mountains. In my early years in Colorado I went to those mountains whenever I had time. I backpacked, climbed, skied, and fished, finding places of true magic that satisfied my deepest passions. The West to me in those years *was* those mountains.

Much as I loved the mountain West, I realized that I was vaguely uncomfortable with other aspects of the region. Beginning with Denver, the cities seemed remarkably characterless. Perhaps because there was so much beauty such a short distance away, it seemed people in the West didn't care much what their cities looked like. Much of the urban growth in Denver and other western cities occurred after World War II, in an era in which the automobile encouraged people to spread out. Urban cores might still serve as business centers, but no one lived there, fewer and fewer shopped there, and not many recreated there. Instead, people retreated to their suburban homes and adjacent shopping centers.

Except in the mountains, most western rivers and streams seemed insignificant compared with rivers I had known in the East. The South Platte River running through Denver, and the Rio Grande passing through Albuquerque, hardly matched the image of rivers upon which great cities are supposed to be built. In the late summer and early fall, these and other western rivers seemed almost to disappear.

And then there were the vast areas of the West that I merely passed through on my way to other mountains or cities. These were places with no rivers and very little rain. To me they appeared harsh, barren, uninviting. Judging from the few people living in such places, I assumed others felt pretty much the same way I did. Yes, these places were *in* the West, but they weren't *my* West.

Yet the more I traveled, the more I realized that such areas in fact made up far more of the region than did my mountains. Those clear blue skies that I loved, I came to understand, meant that little of the West's water came from rainfall. Those gray, overcast skies I knew so well and disliked so much growing up in the East took on a new meaning. When I had moved to the West, one of the exchanges I had made was blue sky for natural vegetation.

Slowly, gradually, I started to discover other parts of the West—first in the extraordinary desert canyons of the Colorado Plateau, then in the pinyon-juniper country at the transition between mountains and valleys, next in the short-grass prairies. Still, at first, I was drawn to those special places where there was water—springs emerging mysteriously from a cliff side, sandstone potholes sometimes filled with water by rain and melting snow, wetland areas fed by a hidden source of underground water, occasional flows in otherwise ephemeral streams. Even so, my West had now grown substantially.

I became aware of the oasislike quality of urban areas in the West. The acres and acres of Kentucky-bluegrass lawns carpeting Denver and its suburbs grew only because they were sprinkled throughout the summer with large quantities of water. Cut off that water supply, and those dark-green grasses would be brown in two weeks. The large, beautiful elm trees that lined residential streets in older parts of the city had been nurtured into life decades ago with regular feedings of water. In the 1960s the loss of the trees, highly susceptible to disease, had caused noticeable gaps in the urban landscape that were not readily replaced. Intensive watering of introduced vegetation in places like Denver, I was told, had produced microclimates with higher relative humidity than would otherwise exist.

I thought little about where that water came from. I gradually learned that western cities often constructed extensive (and expensive) systems for capturing and transporting water—sometimes moving that water hundreds of miles, even through mountains (I vaguely understood, for example, that Denver got an important part of its water supply from the Colorado River Basin, across the Continental Divide). I came to understand that this water supply depended on dams—structures of concrete, rock, or earth that held back the flows of rivers in reservoirs. I saw such reservoirs everywhere I went, and sometimes I used them for swimming or sailing. For about four years I lived in a house supplied with water from a well 120 feet deep. Twice the well "ran dry" for short periods–that is, we had to stop using the pump for several hours to allow enough water to build up. It was inconvenient, but nothing more. For the most part I lived in places where there was always water when I turned on the tap or the shower. And if I thought about the cost of that water, it was probably to think how cheap it was (as I came to learn, less expensive than water in the well-watered East).

In the early 1980s my work caused me to start thinking about water in other ways. I came to the University of Colorado at Boulder to be the first director of the Natural Resources Law Center in 1983. The Center had been officially created the year before, a formalization of efforts already under way involving several members of the law school faculty–particularly David Getches. David, together with Jim Corbridge, Steve Williams, and then Charles Wilkinson, had started an annual conference at the law school in 1980 on topics of natural resources law and policy. Water was a subject of particular interest, and the center took on the responsibility of organizing and presenting a three-day conference each June on issues of water law and policy in the West. I needed to learn more about water law than I remembered from my one law school class more than ten years earlier. Since 1983 most of my research, writing, and professional work has focused on water-related matters.

~

In 1991, with a grant from the Ford Foundation to the Natural Resources Law Center, I got a chance to look firsthand at irrigated agriculture in parts of the West. Walt Coward, then program officer for Ford's Rural Poverty Program, had spent many years studying the efforts of small farmers in Asian countries to meet their water needs, an experience that had convinced him that the local entities people create to represent their interests are generally effective at achieving their intended objectives.[1] The Natural Resources Law Center had just completed a major study of western water policy, culminating in a book, *Searching Out the Headwaters*.[2] Walt wondered why the organizations representing water users in the West were not taking leadership in making the kinds of policy changes suggested in this study. Many years earlier the center had taken a look at these organizations in a book called *Special Water Districts: Challenge for the Future.*[3] Now we proposed to take on Walt's question through the careful examination of a number of places in the West in which irrigated agriculture is prominent and exercises control of much of the available water.

After a good deal of looking around, we settled on four places. I chose the Grand Valley of Colorado and the Lower Arkansas River Valley in Colorado. Teresa Rice decided to look at the Boise Valley of Idaho while helping me in the Grand and Arkansas valleys. And Sarah Bates (now Van deWetering) selected the Verde Valley of Arizona. We put much of our effort into studying the array of irrigation water supply organizations providing water to agricultural users in these areas–their legal structures, their physical diversion and delivery systems, their water rights, the arrangements under which they supplied water to irrigators. We met many of their managers and members of their boards of directors. We prepared case studies of the Grand Valley and the Verde. Based on this work, my conclusions were that such organizations generally do a good job of serving the traditional water-supply needs of their members, but that they have not expanded their focus to include newer concerns such as growing urbanization, water efficiency, water transfers, water quality, or endangered species. They are involved in these issues to the degree that the issues directly affect their water-supply function, but largely in a reactive or defensive mode, not as problem solvers. In general, they are not likely to be key participants in the challenging process of incorporating changing values into the use, management, and protection of western rivers and aquifers. Nevertheless, it seemed clear that irrigated agriculture, as the major user of western water resources, needed to play a major role in finding ways to reach such an accommodation. If traditional water supply organizations were not the key, what was?

It occurred to me how little most of us "new westerners" understand about the world of irrigated agriculture. How did agriculture come to be the basis for settlement of a region with inadequate rainfall to grow crops? How was it that irrigation came into control of the lion's share of the West's developed water? Why has it proved to be so difficult to incorporate changing uses and values of water into this system? What are the implications of changing long-established water management and use practices in the West–does the manner in which change happens matter?

So the book we had been planning to write about water-supply organizations became instead a book about irrigated agriculture. After I left the Natural Resources Law Center in 1995, I started working on this new book. First, I drafted a lengthy piece on the Lower Arkansas Valley, into which I placed much of what I had learned about irrigated agriculture during our study of local water-supply organizations. Then I wrote the stories of the Truckee-Carson and the Yakima–both places I had looked at before in connection with changes in their Bureau of Reclamation water projects. Next I wrote the Grand Valley section, using some material drafted previously. Then I turned to policy matters, drafting what is now part 5 of the book. During all this time I kept drafting and redrafting what is now the book's introduction as I became more focused on the book's purpose.

In a process that now covers more than eight years, it is impossible to acknowledge all the people who have helped me along the way. For example, during the original case-study work many law school student research assistants provided valuable help. Teresa Rice accompanied me on most of the field visits to the Lower Arkansas and Grand Valley and helped with the research for these areas. Anne Drew with the Natural Resources Law Center laboriously transcribed many hours of tape-recorded interviews. We met with many, many more people during the field work than are reflected in this book. I learned from them all.

I imposed very rough early drafts on several good friends who offered both condolences and support. Sarah Van deWetering provided especially valuable editorial review that helped me organize my chaotic early drafts into more logical and readable form. Don Glaser offered helpful observations throughout the manuscript, but especially in the policy chapters. Charles Wilkinson provided advice and encouragement at several points during the process. Robert

Glennon got roped into reviewing the manuscript and shared his insights with me. A. Lee Brown helped me turn a rambling prologue into a more focused introduction. Gabe Carter researched and drafted text for many of the endnotes. Finally, Len Ackland and I shared many hours commiserating (over beers) about the struggles of writing a book.

I thank them all.

FROM RECLAMATION
TO SUSTAINABILITY

Introduction
LIVING IN A LAND OF LIMITED WATER

The American West, despite its unlikely status as the most urbanized region of the country,[1] exists largely between its cities. Here are those distinctive features that most characterize the region: vast open landscapes offering vistas largely unobscured by native vegetation; the earth's crust on display as mountainous uplifts, canyons, arroyos, deserts; bright sunlight in an azure sky. This is the native West—a product of its geology and its aridity.

It is a region that does not readily welcome large-scale human inhabitation. Not only is its rainfall generally inadequate to grow crops, its rivers, lakes, and other permanent sources of water are few in number, small in size, and highly variable in volume compared with the eastern states. Vast areas, including the Great Plains, the Great Basin, and the desert Southwest, are largely devoid of trees. Its numerous, generally north-south-trending mountain ranges present formidable obstacles to travel. Its climate, with its propensity for extremes and its unpredictable changeability, poses hazards for the unprepared.

The lure of mineral wealth brought the first massive wave of in-migration to the American West, but agriculture—including livestock production—made it possible for people to settle and stay. The idea that agriculture would be the basis for settlement and development of a region so apparently unsuited for this use seemed unlikely to those first to come from the eastern United States and from northern Europe. By the late 1800s, however, when the many mining booms had gone bust, that was exactly the conclusion most western promoters had reached. After all, if there was one thing the West had in abundance, it was land–much of it still unowned. Barren as much of the land seemed to most new arrivals, it proved to be surprisingly suitable for growing crops–as long as sufficient water could be artificially supplied in place of rain.[2]

Irrigation seemed almost miraculous in its ability to transform desert into oasis.[3] The Reclamation Act of 1902, setting out a bold national program supporting settlement of the American West, made federally supported projects providing water for irrigated agriculture its centerpiece.

Irrigated agriculture still makes a highly visible human imprint on the West-between-its-cities. Fly over almost any part of the continental United States west of the ninety-eighth meridian, particularly in the summertime, and you will see its distinctive patterns. In the Great Plains–the states of Nebraska, Kansas, Texas, and eastern Colorado–the patterns are green circles: crops irrigated with groundwater by a sprinkler system that pivots around a central well. In the river valleys of the Intermountain and Great Basin West the patterns are rectangles within green ribbons or bands paralleling rivers and streams: crops irrigated with water brought by networks of ditches. Green is divided from upland brown by a line whose contours match that of the country through which it traverses, marking the location of the "highline" ditch. On the rivers themselves you notice places where they widen and seem to become lakes. These are reservoirs where the flows are captured and stored for release and use during the hot, dry summer months.

Enormous amounts of water are captured behind storage dams, diverted out of rivers and streams, and withdrawn from aquifers in the American West.[4] Consider the unit of measurement in which western water uses are described: the acre-foot. An acre-foot of water describes an amount that would cover an acre of ground (43,500 square feet–roughly the size of a football field) to a depth of one foot. Most of us are accustomed to measuring water in cups or quarts or gallons. Individually, we consume about two gallons of water a day for our direct human needs. *One* acre-foot is the equivalent of *325,851* gallons of water.

Consider also that farmers and ranchers took about 140 *million* acre-feet of water from streams and aquifers in the western states in 1990 for irrigation use—more than 45.6 *trillion* gallons of water. This water was used on about 46 million acres of cropland, an average of about three feet of water diverted for every acre of land irrigated. This is water applied in addition to precipitation from rain or snow. Three feet of water for every acre of land. Nearly a *million* gallons of water *per acre*. Roughly another 40 million acre-feet came from streams and aquifers to supply other human uses.

Irrigated agriculture remains one of the key components of the West's economy.[5] In general, much higher-value crops are grown on irrigated lands than on drylands, and the value of irrigated lands is higher than that of drylands.[6] Nevertheless, there is a sense today that irrigation's transformation of what in fact is only 3 percent of the land area of the West[7] is ephemeral: in writer Sam Bingham's image, nothing more than a layer of green makeup on a permanently brown face, a thin veneer that would disappear quickly if it weren't assiduously reapplied every year with trillions of gallons of water.[8]

Irrigated agriculture is part of the "old" West, the extractive West, the West of mining, timbering, and livestock grazing. It is a West in which people struggled to overcome those features that seemed to limit its habitability while exploiting those features that provided a living.[9] It is remarkable that such a place is now the fastest-growing region of the country. In its seventeen-state region live nearly a third of the nation's population, with another 28 million residents projected by 2025.[10] It is the location of nine of the ten fastest-growing states and eight of the ten fastest-growing cities in the country.[11]

There have been other periods of rapid growth in the West. A distinguishing feature of the present period's growth, however, is that it is driven at least as much by the attractions of the native West as by the region's economic opportunities. Indeed, the very qualities that once made this region seem inhospitable now are among its major draws. To westerners today aridity means the comfort of low humidity. It means cloudless blue skies and hundred-mile vistas. Once-fearsome mountains have turned into winter and summer playgrounds. Deserts offer wintertime warmth (while air-conditioning makes summertime tolerable). Instead of isolation, open spaces offer relief from congestion.

The native West no longer seems to limit human occupancy. Large-scale development of western rivers and aquifers makes water readily available for human use. With irrigation people can grow cotton, rice, Kentucky bluegrass, roses, and just about any other kind of vegetation they want. Western distances have faded in significance with the advent of interstate highways, airplanes, and the Internet. With all the standard accoutrements of modern human life available, and with an economy offering an array of opportunities, the "new" West is no longer only for the adventuresome.[12]

~

If, as Wallace Stegner has suggested, aridity is the single most important defining characteristic of the West,[13] then a careful examination of human use of its limited water resources should reveal much about this region and its people. Thus, books such as Marc Reisner's *Cadillac Desert*, Philip Fradkin's *A River No More*, Donald Worster's *Rivers of Empire*, William Kahrl's *Water and Power*, and Russell Martin's *A Story That Stands Like a Dam*[14] tell of the development of the West through the development of its water. In compelling prose they paint vivid portraits of the human will to overcome perceived limitations of life in a land with limited water. Books such as Wallace Stegner's *Beyond the Hundredth Meridian* and *Angle of Repose*, Mary Austin's *The Land of Little Rain*, Marie Sandoz's *Old Jules*, Stanley Crawford's *Mayordomo*, William deBuys and Alex Harris's *River of Traps*, Arthur Maass and Raymond Anderson's *. . . And the Desert Shall Rejoice*, and Charles Wilkinson's *Crossing the Next Meridian*[15] offer a deeper sense of place and of people than of politics and power. They serve as wonderful guides to another West, a place where people struggle mightily—and not always successfully—with the challenge of living with limited water.

Still, I thought there was room for another book. I had started with an interest in the organizations that controlled so much of the West's water—ditch companies, irrigation districts, and the like. I soon realized that these organizations were just extensions of their users, and that the subject of my investigation was people, not institutions.

In particular, it was the people who had chosen to farm in the arid West using irrigation.

The vehicle for my investigation was an immersion into four places I had known little about: the Lower Arkansas Valley of Colorado, the Grand Valley of Colorado, the Truckee-Carson Basin of California and Nevada, and the Yakima Basin of Washington. Over several years I spent weeks in these places, driving roads and byways, meeting residents, learning about their history, their present, and their hopes and concerns. I spent most of my time learning about irrigated agriculture, since I had known little about this world before.

Along the way I met some extraordinary people who shared generously of their time, patiently explained their farming and irrigation practices as we drove in their pickup trucks and walked along their ditches, brought me into their homes and talked about their personal lives and their hopes for their children and grandchildren. Through these experiences I began to understand why people *wanted* to live in these places, why many–perhaps most–would not live anywhere else or do anything else but farm. I grew accustomed to that pervasive pessimism for which farmers are so well-known. Things were never "good," but some years might be better than others. Over and over again I heard people wondering why they were not better appreciated for producing the world's best and lowest-cost food supply. These, I realized, are people *proud* of what they are doing and genuinely puzzled by what they perceive to be a pervasive antifarming bias among many urban people.

I chose these places because they have the good fortune to have a permanent source of water, however modest. They are places in which irrigated agriculture became the basis of settlement in the late 1800s. They are places in which individual and collective efforts first captured rivers for irrigation, efforts later considerably expanded by federal water projects. They are places in which irrigation water use remains dominant today.

They also are places that have changed as the West has changed. Most noticeably, they have urbanized. Residential and commercial development extends onto formerly irrigated lands. Highways cut through agricultural areas, bringing with them more residential and commercial development. Ditch systems passing through now-urbanized areas are regarded as hazardous playgrounds for children.

In these urbanized areas live people more and more separated from the old West, the West of irrigated agriculture. Many are people like me, transplanted easterners drawn primarily by the physical beauty of the native West. We know (and probably care) little or nothing about irrigated agriculture. We see little evidence of the harsh limitations that faced early western settlers. We are offended by the unsightliness of the extractive West—mine tailings in mineralized mountainous areas, clear-cut hillsides, dewatered rivers and streams. We value our recreational time greatly and are rapidly expanding our recreational demands on the lands and waters of the West. We value natural ecological processes and the intricate webs of life they support.

The stories in this book explore the implications of an increasingly urban-centered West for the West of irrigated agriculture. They bring home the divergence of perspectives about water: how traditional westerners tend to view water as an integral part of their lives, as something upon which their lives and livelihoods depend, as something that not only *can* be used but *must* be used, whereas new westerners like me are more likely to view water as a convenience and an amenity, something valued primarily in noneconomic terms.

This dichotomy in views about water is no small matter. For at least one hundred years, white westerners shared a more or less common understanding about the roles water was to serve: meeting basic human needs and providing economic benefits. Based on this understanding, the shared priority was to "develop" water—that is, to make it physically and economically usable. People disagreed about who actually got to use the water, but few questioned that human use was its primary purpose.

For people whose way of life depends on being able to continue to use water—*lots* of water—it sounds threatening to hear talk about what a big mistake it is to have dams, about how water should stay in streams rather than be diverted for irrigation, about how water should be "reallocated" from irrigation to other uses, about how irrigators are wasting and polluting water. The considerable attention now being given to the "new" West—urban centered and high-tech—makes these people part of the "old" and perhaps "expendable" West. They are convinced that the water needs for this new West—for its unending urban growth, its recreational and even aesthetic interests, its environmental concerns—will come from *their* water.

The seeming intractability of some contemporary water conflicts came home to me on a trip to the Rio Grande downstream of Albuquerque, New Mexico, in the spring of 1996. I stood at the San Acacia Diversion Dam, where the Middle Rio Grande Conservancy District diverts water into its Socorro Main Canal for delivery to irrigators within the district. Two weeks earlier the district had closed the dam's gates, blocking virtually all of the river's flow at that point. An unusual snowless winter in the San Juan Mountains of Colorado, where the Rio Grande originates, reduced springtime flows in the river to only 20 percent of normal. Farmers in this Socorro portion of the district needed, they believed, all of the water available in the river to bring their crops to life. The state water right under which the district diverts water at San Acacia authorizes the diversion of all river flows if necessary.

A week after the district closed the San Acacia gates (the week before I was there), state and federal wildlife officials found more than one thousand dead Rio Grande silvery minnows in isolated pools downstream of the dam. This three-inch-long fish is listed as an endangered species under the federal Endangered Species Act, meaning that U.S. Fish and Wildlife Service biologists believe this species of fish is in imminent danger of extinction. These same biologists estimated in 1994, at the time of the listing, that 70 percent of the known remaining population of this species live in the stretch of the Middle Rio Grande that includes this segment below San Acacia.

Which brings us to the heart of the matter: How do we share what is a highly variable but ultimately fixed amount of water with what seems to be a constantly enlarging set of users? How can the limited water resources of the West do more? When the need was for more economic uses, the answer was more water development—more dams, more wells. Now, when the needs are more complex, when additional water development may well mean unacceptable ecological loss, when out-of-stream uses compete directly with important in-stream values, when—nevertheless—new consumptive demands continue to grow, how can this painfully finite resource satisfy these demands?

The answer suggested in this book is it can't—western water resources cannot satisfy all these demands, not in the manner in which they have been satisfied to this point. Despite all the rhetoric about the importance of water, about how water is the "lifeblood" of the West, we have been remarkably cavalier about its use. Users hold claims to water based on what is the easiest and the cheapest rather than, for example, the most efficient way to use the resource. Our water-allocation system effectively locks uses in place, encouraging users to take every bit of water to which they are legally entitled whether they actually need it or not, insulating them from considering other, potentially more valuable, uses. Generous public subsidies encourage overuse of water by reducing its real cost to the user.

As the stories in this book illustrate, changes are occurring. As always, much of this change simply accompanies larger societal changes. Thus, for example, irrigated farmlands turn into housing developments and water that once grew corn and alfalfa now grows grass. Often, however, changes involving historical water-use practices have come grudgingly and only after much conflict. We are far from agreed as a society about the manner in which this process of change should occur.

~

The following stories are told in somewhat different ways. The first, describing the Lower Arkansas Valley of Colorado, is the longest. It focuses heavily on irrigated agriculture, relaying much that I've learned from site visits, guided tours, and interviews, as well as from historical materials. Irrigated agriculture remains an important part of the other three stories, but additional perspectives are provided—particularly those representing environmental values. In an attempt to make this material as accessible as possible, I have tried to minimize the technical and highly fact-specific discussions that are ultimately an unavoidable part of working in water, and to provide explanations where technical aspects seem necessary. I have attempted to make these places visible and real to the reader, providing maps and photographs to supplement words in some cases.

At base these stories all recount human efforts to live in places of limited water and to benefit from use of this water. They are stories of human effort to make the fullest possible use of those limited water resources through development of rivers and aquifers. They are stories about communities that developed, in part, because of water development and use. They are stories about changes in these communities and the places of which they are a part. They are stories about water-use changes that mirror the larger changes in the West. They are stories about the very difficult and important work of making these water-use changes.

The stories recount human efforts to transform the native West for human benefit. They are tales of hardship, of enormous enterprise and hard work, of both failure and success measured in human terms. They reflect human adaptability as well as the ability of humans to change a place to suit their needs. They suggest that our development and use of water and its sources substantially exceed that which is sustainable. They illustrate the very difficult process of change that is under way: in the way rivers are managed, water is stored and released from dams, hydroelectric facilities are operated, water is diverted from rivers and withdrawn from groundwater aquifers, water is used on lands, in businesses, and in homes, and new water development occurs. They are stories without end, for these efforts continue as human presence in the West grows.

The final part of the book explores the significance of the changing West for its water resources. It characterizes the direction of change as moving from the Reclamation West, with its emphasis on overcoming its physical environment, to what might be called a sustainable West, based on "productive harmony"[16] between people and their environment. It discusses four "directions of change" in the movement toward a sustainable West: reducing the gap between diversion and consumption; restoring rivers; changing water uses; and using watershed-based partnership processes for planning and decision making.

Let's turn first to our stories.

PART 1

THE LOWER ARKANSAS VALLEY
AFTER THE WATER IS GONE

After the water is gone, what do I see?
I see things that are foreign to me.

–Frank Milenski, "After the Water is Gone"

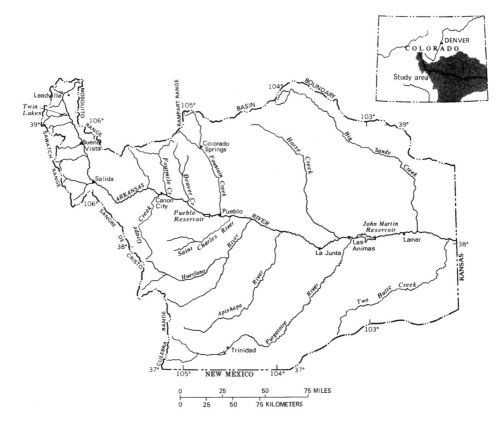

1.1 The Arkansas River Basin, Colorado.

1

COLORADO'S ARKANSAS RIVER

The Arkansas River in Colorado is a modest river, even by western standards. Typical of mountain streams, the flows of water in the Arkansas vary widely. As the snowpack melts in the late spring and early summer, flows increase—sometimes dramatically. In the fall and winter natural flows decrease to just a fraction of the peak flows. The basin's full drainage is about 25,400 square miles, nearly a quarter of the state of Colorado. But the river's annual average yield of water is only about 884,000 acre-feet—only about 6 percent of the water produced annually in the state.[1] A look at a map of the basin explains why (Figure 1.1).

The headwaters of the Arkansas begin high in the central Rockies amid several fourteen-thousand-foot peaks, including Mount Elbert, Colorado's highest. The basin is narrow at this point, like the tail of a dog, pinched between the Sawatch Range to the west and the Mosquito Range to the east. As the river trends generally south out of the headwaters region, past the old mining town of Leadville, it is joined by a few notable streams such as Lake Creek and Clear Creek. Then, blocked by the uplifting of the Sangre de Cristos on the south, the river turns southeast near Salida and then east, descending through a narrow rocky canyon (the spectacular Royal Gorge), emerging near Cañon City and Florence, then flowing east through Pueblo out onto the Colorado plains and into the Lower Arkansas Valley. Although virtually all of the basin's drainage area exists in this lower portion, it is an arid plains region that adds very little water to the river in most years.

To call the lower part of the river basin a "valley" is perhaps misleading, since it is not a distinctively low-lying area bordered on both sides by hills. Rather, it is a valley because a river runs easterly through its lowest point. The land itself is largely flat or gently rolling, revealing the location of the river only by stands of cottonwood trees that grow sporadically along its banks. This is a dry-plains region, west of the ninety-eighth meridian and in the great rain shadow of the Rocky Mountains. It is a short-grass prairie, with little to catch the eye.

Driving east on Highway 50 from Pueblo, you soon leave the city behind and move into rural Colorado. Small to medium-size towns like Fowler, Manzanola, and Rocky Ford appear, but the landscape is largely agricultural. Viewed from above, the Lower Arkansas Valley appears as a narrow band of green paralleling both sides of the river, marking the lands that are irrigated from the many ditches that carry water out of the Arkansas River. If you know the right roads, you can drive down to the river at points where concrete diversion structures channel off some part of the river's flow into the Colorado Canal, the Rocky Ford Highline Canal, the Oxford Farmers' Canal, the Otero Canal, the Catlin Canal, the Rocky Ford Canal, the Fort Lyon Canal, and many others. The ditches on the south side of the road (where the highway runs at this point) cross under the highway as they carry the water of the Arkansas River to the farmlands below. There are no signs, but those who live in the area know the names of the ditches as well or better than the names of the roads that join the highway.

On St. Charles Mesa just east of Pueblo, lands irrigated with water from the Bessemer Ditch raise relatively high-value crops such as corn and onions. But housing subdivisions are competing for use of some of these lands as the city grows to the east. Beyond the mesa to the east, Highway 50 goes through Nepesta, the original Native American name for the Arkansas River, then through the town of Manzanola, so named because of apple orchards that once thrived there. Still farther east, the town of Rocky Ford perhaps feels the most distinctively agricultural of the larger towns along the river. Colorado State University's extension-service office is located in Rocky Ford, as is the U.S. Department of Agriculture's Soil Conservation Service (now the Natural Resources Conservation Service).

Next is La Junta, the county seat of Otero County. Reflecting its origins as a railroad center, it retains a more commercial, less agricultural feel. Across the river and somewhat to the east is a reconstruction of Bent's Fort, a major trading post in the days of the Santa Fe Trail, now operated by the National Park Service.

Another fifty miles east on Highway 50 is Las Animas, the county seat of Bent County. In the early 1870s Las Animas gained prominence for a period as the terminus of the Kansas Pacific Railroad. The Purgatoire River joins the Arkansas just east of Las Animas. Here the Arkansas has been transformed into a large reservoir by the John Martin Dam a few miles downstream. At Las Animas the highway heads north across the river on its way east past the John Martin Reservoir to the town of Lamar, the county seat of Prowers County and the largest town in the Lower Arkansas Valley. Here the highway closely parallels the railroad, finally passing through the town of Holly (birthplace of Colorado governor Roy Romer) on its way into Kansas. From its fourteen-thousand-foot origins, the river at this point runs at an elevation of about thirty-three hundred feet.

The explorations of Zebulon Pike first opened up this part of the West to citizens of the United States. The Louisiana Purchase in 1803 had greatly expanded the land area under American domain. General Wilkinson, governor of the new Louisiana Territory, wanted to know more about the southern reaches of this area and, in 1806, sent the twenty-six-year-old army lieutenant to explore, among other things, the source of the "Arkansaw" River.[2] Pike's journey intercepted the river in present-day Kansas and followed it upstream to the Front Range of the Rocky Mountains, where he took what he thought would be a short detour to climb (in November) the fourteen-thousand-foot mountain that now bears his name. Pike got a quick lesson in the scale of western mountains when his planned twenty-four-hour ascent turned into a three-day journey that got him no closer than sixteen miles from the peak. He then resumed his journey to the headwaters of the Arkansas. Returning downstream, he made his way south over a pass in the Sangre de Cristo Mountains into the San Luis Valley, where, in territory considered part of New Spain (Mexico), the Spanish took him prisoner. Pike pleaded ignorance of his transgression, and, indeed, the border between the

Louisiana Territory and New Spain was not well defined at the time of the Louisiana Purchase. Spain had ceded the Louisiana Territory to France in 1800 without specifying this border. In 1819 the Arkansas River became part of the boundary between the United States and Spanish-controlled Mexico.

The Arkansas River served as something of a border area between Native American tribes as well. According to historian David Lavender, "This stretch of river was . . . the uneasy border between half a dozen or more tribes: Cheyennes, Arapaho, and Prairie Apache wandering the rolling uplifts between the South Platte and the Arkansas; the Utes of the mountains foraging after buffalo and horses; the Comanches and Kiowas south of the river; and roving bands of Crows, Gros Ventre, and Wyoming Shoshoni out to visit friends or raid enemies."[3] The Cheyenne in particular made considerable use of Big Timbers, a reach of the Arkansas below its junction with the Purgatoire River, lined with mature cottonwood trees.

Others followed Pike into this region, largely for trapping and trading. In 1829, at the age of twenty, William Bent set out from Independence, Missouri, with his brother Charles for Santa Fe. Nine years older, Charles was by this time a seasoned veteran of the Missouri River trade who had decided to try his luck in the rapidly developing commerce with Mexico. Charles was elected as leader of the caravan of thirty-eight wagons with seventy-nine people. The journey was a harrowing one, marked by fights with American Indian tribes after crossing the Arkansas River into Mexican territory. The caravan was rescued by a group of about ninety-five American "mountain men" from Taos that included Ceran St. Vrain and Kit Carson.

In the fall William joined up with trappers heading into the Rocky Mountains, ending up in a winter camp along the Arkansas River, where he began his close relationship with the Cheyenne. Charles launched an association with St. Vrain, placing him in charge of the Mexican end of the trade while Bent handled the American side. William initiated trade with the Cheyenne, operating from a base near the present site of the city of Pueblo. Seeing the obvious benefits of linking their activities, the brothers (two younger brothers, George and Robert, also were involved) carved out a new wagon road from Taos, north and east over the mountains, through Raton Pass and ultimately into the Arkansas Valley.

In 1833 they built a fort at a place on the north (American) side of the Arkansas River a few miles east of where the mountain route of the Santa Fe Trail joins the river, near what became the town of La Junta.[4] Built of adobe bricks, in the style of buildings in Santa Fe, the fort was a substantial rectangular structure with a main gate through which freight wagons could pass, with living and storage rooms along the sides. The walls were fourteen feet high and thirty inches thick.

With the establishment of Bent's Fort and the wagon road link with Taos, the Bents created a major branch to the Santa Fe Trail. Longer and more physically arduous than the original trail that cut through the desert country of the Cimarron River, the mountain branch was considered safer, or at least more protectable, because it stayed in American territory longer. The Lower Arkansas Valley became a trade route and a trading center.

One traveler of the Santa Fe Trail was Lewis Garrard, who in September 1846, as a seventeen-year-old, joined Ceran St. Vrain in a caravan departing from the site of present-day Kansas City. The wagon train headed first for Council Grove, at about the ninety-eighth meridian the last substantial wooded area along the route, where the wagons were made ready for the open prairies ahead. Hardwoods such as hickory and oak provided spare axles for the wagons. In his journal Garrard reported his first encounters with buffalo, mirages in the open plains, and American Indians.

Encountering the Arkansas River for the first time in eastern Kansas, he noted it was: "here quite broad, with two feet of water, sandy bottom, and high sand buttes on either bank, as bare & cheerless as any misanthrope could wish."[5] Farther west, the trail came to its junction at the "Cimarone Crossing," the junction between the original Santa Fe Trail and the mountain route that continued along the Arkansas River. Following the mountain branch to a point just inside the present-day boundaries of the state of Colorado "where a creek fringed with timber made a graceful curve, emptying its modicum of water" into the Arkansas, Garrard commented: "The pleasing position and grouping of the trees render this spot picturesque, and it is well known to travelers as the 'Pretty Encampment.' "[6] Mov-

ing upstream toward Bent's Fort, Garrard and the wagon train passed
through Salt Bottom, "so called from the salt marshes and saline
efflorescence appearing in spots as if flour had been sprinkled on the
ground."[7] After a journey of fifty days they arrived at Bent's Fort in a
cold rain. The next morning was clear, and Garrard describes seeing
both Spanish Peaks ("apparently fifteen miles distant–in reality *one
hundred and twenty*") and Pike's Peak.

Garrard's journal gives the first good account of life at that
time in the Lower Arkansas Valley. He reports, for example, efforts
to grow corn and squash in the bottomlands adjacent to the river,
diverting water from the river to help them grow. He describes William Bent's farm, located along the Purgatoire River in Mexican
territory, in almost poetic terms: "The gentle curves of the shallow
River of Souls, its banks fringed with the graceful willow and thorny
plum, on which were affectionately entwined the curling tendrils of
the grape and hop; the grouping of the slender locust and the outspreading umbrageous cottonwoods, with the clustering currants
dotting the greensward, gave a sweet, cultivated aspect to the place;
while the surrounding hills, within their sheltering embrace, seemed
to protect the new enterprise."[8] Garrard helped construct an acequia
(ditch) to help irrigate Bent's fields and was impressed with this means
of assuring that plants received the water they needed to grow in
such places.

The Bents were not the first to settle this valley. As mentioned,
the Cheyenne and the Arapaho shared the open treeless plain between the South Platte and the Arkansas, hunting buffalo in the summer when the herds moved through the area, and wintering along
one of the rivers. The Sioux lived primarily to the north, and the
Kiowa and Comanche lived to the south. The Treaty of Fort Laramie
in 1851 dedicated the land between the South Platte and Arkansas
rivers as the domain of the Cheyenne and Arapaho, an arrangement
that worked reasonably well so long as there was no settlement interest in this land.

The great gold rush that came to Colorado in the late 1850s
brought thousands of hopeful gold seekers, on their way to "Pike's
Peak or bust," through the valley. Considerable mining occurred in
the vicinity of Cañon City, and a few of the unsuccessful prospectors

returned to the Lower Arkansas Valley to live, while many more settled in and around Denver and the northern Front Range. One tangible outcome of this rapid influx of new people was congressional creation of the territory of Colorado in 1861, with a southern border including all of the tributaries of the Arkansas River—an area previously considered part of what was to become New Mexico.[9]

With the enormous influx of settlers to the region beginning with the 1858 gold rush, conflicts inevitably arose. William Bent, married to a Cheyenne woman who bore him five children, eventually became the U.S. agent for the Cheyenne and Arapaho. In 1859 he wrote: "The concourse of whites is therefore constantly swelling, and incapable of control or restraint by the government. This suggests the policy of promptly rescuing the Indians, and withdrawing them from contact with the whites. . . . These numerous and warlike Indians, pressed upon all around by the Texans, by the settlers of the gold region, by the advancing people of Kansas, and from the Platte, are already compressed into a small circle of territory, destitute of food, and itself bisected athwart by a constantly marching line of emigrants. A desperate war of starvation and extinction is therefore imminent and inevitable, unless prompt measures shall prevent it."[10]

Desperate for some means by which the American Indians could hold on to their lands, Bent urged the tribes to take up agriculture. Under the Treaty of Fort Wise in 1861 the tribes agreed to reduce their land claims to an area north of the Arkansas River and west of Big Sandy Creek in the vicinity of Bent's Fort, in return for annual payments from the United States of thirty thousand dollars for fifteen years and help in developing the agricultural potential of the area. In 1863 the army began construction of an irrigation ditch from the river at a place called Point of Rocks. Otherwise, the treaty went unimplemented.

There is a sad sense of inevitability that surrounds the events leading to the Sand Creek Massacre in November 1864 (Figure 1.2). The number of incidents between Native Americans and whites in this part of Colorado Territory and Kansas and Nebraska increased during the 1860s, provoked and instigated on both sides. The War Between the States was taking its deadly toll, and there was a sense of vulnerability among white settlers in this area who felt unprotected with the army committed so deeply to the war. Among white leaders there seemed to be a growing feeling there could be no security without some decisive military action against the tribes. Colorado territorial governor John Evans issued a proclamation in August 1864 "authorizing all citizens of Colorado, either individually or in such parties as they organize, to go in pursuit of all hostile Indians on the plains . . . also, to kill and destroy, as enemies of the country, wherever they shall be found, all such hostile Indians."[11] Under the influence of Bent, Black Kettle and other Cheyenne chiefs negotiated a peace understanding with Major Wynkoop, commander of Fort Lyon, in September and then went to Denver to meet with Governor Evans. Once again Black Kettle and the others made clear their intention not to participate in the hostilities then under way. Colonel John M. Chivington, commander of all army troops in Colorado Territory, appeared to direct the Indians to submit themselves to the direction of Major Wynkoop at Fort Lyon. Not long after returning to Fort Lyon, Wynkoop was replaced by Major Scott J. Anthony, apparently because the army command in Kansas with direct control over Fort Lyon considered Wynkoop overly sympathetic to the tribe. Anthony arrived in early November and advised Black Kettle and the other tribal members to remain in their encampment at Sand Creek.

Sand Creek is one of the more prominent tributaries to the Arkansas River from the central Colorado plains, joining the river on the north perhaps ten miles downstream from Lamar. It is an ephemeral creek, flowing water only a few times of the year—spring snowmelts or summertime thunderstorms. The creek bed meanders through the plains, marked by occasional stands of cottonwood trees such as are found at the site where the Native Americans had set up camp. High bluffs to the west create a kind of protected valley, which must have drawn the tribe to the location. The creek bed forms a bend from south to east that mirrors the shape of the bluffs.

Chivington arrived unannounced at Fort Lyon on November 28 with the Third Regiment of the Colorado Volunteer Cavalry, hundred-day enlistees recruited specially for the Indian war declared by Governor Evans, and three companies of the Colorado First—

1.2 Site of the Sand Creek Massacre.

approximately 575 troops in all. Joined there by 125 Fort Lyon troops, he set off that night to cover the roughly forty miles northeast to a point along Sand Creek where several hundred Cheyenne and Arapaho were encamped. The army troops reached the camp shortly after daybreak on the morning of November 29 and attacked immediately, killing perhaps a hundred Indians, including women and children. Though fighting continued sporadically in this area for a few years thereafter, American Indian claims to lands in the Lower Arkansas Valley disappeared—opening the way for white settlement.

2

WATERING AND CULTIVATING THE PRAIRIE

In 1871 George Washington Swink arrived at Rocky Ford, Colorado.[12] He was thirty-five. He had left his wife and eleven children in Illinois while he came west to establish a new life. He acquired land with the intention of raising livestock and started a mercantile store at Rocky Ford—so named because the Arkansas River's rocky and shallow bottom at this location provided a good crossing. When the railroad bypassed Rocky Ford, Swink and others in 1877 simply picked up their businesses and moved the town three miles from the river to its present location.

At his store Swink sold a few vegetables, obtained from the only two farmers in the area. He began experimenting with growing his own vegetables by filling barrels of water from his well, allowing the water to sit for a day to warm up, then using the warmed water to irrigate the garden. He had good success with this technique, but he could cultivate only a small area.

The next step was to move water directly from the river to his lands. Swink and other neighboring landowners joined together to build the Rocky Ford Ditch. Twelve feet across at its bottom, where it took off from the south side of the river several miles upstream of the town, the ditch by 1874 extended to beyond Swink's lands, and in 1875 it reached to Timpas Creek—a distance of ten miles. Its estimated cost was twenty thousand dollars, a major commitment from limited local sources.

To build a ten-mile ditch with an initial bottom width of twelve feet was no small task in those days. Water in a ditch must be able to move by gravity, so the line of the ditch must be contoured in a gradual fall, dictated by the topography of the land through which it traverses. Moreover, the ditch must run at an elevation higher than the lands to be irrigated. As a result, the headgate through which water is diverted from the river into a ditch typically is located some distance upstream from the lands to be irrigated. The line of the ditch represents some compromise between one running as straight as possible and one following the natural slope of the land. In either case the task in those days of moving dirt had to be accomplished by the use of horse- or mule-drawn plows and scrapers. As the ditch got deeper, wagons were used to move the dirt out. Particularly in these early efforts, the work was done primarily by owners of lands that would be benefited using whatever equipment was available.

Another of Swink's permanent contributions to the area was the introduction and successful cultivation of cantaloupes. After discovering that cantaloupes and watermelons grow especially well in this warm, dry climate with the careful use of irrigation, he systematically worked on developing a cantaloupe that could be shipped to market by rail. Recognizing the need for earlier pollination of plant blossoms, he introduced honeybees to the area. The honeybees helped the pollination of the cantaloupes, but they thrived on another crop introduced in a major way to the area by Swink—alfalfa.

Finally, it was Swink's successful propagation of sugar beets from seeds acquired from Germany that launched what became the dominant agricultural activity in the Lower Arkansas Valley for much of the twentieth century—sugar processing. Swink persuaded a large number of farmers in the area to grow sugar beets in the 1890s, providing enough production to support the construction of the American Crystal Sugar Company factory in Rocky Ford in 1900. According to one observer: "By 1901 the farmers of the Rocky Ford Ditch Company, under the shrewd boosterism of Swink, found themselves operating the most stable and envied irrigation enterprise in the valley."[13]

Nevertheless, agriculture was slow to develop in the Lower Arkansas Valley of Colorado. Writing in 1883, agricultural promoter William Pabor noted: "Yet this state of affairs is not brought about by the absence of water or of arable land. A noble river runs unfettered by, with an abundant volume of water entirely unappropriated, and so not hampered by any priority of right as to the possession and use. Wide table lands–capable of producing corn, oats, amber cane, potatoes, and all kinds of vegetables–with gentle undulations slope up from each side of the river, at an altitude of about four thousand feet above the level of the sea, more promising than can be found in valleys having a higher altitude and a colder soil, such as prevails in Northern Colorado."[14]

Pabor's rhapsodizing is very much in tune with the times. William Gilpin, Colorado's first territorial governor, looked out on the plains of eastern Colorado and pronounced them the "Pastoral Garden of the World."[15] These are the very lands that Zebulon Pike described as a desert in 1810 and that Dr. Edwin James, official chronicler for the 1820 expedition led by Major Stephen Long, described as "a dreary plain, wholly unfit for cultivation, and of course uninhabitable by a people depending upon agriculture for their subsistence."[16] Prairie grasses, it had been discovered in the interim, provided a remarkably nutritional forage for domestic livestock. And contrary to Dr. James's assertion, the practice of irrigation made agriculture possible in this region–indeed, not just possible but even superior (in the view of western boosters) to agriculture in the more humid East, because it was not subject to the vagaries of rainfall. In their enthusiasm many came to believe that "rain follows the plow"– that the very act of cultivation somehow helped produce the moisture needed to grow crops.

Irrigation came to the Lower Arkansas Valley well before George Swink built the Rocky Ford Ditch. There are reports of irrigation-watered crops grown on the bottomlands of the Arkansas River adjacent to Bent's Fort as early as 1839.[17] Garrard's account of Bent's farm along the Purgatoire River also speaks of the use of irrigation. And there are early reports of irrigation along Fountain Creek, just to the north of Pueblo.[18] For the most part these efforts involved little more than periodically placing some kind of obstruction in the stream bed to flood water onto adjacent, low-lying lands–a practice possible only in very few places.

Promoters of Colorado agriculture like William Pabor preached the need for larger-scale, permanent irrigation systems, constructed using cooperative efforts like those of Swink and the others who built the Rocky Ford Ditch. He noted that "[o]ne man alone cannot build an irrigating canal many miles in length, and so redeem broad prairie land from the curse of sterility."[19] He went on: "Seldom can ten men do it, save where the land lies close to the water's edge. It takes combined energy, skill, and capital to construct them." But the effort was worth it: "Once built, however, and the land cultivated, the harvest is sure for the farmer who sows his seed, and, without watching the clouds, provides his land with the moisture it needs during the season of crop-growing."

The history of permanent irrigation development in the Lower Arkansas Valley can be traced by looking at the water rights on the river.[20] Contrary to Pabor's assertion in 1883 that the water of the Arkansas River was unclaimed, in fact its reliable summertime flows had already been fully appropriated by this time. First to develop were the lands in the vicinity of Cañon City and around Pueblo. Mining in the nearby mountains brought settlers who needed to eat. Between 1861 and 1869 there were thirty-one separate appropriations of Arkansas River water made by seventeen different claimants between Cañon City and Nepesta, the majority of which were for irrigation. The largest of these appropriations was to divert forty cubic feet per second (nearly eighteen thousand gallons of water per second); most were much smaller. In the 1870s most of the irrigation development occurred on lands around Pueblo. The striking exception is the Rocky Ford Ditch, which, at 111 cubic feet per second, was the largest single irrigation appropriation from the Arkansas River at that time (1874). As it turns out, the Rocky Ford appropriation is the last one in the Lower Arkansas Valley that reliably produces water from the natural flow of the river during the summer irrigation season.

Pabor was wrong about the availability of water, but he was certainly right about the availability of land. A massive Mexican land grant encompassing essentially the entire Purgatoire Basin governed most of the land on the southern side of the river.[21] As mentioned, Native American tribes controlled much of the land on the northern side until the Sand Creek Massacre. Large-scale cattle operations first dominated nonnative uses of lands on both sides of the river. Early settlers like John Wesley Prowers and James C. Jones controlled much of the Lower Arkansas Valley in the 1870s and into the early 1880s. In 1881, for example, Prowers (for whom Prowers County is named) owned forty miles of land along the Arkansas River and controlled four hundred thousand acres of land.[22] In that same year Jones sold his holdings along the south side of the river east from La Junta to the Scotch-owned Prairie Cattle Company, the largest of the American cattle companies.[23] In its so-called northern or Arkansas division in Colorado, this giant company controlled more than 2 million acres of land.

The 1880s marked an extraordinary period of irrigation development in Colorado. Private investors, influenced no doubt by the enthusiasm of people like Gilpin and Pabor, believed there was money to be made. Thus did a Denver real-estate developer named Otis L. Haskell establish the Arkansas River Land Town and Canal Company in 1884 for the purpose of building a "canal" capable of carrying enough water to irrigate three hundred thousand acres of land. Haskell's company acquired a small existing ditch taking off to the north from the Arkansas River a few miles above the town of La Junta—the very ditch constructed by the U.S. Army in 1864 to provide the water that William Bent hoped would turn the Cheyenne and Arapaho into farmers. Haskell expected to recoup his investment by selling shares of company stock to landowners in the vicinity of the canal, entitling the owner to a portion of the canal's water.[24]

Irrigation water supply companies are an innovation of the frontier American West, bringing the organization and incentives of corporate business to the task of building and operating systems that could take water out of rivers and carry it to places where its use would earn money. Sometimes these companies were privately owned. Investors, often from the East or even from England, expected to profit from their investment, either through the sale of water, shares in the company, or lands made arable by the availability of water for irrigation.

Eventually most of these companies failed. Often they transformed into "mutual" companies, owned by those with lands that could be served with water from the main ditch or canal. Like Swink and his neighbors, adjacent landowners wanting water for irrigation

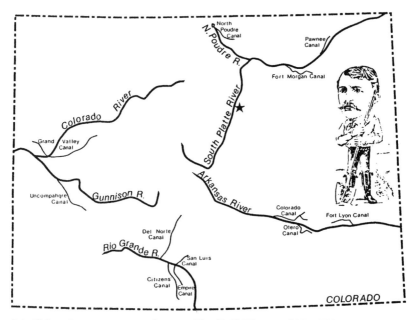

2.1 Colorado irrigation canals started by T. C. Henry, 1883–1892.

from a nearby river could join together in the work, build one diversion structure and one main ditch, share in the expense of construction and ongoing maintenance roughly in proportion to the amount of land each wanted to irrigate, and share in the supply of water available in the ditch. It was cooperative capitalism, whereby the owners of the company were also the operators and the users of its product–delivered water.

In February 1884 Haskell's company employed fifty men and forty teams of horses to begin enlarging the existing ditch and extending it east. By 1886 only seventeen miles had been completed, and Haskell found few buyers for his water stock. Unable to supply water to even these few users in 1887 because of operational problems, Haskell sold his company that fall to a group of investors led by T. C. Henry.

Henry is one of those people now generally lost to history who had been unusually important in their time (Figure 2.1).[25] He had been a wheat farmer in Kansas whose failed fortunes resulted at least in part from drought, making him a fervent believer in the virtues of irrigation. Upon moving to Colorado in 1883 he immediately began raising money to support the construction of the Grand Valley Canal in western Colorado (described in part 2). By the fall of 1887 Henry had been involved with the construction of eleven other ditch systems around the state. The Fort Lyon marked his first foray into the Arkansas Valley.

Henry's success as a promoter derived, at least in part, from his unbridled, perhaps somewhat naive, enthusiasm for the ability of irrigation to transform desert land into cropland. He persuaded the Travelers Insurance Company, for example, to invest more than $1.5 million in the construction of four irrigation systems in Colorado in 1883 and 1884—an investment secured by bonds that were to be repaid by sales of stock in the canal companies. Construction costs escalated, and stock sales failed to generate the funding needed to repay the bonds—eventually leaving Travelers with the ownership of companies worth considerably less than its investment. Nevertheless, Henry continued to find other sources of funding for his ventures, including the Fort Lyon.

The Fort Lyon Canal charged T. C. Henry's imagination. He envisioned building the largest irrigation ditch in the state, one that might eventually extend all the way to Kansas. Initially things went well. In particular the extension of the Atchison, Topeka and Santa Fe Railway Company to Lamar in 1889 spurred interest in extending the canal to lands in this vicinity. By 1893 Henry's company completed the canal to its junction with Big Sandy Creek (not too far from the site of the Sand Creek Massacre), a distance of about 110 miles. At this point the bubble burst. Water rights for the canal, with appropriations dated 1884, 1887, and 1893, are relatively "junior" on the Arkansas River. Under the priority system of western water law, those first to appropriate water from a river are allowed to divert and use the full amount of their appropriation before those who come later. Thus the more senior Rocky Ford right can take up to 111 cubic feet per second of the Arkansas during the irrigation season, potentially leaving nothing in the stream for more junior downstream appropriators.

It is one thing (remarkable in its own way) to build a canal 110 miles long, with a beginning width at its bottom of fifty feet (remember

the twelve-foot-wide Rocky Ford Ditch?) and with a volumetric capacity of eighteen hundred cubic feet per second of water (imagine one-foot cubes of water fifty feet wide and thirty-six feet high
moving into the canal *every second*–over eight hundred thousand gallons of water!). It is another thing to fill something this large with
water, especially when the source of that water is the lower Arkansas
River in Colorado. By the time Haskell and then Henry sought to
lay claim to this large share of the limited water supply, many others
were ahead of them in line.

The 1884 appropriation of 164 cubic feet per second for the
Fort Lyon marks the beginning of large-scale irrigation development
in the Lower Arkansas Valley. The Catlin Ditch, its diversion point
located about thirty miles upstream of Fort Lyon's, holds an appropriation for 226 cubic feet per second, also with an 1884 priority
date. The Catlin's appropriation, however, is dated December 3,
whereas the Fort Lyon's is dated April 15–a critical difference in the
West. By the time Henry appropriated another 597 cubic feet per
second in 1887 for his greatly enlarged Fort Lyon Canal, he was claiming water that simply wasn't in the river after June most years. This
was even more true for the 171 cubic feet per second appropriated in
1893.

Henry had promised Fort Lyon shareholders that, as soon as
the capital costs of the irrigation system were returned to the investors, they would become owners of the canal and the water rights.
Irrigators depending on water from the Fort Lyon could not wait.
Led by John Hess, an irrigator with six hundred acres near Lamar,
many of the farmers sought to take control of the Fort Lyon from
Henry and the First National Bank of Denver, which held the primary mortgage on the system.[26] In 1893 and 1894 the Arkansas River
seemingly sought to make up for a preceding period of drought.
Flooding filled the canal with sand and sediment, blocking delivery
of water for thirty days in 1893. In 1894 floods washed out the Fort
Lyon diversion dam two separate times. A court-appointed receiver
took over operation of the system in 1894. In 1897 Fort Lyon shareholders organized themselves into the nonprofit mutual corporation
under which it operates today. Then they spent five years in court
validating their control of the old company's assets.[27]

As Gilpin, Pabor, Henry, and others were busily promoting western development, people like John Wesley Powell, Dr. Ferdinand Vandever Hayden, and Lieutenant George M. Wheeler were conducting congressionally funded surveys of the lands and resources that would support this development. In 1878 Powell—then head of the Geographical and Geological Survey of the Rocky Mountain Region—issued his *Report on the Lands of the Arid Region of the United States, With a More Detailed Account of the Lands of Utah.*[28] In decided contrast to the unbounded enthusiasm of the promoters, Powell offered a sober assessment of the implications of aridity for western agriculture. First, he challenged the 160-acre homestead model as unworkable. He argued that the minimum acreage needed to support a viable grazing operation in areas of limited rainfall was 2,560 acres. From his direct observations of Mormon irrigation-based communities in Utah, he understood both the value and the limits of irrigated agriculture. Thus he asserted that all homestead units should be surveyed in a manner that assured they would have access to water. Throw out the rectangular survey, he argued, and carve up lands according to usability of the soils and availability of water. Farms with fully irrigable lands need only be eighty acres, he believed, because of the intensive development they would require and the considerably higher yields they would produce. Even grazing homesteads should be surveyed to include access to water and to twenty acres of irrigable land. His careful evaluation of Utah concluded that only 3 percent of that state's land area was suitable for irrigation.

At the same time that Henry was pressing ahead with expansion of the Fort Lyon and with development of the equally ambitious Colorado Canal, F. H. Newell, later to become the first director of the Reclamation Service, was at work in the Arkansas Valley gathering data for the 1890 agricultural census. In his "Report on Agriculture by Irrigation in the Western Part of the United States," published as part of the 1890 census, Newell explicitly notes that "the united capacity of the canals [in the Lower Arkansas] is so great that it is a matter of doubt whether the river can supply them all when completed."[29] He reported complaints of area farmers (almost certainly including some from the Fort Lyon) about receiving only half or three-quarters of the water for which they paid.

The severe drought that gripped the Arkansas Basin in 1889 and 1890 prompted hearings by a special committee of the U.S. Senate.[30] What emerged from the hearings was agreement that reservoirs needed to be constructed in the basin to store water available in high-flow periods for use in drier times. At that time only 13,000 acre-feet of storage capacity existed in the basin, but between 1890 and 1910 irrigators and cities constructed three reservoirs in the headwaters of the basin and another eleven reservoirs in off-stream locations below Pueblo, adding a total of about 576,000 acre-feet of water-storage capacity.[31] The Fort Lyon Canal Company, for example, built reservoirs on Horse Creek and Adobe Creek between 1900 and 1910, as well as a new canal from the Arkansas River just to carry unclaimed springtime flows for storage when available. It seemed just possible the storage of water in periods of high flow could later provide the water that nature did not otherwise make available.

Perhaps the single most significant storage facility constructed during this period was the Twin Lakes Reservoir on Lake Creek. With its headwaters on Independence Pass, Lake Creek is the Arkansas River's largest tributary. The private company that took over construction and operation of the Colorado Canal from T. C. Henry built Twin Lakes between 1896 and 1900. Company investors realized that their already considerable investment in the purchase of lands and construction of the Colorado Canal was in jeopardy without a more reliable supply of water.[32] In 1913 a Colorado court decreed storage capacity at the Twin Lakes Reservoir to be about fifty-four thousand acre-feet, though the annual yield from the reservoir was in fact much smaller. The company developed as well two smaller off-channel sites for storage within the area served by the Colorado Canal–Lake Meredith and Lake Henry.

The work of George Swink and others to develop and use the water supplies of the Arkansas Basin for irrigation brought large-scale agricultural processing to the area for the first time. In 1900 the new town of Sugar City was incorporated. Located along the Missouri Pacific Railroad line, Sugar City grew up adjacent to a sugar beet processing factory constructed by the National Beet Sugar Company. George Swink already had demonstrated that sugar beets would grow well in the area, and he had attempted to encourage outside

THE ARKANSAS VALLEY
: : : IS THE : : :

"Garden Spot"

OF COLORADO.

If you are interested and want a beautifully illustrated book telling all about the choicest Fruit Lands, Sugar Beet Lands, Cantaloupe and Melon Farms, address

The Twin Lakes
Land and Water Co.

Central Block, Pueblo, Colo.
or Ordway, Colo.

Lands under the Colorado Canal are in direct connection with the Twin Lakes reservoirs and other immense reservoirs in the vicinity of Ordway. This guarantees all the water that is needed for irrigation.

2.2 Typical Twin Lakes Land and Water Company Advertisement (Source: *Pueblo Chieftain,* 1 Jan. 1901).

investors to construct a processing facility. The McKinley Tariff of 1890 made domestically produced sugar very attractive. The factory at Sugar City was actually financed by some of the same investors from Buffalo who had taken over the Colorado Canal from T. C. Henry and then had constructed the Twin Lakes Reservoir. Just as the investment in the Twin Lakes Reservoir was intended to bail out earlier investments in the land and the Colorado Canal, so too was the commitment to sugar beets. The National Sugar Beet Company not only committed to the construction of the processing facility at Sugar City, it also acquired twelve thousand acres of land within the Colorado Canal development and the associated water rights in order to assure there would be sugar beets available to be processed.[33] In the words of historian Dena Markoff, "This group had undertaken a task immensely more difficult than a typical sugar factory promotion. They also built a town, completed an irrigation system, raised a beet crop, and recruited workers and settlers."[34]

The story of the struggles to keep this facility in business provides a tale of enterprise and hard work.[35] Energized by the new sugar-beet industry, the land company initiated an aggressive promotion effort. It advertised its lands and the Arkansas Valley as the "Garden Spot" of Colorado (Figure 2.2). Its brochures "spoke of Colorado as the 'Paradise of the West' with fertile lands, sufficient water, and glorious climate, a land 'Kissed by the Sun and Blessed by Irrigation.' The Arkansas Valley, the choicest of locations, needed 'farmers with energy and industry to go upon this land and become neighbors for the many newcomers already here.' The area offered an idyllic life, filled with 'blessings of independence and contentment.' "[36]

Sugar can be produced considerably more cheaply from sugar cane than from sugar beets. The viability of the sugar-beet industry depended on protective tariffs applied against imported sugar.[37] There were repeated efforts between 1897 and 1913 to eliminate the tariff. For example, in 1902 Congress gave serious attention to providing duty-free status to sugar imported from Cuba.

Protected by tariffs, beet sugar took hold in the Lower Arkansas Valley as well as in other places in the West. In the six years following construction of the processing facility at Sugar City, other beet-sugar factories were built in Rocky Ford, Lamar, Holly, Swink, and Las Animas. By 1911 Sugar City had become "a trading center for farmers in a twenty-five-mile radius. Everything within its limits had been built in a short time and had a glow of newness and well-being. Houses had well-established yards with grass, flowers, and trees. A neatly kept lawn and beds of zinnias gave the factory grounds a park-like appearance."[38] Population in the area had grown to such an extent that a new county–Crowley County–was carved out of the northern portion of Otero County. Things were good in the Lower Arkansas Valley, largely due to sugar beets.

3

STRETCHING A LIMITED WATER SUPPLY

To build a heavily water-dependent economy in the Arkansas Valley was, in many respects, an act of human defiance. Yet by the turn of the century the fortunes of many people living in this valley were closely linked to the use of the limited water resources of the Arkansas River. Most obvious was the substantial irrigation economy now developing rapidly along the length of the valley.[39] In addition, the city of Pueblo boasted the Rocky Mountain West's only iron-and-steel works, run by the Colorado Fuel and Iron Company.[40] This facility was itself a major user of water from the Arkansas River.[41] And, of course, the growing urban populations in Pueblo and Colorado Springs demanded additional water.

If white settlement and the development of an economy were the major events of the Arkansas Valley in the nineteenth century, development of sufficient usable supplies of water to maintain that economy dominated the first half of the twentieth century. Adding to this challenge was the increasingly insistent claim of Kansas irrigators to some share of the river that also passed through their lands on its way to the Mississippi.

In 1901 the state of Kansas filed an action against Colorado in the U.S. Supreme Court.[42] It sought an order from the Court prohibiting any additional water development in the Arkansas Basin of Colorado. Colorado responded that Kansas had no legal basis on which to dictate uses of water in another state. A more technical aspect of the case turned on the contrasting legal doctrines in the two states governing who could use water: Colorado followed the rule of appropriation, whereas Kansas followed the "riparian" doctrine. Riparian principles, developed in well-watered England, attached permanent rights to enjoy the benefits of water to those owning adjacent lands. Unlike with appropriation, riparian landowners need never take any overt action to claim water. Their rights simply inhered in their ownership of land adjacent to a river or lake. Moreover, under traditional riparian principles those rights included a continuation of the river's flows "substantially undiminished" in quantity or quality. Active water development upstream in Colorado, particularly since the 1880s, had undeniably reduced the flows of the Arkansas River.

Within Colorado the priority system of water law sorted out competing interests using the simple rule of first-in-time, first-in-right. It was this rule that gave relative security to irrigators under the Rocky Ford Ditch as compared to those operating under the Fort Lyon or the Colorado Canal. But what was the rule as between states? After all, the Arkansas River did flow (sometimes) into Kansas (where it became known as the "Ar-*KAN*-sas" River). Water users in Colorado were in the enviable position of being upstream. Did that mean they could take as much of the Arkansas River as they could use? Or did users in Kansas have something to say about what happened upstream?

Colorado appropriators made much of their substantial investment to turn the water of the Arkansas River into an economically productive asset. They pointed out the questionable wisdom of interfering with such productive uses simply to assure that water flows downstream through the riparian lands in Kansas. Of course, it wasn't just for the pleasure of seeing water in the ArKANsas River that Kansas filed its lawsuit. Irrigated agriculture had taken root in this part of western Kansas as well, and Kansas farmers wanted to be able to divert water from the river during the irrigation season.[43]

The federal government, though not itself a party to the suit, had a more than passing interest in this dispute. The Reclamation Service, formed in 1902 to construct water-supply systems for agriculture in the western states, feared that ratification of a riparian rule would greatly complicate its task of establishing clear legal rights to capture and deliver water. Reclamation also feared Colorado's assertion of absolute sovereignty over its water. Despite the admitted nonnavigability of the Arkansas River, eliminating the assertion of federal constitutional authority over interstate commerce (through navigation), the United States nonetheless argued that its authority was implied by the multistate nature of the resource.

The decision of the U.S. Supreme Court in 1907 rested on a principle that has come to be known as "equitable apportionment."[44] States were free to devise their own rules governing rights to use water, but the Supreme Court would sit as arbiter to ensure that actual uses of water between states were equitable. In this case, the Court determined that although development in Colorado had in fact reduced the flows of the Arkansas River into Kansas, the benefits to Colorado outweighed the harm to Kansas. Warned the Court, however, "there will come a time when Kansas may justly say that there is no longer an equitable division of benefits, and may rightfully call for relief."[45]

To some the way to get around this problem was straightforward enough: increase the usable water supply so there was more to go around. Not much could be done to make more water, but a great deal could be done to manage the available supply to make it better match up with human needs. Most important, the flows could be dammed and stored during peak runoff periods and then released for use as needed. Thus, high flows that would otherwise pass downstream unused in the spring could be captured and then released during the warm, dry summer months to meet downstream irrigation demands.

In the 1920s Michael Creed Hinderlider, Colorado state engineer, proposed construction of a dam across the Arkansas River at the small town of Caddoa, about sixty river miles from the Kansas border. Storage low on the Arkansas River in Colorado would help firm up water supplies for the ditches at the other end of the river, as well as improve water availability for ditches in western Kansas. He also envisioned building tunnels through the mountains to bring additional water from the less-developed and wetter western slope of the Rocky Mountains into the Arkansas Basin. The major problem was money. Water users on the lower Arkansas River, though they would obviously benefit, could not begin to pay the costs of building a dam at Caddoa or for bringing water from the other side of the Continental Divide.

In the mid-1920s Hinderlider and representatives of local water users turned to the U.S. Department of the Interior for help. Would the Bureau of Reclamation finance and construct the Caddoa dam? Their timing was poor. Reclamation was going through an agonizing reevaluation of its role in constructing irrigation projects. Expectations about the ability of irrigators to return the costs of projects to the U.S. Treasury had proved unrealistic.[46] A Reclamation study of the proposed dam at Caddoa concluded that its costs outweighed its benefits.[47]

The Great Depression that gripped the United States in the 1930s was also the period of the dust bowl in the American Southwest. An unparalleled drought struck much of the West, reducing stream flows to historical lows and drying out plowed soils. Winds scooped up the powdered dirt, turning daytime into night in some places, and carrying the soils of the Great Plains all the way to the White House.[48]

The occupant of the White House at that time, Franklin Delano Roosevelt, was convinced the federal government bore a responsibility to assert itself into the economy and other aspects of society as necessary to combat the depression and to improve people's lives. One of his administration's major weapons in this war was the so-called "public works" program: large-scale, publicly financed construction projects providing employment. Projects with widespread public benefits were desirable, but the most important criteria were strong local and state support and the number of jobs that would be provided. Colorado interests, working through their congressman John Martin, sensed an opportunity in 1933 to obtain the federal support that was not forthcoming in 1926. That support came not from the Bureau of Reclamation but from the Army Corps of Engineers.

Established in 1824 to provide engineering know-how for the planning of roads and canals "of national significance,"[49] the Army Corps of Engineers has been described as "the engineering department of the Federal Government."[50]Over the years its mission expanded from navigation improvements to flood control to multiple-purpose projects. Large water projects providing generalized

3.1 John Martin Dam and Reservoir.

benefits such as flood control fit well with the Roosevelt administration's interest in supporting public-works projects.

In 1936 Martin managed to get the project authorized for construction in the Flood Control Act. The corps asked local water users to provide the land for the reservoir and to assume operation and maintenance costs.[51] Even this modest level of contribution exceeded the financial capability of the water users. A recession in 1937, however, persuaded Congress that it should pump up federal expenditures, and, in 1938, it authorized 100 percent federal funding of flood-control projects. The project at Caddoa, characterized as flood control, could go forward. In 1949 the corps completed the John Martin Dam and Reservoir (Figure 3.1).

The other piece of Hinderlider's strategy for the Arkansas River, increasing the water supply through "transmountain" diversions of water, followed a different tack. Bureau of Reclamation planners came up with an ambitious scheme for transporting water out of the Gunnison River Basin and from the Roaring Fork, a tributary to the Colorado River, into the Arkansas Basin. The proposal became known as the Gunnison-Arkansas Project.[52] Unable to gain congressional support for the full project, Reclamation redesigned the project into phases, proposing initial development of water out of the Roaring Fork. Congress finally authorized construction of the Fryingpan-Arkansas Project in 1962.[53]

During the twentieth century irrigators in the Arkansas Valley discovered another way to tap the water resources of the basin: by pumping groundwater. The channel of the Arkansas River as it makes its way eastward out onto the plains of Colorado rests on a bed of alluvial fill materials up to two hundred feet in depth, and one to fourteen miles in width, with an average width of three miles.[54] Though this is a greatly simplified picture, imagine a long, shallow U-shaped trough, like a huge bathtub, mostly filled with unconsolidated rocks, gravels, clays, and sand. A modest indentation in the surface of this alluvium represents the channel of the river with its visible flow of water. Far more water exists in the interstices of the unconsolidated fill, but it is hidden from view. This is known as alluvial groundwater.

As water on the surface moves through the indentation in the trough, it passes through places where the underlying material is highly permeable and the elevation of the alluvial groundwater level (the groundwater table) is below the channel. In these places water will percolate out of the surface channel and into the underlying groundwater aquifer. Similarly, as water falls on (or is placed on) the surface area of lands adjacent to the river channel, some will percolate down into the alluvial fill. The source of this water could be rainfall or snow; it could be water applied for irrigation of crops.

Water underground moves downward and laterally, under the influence of gravity, through the openings available in the alluvial materials. At the perimeters are the walls of the trough, the more or less impermeable bedrock in which the alluvial materials are contained. As these alluvial materials are saturated, the water table begins to rise. At times, and in some locations, that level may even exceed that of the stream channel. At such points groundwater then moves into the surface flows.

It is a dynamic system, constantly in movement, constantly changing. Conceptually, though, it is useful to understand that the

Arkansas River is part of a hydrologic system much greater and more complex than can be seen with the human eye. The alluvial aquifer in that portion of the basin downstream from Pueblo is estimated to contain about 2 million acre-feet of water.[55]

The existence of groundwater in the basin, sometimes at depths not far below the surface, has long been known. Pumping of that groundwater for irrigation use, however, did not really begin in any significant way until the 1940s with the advent of the vertical turbine pump and the widespread availability of electricity in rural areas. In 1940 there were an estimated 16 irrigation wells in the Arkansas Valley.[56] By 1950 there were 186 irrigation wells; by 1960 there were 822 wells; by 1970 there were 1,466 wells. In 1940 an estimated twenty-five hundred acre-feet of groundwater were pumped; in 1972 pumping of groundwater was estimated at more than two hundred thousand acre-feet.[57]

This phenomenal growth in the number of wells and the amount of water pumped reflects the many advantages of groundwater. Lands not already provided water-delivery service by one of the ditch-company systems—for example, those located at higher elevations than the closest irrigation ditch—could now be irrigated. Wells also could provide supplemental water for lands served by ditches with junior priorities, avoiding or reducing risk of crop damage or loss if surface water supplies were not available. Water is available at the flick of a switch, anytime an irrigator wants to water his crops, not just when his turn comes up in the ditch system's pattern of surface-water delivery. In some places, where lands had become waterlogged because of rising groundwater levels from irrigation recharge, wells could reduce that water table, perhaps eliminating water-hogging phreatophytes such as willows and salt cedar that had taken root.

There were, of course, some limiting factors. One was the expense of drilling the well and installing the pump. Another was the cost of the electricity and maintenance to operate the pump. A third was the variation in the quality of the aquifer at different locations, including depth to water table and the permeability and porosity of the alluvial fill. Generally, wells located closer to the river are likely to be more productive than upland wells. Moreover, wells located too close together will compete for the same water. And, finally, pumping groundwater that is physically connected to surface flows will at some point cause a loss of the surface flows.

A well is like a straw punched into the ground. Sucking water through that straw drains an area around the straw in the general shape of an upside-down ice-cream cone (called a "cone of depression"[58]), with the opening of the cone at the bottom of the straw and the point reaching up to the surface. As water is withdrawn, the circumference of the cone increases. Groundwater that normally would move through an aquifer to an adjacent stream or another well is intercepted by the pumping. A well located close enough to the river may create a cone of depression that actually extends into the aquifer beneath the stream bed, eventually encouraging a portion of the flow to move into the aquifer—even possibly to the well for withdrawal.

In a water system as heavily used as the lower Arkansas, it wasn't long before the effects of this expanded groundwater pumping became apparent. Ditch systems with priority rights to surface water dating back to the 1880s were going without water, while wells installed in the 1950s and 1960s were pumping without limitation.

Roger Fellhauer farmed bottomland along the south side of the Arkansas River about thirty miles downstream of Pueblo. In 1935 he dug a well thirty-five feet deep about a quarter mile from the river and used water from the well to irrigate his 150 acres of land.[59] Over time the river channel changed course, moving to within four hundred feet of the well. In late June 1966 flows in the Arkansas River were so low that the Fort Lyon Canal, with its point of diversion about another thirty miles downstream, was required to stop diverting water. Unlike many western states at this time, Colorado water law did recognize that groundwater and surface water are connected.[60] Fort Lyon asked the Colorado state engineer to shut down the Fellhauer well.

In 1965 the Colorado General Assembly had directed the state engineer to administer groundwater uses within the same priority system that applied to surface-water users. Pumping from a well that takes water legally committed to senior water rights could be enjoined, and the Colorado attorney general sought and obtained an injunction stopping Fellhauer's pumping in 1966.

On appeal the Colorado Supreme Court was introduced to the Arkansas River alluvium and the rapidly developing science of stream-aquifer hydrology. It had little trouble concluding that well pumping from the alluvium in the Arkansas Valley was taking water from senior surface users. Nor did it have any difficulty with the state's authority to require wells to stop pumping if determined necessary to protect senior appropriators. It did, however, overturn the injunction in this case. In essence the court told the state engineer to develop a planned basis for administration of surface-water and groundwater use rather than simply shutting down wells close to the river.

Writing for the court, Justice James K. Groves recognized that stopping groundwater use just because it was more "junior" did not necessarily make sense. Groundwater provides a critical source of supply in the Lower Arkansas Valley. Its use should be encouraged, so long as that use does not take water from senior appropriators. The broad public interest in "maximum utilization" of water, he concluded, overrode the traditional prior-appropriation rule that a junior could never take water from a system in which a senior is not able to divert his full appropriation. The important thing was to be sure that this pumping would be managed in a way that did not interfere with other, already established water uses.[61]

While Colorado surface and groundwater users were working out their differences, downstream users in Kansas were contemplating still another original action in the U.S. Supreme Court seeking more water from the Arkansas River. In 1949 the two states reached agreement on the Arkansas River Compact.[62] The John Martin Reservoir, with a total capacity of 700,000 acre-feet (including 400,000 for storage and 280,000 for flood control), was finally completed in 1948, and the development of operating criteria for the dam was a principal purpose of the compact negotiations.[63]

In 1985 Kansas filed an action against Colorado arguing that water users in Colorado, primarily those groundwater pumpers who had installed wells after the compact, had materially depleted Arkansas River water that should have been available for users in Kansas. Trial before Special Master Arthur Littleworth commenced in 1990 and ended in late 1992. In February 1994 the special master issued his report, concluding that groundwater pumping in Colorado from wells installed between 1948 and 1969 (virtually all of them) violated the provision of the Arkansas River Compact regarding material depletion of Arkansas River water. The U.S. Supreme Court affirmed this finding in 1995.[64] As a direct result of this decision, all large-scale groundwater pumping in the lower Arkansas now is required to account for and replace its depletions of Arkansas River water—a requirement that will force at least some of that pumping to cease.

Justice Groves, in his call for maximum utilization of Colorado water, reflected fully the sentiments of most water users in the Arkansas Valley who were struggling mightily to make the water resources of the basin (and those that could be imported) meet their oversized demands. One of the more successful efforts to match supply and demand in the valley is the winter water storage program. Made possible by completion of the Pueblo Dam in 1974, this program addresses the problem of ditches in the valley that, in a futile effort to build soil moisture, formerly diverted water from the river during the winter months for flood irrigation of fields. The program now allows these ditches to store the water in the Pueblo Reservoir (and other reservoirs) for release in the early part of the irrigation season.[65] Thirteen ditch and reservoir companies participate in this program, which has markedly improved the availability of water during the irrigation season for most participants.

The winter water storage program is one of the many legacies of Charles L. (Tommy) Thomson to the Arkansas Valley. Thomson began his career as manager of the Salida Chamber of Commerce in the early 1950s. From there he moved to Pueblo to run the chamber. In 1966 he became general manager of the Southeastern Colorado Water Conservancy District, a position he held until his death in 1994. Thomson understood that the Fryingpan-Arkansas Project, important as it was, would supply only a modest amount of additional water to irrigators in the valley. He became persuaded that the traditional practice of wintertime irrigation produced few real benefits, particularly when compared to the cost and effort involved in operating canal diversion and delivery systems in sometimes freezing conditions. Slowly, carefully, he set about the difficult work of convincing all of the ditch companies in the Lower Valley that had practiced winter irrigation for many years that they would be better off to store this water and use it during the irrigation season. "In the beginning, I started meeting with individual companies to talk to them about the advantage of storing some of their winter water rather than using it when their decree was in [priority]. If the weather was 20 below on Christmas Eve, they had to use it or lose it! Instead of that, I talked to them about working cooperatively, storing some of their water in Pueblo Reservoir and others like the Holbrook, Fort Lyon, Colorado and Amity storing their water in their privately owned reservoirs."[66] Among the issues Thomson helped to negotiate were the number of months in which storage would occur and, perhaps most difficult of all, how to divide the stored water. "The interesting part in all this is that it had to be done by unanimous agreement. If any one company had objected—that is, kept their call on the river—that would have meant the whole program would have been dead." Now the program has been formalized and has even been granted a water-court decree. Moreover, the Supreme Court's special master determined that it did not violate the 1948 compact.

~

Most irrigators in the Lower Arkansas have improved the irrigation systems on their farms. Carl Genova's farm east of Pueblo provides a good example. Genova operates a 750-acre farm together with two brothers on the St. Charles Mesa. His surface water comes from the Bessemer Ditch. He is one of the acknowledged leaders on water issues in the valley; he is on Bessemer's board, the board of the Arkansas Valley Ditch Association, and the Southeastern Colorado Water Conservancy District board.

When we met at his farmhouse, he was wearing the omnipresent farmer's baseball cap, this one saying "Brand Chief Beans." Carl and his brothers operate a cattle feedlot. They grow mostly feedstocks for their cattle but also pinto beans, dry onions, and pearl onions. Carl figures that he gets about two and a half acre-feet of water for each of his irrigated acres each year from Bessemer Ditch rights. He supplements this supply with another half acre-foot per acre from five wells.

"My dad started this farm in the 1920s," Carl said. "My grandfather immigrated from Italy to work at CF&I [the steel mill in Pueblo].

3.2 Carl Genova setting gated pipe.

He was killed in a blast furnace explosion at the time his family was coming from Italy to join him."

We took a tour of his farm. Carl showed me how the water from wells is piped to go anywhere on his property. His waste ditches carry unused water to a tailwater detention pond. He has installed a pump at this pond that can move water back to his irrigated lands, creating a water recirculation system. He uses gated pipe to provide a measured flow of irrigation water into the furrows of his field (Figure 3.2). Carl pointed out to me a white tank next to one of his ditches from which he dispenses fertilizer directly into the irrigation water. Every ditch on his land is concrete lined.

"I get the feeling that people think the Arkansas Valley is expendable. And I don't think it is. I guess I can't figure out why people can't come to the water instead of wanting the water to go to them."

Vernon Procter farms seventeen hundred acres of land served by water from the Rocky Ford Highline Ditch, the Rocky Ford Ditch, the Catlin, and the Oxford. He is president of the Rocky Ford Highline Canal Company. With financial assistance provided under the Patterson Hollow Water Quality Improvement Program (a Depart-

3.3 Retention pond for return water.

ment of Agriculture program), he has made major improvements to his irrigation systems. Like Genova, he has built ditches to carry unused water to tailwater ponds, where it is collected and pumped back to his fields for irrigation use (Figure 3.3). With these and other improvements he believes his water supply has improved 40-50 percent (Figure 3.4). He uses trash screens to keep the water clean.

In addition to improving the usable water supply, water-quality management is another important motivation for these on-farm improvements. The lower Arkansas River in Colorado is *five times* more saline than the "Salty Colorado."[67] In the Lamar area the salinity concentration measures more than 4,000 parts per million of total dissolved solids most of the time, compared to approximately 850 parts per million of TDS measured in the Colorado River just above the border with Mexico.[68] Only in the Pecos Valley of New Mexico are lands in the United States irrigated with water more saline than that of the Arkansas.

The headwaters of the Arkansas emerge almost pure from snowmelt in the mountains, containing perhaps thirty parts per million of TDS. Only modest additions of salts occur until the river

3.4 Extension Service Agent Jim Valliant explaining surge irrigation demonstration project.

passes Cañon City, at which point the channel cuts through highly saline sedimentary materials and the salt load of the river more than doubles.[69] Additional salts are added to the river as it moves through the eastern plain, largely from natural sources, but also from irrigation return flows.

It is in this portion of the river below Cañon City where virtually all of the irrigation uses of Arkansas River water occur. Here the salts added largely from natural sources become concentrated–the result of the intensive use and reuse of the river's water. Don Miles, former agent for Colorado State University Extension Service located in Rocky Ford, produced a thorough analysis of salinity in the Lower Arkansas Valley of Colorado in the mid 1970s. He estimated that about 98 percent of all Arkansas River water passing Cañon

City is consumed before it reaches the Kansas border.[70] This depletion of water drives up the concentration levels of the salts in what remains. As a result, more than two hundred thousand acres of lands in the Lower Arkansas Valley of Colorado were being irrigated in the 1970s with water classified by the U.S. Salinity Laboratory as its "highest salinity hazard."[71]

Not surprisingly, cropping patterns in the basin reflect the salinity levels of the water used for irrigation. Salt-tolerant crops like alfalfa, grain sorghum, and barley predominate downstream, whereas low-tolerance crops like corn, onions, and beans are grown upstream. In general, crops with low salt tolerance tend to be higher value than higher-salt-tolerant crops. Nevertheless, there is no strong indication that farmers in the Lower Arkansas nearer to Kansas are worse off than those upstream. Indeed, it appears that the irrigators of the Lower Valley have adapted remarkably well to the disadvantages of the more saline water.

4

IRRIGATION WATER FOR SALE?

Following World War II, the Front Range of Colorado boomed. Fueled in significant part by massive federal investments in the region, urban areas like Denver, Colorado Springs, and Pueblo grew rapidly. Drought seized Colorado in the early 1950s, reducing stream flows to at, or even below, those of the dust bowl years. Touring the drought-stricken Arkansas Valley in 1955, Agriculture Secretary Ezra Taft Benson could only suggest a day of prayer.[72]

Growing urban areas needed more water; agricultural users controlled the water. Slowly, beginning in the 1950s, cities (and brokers wanting to sell to cities) began acquiring portions of the water supply in the Arkansas Valley that had been developed by agricultural interests. Particularly active was the city of Pueblo and its Board of Waterworks. The first transaction occurred in 1955 when the city of Pueblo purchased the Clear Creek Reservoir and the associated storage rights from the Otero Ditch Company.[73] In 1971 Pueblo worked out a deal with the Rocky Ford Highline Ditch Company for the transfer of its Busk-Ivanhoe transmountain diversion system in trade for the diversion rights of the Las Animas Town Ditch. In 1972 Pueblo purchased the Booth Orchard Grove Ditch just downstream of the city and shifted the diversion of water to its upstream outtake.

Private investors also got involved. In 1968 a group of investors styling themselves the Crowley Land and Development Company (CLADCO) sent letters to every shareholder of the Twin Lakes Reservoir and Canal Company offering $380 an acre for their farms

in Crowley County. The price included land, improvements, and, most important, water rights. Claiming it intended to operate Christmas-tree farms and raise lettuce, CLADCO extended its offer at an opportune time.[74] The year before, the National Sugar Manufacturing Company went out of business, closing its Sugar City mill.[75] Even with the mill in operation, farmers served by the Colorado Canal had struggled to stay viable. Now, many believed, it was time to get out. By 1970 CLADCO had acquired about 23 percent of all Twin Lakes stock. Just two years later it owned 55 percent of the stock.[76]

Formed in 1913, the Twin Lakes Reservoir and Canal Company was a nonprofit mutual ditch and reservoir company with ownership, at the time of the CLADCO purchase, of the fifty-mile Colorado Canal; the Twin Lakes Dam and Reservoir with about fifty-four thousand acre-feet of storage capacity located on Lake Creek; a transmountain diversion system consisting of water-collection ditches; a holding pond on the west slope of the Rocky Mountains in the Roaring Fork drainage (a tributary of the Colorado River); and the 504-cubic-feet-per-second-capacity Independence Tunnel for carrying water under the Continental Divide. In addition, it owned a series of decreed water rights, including one providing for the direct diversion of 756 cubic feet per second from the Arkansas at its headgate near Boone with an 1890 priority; a 1913 storage right in Twin Lakes for fifty-four thousand acre-feet of water from the Lake Creek drainage; and a 1935 right to divert up to 625 cubic feet per second from the Roaring Fork drainage for temporary storage in Twin Lakes Reservoir. By far the most valuable of these assets were the Twin Lakes Reservoir and the transmountain diversion rights that provided most of the storage water. Located high in the upper Arkansas Basin, water stored in Twin Lakes is exceptionally versatile. It can, of course, be released down the Arkansas River. But, with pumping, water from Twin Lakes can be moved relatively easily into Colorado Springs' Fountain Creek drainage or into South Park and thus into the South Platte Basin and downstream to the rapidly growing Denver metropolitan area. It is high-quality water, not originating or passing through the heavily mined Leadville area of the upper Arkansas Basin. And because there had been relatively little water development in the Roaring Fork at that time, the 1935 diversion right provided a reasonably reliable supply of water.

As it turned out, CLADCO was primarily interested in the Twin Lakes Reservoir water—and not for raising Christmas trees. Its first buyer was a newly formed water-supply district for the rapidly growing area west of Pueblo. Thereafter CLADCO negotiated sale of Twin Lakes shares to the cities of Aurora (located in the South Platte drainage), Colorado Springs, and Pueblo. Meanwhile, some of the farmers who had not sold their land and water rights to CLADCO organized themselves to sell their Twin Lakes rights directly to the cities. They found the cities willing to pay $1,075 per share just for their Twin Lakes interests, leaving them with their land, their homes, their direct-flow rights from the Arkansas River, and their storage rights in either Lake Henry or Lake Meredith. By 1980 CLADCO had ceased to exist. At this point the four cities owned 94 percent of all Twin Lakes shares.[77]

A variation on this same theme took place in the 1980s, this time involving the Rocky Ford Ditch. In 1979 the Arkansas Valley's last remaining sugar beet processing facility (located in Rocky Ford) shut down. Its owner, the American Crystal Sugar Company, sold the plant, six thousand acres of land, and its water rights in the Rocky Ford Ditch in 1980 to an entity called Colorado Land and Water Supply, Inc., which in turn sold these interests to Resource Investment Group, Ltd., in 1981. With this purchase RIG automatically became majority shareholder of the Rocky Ford Ditch Company. In 1983 RIG and the city of Aurora entered an agreement for the transfer of half of the ditch-company shares, at a price of twenty-two hundred dollars per acre-foot of water ultimately determined by the water court to be transferable with each share.[78] Aurora took an option on the other half of the shares for twenty-three hundred dollars per acre-foot. A 1987 settlement agreement set the total transferable quantity of water at 8,250 acre-feet per year, resulting in the permanent dry-up of four thousand acres of land in the vicinity of Rocky Ford.

The sale of Twin Lakes and Rocky Ford Ditch water reflected primarily the decline of the sugar-beet industry. Sugar beets brought periods of prosperity to the Lower Arkansas Valley until the 1960s. In the good years, when sugar prices were high and beet production was successful, the sugar companies made money, the factories employed hundreds of people, and farmers who chose to grow beets found a ready market. There were not many such years, however. As support for free trade gained political support over the years, tariffs declined and domestic beet sugar struggled.

Beet production was itself sometimes the problem. Growing sugar beets is a highly labor-intensive process, requiring perhaps one hundred hours of work per acre per season.[79] Sugar beets also require a good water supply. A sustained period of drought in the Arkansas Basin between 1950 and 1957, coming only twenty years after the "dirty thirties," severely eroded sugar-beet and other agricultural production. Without water from their transmountain diversion right, farmers under the Colorado Canal in 1954 would have had no water at all.

Sociologist Kenneth Weber has made an exhaustive study of the causes of the Twin Lakes and Colorado Canal water sales and the effects of the sales on Crowley County, site of the formerly irrigated land. Crowley County came into existence in 1911, largely as a consequence of the growth of Sugar City with the National Sugar Manufacturing Company's plant. Formerly part of Otero County, this land area was cut off by the Arkansas River, and there was no bridge joining the two places at the time. Crowley County's first census (1920) marked the peak of its population—about sixty-four hundred people. By 1980 only half this number lived in the county.[80] Since the county's inception its fortunes were tied closely to the fortunes of the lands irrigated by the Colorado Canal—which, in turn, depended heavily on the fortunes of National Sugar.

As Weber demonstrated, farmers irrigating with water from the Colorado Canal never had the supply necessary to assure reliable and consistent production. Proponents of irrigation like Gilpin, Henry, and Pabor had boasted of the freedom that irrigation brought from the vagaries of natural rainfall. They failed to reckon fully, however, with the vagaries and limitations of the water supply in western rivers like the Arkansas.

John Carlson, perhaps Colorado's finest contemporary water lawyer, represented the Twin Lakes Reservoir and Canal Company during the period of its transition from an irrigation to an urban water supplier. When we discussed this transition (prior to his untimely death in 1993), he urged me to look carefully at the record of the water supply to irrigators in Crowley County. It is, indeed, revealing. Between 1941 and 1973 the largest amount of water available in any year was about 189,000 acre-feet (in 1957).[81] The smallest was about 39,000 acre-feet (in 1954). The year-to-year variation was like an out-of-control yo-yo, bouncing unpredictably up and down, reflecting primarily the enormous variability in the flows of the Arkansas River and the junior priority held by the Colorado Canal.

Weber compared the availability and reliability of the Colorado Canal farmers' water supply with those supplied from the Rocky Ford Ditch. Between 1950 and 1969 the per-acre supply to Colorado Canal farmers averaged only 14 percent of the water available to Rocky Ford farmers.[82] Moreover, he found the year-to-year variability from its twenty-year mean to be ten times greater for the Colorado Canal farmer than for the Rocky Ford farmer.[83] And, as it happens, there is little usable groundwater in the shallow formations underlying lands in Crowley County. Sugar factory or no sugar factory, growing crops with the water supply available to irrigators served by the Colorado Canal was a chancy and difficult business.

In answer to the question "Who sold their water?" Weber answers "almost everyone."[84] In part he seems to be taking issue with the economists' assumption that only those farmers operating "at the margin"—that is, at or below cost—are likely to sell. In this instance, at least, virtually all of the landowners sold their reliable (and highly valuable) Twin Lakes water. Many also eventually sold their much less reliable (and less valuable) Colorado Canal and related storage rights.

What happened? One of the few holdouts, Orville Tomky, thinks people were afraid they would be left with nothing.[85] Tomky's daughter, Karen, said: "CLADCO came in and said, 'We'll offer you this money, and if you don't sell, then you won't get your water if you're the only one left on the lateral. If everybody sells their water, then you won't get yours.' " She added: "These guys [irrigators] were overextended." Weber's research backs up this statement. Using 1974 Census of Agriculture data, Weber found that the average farm operator debt in Crowley County nearly doubled that in the adjoining three counties of Bent, Otero, and Prowers.[86]

At the time of most of the water sales (around 1970) Tomky was a vigorous man in his forties. Again, Weber's examination of census data reveals that in 1964 about 62 percent of all farm operators in Crowley County were forty-five or older. By 1974 that percentage had risen to 78. Weber concludes that some sellers were attracted because they had no economic options: "Many had farmed to the edge of bankruptcy, had nearly exhausted their lines of credit, and, for them, the opportunity to sell their water shares offered much better options than the increasing likelihood of foreclosure in the near future."[87] Others saw this as an opportunity to pay off their existing debt and have enough left over for retirement. Some worked out an arrangement allowing them use of the water for up to fourteen years, at which point they planned to retire anyway.

Weber also pursued the question of what happens to those who sell their water. Do they, in fact, move to San Diego and drink martinis, as some have casually asserted? To the contrary, Weber found—nearly all of the sellers of Twin Lakes and Colorado Canal shares stayed in Crowley County. According to Weber: "In 1980, some eight years after the Twin Lakes sale, 62 of the 70 (88.6 percent) farmers who sold 80 or more shares of Twin Lakes stock remained in Crowley County. In 1988, three years after the Colorado Canal Company sale, 35 of 36 (97.2 percent) farmers who sold 80 or more shares of stock in that company remained in Crowley County."[88]

Robert Young, an eminent agricultural economist at Colorado State University, took a careful look at the economic effects of the removal of water from Crowley County.[89] He focused first on what he termed "foregone direct benefits," roughly the addition to regional income directly attributable to the use of an acre-foot of water in irrigation. This amount he calculated to be $21.00 per acre-foot of water, the equivalent of about $0.065 per one thousand gallons of water. By comparison, he noted that residential water users in cities to which the water moved pay roughly $1.50 to $2.00 per thousand gallons—more than twenty times as much. He estimated total direct farm employment losses to reach, eventually, about 150 full-time jobs, with perhaps another 100 indirectly linked job losses. Is this a lot? Certainly it is for a place like Crowley County.

4.1 Downtown Ordway.

Charles Howe, a distinguished economist at the University of Colorado, Boulder, and longtime water expert, also has examined the economic impact of water transfers in the Lower Arkansas Valley.[90] His analysis suggests that one job is lost for every 308 acres removed from irrigated agriculture, "state net income" decreases fifty-three dollars for every acre-foot removed from irrigation, and local and state government revenues decrease five dollars for every acre-foot removed. Though he does not attempt to measure the benefits of the water in its new uses, he assumes, like Young, that they are substantially higher. The problem, as he notes, is that "the incidence of the costs is upon the rural areas, while the benefits accrue largely to the urban buyers."[91]

A drive through Crowley County today readily confirms this observation. The number of irrigated farms in the county declined from 390 in 1950 to 101 in 1987.[92] Total irrigated acreage in 1987 was about 114,000 and dropping. Despite the expected benefits of a new state prison constructed in Ordway in the 1980s, there are a lot of closed businesses in the town (Figure 4.1). Sugar City is virtually

4.2 Side oats—a native grass.

deserted. And Olney Springs is little more than a gas station. Deserted farmhouses, marked by dying stands of trees, dot the landscape. Weeds dominate the vegetation on much of formerly irrigated
land. It is not a pretty picture.[93]

Dave Miller works for the Natural Resources Conservation
Service out of Rocky Ford. The NRCS emerged in the 1930s in response to the problems of the dust bowl. Dave works like a free
consultant to farmers and local soil-conservation districts, advising
them on ways to improve their practices to prevent soil erosion, and
now to reduce water-quality impairment. As we drove out to look at
some lands near Rocky Ford, he explained: "Large areas of the Arkansas Valley are no longer in cultivation. Weeds soon took over
much of this dried-up land area and started to spread into adjacent
farmed lands. No one had thought much about what would happen
with these lands, but those that had expected that they would return
to some kind of native vegetation and be usable for grazing cattle
(Figure 4.2).

"Instead," said Miller, "what we found on our irrigated lands
was that, over the years, the silt that the river traditionally carried

and the salinity–remember, the Arkansas is the saltiest river in the U.S. after the Pecos–passed into the soils. So those soils no longer resemble any native-type of soil. Native grasses can't live in these soils without irrigation–rainfall is not enough." Showing me some native grasses, Miller added: "We're learning how to revegetate this kind of land with plants that can live eventually without irrigation, but it's not easy. You have to work with the conditions at every site, the basic soil types and how they've been changed. You want a diversity of cover, not just one type of plant. You need to keep paying attention to them until they are established, or the weeds can still take over. Eventually it should be able to be grazed, but it won't take the abuse that native grasslands do. Overgraze this land, and the grasses will disappear. Next year weeds will be everywhere."

Orville Tomky, a lean, strong-looking man in his late sixties, irrigates 320 acres of land with water from the Colorado Canal. About half of his land is in alfalfa. On the remainder he grows tomatoes, melons, and corn to sell to feedlots. He also runs about two hundred head of cattle on an adjacent three thousand acres of grazing lands. One of the few Colorado Canal irrigators still holding rights to Twin Lakes water, he figures his Twin Lakes shares are worth over $1 million. Tomky grew up on a farm near the South Platte River in the vicinity of Fort Morgan, Colorado. He went into the famed Tenth Mountain Division during World War II because they were looking for farm people. After the war, he worked for the Colorado Construction Company and came to the Lower Arkansas Valley to help rebuild Highway 71 during the winter of 1947–48, where he met his wife-to-be in La Junta. They started off with eighty-eight acres. They have four children, two sons and two daughters, all college graduates. One son is a bank manager in Rocky Ford, and another has a farm. Tomky still water-skis regularly on nearby Lake Henry–one of the storage reservoirs connected to the Colorado Canal.

Ironically, Orville Tomky and the others who chose to stay in irrigation in Crowley County probably have a more reliable water supply today than before the sales. The system now operates on a rotation basis, with check structures in the canal used to control the "run" of water. The rotation system means that all of the irrigators have to be ready to take water when it is available in their part of the canal, so Allen Ringle, superintendent of the Colorado Canal, spends much of his time coordinating the timing of water deliveries. The morning I spent with Allen and Orville touring the Colorado Canal, they were working out when to schedule the next run of water. "I have to coordinate with eighty to ninety people just to figure out when I can get water to Orville," says Ringle.

"One of the problems we have is the different interests in crops and the timing of the water delivery, " says Tomky. "I grow some crops like cantaloupes and tomatoes where the timing of my irrigation is critical. Others grow crops with different needs.

"The Southeastern Project [the Fryingpan-Arkansas] has been the lifesaver of the valley. I can get a run of winter storage water and, some years, a good run of project water. The only downside is that now the recreational people think they own Pueblo Reservoir. And the rafters think they own the whole damn system!"

Tomky added: "You know, you can say a lot of things about this sale of water, but one thing is that it has made us better irrigators."

5

A HOSTILE TAKEOVER?

Colorado Interstate Gas Company, based in Colorado Springs, and its parent company, Houston-based Coastal Corporation, thought they saw a unique opportunity in the Arkansas Valley in 1991. The rapidly growing Front Range of Colorado needed water, and urban-water suppliers had been unsuccessful in obtaining permission to build a large dam on the South Platte River called Two Forks from which to supply this expanding demand.[94] These water suppliers had been willing to spend as much as a billion dollars to build a project that would provide—at most—one hundred thousand acre-feet of water annually. CIG believed it could supply at least half of this water at a lower cost from a completely different source: irrigated agriculture in the Lower Arkansas Valley. Here was its plan.

A wholly owned subsidiary, Colorado Water Supply, would purchase a majority interest in the Fort Lyon Canal Company. It would take a portion of the water now supplied by this company for irrigation use, put it in a newly constructed pipeline within its existing right-of-way that ran nearby (CIG is an interstate gas pipeline company), and pump it as much as 150 miles back uphill to users along the Front Range of the Colorado Rocky Mountains. CIG and Coastal calculated they could afford to buy the shares, go through the legal procedures necessary to allow them to move the water, build and operate the pipeline, and still make a profit. Strictly a business deal. Willing sellers and willing buyers. Let the market decide. They didn't know much about western water.

In December 1991 Ed Blackburn, Kent Rehyer, and the other owners of the roughly ninety-four thousand Fort Lyon shares received in the mail an inch-thick document offering them about twenty-two hundred dollars for each share. Fort Lyon's primary assets are two diversion dams in the lower Arkansas River, about 160 miles of right-of-way through which two large water-supply ditches run, and three small reservoirs—all valued on the company's books at the original acquisition and construction cost of about $1.4 million.[95] In addition, the company holds legal title to a series of water-court decrees establishing priority dates under which it can divert water out of the Arkansas River at specified maximum rates.[96] The shareholders are primarily farmers who own about ninety-three thousand acres on the north side of the Arkansas River between La Junta and Lamar that can be irrigated with water from the 110-mile-long Fort Lyon Canal. Ownership of a share of the Fort Lyon Canal Company represents 1/94,000 ownership of the company's assets and the legal right to 1/94,000 of the water available to the Fort Lyon system in any given year.

For three months Fort Lyon shareholders debated the offer among themselves over fence posts, at ditch headgates, in local coffee shops, and in a series of public meetings organized by the canal company and others. Blackburn, then president of the Fort Lyon board of directors, called the offer a "hostile takeover."[97] "They want 51 percent, then they can control the company and change the by-laws. They'll put three directors on the [five man] board, then they can do whatever they want." Don Zinko, a CWS (and CIG) vice president responded: "This is not a hostile takeover. If the people don't want to sell, we don't want it. If we can get 51 percent or more, we still want to keep the water available for those who don't want to sell."[98]

CWS knew there were Fort Lyon shareholders interested in selling. In 1987 a group of shareholders offered to sell as much as 65 percent of the company's shares for $4,210 per share.[99] They found no takers. Among those still interested were fifty-six-year-old A. C. Rowan and his wife Bonnie.[100] After twenty-two years of farming they found themselves with a half-million-dollar debt, largely the result of a failed effort to raise hogs in the 1980s. With money from the sale of some or all of their 393 shares, they figured they could pay off their debts and retire to the foothills of the Rockies.

The public meetings attracted widespread (even national) attention. Colorado Governor Roy Romer, himself a native of the Lower Arkansas Valley, weighed in on the proposal. Advice came from all directions, causing Ed Blackburn to say, "Many well-intentioned people are trying to solve the problem for us. It's high time we solve our own problem."[101]

At one level, the "problem" was simply deciding whether twenty-two hundred dollars is a good price for a share of Fort Lyon stock. Few in the Arkansas Valley directly challenged the right of Fort Lyon irrigators to sell their shares. Because shareholders using water from a common ditch are so closely linked through the operation of the diversion dam and the delivery system, however, Colorado courts have recognized the authority of the mutual ditch company to impose conditions on the transfer of shares, including restricting the transfer to those owning lands that can be directly served with water from the main ditch.[102] Fort Lyon Canal Company bylaws restrict the sale of company shares in this manner and require approval of transfers by the board of directors. Even so, company shares do change hands periodically among the farmers in the area. Sales around that time had been in the seven to eight hundred dollar range. By this measure the CWS offer looked attractive.

Built into the complex CWS offer, however, were a number of conditions that had to be satisfied before sellers would receive their full compensation. For example, the shares had to produce a reliable annual yield of 1.1 acre-feet of water–that is, CWS had to be able to take at least that amount of water out of the canal for use elsewhere for every share it acquired. The water-court decree approving the change of use of the water could not impose conditions that would delay the project or increase its costs. All permits necessary to complete and operate the project had to be obtained. And "revegetation" of formerly irrigated lands–planting a permanent ground cover that would survive without special irrigation–had to be 90 percent complete.[103] One analysis of the offer suggested that the effect of the conditions was to reduce the "net present value" (the value taking into account the likelihood that full payment would not be received for eight to nine years, and that money received nine years from now is worth much less than money in hand today) to between five hundred and one thousand dollars per share.[104]

Why all the conditions? Like any investor, CWS was trying to cover its risks. It needed majority ownership to be able to change the bylaws and to be sure its efforts to move water out of the Fort Lyon system would not be blocked by other shareholders. It needed to go through a so-called change-of-water-right proceeding in a special district court in Pueblo, created under Colorado law to deal only with water issues. In that proceeding CWS would bear the burden of proving that its new use of Fort Lyon water would not "injure" any other water user within the Fort Lyon Canal Company or elsewhere on the Arkansas River. Through the use of detailed engineering analysis it would need to demonstrate that other water users would still receive water in the manner to which they were legally entitled under their water rights. Almost certainly other water-right holders would "object" to the proposed change of use. The court process itself likely would take three to five years.[105] Only then would CWS know for sure how much water it would be able to take out of the Fort Lyon system. Finally, it wanted to be sure vegetative ground cover not requiring ongoing irrigation could be successfully established on the lands from which it would permanently remove the irrigation-water supply. Recent experience on other lands in the Arkansas Valley made it clear that such revegetation took time and was expensive.

Then, of course, CWS had to be able to sell the water to users willing to pay enough for CWS to recover not only the costs of purchasing the shares and completing the change of use but also building and operating a pipeline and pumping facilities. CWS suggested that water marketed to cities would probably have to be treated to reduce existing high levels of total dissolved solids (salts). The purchase of 51 percent of Fort Lyon shares alone would cost about $110 million. Press accounts suggested that completion of the project probably would cost at least another $200 million. At a minimum CWS needed to recover a $300 million investment.

Obviously CWS believed it could find buyers willing to pay enough for the water to justify the investment. How much might this be? The price of an acre-foot of water in the West depends on where you are, who you are, and what kind of use you make. If in 1992 you were an irrigator with shares in the Fort Lyon system, you paid an annual "assessment" per share of about twelve dollars, for which you likely got about two acre-feet of water. If you were are an irrigator in the Lower Arkansas Valley of Colorado who purchased an acre-foot of water from the Southeastern Colorado Water Conservancy District and its Bureau of Reclamation–constructed Fryingpan-Arkansas Project, you paid eight dollars. If you were a homeowner in Boulder, Colorado, paying for the use of an acre-foot of potable water at the lowest possible rate, you paid about three hundred dollars. A big difference, and one that CWS planned to take advantage of.

At another level the problem facing Fort Lyon shareholders was far more complex. To many it involved the future viability of the Fort Lyon Canal Company as an irrigation-water supplier and, perhaps, the continued viability of irrigated agriculture itself in the Lower Arkansas Valley of Colorado. What would it mean for those still wanting to irrigate their farmlands through the Fort Lyon Canal to have a gas pipeline company in control of the ditch company? What would it mean to have at least fifty thousand acre-feet less water available for irrigation use? What would it mean to have more than half the lands now irrigated with Fort Lyon water permanently removed from irrigated agriculture? What would it mean for the irrigation farmers' water supply? For the cost of their water? For the continued care of the canal? For the businesses in adjacent communities closely tied to irrigated agriculture (seed companies, farm-equipment suppliers, processors, shippers)? For the businesses that benefit more indirectly (hardware stores, clothes stores, supermarkets)? For the schools, roads, and other county services supported by property-tax assessments?

⁓

I spent several days in the fall of 1992 looking at the Fort Lyon Canal and related facilities, and meeting members of the board and other shareholders who farm lands supplied by Fort Lyon water. Even a casual glance makes it clear that alfalfa dominates the crops grown on these lands, particularly in the eastern part of the system.[106]

The Fort Lyon service area is broken into five divisions for purposes of managing water deliveries. Water is supplied to the users in each division on a rotating basis. There are 365 separate headgates at which shareholders in each division, when the canal is full, divert water at the rate of 0.015 cubic feet per second per share for forty-eight hours. Some of these headgates take water directly out of the Fort Lyon Canal, but most are located on laterals (ditches branching off the main canal). There are eighteen major laterals along the canal, owned and maintained separately from the company by the landowners who receive their water through them. Company ditch riders who manage this water-delivery process attempt to ensure that each shareholder receives the same amount of water per share during a rotation. When the canal contains less than the fullest possible amount of water (most of the time), less water passes through the headgates, but they remain open for a longer period of time. The difference is in the number of times during an irrigation season that an irrigator can expect to see water at his headgate. Under peak-supply conditions shareholders receive water two out of every four days. When conditions are dry, shareholders are likely to receive water only four days a month.[107]

The year-to-year variations in the total amount of water diverted out of the Arkansas River into the Fort Lyon Canal are pronounced: averaging about 191,000 acre-feet on an annual basis between 1950 and 1985, the canal diverted as little as 94,000 acre-feet in 1954 and as much as 337,000 acre-feet in 1984. The actual water needs of plants, of course, vary little from year to year. Based on water availability during this period, the Fort Lyon system has a 90 percent probability of receiving only 110,000 acre-feet a year—not much more than one acre-foot per acre of irrigated land.[108] With this kind of water supply, it probably doesn't make much sense for farmers/shareholders in the Fort Lyon Canal Company to plant crops that absolutely require large amounts of water every year.

Kent Rehyer's eight-hundred-acre farm is located in the western part of the Fort Lyon system. First elected to the board of directors in 1985, he had also served as secretary since that time. He graduated from Colorado State University in 1972 with a major in agricultural education and taught for a year at Crowley County High School.

He got married in 1973 and decided to join with his father in his farming operation. Even though he grew up on a farm and has been farming himself for twenty years, he considers himself a "young kid, really, compared with some of the farmers under the system," and he *does* seem a lot younger than most of the other farmers I met in the valley. He laughs easily when he talks.

Like most of the farmers in the area, he grows some alfalfa, but not as much as they do in the eastern part of the system. He also grows corn, wheat, milo, and, since 1991, watermelons. "When I started, I tried to follow the rule book. I set high yield goals, took soil tests, did everything they told us to do at CSU. Pretty soon I was looking at an eight-thousand-dollar fertilizer bill, and I said, 'This isn't the way to go.' So then I switched my focus to management, getting the most production out of the least money through crop rotation, careful irrigating, doing things at the right time. And it worked–for a while. I still think it's the best way to go."

Kent talked about the fact that lands in this part of the Fort Lyon system started off with twice as many shares per acre as in the eastern part of the system–partly due to the soil differences and partly because the original developers wanted to spread the water supply to a larger area as they expanded the system. "It's a lot more expensive growing row crops than alfalfa. We've got more water up here, but we pay for that extra water. We've got the expense of more labor, more supplies, checks, irrigation dams, syphon tubes, gated pipe, or whatever system the farmer is using. We spend a lot managing that water. There were places on this farm where there were five ditches. Now there's one. Water used to run off of these fields in three different directions. Now most of the fields have been leveled so they run to the south. All our main carry ditches from the headgates go north and south, our carry ditches to the fields go east, we irrigate to the south. Wastewater is picked up and runs to the east. We try to use every drop that belongs on this farm." Kent pulled the pickup over to the side of the road and pointed. "See that bare spot there in the middle of the field? That's a place we probably shouldn't have leveled because we cut into a foot of shale. It was about the third year I was here. It took a guy with a big old Cat with a chisel on the back and a loader on the front to break it up, and it took us a day

5.1 Saline soils in the Lower Arkansas Valley.

and a half to haul the shale away. There's just no organic matter in the soil. Even after all these years nothing grows there."

As we drove on, he pointed to a ditch running with water. "That's groundwater I'm pumping from one of my two wells. I'm trying to get my winter wheat crop planted here, and I missed getting canal water when it was available last weekend. Too busy loading watermelons! Your whole farm operation pivots around water. The Fort Lyon's a 'flood right' ditch, really. The only reliable supply is our first decree for 165 feet [cubic feet per second]. You've got 110 miles right through ninety-three thousand acres. You're not going to irrigate anything with 165 feet, so, really, we depend on that second and third right, which gets us up to 700 and some feet and then up to 933. So unless you have a good river, you're hurting. If this system had 400 feet, 500 feet all season long, I think it'd be better than this 933 for a few days and then drop down to 200, then back up to 500 and then down again."

Pointing to some white-crusted soil (Figure 5.1), Kent remarked: "One of the other problems we don't have control over right now is the quality of our water—lack of good quality. The salt is limiting our ability to try new things—things that have extra yield. We used to grow pinto beans, but they just don't do as well here as they do up west. Soybeans have the same problem. Alternative crops have been limited because of the water quality."

Later, as we walked along a ditch carrying water to one of his fields, he said: "We're right here in no-man's-land. We can't grow the high-income crops like they can up west. And we don't seem to get the yields of milo and alfalfa that they get down east. In your traveling, I don't know if you've noticed it, but I think you'll see nicer, more modern homesteads, farm buildings, down east than you will in this fifteen- or twenty-mile stretch right here. Why? I can't believe it's just the people. I think we're having a little tougher job right here. I'll bet that 90 to 95 percent of the people that Colorado Water Supply signed up live within five to fifteen miles of this house."

On our way back to Kent's farmhouse I asked if he had children. "Yes, three: two girls and a boy. They are allergic to farm work! One really is. She's allergic to anything and everything that grows or walks. Allergic to cats, allergic to trees and pollen and weeds and grass and everything. So she's never been a farm girl. The second one, well, I guess I've never pushed her. The youngest is a boy, and he enjoys electronics and machinery. His hobby is trains. He can get on a piece of equipment, watch how I operate it, and he can do it. I guess we don't give our kids the same kind of opportunities I had as a kid. Shoot, I was driving a pickup when I was six years old and driving a tractor in the fields when I was ten. I don't know if it was crazy or they just needed the help. But, of course, we loved that stuff. There weren't any air-conditioned cabs and we'd come back covered with dirt, but it was fun." Do you think your son might be interested in farming, I asked? "Yeah, I think so. Darn it! For fear of being accused of child abuse, yeah, I guess. I shouldn't want to instill in him the idea that 'this is what you want someday' because the economics of agriculture is so bad. But, you know, my wife and kids were at the local coffee shop one day with a bunch of other farmers. And they were talking about the Colorado Water Supply deal. And my son said: 'Well, we can't sell ours. We've got to be farming here. Even if I had a job somewhere else, I've still got to be able to come back to this farm.' Well, that kind of shocked me. I had never heard that. I didn't know that's how he felt."

As we pulled into his driveway, Kent said: "We put in this windbreak in seventy-five when our daughter was three weeks old. The hardest thing to get going was the ponderosa pine. I've had to replant some, and you can still see a gap here. Those Russian olives, they're almost like weeds you can't control. Six hundred forty trees. Planted by hand." He paused. "I hope you're getting what you need. You know what this place would look like if you took the water out. Just drive across to the other side of the canal, and you can see what it's going to be, you can see what effect it would have. But—we're still going to try to protect that right [to sell water] because we might be the ones tomorrow that want to have that ability."

As I was about to leave, he said: "So the water issues in the valley—they're from the heart. They have an impact you probably can't imagine unless you were in it. Maybe we can come up with some ideas for other ways to use water in the valley. If the water's not used for agriculture, at least maybe they can get some industry in the valley that will keep the people and the businesses here."

〜

As described in chapter 4, other sales of ditch-company shares in the Lower Arkansas Valley had taken water out of irrigation use and out of the valley. But this sale of Fort Lyon shares would be the single largest such transaction. Already by 1991 other sales had resulted in the dry-up of about 56,000 acres of the roughly 320,000 acres of irrigated land between Pueblo and the state line.[109]

Transactions like the CWS offer have come to be referred to as "water marketing."[110] Such a description is perhaps unfortunate, since it implies there is a market in which water is being bought and sold. Far from it. Water never has been traded like a commodity in the West. To use the vernacular, it has been "appropriated"—which is to say that a claim to its use has been made according to state-law requirements. Appropriation involves the construction of the physical structures that make possible control and use of the water. Users pay the cost of the facilities; they do not pay for the water. Actual beneficial use of the water creates a water "right"—legal recognition of the diversion and use of water for the described purposes and protection of that use against harm by subsequent users.

CWS wanted to obtain water that it could provide to others at a profit. It could not simply go out into a marketplace and purchase water. There is no such marketplace. Instead it had to buy majority ownership of a company through which it could get access to water. It had to deal with company shareholders whose lives and livelihoods are tied directly to the use of the water. To these shareholders, selling these shares meant getting out of irrigated agriculture, probably forever. To CWS, buying these shares meant taking over an irrigation company. Getting use of the water meant going through a complicated court proceeding. Only then would CWS actually have water for sale. Calling all of this water marketing hardly captures the nature of the process or the kind of fundamental change implied by such transactions.

~

The February 28, 1992, deadline set by CWS for responses to its offer passed without the requisite 51 percent acceptances. CWS never revealed how close it came to reaching this target, but indications are that it wasn't very close. One explanation is simply the price. Those offering to sell a few years earlier wanted over four thousand dollars a share, compared to the twenty-two hundred dollars offered by CWS. Another explanation was the nature of the offer itself: a complex, highly legalistic document filled with protections for the buyers. And then there were suspicions about the large corporate interests behind the buyers.

Ed Blackburn farms five hundred irrigated acres under the Fort Lyon Canal. Trained as a geologist at the Colorado School of Mines, he worked for ten years as an exploration geophysicist looking for oil. He tired of the traveling and the separation from his family, returned to the Arkansas Valley, where he was born and raised, and bought a farm next to his father's property, which he now owns as well. He grows primarily alfalfa, together with some wheat and silage corn, and also runs a cow-calf operation on about six thousand acres of adjacent drylands.

As president of the Fort Lyon board of directors, Ed was actively involved in the discussions surrounding the Colorado Water Supply offer. In his thoughtful, careful way he worked hard to convince other Fort Lyon irrigators not to take the offer. "I have often thought it would be nice to sell your water and have a million and a half dollars and walk off. But, really, when the time comes, that isn't what it's about. There is a lot of tradition here—you know, your dad and your grandfather, all these people that worked very hard to make the canal company what it is. And then you've had a part in it too. And for me it became very, very difficult to think that you could sell it."

Joe Cline is another Fort Lyon shareholder and member of the board of directors. He too opposed the CWS offer. He farms over two thousand acres, built from the original quarter section of land purchased by his grandfather in 1902. "Well, I'm not interested in selling water. Now, that's me—but I don't want to tell my neighbor he can't sell his. I don't go that far."

Kent Reyher was a member of the board at the time of the CWS proposal. "I had a guy call me up, tell me he's eighty-some-thing years old, he's got a hundred or so shares of water. Kids are gone, nobody else wants it—what's he going to do with it? We need to have an option for people like him." He added: "My job as a member of the board is to be sure that the guy who wants to be the last irrigator on this system, when everyone else is gone, is protected." He paused for a moment, shifting thoughts. "If you want to bring in the issue of how I'm going to affect the clothing store downtown Las Animas, forget it. Yes, I'm concerned. I've been on the chamber of commerce, and I'm for the community, but first we're trying to look after ourselves."

Dave Rehyer is a vice president of a bank in Lamar. He also owns and leases 160 acres of nearby farmland held by his family for more than one hundred years. "Farming's a tough business, no doubt about it. Some people are having a pretty tough time. However, on the other side of that, there are some people that are doing very well. The press or the six o'clock news has a way of only telling you about the poor farmer who is down on his luck and the bank is pounding on his head, and yeah, that happens from time to time, but for every one of those, I could name you ten that are doing great." He took another drink of coffee. "I understand people wanting to be able to make up their own minds about what they do with their water, but I hope they think about what they're doing. Because when it's gone, it's gone. It's never coming back. Selling water out of this valley would be an economic and environmental disaster. I wish I had time to sit down and track a dollar through this community. If I have a ton of hay sold out here, every dollar probably turns over in the community five to seven times." Sitting back in his chair, he said, "You've got young people in the area that want to farm, who are energetic, forward-thinking people, and then we've got the old, established farmers who came up through tough times when they didn't know where the dollar for their next dinner was coming from, let alone how they were going to put fuel in the tractor. But in my opinion there's a lot of things we can do to preserve the water, make us more efficient, that really would add economic value to our property." As he got up to go, he said: "The deal that was offered by the company trying to buy the water was a bad deal. But if somebody came to me and said, 'Dave, we're going to give you two thousand dollars a share *today*,' I'm not sure how smart I'd be to turn that down, to be honest with you. Two thousand dollars, and my land's only worth eight hundred dollars an acre."

Paul Springer lives on the far eastern end of the Fort Lyon system on 835 acres. His father started farming in this area in the 1890s, coming out from Missouri. He is in his mid-seventies, spry and vigorous. Along with his wife and his son, he grows mostly alfalfa and some wheat and milo. "I used to raise chickens and sold the eggs for hatching. Kept careful books on them. Found out I wasn't making anything, so I eliminated the chickens. Had sheep. And I kept careful books on them. Found out I wasn't making anything, so I eliminated the sheep. Now I'm straight farming." Winking at me, he laughed. "I don't keep any books on it, because I'm afraid if I found out I wasn't making any money, I'd eliminate the farm!"

As we toured the lower end of the Fort Lyon Canal, he said: "That water company called me, and I told them, 'Hey, I love farming and my son loves farming. And I got a great-grandson running around yelling 'tractor, tractor,' and he wants to farm. And I said,

'What do I want to sell it for?' I said, 'There's a heritage of people out here on the land doing what they love to do. Why should I sell that to Denver?' I wouldn't sell."

As I got ready to leave, he said, "Farming's not for everyone. My son-in-law thought he wanted to be a farmer. But what he really wanted was an eight-hour-a-day job and lots of time to go off hunting and fishing. He didn't like getting up in the middle of the night to go set irrigation water."

6

LOOKING AHEAD

Once a month, at half past six in the morning, people from the town of La Junta gather together at the junior college for a breakfast known as "Wake Up La Junta." Several hundred people fill the large cafeteria, filing through buffet lines to load up on eggs and bacon, toast, coffee and more. Soon the tables are filled and breakfast is eaten. As soon as everyone is seated, two men—dressed in long-underwear tops, jeans, and suspenders—ascend the stage in front and start up a friendly banter—like a morning radio talk show with two hosts. The first official order of business is to give special recognition to passengers from a car "kidnapped" the night before from Highway 50 with the help of town police. A car is picked at random as it passes through La Junta, pulled over, and the passengers are "arrested"—that is, they are invited to stop overnight at a local motel, have dinner, and come to the "Wake Up La Junta" breakfast the next morning, compliments of the town. This month's "detainees" are from Kansas, on their way to visit relatives in Colorado Springs. They smile gamely when introduced and mumble a few words about hospitality. Another standard feature of the monthly program is to introduce any new arrivals to La Junta since the last breakfast and to introduce every new business that has started. It's purely chamber of commerce stuff, but fun and effective, and all there seem to be enjoying themselves.

Communities in the Lower Arkansas Valley of Colorado are working to build a future. As with rural communities generally, the postwar era has not been good to such places. Perhaps the single biggest factor in the Arkansas Valley was the loss of the sugar beet processing facilities, but the general decline of rural areas transcends any single economic factor and reflects broader economic and societal trends. There is growing evidence, however, that these urbanizing trends now have peaked and that people are once again seeking out rural areas in growing numbers, both to live and to work in.[111] Moreover, this rural migration is occurring in places other than Sun Valley, Jackson Hole, Aspen, and Sedona.

What does this mean for the Arkansas Valley? It's hard to tell. Towns like Lamar, La Junta, and Rocky Ford seem healthy enough, but some other communities in the valley are clearly declining. Ordway in Crowley County is one prominent example.

When all is said and done, land and natural resources remain the economic base of the valley. Grazing cattle is still the only use of most of the land area of the Lower Valley that can generate an economic return, small as it might be. Irrigated lands produce considerably more return, but such lands comprise only a small (and shrinking) portion of the land area—perhaps 3 percent. Dryland agriculture, particularly for wheat, yields good returns in some years.

In the foreseeable future agriculture and ranching are likely to remain the core of the valley's economy, and irrigated production will remain a modest but valuable part of that agriculture. Too much, perhaps, has been expected of irrigated agriculture in this valley. Enticed by the almost miraculous transformation of dry prairie lands into productive farmlands, people like T. C. Henry greatly overextended the valley's water supply. Despite almost continuous efforts to overcome this reality ever since, the fact remains that there is simply not enough water in the Arkansas Basin to supply existing irrigation demands reliably. Cities are able to pay far more to use the limited supplies of the Arkansas River than are irrigators. Some irrigators find it increasingly difficult to justify their farming in the face of offers for their water that exceed the value of their land, their improvements, and their water in agriculture. Others can't imagine living any other way.

Much has been done to improve the usability of the available water supply, by increasing water-storage capacity, by enlarging the amount of water imported into the basin from the Colorado River

Basin, by tapping into the groundwater supply, and by improving water management and use both within ditch systems and on farm. It seems likely the productivity per unit of water used in Arkansas Valley irrigation is higher than it has ever been. That productivity seems sure to increase as additional claims are placed on the Arkansas River and its tributaries, both surface and subsurface—by Kansas, by upstream cities, and by recreational interests.

And yet there is a sense of a downward spiral pervading irrigated agriculture in the Lower Arkansas Valley. Right now, most people in the valley see only their piece of the water—their ditch-company shares, their winter water-storage rights, their groundwater rights, their transmountain diversions. They have been concerned mostly about getting as much of this water for their own use as they can and, more recently, about holding on to what they have from what they see as outside forces wanting to take "their" water away. This is a pattern repeated all across the West.

The Colorado Water Supply proposal to buy up majority ownership in the Fort Lyon Canal came as a kind of wake-up call for many people in the Lower Arkansas Valley. Images from Crowley County and the Colorado Canal foretold a future that few wanted. But what are the alternatives? There does not yet seem to be much of a consensus about this, except perhaps that the water of the Arkansas should somehow remain in the valley—for irrigation if that can be sustained; for other uses if it cannot.

If that use is not likely to mean irrigated agriculture to the extent it has in the past, what does it mean? If irrigated agriculture remains important to the economy of these areas, are there changes that can strengthen this sector and help bolster its long-term sustainability? These are the kinds of questions facing those who live in the Lower Arkansas Valley. They are the same questions facing other rural areas of the West historically developed around irrigated agriculture.

Because of the Colorado Water Supply proposal, valley residents started considering alternatives that might help to keep at least some of the Fort Lyon water in the Lower Arkansas Valley. For a short time there was interest in the possibility of unified ownership of all irrigation-water rights under a single district, with water leased back for irrigation and other use in the valley.[112] The Colorado General Assembly directed the Colorado Water Conservation Board to examine alternatives to the transfer of water from the Fort Lyon Canal. The consultant's study favored establishing some kind of water-banking mechanism operated by the Fort Lyon company itself that could make possible temporary transfer of water from fallowed land to other uses, presumably within the valley.[113]

The study identified several possible uses of water that would be made available through such a water bank. One is as a source of replacement water for new or existing groundwater diversions to meet municipal needs in the valley.[114] Another is to meet potential water needs for expanded feedlot operations expected in the valley. A third is as a source of water to improve and stabilize storage in the Great Plains Reservoirs and other off-stream reservoirs in the valley that offer valuable recreational uses and wildlife habitat.

For many years the state of Colorado has been interested in improving recreational opportunities in the Lower Arkansas Valley. In the early 1970s the Colorado Division of Wildlife purchased shares of the Catlin Canal Company, with the intention of transferring the use of this water to the John Martin Reservoir. It made the mistake, however, of failing to consult with Frank Milenski before doing so (Figure 6.1). Frank, who died in 1998, is something of a legend in the Arkansas Valley. In 1990 he published a book called *Water: The Answer to a Desert's Prayer*,[115] and in 1993 he published a summary of the board proceedings of the Southeastern Colorado Water Conservancy District between 1958 and 1990 called *In Quest of Water*.[116] Over the years he was a highly effective advocate for irrigated agriculture in the valley and across the state. He always had an opinion or two about everything, and the personality to back it up.

Frank believed in his every fiber that the best use of water from the Arkansas River is for irrigated agriculture. He was proud of how effectively that water is used and reused as it makes its way through the eastern plains of Colorado, and not at all interested in the ideas of those who say water should be used more efficiently (he called them the soil "conversationalists" instead of the soil conservationists). Putting water in a "fishpool" in the John Martin Reservoir is just plain foolish, said Frank. It will evaporate instead of growing

6.1 Frank Milenski at the Catlin Canal Diversion Dam.

crops the way it should. The sediment will drop out into the reservoir, making the water that is released to downstream irrigators "hungry" for soils instead of soil replenishers.

Frank, Catlin's longtime lawyer Rex Mitchell, and the Catlin Canal Company succeeded in convincing the Colorado Supreme Court that the Catlin Canal Company, as a mutual ditch company, could legally restrict the transfer of shares for use outside the company service area.[117] Milenski brought the same passion for protection of irrigated agriculture in the Lower Arkansas Valley that he brought to protection of the Catlin. It was a passion born of belief in a way of life: hard work, productive work, work that provides a decent living while providing food for others. Moved by the threat of the transfer of more than half the water from the Fort Lyon Canal system, Frank wrote "After the Water is Gone":[118]

After the water is gone, what do I see?
I see things that are foreign to me.
The dream of the men that used to be,
The pioneers who by their ingenuity
Built the canals with horses and mules that pulled
　the slips tied on with a whippletree.
The men with the old transits putting in the stakes of the grade of
　　the canal that would be.
The old timers looking at the wooden headgates and the twenty
　　foot culverts that from the canal turned the water free.
To water the land broken from prairie,
The land of the rattlesnake and sage brush,
　turned into irrigated land to grow food for you and me.
The land that the settlers homesteaded–that the U.S. Government
　　gave them free
To start a civilization in the West so all the world could see
The glory of nature and man working in harmony.

And now what do I see?
I see the cities growing
Bold and wanting much more of what is a necessity
To be used they say for the finer things of life,
Or so they say to me.
To develop green belts and golf courses
　and things they say need be.
To have in the garden, grass and shrubs and the posy
　that are grown by the water of the farmers that used to be.
The water is supposed to produce recreation for those
　whose time is free.
The cities have to have supplies for as far as you can see.
Not withstanding that mama nature is the one
　that says what will be.
It is not a case of pulling up the belts in time of scarcity.
If you live in a city
　you are instilled to have the luxury,
Of having a supply of water for the next century.
It is not what is to be used as a necessity,
　as the farmers put up with nature in good time and adversity.

I know water flows up hill to money.
It used to be it was a battle of the have-nots and the haves
　as agriculture in its way of life used the most valuable
　thing it's plain to see.

Now that the people who till the soil are down to
　two percent or three
And the God all mighty
　dollar has all the power to be,
The people in agriculture have fallen on hard times and misery.
And yet, Roosevelt said food would win the war and write
　the peace after victory.
God help the people if all the water Brains are in Washington
　and the politically are to be the judge in every case.
Common sense has to be a sustaining light.
In a time of the farmers trying to keep the wolf from the door
　came the bargains galore
For developers and the fast buck artists,
　the ones who rich in one stroke want to be.
The water they could grab from drilling holes and augmentation
　which they say are produced by men of three–
H2O to you and me.
One of the reasons the Canal Company people are broke
　is that it takes money to protect what you thought was a
　　property right from the guy who'd like to have it for free
And now to a water court go those
　who want a change of use to be.
In all the pomp and ceremony
　go the learned lawyers for a fee.
The lawyer being a professional debater has to use all his
　cunning, you see.
When as a witness they call a man with a pedigree
He has graduated from college and has a string of letters
　of his education for all to see.
Makes no difference if a Mexican dragline (an irrigating shovel)
　on his back he has not packed with glee,
Or how long a tenure on the river he has had,
　it's what the book says, you see.
I know the learned Judge has great decisions
　for the facts presented to him he must sort with great care
And make a decision just and brave that will withstand a Supreme
　　Court appeal in the face of a lawyer who wants to rave–
　a lawyer whose reputation has to be upheld to help his image
　as the famous water lawyer that he would like to be.

Now I know water was put on this earth to be used as a necessity,
It just may be that the food we produce by water to the
　land is a blessing for you and me.

And the fact that generally speaking no one goes to bed hungry
  may be one of the greatest Blessings that there will ever be.
The day in this country when to the grocer you do go,
  and find that all the food to which you've grown accustomed
  has become a luxury,
Just may be the time when some of the smart ones will have to
    eat the smog that they helped to be.
Surely there are users of water in the country
That should draw some kind of use at home
  where the water should be.
When you push people by droves to the cities
  they miss the greatest joy of life, you see.
On a farm all my life I have spent—it develops humility.
To live with wonders of nature has been a privilege to me.
So I hope to God there will always be a place to farm for others
  who believe like me.

It was, I think, the wish of the Lord that the earth be used—
  otherwise, why would it be?
To use the earth with care
  to use it any other way no one should dare.
But if we wish to survive, I surely hope the do-gooders are not
  the ones we depend on for the groceries in times to be.
For a city to survive in the style they have projected will be,
Without storage of water, under the Colorado Constitution the
    right to appropriate unappropriated water should always be.
So maybe a storage of water is a necessity.
It might just keep the water on the farms to be used at where it
  ought to be.
In the Arkansas Valley the land to be dried up you see.
At the present time water sold adds up almost to a hundred square
  miles of dried up land with a future that's not good to see.
T'was better the land had not been broken from sod than to grow
  weeds and produce a land of misery.
There are people who say grass without water can grow on the land
  after the water is taken to the cities.
Now, between you and me and the gatepost, I have lived in
Colorado all my life. But now I come from Missouri—show me!

Congress authorized a ten-thousand-acre-foot "permanent pool" of water in the John Martin Reservoir in 1965. The Arkansas Compact Commission allows the Division of Wildlife to store up to another five thousand acre-feet. Replenishing the water evaporated from this pool requires from two thousand to five thousand acre-feet per year to be added. In May 1992 Governor Romer appointed the Lower Arkansas River Commission to look at options for establishing a state park in the valley and for providing water for recreational and wildlife uses at John Martin and Great Plains. This commission recommended obtaining a permanent supply of replacement water for John Martin, acquiring a water supply for the Great Plains Reservoirs from the Amity's storage decree, and establishing a state park at Great Plains.[119]

On one of my trips to the Lower Arkansas Valley I went out to visit the Great Plains Reservoirs. It was an early evening in September. The fading light reflected off clouds scattered high in the pale sky. I picked the reservoir called Nee Noshe to visit first (Figure 6.2). With a little exploration I found a dirt road that led me to a point perhaps one hundred yards from the water. I walked across this open, flat area, sometimes inundated by water, to reach the edge of the reservoir itself. The water is shallow, no more than a few feet deep. Hardly what I would call beautiful in a classic sense—and yet there were some ducks floating out on the open water, and flycatchers cut through an evening sky filled with insects. Some tamarack bushes grew off to the sides of the reservoir bed, providing valuable habitat for birds and other wildlife. In a land with few such places, it had its own special kind of value.

Certainly these four reservoirs have never quite fulfilled their promise as a "chain of inland seas, holding in reserve immense bodies of water beneficial not only for direct irrigation, but necessarily tending by evaporation to increase moisture and induce rainfall."[120] Shallow depressions of unknown origin, they collected and held water periodically from local cloudbursts—serving as buffalo "wallows." Beginning in 1895, canals were constructed from the Arkansas River to carry water from the river for storage in these natural buckets. Unfortunately, these reservoirs proved to be highly inefficient. First, there is the problem that much of the water deposited into them can

6.2 Sunset at Nee Noshe Reservoir.

never be retrieved–it goes into what is called "dead storage." Then there is the problem of evaporation. Not only is the area warm and dry in the summer, but the relatively large extent of surface area compared to depth further accelerates this evaporation. Next there is the roughly 20 percent of water lost in its conveyance from the river. And, of course, there is the highly constricted and erratic nature of the water supplies in the Arkansas River itself. The owner of these reservoirs, the Amity Mutual Irrigation Company, now uses storage in the John Martin Reservoir instead.[121]

The Nee Gronda and Queen reservoirs offer more traditional recreational opportunities. Both have a line of cottonwood trees growing along their north shores. With their greater depth they are already popular for fishing and water-skiing. With a more consistent water supply, their usability would be improved. Thirty years ago, when I first came to Colorado, reservoirs seemed to me undesirable places to go. Now I am a regular user of Lake McConaughy in Nebraska and other eastern-plains reservoirs. I have learned that you go where the water is, just as Carl Genova wants (though you might not live there).

Recreation is part of the answer to the question of what uses should be made of the Lower Valley's water supplies in the future. Dave Rehyer, son of an irrigator turned bank vice president, sees that: "What to do with your weekend now is one of the big things we're concerned with, and, of course, recreation is getting a lot of focus. What if some of the water off those irrigated lands went into a permanent pool in the lakes in the valley? You might have some little industry sprout up for recreation: marinas, boat dealers, additional motels and hotels."

But the central question still concerns irrigated agriculture. What is its future? Is it an activity that simply no longer is viable and should be allowed to disappear slowly but surely in the manner that it has since the 1950s? Irrigator Kent Rehyer articulated the problem well: "This nation does not need farming in the Arkansas Valley. But maybe the state of Colorado does, and everyone who lives in this valley does. So who can afford us? I don't know. I don't know if the state can afford us. I don't know if the rest of the community can afford us. Everyone has to pay their own way."

PART 2

THE GRAND VALLEY, COLORADO
WHERE FRUIT, FISH, AND
GROWTH COLLIDE

Fair Fruita in the sunshine lies,
The fairest village 'neath the skies;
Broad sweep of fertile land around,
Where prosperous farmer homes abound;
Home of the almond, apple, peach,
And vines, whose purple clusters teach
That bounteous Nature offers here
A generous summer with each year.

–William E. Pabor, 1900

7

GROWING PEACHES IN AN ARID
MOUNTAIN VALLEY

Few orchards now grow in the vicinity of the town of Fruita, Colorado, located toward the west end of the Grand Valley, but when William E. Pabor founded the Fruita Town and Land Company in 1883, he planted apples, pears, peaches, cherries, plums, and grapes with such success that, by 1886, a five-acre plot was selling for five hundred dollars.[1] The Grand Valley had been opened to non–American Indian settlement only a few years before but already a good-size town called Grand Junction existed at the confluence of the Grand (later to be called the Colorado)[2] and Gunnison rivers (Figure 7.1). The Denver and Rio Grande Railroad linked the valley with Gunnison to the east, and the Rio Grande Western with Salt Lake City to the west, and three separate irrigation ditch systems were carrying water from the Colorado River to arable lands along the river. Valley boosters–touting the mild climate, the abundance of land and water, and the early success in growing vegetables, grains, and fruit–predicted a glorious future.[3]

Some who previously had passed through this area might have been surprised at its rapid transformation. Most early visitors arrived via the Gunnison River Valley from the southeast, where the Gunnison joined the larger but less accessible Grand River. Their reports commented on the valley's barren landscape (featuring primarily greasewood and sagebrush) and its desertlike dryness (eight to ten inches of precipitation annually).[4] Until the 1877 Hayden Survey suggested the feasibility of irrigation, few saw much agricultural potential for

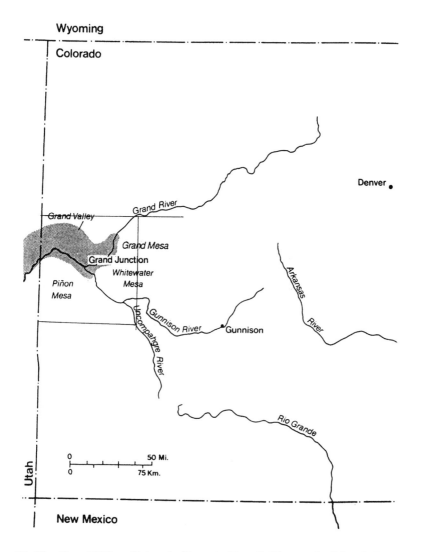

7.1 The Grand Valley, Colorado (Source: *Town Building on the Colorado Frontier*, Kathleen Underwood, University of New Mexico Press, 1988).

the valley.[5] Even George Crawford, one of the founders of Grand Junction, would say in his diary at the time the town site was located: "Not a tree, not a house, not a drop of water, not a green thing dotted the valley. . . . Nothing but a barren waste."[6]

The Grand Valley is shaped like the side of a riding boot, with

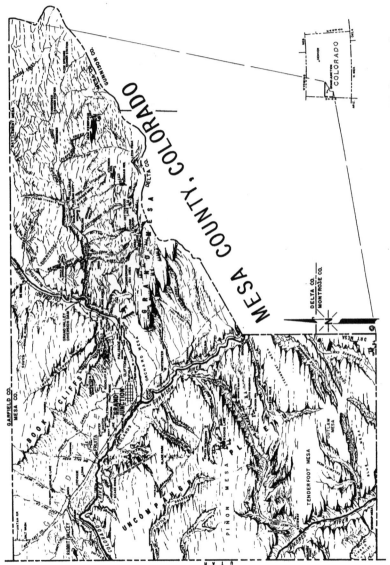

7.2 The Grand Valley Region (Source: *Mesa County, Colorado, A 100 Year History*, Emma McCreanor, Lani Duke, & Judy Prosser, The Museum of Western Colorado Press, 1986).

7.3 Book Cliffs as seen from Orchard Mesa.

its leg pointing toward the northwest and its foot tipped slightly upward to the east (Figure 7.2). The city of Grand Junction (and the junction of the two rivers) sits at the ankle of the boot. To the north are the Book Cliffs, highly erodible sediments permanently brown in color because of their lack of vegetation (Figure 7.3). The southern edge of the upper boot, by comparison, features striking reddish walls and spires of hard sandstone–a portion of which is included in Colorado National Monument. At the easternmost point of the foot rises the Grand Mesa, rolling forested lands dotted with small lakes lifted high above the valley. From toe tip to the calf of the boot is about forty miles. Its width ranges from roughly four to twelve miles.

Ute Indians officially controlled this part of Colorado by treaties ratified by the U.S. Senate in 1863 and 1868, for which they ceded their claims to the central and eastern part of the state and by which a reservation including the Grand Valley was established.[7] In

1879 disgruntled Ute in northern Colorado killed Nathaniel Meeker, at that time Indian agent on the reservation and, formerly, founder of the Union Colony at Greeley, Colorado. In response the United States decided in 1880 to remove the Ute from all of western Colorado except for two small reservations in the southwest corner of the state. In August 1881 Ute residing in the Grand Valley were forced to move to the Uintah Reservation in Utah.[8] Settlers immediately came into the valley and laid out claims to land.[9]

The primary initial attraction of the Grand Valley in 1881 was the availability of large areas of unclaimed land, level enough to be farmable, with a large, essentially unused river running through it, at an elevation lower than Denver's (about forty-six hundred feet at Grand Junction compared to about fifty-two hundred feet), and with a surprisingly mild climate. Somewhat sheltered from Canadian cold fronts by the mountains to the north and east and warmed by desert air from the southwest, the Grand Valley turned out to have an average growing season of 182 days, nearly a month longer than around Denver.[10]

Only with irrigation was settlement of the Grand Valley possible. Getting water from the Colorado River to lands in the valley, however, was no easy matter. As the Colorado leaves the confines of DeBeque Canyon and enters the valley, its channel cuts down through the alluvial valley floor. Not until the river is well into the valley does it make an arcing turn to the south, causing it to run almost even with its banks to the west, thereby making it possible to divert water directly out of the river. It is along this stretch that the first three ditches built their headgates. As the river turns once again to the west, it soon moves back into a channel cut well below the adjacent lands, through which it continues to its junction with the Gunnison River and beyond.

Work began on the Grand Valley Ditch shortly after settlement in 1881 and on two other small ditches the following year.[11] Initially, these ditches extended only to lands in the vicinity of Grand Junction. In 1883 settlers in the valley west of Grand Junction constructed their own ditch, with a takeout point from the Colorado River a mile downstream of Grand Junction.

With its headgates located the farthest upstream, the Grand Valley Ditch offered the means to provide irrigation water to more lands than the other ditches combined. Seeing this opportunity, an entrepreneur from the Gunnison area named Matt Arch bought control of the ditch in 1883 and launched ambitious plans to enlarge and extend it. Even though the ditch began delivering water to irrigators in May, costs of constructing and operating the ditch far exceeded revenues. Arch sought outside financing, first obtaining a loan from the Colorado Loan and Trust in Denver in August, then selling his interest in the ditch outright. The president of the Colorado Loan and Trust was a former Kansas wheat farmer named Theodore C. Henry.

We have, of course, already met T. C. Henry in our look at the Lower Arkansas River Valley. The Grand River Ditch was one of his first large-scale irrigation-development ventures. By spring 1884 construction of the main ditch and a major lateral reached its final destination at Big Salt Wash beyond the town of Fruita, a distance of about twenty-five miles. When water was turned into the system, however, major problems developed. Large sections required "puddling"—soaking with water so they would settle and hold the water. In some cases the lands settled as much as eight feet, requiring considerable reconstruction. Additional wasteways—ditches used just to carry off excess water from the main ditch—had to be constructed. Henry raised the price of delivered water to cover these substantially increased costs, provoking a strong reaction from the users. Deciding the project would not pay for itself, Henry and the Colorado Loan and Trust sold the ditch in November 1884. By May 1885 the Travelers Insurance Company in Hartford, Connecticut, had become the major stockholder.

Management appointed by Travelers decided that the answer was to consolidate all of the existing ditch systems into one corporate entity and sell water rights to users rather than charge a yearly water-rental fee. Thus, rather than charge two dollars per acre per year for water, the plan was to sell permanent water rights for ten dollars per acre (a share) and charge an additional small annual assessment fee for ditch operations and maintenance. Irrigators could purchase shares over a five-year period. By the spring of 1886 the new arrangement was in place. Nevertheless, the company could not meet its bond-payment obligations and was sold at public auction in September 1888.[12] The buyer: Travelers Insurance Company.

At this point T. C. Henry and the Colorado Loan and Trust Company once again got involved. They filed suit challenging the legality of the sale of the ditch company to its previous owner. In 1894 a Colorado district court ruled that the sale was "null and void." Instead of holding that Colorado Loan and Trust was the owner, however, the court determined that the company instead reverted to the water-right shareholders. It ordered the company to be put up for sale once again.

This time interests in the Grand Valley put together a deal by which a local investor purchased the company and then sold it to the newly formed Grand Valley Irrigation Company, owned by those holding water-right shares in the original company. The capital stock of the company was divided among these individuals according to the number of water-right shares they had held. In short, the company transformed itself from a for-profit corporation to a nonprofit mutual ditch company, owned by its users.

An "apple boom" hit the Grand Valley in the mid-1890s.[13] Promoters planted apple and pear trees on thousands of acres of land in small lots of from five to forty acres, which they sold to people with little knowledge of orchards. Fruit trees virtually covered the area between Grand Junction and Fruita. In 1909 and 1910 the sale of apples from orchards in the Fruita area "yielded a net annual income per acre equal to the net annual income of any farm land in the world."[14]

Drawn by the inevitable promotion accompanying such success, the forty-four-year-old Edward Joshua Currier and his fifteen-year-old son, Charles, came to the Grand Valley from Iowa in 1892.[15] The year before, the elder Currier had bought 160 acres of land in this part of western Colorado, sight unseen, from a land promoter he encountered in Colorado Springs. The area, he was assured, enjoyed a Mediterranean-like climate, good soils, and an abundant water supply for irrigation. The successful development of orchards in the valley was especially enticing. They arrived in Grand Junction by immigrant car–railroad boxcars outfitted with beds that provided room to bring along their possessions, including livestock. Among other things, they were accompanied by a single white dairy cow.

The early years were hard ones, causing Edward to write in

7.4 View of Grand Valley lands prior to the Grand Valley Project (Source: Bureau of Reclamation).

1895: "I don't believe the Lord wants us to be as poor as we have been since we came here." Rather than Mediterranean-like orchard land, the land he had purchased was itself a shock: laced with gullies and sinkholes, crusted with alkali, and overgrown with greasewood brush (Figure 7.4). Nevertheless, they set to work immediately, building a cabin and planting apple trees. Edward's wife, Melinda, and her four younger sons arrived shortly thereafter. In a letter to one of her sisters Melinda wrote: "Our land has patches of alkali which may be soaked and washed and the alkali carried off before anything will grow on it and then it will have to be graded up into shape before we put crops on it, but when it is worked over it is the best kind of soil for crops of all sorts." Edward's parents, in their eighties, had come to live with the family in 1893. In 1897 his mother wrote: "In this desert land every body young and old has to do his best to keep the wolf from the door for *years* if he undertakes to scrape a living for his family off from these rough lands. People once settled here do not like to tell of all the rough

7.5 Waiting for project water in the Grand Valley, 1913 (Source: Bureau of Reclamation).

raps he got in starting a ranch for a home here" (Figure 7.5).

Failing to earn a living from apples, the Curriers turned their single cow (and its offspring) into a dairy operation in 1896: "The Golden Rule Dairy, E. J. Currier, Proprietor." The dairy operation expanded into a cattle operation, and Edward bought 160 acres of good grazing lands up on Grand Mesa, east of the valley, in the early 1900s. When Edward J. Currier died in 1938 at the age of eighty-nine, he had built a prosperous livestock and farming operation.

By the 1890s orchardists in the Grand Valley–particularly those growing peaches–had begun to notice that the higher-elevation lands at the east end of the valley in the vicinity of the town of Palisade encountered fewer problems with cold temperatures in the spring after the buds had flowered than did lower-elevation lands. Hydraulic pumps were used to lift water out of the river to these lands as were Ferris-wheel-like devices that scooped water out of the channel and lifted it above the banks to a flume, which then carried the water to a

7.6 The Roller Dam on the Colorado River (Source: Bureau of Reclamation).

ditch. Though capable of getting water up to orchard lands, such devices were highly susceptible to destruction by floods and had to be
replaced almost yearly.

The real opportunity, local developers believed, was in diverting water from the river farther upstream, in DeBeque Canyon,
and building a canal that would bring the water to the considerable
land areas not irrigable from the Grand Valley Canal–both at the
eastern end of the valley and at the higher-elevation lands north of
the canal in the main part of the valley. This was an undertaking that
exceeded the financial means of valley residents but was exactly the
sort of project that the Reclamation Service had been created in 1902
to build.

The Grand Valley Water Users Association was formed in 1905
to promote this reclamation project. To induce Reclamation to build
the project, valley promoters in 1907 had assured the Department of
the Interior that they would be able to pay back the costs of its con-

struction within three years from the time it was completed.[16] It was a time of great optimism in the valley, and irrigation was the basis of this optimism. Orchards covered large areas of irrigated land. Sugar beets too had been determined to do exceptionally well, and a sugar-processing facility had come into operation in the valley in 1899.[17] There was plenty of land. All that was needed was more water.

Reclamation evaluated the feasibility of the project in 1908, and President Taft approved the project in 1911. To make it possible to divert water out of the Colorado River, Reclamation constructed a 14-foot high, 546-foot-wide dam in DeBeque Canyon. The dam utilized six "roller" gates to control flows (and thus is commonly referred to as the Roller Dam)—the first dam of this type ever to be constructed in the United States (Figure 7.6). Water is diverted out of the north side of the river into a canal thirty-eight feet wide at its bottom and more than ten feet deep, with a physical capacity at its headgate to move 1,620 cubic feet of water per second. The fifty-five-mile Government Highline Canal, completed in 1917, parallels the river downstream into the valley, moving through three tunnels cut more than two miles through adjacent cliff sides, and then following a course roughly paralleling the Grand Valley Ditch upland to its north (Figure 7.7).[18]

Later, Reclamation enlarged the Grand Valley Project to provide water to lands within the Orchard Mesa Irrigation District on the south side of the river.[19] Orchard Mesa is an elevated area of land extending west from the Grand Mesa, separating the Colorado River from the Gunnison River. Fruit trees grow well on much of this land, and there had been at least five private efforts to pump water up onto the benchlands high above the river that all ended in failure because the diversion facilities washed out in high spring flows. Between 1909 and 1910 the Orchard Mesa Irrigation District (OMID) attempted to solve its water problems by building a water diversion and delivery system, taking water out of the river up in DeBeque Canyon and running it through flumes and a canal along the south side of the river to a point where it was then pumped onto the mesa.[20] OMID used its taxing and bonding authority under state law to issue nine hundred thousand dollars' worth of bonds to finance the project. Final construction costs totaled more than $1.3 million, however—more

7.7 Irrigating oats with water from the Grand Valley Project, 1917 (Source: Bureau of Reclamation).

than the district and its users could afford to pay. In 1922 the Reclamation Service entered into a contract with OMID under which the United States would divert additional water at its diversion dam for the Grand Valley Project, split the water off from its main canal, and move it under the Colorado River in a reinforced concrete siphon to the 3.5-mile concrete-lined Orchard Mesa Power Canal. The Orchard Mesa Pumping Plant then would lift the water as much as 130 feet to two canals supplying about eight thousand acres of irrigated land on the mesa.[21]

Fruit production in the Grand Valley has gone through a number of ups and downs. There *is* something undeniably incongruous about growing peaches in a Colorado mountain desert. And yet they do grow—in most years very well. They grow best in the eastern part of the valley, closest to the mountains, on the higher-elevation lands that benefit from the fact that warm air rises, providing a frost-free growing season averaging forty-seven days more per year than for lower-elevation lands in the western part of the valley closer to the river bottom.[22]

Beyond problems with climate, fruit production in the Grand Valley suffers from salinity in the soils and from pests and disease. Salinity long has plagued irrigated agriculture.[23] To a considerable degree this is a problem that can be managed through good drainage practices, but in the Grand Valley (and in most irrigated areas of the West) no one thought about drainage until problems appeared. In retrospect it is not surprising that lands accustomed to receiving perhaps eight *inches* of moisture per year would not readily absorb an additional four or five *feet* of irrigation water.

The major source of salinity in the Grand Valley is the Mancos shales. The soils of the valley are primarily alluvial in origin and are underlain by the shales. With the addition of large amounts of water to valley lands beginning in the 1880s, groundwater levels started to rise. A 1916 Department of Agriculture report noted the highly saline character of the valley's groundwater and concluded that successful crop production would require keeping the water table far enough below the root zone to avoid salinity damage. "In many instances," the report noted, "the existence of a problem in the Grand Valley was first realized when some of the older apple orchards began to fail. Almost invariably the older trees in any particular orchard died first. Frequently the land upon which apples trees 15 to 25 years old had died and had been removed would be reset to apples and the younger trees appear to thrive for a period, sometimes for several years. These younger trees would then die and finally the owner would remove the orchard and plant the tract to alfalfa or small grain. It was not unusual for either of these crops to do well at first and sometimes for several years, although almost invariably the end has been the same, i.e., the land finally became unproductive. In some cases the trouble has so far developed as to cause the land to be entirely abandoned."[24]

Between 1917 and 1921 the Reclamation Service constructed an extensive network of drainage ditches for the Grand Valley Project that also benefited lands within the Grand Valley Irrigation Company.[25] Deep enough to drain subsurface water from adjacent lands, these ditches carried unused water directly back to the Colorado River. In 1923 irrigators in the valley voted to levy an assessment on their lands to pay for the installation of additional drainage ditches. The work was essentially completed in 1930.

Particularly devastating to the apple orchards in the valley early in the century was the codling moth. Eggs laid by the moth turned into worms, which then infested the apples. Despite spraying lead arsenate on fruit trees as many as ten to twelve times a year in the mid-1920s, worm damage continued.[26] A federal requirement established at that time under the 1906 Pure Food and Drug Act required removal of lead from all agricultural products before shipping, a process that itself damaged the fruit and added considerable expense until automated means were devised.[27] In 1927 one state official estimated that orchard areas in the valley had decreased by 40 percent since 1915, whereas the cost of spraying had increased by 365 percent.[28] DDT and other high-potency pesticides eventually brought the codling moth and other pests under control.

Valley peach orchards in the 1930s and 1940s were devastated by the budmite-transmitted peach-mosaic virus. The only effective means of control is to remove and burn infected trees. Between 1935 and 1949 over 125,000 peach trees were removed from orchard lands in the Grand Valley in an attempt to control the virus.[30]

Today spring frosts are the primary factor limiting fruit production in the Grand Valley. Record-cold temperatures in the winter of 1962–63 killed more than one hundred thousand peach trees, and in the spring of 1989 a severe frost caused the most complete bud kill in the valley's history. Wind machines that mix in warmer air from higher elevations now are common in the peach orchards, replacing smudge pots used in the past.

~

Marcus Klocker grows seventeen varieties of peaches, as well as apples, sweet cherries, peppers, tomatoes, corn, and pumpkins on thirteen acres of land near the town of Palisade. In the late 1980s Klocker retired from his state job as water commissioner (responsible for administering the use of water rights in his area according to their priority) to spend all his time on the farm he had started thirteen years before. He sells everything he produces primarily through a stand he and his wife operate on their farm. Pumpkins and some tomatoes are sold on a "pick your own" basis. He sells popping corn in the winter. "You have to keep your name in front of the people most of the year, not just in the summer," he believes.

Like other farmers in the Grand Valley, he has tried a lot of different crops. Until the mid-1970s, when the Holly processing plant in Delta closed, many grew sugar beets. They used the leftover pulp and pulp pellets to feed cattle. Then many tried sunflowers. Some grew barley for Coors Brewing Company for a while, until Coors decided that it could do better elsewhere. More recently soybeans are being grown with some success.

Klocker is happy growing peaches, but, as he explained to me, there are some problems. According to Klocker, "Rain can be real bad on the peaches. A drop of cold rain on a hot peach will split the skin. Hail will bruise them so no one wants to buy them." Then there is the cold: "I've been froze out five of the last thirteen years I've been on this farm. I even lost trees—not just fruit but trees—in 1989 and 1991."

The first time I went to talk to Harry Talbott at his peach-packing plant on Orchard Mesa, he couldn't see me because the skins on peaches his company was packing for shipment were developing inky-black spots (Figure 7.8). He looked much more relaxed when I came back to visit several months later. "The day we got it turned around," said Talbott, "was the day you were here. We tried dry-brushing the ink spots with some horsehair brushes we had in storage, and it worked pretty well! Ended up having a pretty successful season."

Talbott operates the largest fruit-packing and distributing plant in the Grand Valley (Figure 7.9). "We have about two hundred acres of our own orchards. But about half of our fruit comes from other growers in the area who consign us their fruit, and then we pack and ship for them." We talked in his office on a second-floor landing above the fruit-packing floor. "My dad was a cattleman originally," he said. "He married a fruit grower's daughter, one of the early fruit growers in the valley. He first went to work for a company in Kansas buying produce for them. Then they moved back to Colorado and he started

7.8 Talbott Farms on Orchard Mesa.

buying orchards in 1943 or 1944. That's been the family business ever since."

Talbott pulled out a chart showing the number of packed bushels of peaches annually in western Colorado since the 1930s. The chart showed a more-or-less steady increase until the early 1950s, when it reached about a million and a half packed bushels. "See, we went from a million four or a million five down to here [about 200,000 bushels]. And now we think it's back up to about 350,000 bushels. Not exactly a success story, is it?" he asked. "The growers here stuck with the old standard Alberta peaches instead of diversifying into other varieties that ripen earlier and at different times of the season. The standard Alberta peach comes off from about August 25 through September 15, peaking at Labor Day. Labor Day is a terrible time for selling fruit. It was the wrong peach, but those guys had lived with the past and don't change very readily." He laughed and said, "As a kid I used to wonder why the children of Israel had to wander in the wilderness for forty years before they could come into the Promised Land. Now I know that it was so the old ones that remembered Egypt

7.9 Packing peaches at Talbott's Plant.

could die off and a new generation take over. Well, it's almost like that in the fruit industry. The old generation is just now passing from the scene, the ones who remember the boom days of the 1940s and early 1950s. The new generation is going to go in its own direction."

Today the Grand Valley is urbanizing. The city of Grand Junction has a population of nearly thirty thousand, and subdivisions are filling in fields that once grew crops. Agriculture, virtually all of it irrigated, continues to be an important part of the economy of the valley, particularly the orchard lands in the higher, eastern end of the valley and the croplands in the more rural, western part of the valley. In total there are about seventy thousand acres of irrigable lands in the valley, and from a vantage point up on the high red-colored sandstone ridge that is the Colorado National Monument, irrigated fields still dominate the landscape. But the average farm size in the valley now is less than thirty acres. To the north, beyond the irrigated areas, sage- and greasewood-covered desert lands that once dominated the valley are still readily visible.

There are still a lot of Curriers in the Grand Valley and up on the Grand Mesa. The original Currier land now is part of the airport development. Ed Currier, Edward's grandson, is a retired engineer who, when we met in 1992, was president of the board of directors of the Grand Valley Irrigation Company. He is selling off some of his land in the valley for residential development and rents the rest, as well as land he still owns up on Grand Mesa. "By about 1970," Ed says, "it was no longer possible to run a livestock operation here in the valley the way we used to. There was too much development, too much traffic to move our herds between the valley and the mesa." His brother, Bruce, still runs livestock, but he recently sold his land to the adjoining airport and plans to move to the more agricultural "middle valley."

Carlyle Currier, a great-grandson of the first Edward, lives with his family and his parents on a 1,140-acre ranch on Grand Mesa. They run between four hundred and five hundred head of mother cows and their calves, summering them on an allotment in the Grand Mesa National Forest and wintering them on their own lands with corn silage and alfalfa they grow. "There really aren't that many working ranches up here now," Carlyle remarked. "Mostly the people who live up here now have full-time jobs and maybe farm a little on the side. But it's a great place to live, and a very good lifestyle. I like the work I do. It's home. We're never going to get rich at it, but so far we've been able to make a decent living."

Those like the Curriers whose families long have supported themselves in the Grand Valley through irrigated agriculture find themselves living in a much-altered place. The circumstances that so clearly favored the dedication of much of the water of the Colorado River in Colorado to agriculture in the Grand Valley have changed. Other interests have emerged and are expressing a desire for water uses that would allow them to enjoy more of the benefits of the river.

Irrigators in the Grand Valley understandably are uneasy about what will happen to them. As I discovered on one visit, there is a deeply ingrained sense that Grand Valley farmers must protect "their" water from others who want to take it from them. For years the Denver Water Board and its aggressive efforts to take water from the Colorado River Basin for use in Denver were the cause of this fear. I spent the first ten minutes of a meeting with board members of the Palisade Irrigation District trying to convince them that I was not an agent of the Denver Water Board. Once I had explained my purpose, one board member said, "We've done okay up to now. We don't need any outside help."

8

THE PROBLEM OF SALT

Imagine an inland sea covering at times much of the continental landmass of what is now western Colorado, a sea coming in from the north and, at one period, extending all the way to what is now the Gulf of Mexico. Such was the state of the earth during a period geologists call the Cretaceous, more than a million years ago. The Mancos shale that is the product of this period underlies the entire Grand Valley, emerging from underground in the Book Cliffs, which form a distinctive northeast boundary for the valley. The sandy shores of this former sea are now found in the Dakota Sandstone formation, while the Mancos shales are remnants of "the shells and skeletons of innumerable marine animals: coiled ammonites, giant oysters, clams, and swimming reptiles."[30] This area of western Colorado is the easternmost extension of the Colorado Plateau, with its uplifted sedimentary layers still remarkably horizontal, though deeply carved by water. Somehow this plateau escaped the mountain-building processes that occurred in the Rockies to the east and the Sierra Nevada on the west.

As already discussed, the salinity of these shales created problems with growing crops in parts of the Grand Valley around the turn of the century—problems largely addressed by the construction of a substantial drainage system. In effect, however, the problems were just transferred downstream.

There are many sources of salinity feeding into the Colorado River: Nearly half of the salts found in the river at Hoover Dam are thought to come from natural sources, whereas 37 percent are attributed to irrigation.[31] Salinity affects the quality of the drinking water that comes from the Colorado River in the lower basin and also makes the water less desirable for other domestic, municipal, and industrial uses. It can limit the types of crops that can be grown, as well as crop yields.

In 1961–when highly saline drainage water from the Wellton-Mohawk Division of the Gila Project in Arizona pushed salinity levels in the Colorado River at the Mexican border to more than two thousand parts per million of total dissolved solids–damage occurred to crops in the Mexicali Valley.[32]

One response to this incident was passage of the Colorado River Basin Salinity Control Act in 1974,[33] providing federal funding to construct projects in the basin that would reduce salt loading to the Colorado River. Among the first of these projects was the Grand Valley Salinity Control Unit. Initial expectations were that this project would reduce salt loading to the river by as much as seven hundred thousand tons annually.

The Bureau of Reclamation completed stage one of the Grand Valley Salinity Control Unit in 1983. The work focused on a 6.8-mile section of the Government Highline Canal in the western part of the Grand Valley, lining this portion of the canal with concrete and rebuilding diversion structures for the laterals. In addition, 30 miles of plastic pipe replaced 34 miles of open dirt laterals. In stage two 38 miles of the Highline Canal in the eastern part of the valley are being lined with an impervious membrane, and 144 miles of open ditch laterals in the Grand Valley Water User Association system are being replaced with pipe.

An unintended consequence of the salinity control project was to highlight water-use practices that had been in existence for at least fifty years with virtually no change. A system, or more accurately a collection of systems, that had met its original objective of providing a reliable and low-cost supply of water for irrigation now was found to be antiquated and even harmful.[34]

The good news, however, was that federal assistance, through the Colorado River Salinity Control Act's Grand Valley Salinity Control Project, was available to fix the problem. In fact, the even better news was that improvements made to the water-delivery systems would actually make things better for the irrigators themselves: Leaky portions of the main canals would be lined, providing more usable water; check structures (gates regulating the depth and flow of water in a section of the canal) would be built, allowing better control of water; new diversions structures for laterals would be constructed, and old dirt laterals would be replaced with piping, allowing more efficient delivery to irrigator headgates; trash cleaners would be installed to keep the water free from branches, leaves, and other debris–reducing the need for irrigators themselves to perform this task; water delivered through pipes would be under pressure, allowing irrigators to install more modern irrigation equipment such as surge systems or sprinklers that could take advantage of this pressure. Moreover, funds would be available through the Department of Agriculture to cost-share on-farm improvements that also would reduce drainage.

But things are rarely what they seem. As government analysts examined more carefully the salinity-reduction benefits compared to project costs, the Grand Valley salinity project was scaled back considerably. Reclamation dropped its expected reduction of salinity loadings to the Colorado River from the Grand Valley from 700,000 to 580,000 tons per year. As of 1994 total reductions amounted to an estimated 99,000 tons,[35] at a cost of approximately $145 million.[36]

In part, human nature got in the way. Understandably, Reclamation didn't want to have to deal with every individual lateral system, preferring instead to work with the organizations responsible for the main ditches. This approach, however, revealed some of the deep splits that existed between water users on the same laterals, between water users and the management of their ditch companies or districts, between different ditches, and, of course, between the local community and the federal government. Within the private Grand Valley Irrigation Company these differences proved insurmountable–blocking federal support for improvements in irrigation practices on lands closest to the Colorado River where salinity reduction would be most cost-effective.

Mutual ditch companies and irrigation districts typically own and manage the main water-supply canals or ditches, whereas laterals generally are owned and managed by the water users. There are 250 private laterals in the GVIC system alone. Once water is delivered to the diversion structure for the lateral, management of that water is left up to the users. In most cases users on a lateral are not well organized. Urbanization and suburbanization of previously irrigated lands further complicate matters. In many areas residential users continue to irrigate lawns with water out of laterals. But they don't take their water like farmers. Residential users tend to irrigate at the same time—mostly at night and on the weekends. Often there are large numbers of users on a single lateral—in Palisade, for example, there are two hundred users on one lateral serving fifty-nine acres. Only in the Grand Valley Water Users Association system are deliveries of water to laterals based on orders or requests; in other systems water is simply turned into laterals on the basis of the direct-flow rights held by the users.[37]

For the most part, irrigators in the Grand Valley Water Users Association who are on laterals now supplied from the improved canal and pipeline system seem happy with the changes. The cleaner water makes the use of siphon tubes and surge systems easier, since there are fewer sticks, leaves, paper, and other obstructions to be cleared. The improved on-field irrigation systems tend to be much less labor intensive than traditional methods used in the area.

One unexpected effect is the flip-flopping of advantages and disadvantages of location on the lateral. In the old earthen-ditch system, irrigators at the head of the system enjoyed first crack at the water and could be sure to get their water if any flowed into the ditch, while those at the end of the ditch might sometimes find themselves with little or no supply. With water in pipes, irrigators at the end of the lateral find they have the best pressure when water is turned into the pipe, whereas those at the top of the system must operate with lower water pressure.

Is this federal investment of $145 million in the Grand Valley ($354 million as of 1994 in the Colorado River Basin) worthwhile?[38] Not surprisingly, opinions are mixed. Estimates of actual damages from salinity vary widely.[39] Some believe that more has been spent on salinity control within the Colorado River Basin than can be justified.[40]

Nevertheless, there is no doubt that the salinity control program has permanently changed irrigated agriculture in the Grand Valley. The opportunities to modify long-standing practices in a manner that reduces the need for the historical level of diversions are now well understood. Improvements made to date demonstrate the potential for irrigating lands in the Grand Valley with less overall demand on the Colorado River. In an era of growing demands for water, those who would like to enjoy the benefits of this Colorado River water are lining up. First in line after the irrigators themselves are those wanting to make more upstream uses of Colorado River water.

9.1 The Colorado River Basin.

LEGEND

• CITIES AND TOWNS

RESERVOIR

—— BASIN BOUNDARY

⊠ U.S.G.S. GAGING STATION

N

0 5 10 20
SCALE IN FEET

① GRAND VALLEY DIVERSION DAM

⊠ ② CAMEO GAGE

⊠ ③ DOTSERO GAGE

9

COMPETITION FROM ACROSS THE DIVIDE AND CLOSER TO HOME

The west slope of the Rocky Mountains in Colorado is one of the great "water holes" of the West.[41] Moist air coming from the Pacific west struggles to hurdle the vertical barrier of these mountains, leaving behind large amounts of precipitation in the process. Generally abundant wintertime snowfall provides the source for much of the spring and summer surface flows in the many rivers and streams that are part of the Colorado River Basin (Figure 9.1). A large number of interests compete to claim and use these valuable flows of water, both within Colorado and in other, downstream states.[42]

The collective total rate of diversion of water from the Colorado River for users in the Grand Valley is 2,260 cubic feet per second during the irrigation season. The seniority of these rights varies, with the Grand Valley Irrigation Company holding both the most senior (an 1882 priority) and the most junior (a 1914 priority) of these appropriations. When this collective package of senior rights places a "call" on the river, upstream junior diverters must stop taking water as necessary to ensure that they are not reducing below 2,260 cubic feet per second the amount of water available in the river in the Grand Valley.[43] Of the roughly 3 million acre-feet of water generated each year from the upper Colorado River watershed above Grand Junction, users in the Grand Valley divert about 1 million acre-feet of water.[44]

Aside from irrigation in the Grand Valley, economically driven water uses of the Colorado River in Colorado were slow to develop.

In 1905 the Glenwood Power Canal and Pipeline claimed up to 1,250 cubic feet per second of water from the Colorado River in the vicinity of Glenwood Springs to generate hydroelectric power at the Shoshone Power Plant. Now owned by the Public Service Company of Colorado, the seniority, size, and year-round nature of this diversion ensure that a considerable amount of water stays in the Colorado River to at least this point.

Others have, of course, been interested in tapping this great water hole. Within the basin itself, modest amounts of water long have been diverted for irrigation of haylands in those places where topography allows. But, until recently, most of the interest in developing Colorado River Basin water came from the much more rapidly growing Front Range of Colorado. Irrigators needing to bolster their water supplies were the first to take advantage of places where the geography made it relatively easy to move water across the Continental Divide.[45] The city of Denver, through the Denver Water Board, constructed the first large-scale transmountain diversion project taking water out of the Colorado River Basin.[46] Piggybacking on the construction of the Moffat Tunnel—built under the Continental Divide to provide direct rail service west from Denver through the mountains—the Denver Water Board brought water from the Fraser River, a tributary of the Colorado, through the Moffat Tunnel's "pioneer" bore beginning in 1936. In the 1930s Denver began construction of the Williams Fork system, by which water from this drainage is brought to the Front Range.

Beginning in 1938, the Bureau of Reclamation began construction of the Colorado–Big Thompson Project—a large transmountain diversion project that would carry water from the headwaters of the Colorado River itself to the northern Front Range.[47] Completed in the late 1950s, the C-BT Project provides as much as 310,000 acre-feet of water per year to the Front Range from its collection system on the West Slope through the project's Alva B. Adams Tunnel. Reclamation also constructed the Green Mountain Reservoir on the Blue River near its junction with the Colorado as part of the C-BT Project. This 152,000-acre-foot reservoir serves as "compensatory storage"—water to be used only in western Colorado.[48]

Then, in the 1950s, Denver began construction of the Dillon Reservoir, soon to become its major source of water supply from the West Slope. With a storage capacity of about 250,000 acre-feet, the reservoir impounds the Blue River at the town of Dillon. Up to 1,020 cubic feet of water per second (more than 2,000 acre-feet per day) can be moved through the twenty-three-mile-long Harold D. Roberts Tunnel to the Front Range.

In the 1960s the Bureau of Reclamation constructed the Fryingpan-Arkansas Project, described in part 1. Water is collected from the Fryingpan River Basin on the West Slope and carried through a tunnel into the Arkansas River Basin. Expected to bring about 72,200 acre-feet of water per year from the Fryingpan, actual annual diversions between 1982 and 1992 averaged 53,500 acre-feet.[49]

The city of Colorado Springs has built two significant transmountain diversion projects moving water out of the Colorado River Basin to the Front Range. The first, on the Blue River, yielded about 11,600 acre-feet in 1993.[50] The second, the Homestake Project, collected 25,900 acre-feet from the Eagle River drainage in 1993.[51]

Beginning in the 1950s, and accelerating rapidly in the 1970s, boom came to the West Slope of Colorado. The long-anticipated oil-shale industry at last appeared ready to become a reality. Companies seeking to capitalize on the massive shale-oil reserves and the skyrocketing price of oil aggressively filed claims for the substantial quantities of water expected to be needed to turn rock into oil.[52] Despite the collapse of this effort in the early 1980s, these companies remain concerned with protecting the value of these rights, pending their future use—either in oil shale or, more likely, for other purposes.

A more enduring engine of growth on Colorado's West Slope has been its increasingly valued recreational assets and its quality of life. Anchored by its world-class skiing, the town of Aspen led the way—followed by Vail, Steamboat, Telluride, and a collection of areas in Summit County. The brand-new town of Battlement Mesa, constructed to house oil shale industry employees but scenically sited on a bench above the Colorado River, transitioned remarkably easily to a retirement community. These growing urban areas, and the resort economy that feeds them, now place an increasing claim on the water of the Colorado River and its tributaries in Colorado.

Despite these many uses, the water resources of the upper Colorado River have not yet reached full physical and economic development. As already described, one important reason is the senior demand at the Shoshone Power Plant and the Grand Valley that requires a considerable amount of the basin's water to flow downstream, out of reach of upstream users.[53] Upstream appropriators have a strong interest in reducing these downstream uses. For different reasons some environmental interests also want to reduce out-of-stream uses in the Grand Valley.

10

WATER FOR NATIVE FISH

Once, not so long ago, there lived a minnow in the Colorado River that grew up to six feet long and weighed as much as eighty to one hundred pounds. That minnow, the Colorado pikeminnow, still inhabits the basin. But now it is an endangered species, occupying about a quarter of its original habitat in the Colorado River and its tributaries. The largest of these fish today reach no more than half their original size (Figure 10.1).

The pikeminnow and three other species native to the Colorado—the humpback chub, the bonytail chub, and the razorback sucker—thrived in a habitat that has been called by Philip Fradkin "A River No More."[54] In its "untamed" form, as experienced by Major John Wesley Powell and his crew in their remarkable journeys down the Colorado in the early 1870s, flows in the Colorado River peaked with the spring runoff—often flooding over its banks and scouring out its channel—and then declined slowly during the summer months. Sediment loads from the many tributaries feeding the river made the water turbid and brown-colored. As the currents slowed and air temperatures heated up in the river canyons, the water warmed.

Fradkin called the Colorado "A River No More" because of dramatic changes wrought by Bureau of Reclamation construction of ten major dams in the basin during the past eighty years. These dams capture and store the peak spring flows. Flooding in the Colorado River Basin now is an infrequent—though occasionally still spectacular—event. The dams transform portions of the river into lakes—

10.1 A Colorado pikeminnow caught in the Yampa River, 1935 (Source: Connie Young, U.S. Fish and Wildlife Service).

sometimes massive ones. As the sediment-loaded water backs up behind a dam, the sediments tend to drop out. Nearly 2 million acre-feet of water is lost to evaporation from basin reservoirs each year.[55] Although the surface area of the reservoir is exposed to the sun, the underlying waters are not. Thus water released from the reservoirs, drawn from this lower level, tends to be considerably clearer and colder than native river flows. Moreover, dams create insurmountable barriers to fish migration, effectively segmenting the river and closing off access to potential spawning and rearing areas.[56]

Colorado River dams have created highly desirable trout habitat in the clear, cold water that is released, and large numbers of introduced species of trout and other fish now reside in the river.

Good habitat for trout, however, is not good habitat for native fishes such as the Colorado pikeminnow—a fact underlined by the precipitous decline of these species since water development began during this century.

The Colorado pikeminnow was listed as an endangered species in 1967. Despite more than twenty-five years of study since that time, the biological requirements for recovery of the pikeminnow still are not fully understood. What is known is that the pikeminnow has entirely disappeared from the lower Colorado River Basin, occurring now only upstream of Glen Canyon Dam.[57] Spawning occurs between July and September and appears to be closely linked to water temperature (which must reach or exceed twenty degrees centigrade). Eggs are deposited in coarse cobble beds that must be relatively free of sediments. Hatching and survival of the larvae are most successful under conditions in which water temperatures are even warmer. Upon hatching, the larvae apparently drift downstream, seeking backwater areas out of the river's current. In the fall and winter the pikeminnow search out pools and other deepwater areas. Colorado pikeminnow can migrate considerable distances—in one case a documented distance of nearly two hundred river miles between April and September.

The pikeminnow is protected by the federal Endangered Species Act, enacted in 1973. Among other things, this law directs the secretary of the interior to develop and implement "recovery" plans for listed threatened and endangered species.[58] Accordingly, the U.S. Fish and Wildlife Service formed the Colorado Pikeminnow Recovery Team in 1975 and expanded the scope of the effort to include all endangered fishes in the upper basin in 1976.[59] The energy boom in the late 1970s prompted a flurry of proposed water-development projects in the upper basin, requiring the Fish and Wildlife Service to consider the effects of this water development on recovery of the listed fishes. As a result, "[b]y 1984 the USFWS had issued nearly a hundred biological opinions, concluding that the site-specific cumulative effect of water developments and depletions was likely to jeopardize the continued existence of endangered Colorado River fishes."[60] The opinions, however, also proposed "reasonable and prudent alternatives," which, if implemented, would allow water development to go forward. In general the "alternatives" included support for the activities of the recovery program and a suggestion that, as long as recovery was proceeding, so too could water development. In 1987 this approach was formalized in the "Recovery Implementation Program for Endangered Fish Species in the Upper Colorado River Basin."[61]

I spent a day in the late fall of 1993 along the Colorado River in the Grand Valley area with John Hamill, then director of the Fish and Wildlife Service's Upper Colorado River Recovery Program. We turned east from the airport in Grand Junction on I–70, cutting through peach orchards at Palisade, headed first to the bridge on Highway 6 crossing the river just east of town. From there we could look downstream and see the diversion dam for the Grand Valley Irrigation Company. Across the river we could see the Orchard Mesa Pumping Plant and the Grand Valley Power Plant. Just upstream we saw some old structures in the riverbed, where, at the beginning of the century, water was pumped out of the Colorado River into the Price-Stubb Ditch. "Pikeminnow and razorback suckers are migratory," John explained. "These structures in the river slowed that migration down. Reclamation's Roller Dam [upriver in DeBeque Canyon] totally blocked migration above that point." Then he pointed downstream on the south side of the river. "That is where water from the [Orchard Mesa] pumping plant can be checked back upstream so it is available for diversion by GVIC. You've heard about the Orchard Mesa check case, haven't you?"[62]

We got back on I-70 and drove east, heading first into DeBeque Canyon, past the Roller Dam, and then toward Rifle. East of the canyon the Colorado River passes through open, rolling terrain. The floodplain of the river broadens noticeably. "See those ponds along the river?" John asked. "Historically the river moved up out of its banks in the spring, flooding adjacent lands and filling low areas, creating ponds of water. We think the fish moved into these adjacent pools of water in the spring, fattened up on the invertebrates readily available in these warmer, shallower waters, and then returned to the river for spawning." We pulled off the highway and walked over to a pond. "Over the years we have channelized the river, built dikes and levees, to keep the river in its banks so the bottomlands could be used for farming or grazing or other development. What we need to do is to reestablish these natural connections between the river and the floodplain, especially these pools that the native fish can use."

Appreciation of the importance of this off-river habitat is relatively recent. In 1991 razorback suckers were found in one of the ponds in this area on private lands. Researchers believe the suckers washed into the pond in the flood flows of 1983–84 and were stranded when the river receded. "The landowner let us take a few of the razorbacks out of her pond so we could get them to a hatchery in New Mexico," John recalled. "But when we came back, she wanted six hundred thousand dollars for access and she wanted us to stock her pond with trout for the next forty years." Fortunately, some of the land along the river already is in public ownership, and other areas are for sale. John envisions a large-scale native fish habitat restoration project in this area, with ponds reconnected to the river so the fish can use these areas for feeding.

Next we went to the Redlands Diversion Dam on the Gunnison River, a few miles upstream of the point where it joins the Colorado. "We want to rebuild this dam so the fish can get past it," said John.[63] Water is diverted at Redlands, both to irrigate lands on benches west of the Gunnison and south of the Colorado and to generate electricity, much of which is used to pump water up to these lands through three separate lifts. Once covered with orchards, lands served through the Redlands system now are rapidly urbanizing.

"There is a lot of good potential habitat for native fish upstream on the Gunnison, but this dam has blocked off this reach for most of this century," he explained. "Redlands takes about seven hundred [cubic feet per second] out of the river, which can be the entire flow. We looked at trying to buy out the hydroelectric plant and its water right so the water could stay in the river, but it was too expensive. So we're going to rebuild the diversion dam instead in a way that fish can pass." We walked down to the river and looked at the dam. "This was first built in about 1910," John said. "The Redlands people apparently have some financial problems and can't afford to maintain it very well." The disheveled state of the structure underlined his point.

Finally, John took me to a series of six specially constructed ponds on the south side of the Colorado River, west of the point where it is joined by the Gunnison. "These are holding ponds for populations of the endangered fishes that have been spawned at hatcheries," John explained. "If the fish tolerate being kept in ponds like these, we intend to keep a number of brood stock, so if we have a catastrophe on the river like a chemical spill, we can put some live fish back in the river." The fish in these ponds represent a last stand—if all else fails, at least some of the native fishes can be artificially maintained. "The goal of the recovery program," John pointed out, "is to reach a point where these fishes are reproducing naturally in the wild on a sustainable basis, not just to keep fish alive in ponds like these. We've got a ways to go."

The upper Colorado River is important habitat for the Colorado pikeminnow. At present the upper limit of occupied habitat is the Grand Valley—apparently because of the obstructions John pointed out. Relatively large numbers of pikeminnow have been found in the "Fifteen-Mile Reach"—the river segment from below the Grand Valley Irrigation Company's diversion dam to its confluence with the Gunnison River—and the area has been identified as a "suspected Colorado pikeminnow spawning area." Consequently, the Fifteen-Mile Reach has been a focal point of recovery efforts.

For reasons that are not entirely understood, successful spawning by the Colorado pikeminnow is closely correlated with significant spring runoff periods. Possible explanations include the flooding of adjacent areas into which the pikeminnow move for feeding and warming prior to spawning, and the cleansing of gravel substrates used for egg incubation. Irrigation diversions for the Grand Valley markedly reduce flows in the Fifteen-Mile Reach, potentially limiting access to adjacent backwater areas and limiting the flushing effect of the remaining flows. These effects are most pronounced between the months of July and September, when diversions are the highest (and as flows naturally decline).

Efforts are being made to improve stream flows through the Fifteen-Mile Reach. The Fish and Wildlife Service recommends flows in this stretch of between seven hundred and twelve hundred cubic feet per second during July, August, and September, with a six hundred cubic feet per second floor in especially dry years. An analysis of historical flows in the reach suggests that an additional forty-seven thousand acre-feet of water is needed to support this minimum flow objective.[64]

A 1992 study by the Bureau of Reclamation examined additional sources of water potentially available for enhancement of flows in the Fifteen-Mile Reach.[65] These sources included unallocated water stored in the Green Mountain Reservoir and Ruedi Reservoir, purchase and transfer of agricultural water rights, and improving the efficiency of water use within the Grand Valley. The least-cost alternatives identified in the study involved changes in Grand Valley water uses.

11

THE PROMISE—AND PROBLEMS— OF WATER CONSERVATION

Bob Norman, an engineer working for the Bureau of Reclamation in Grand Junction, knows that there is nothing particularly mysterious about how to reduce diversions of Colorado River water for irrigation in the Grand Valley. "We estimated the efficiency of the irrigation systems in the Grand Valley in the 1970s to be between 25 to 35 percent," he told me. That means that for every three to four acre-feet of water diverted out of the Colorado River for irrigation use in the Grand Valley, only one acre-foot was actually being used to grow crops. The Grand Valley Irrigation Company Canal and the Government Highline Canal both are gravity systems, designed to run a continuous flow of water essentially throughout the irrigation season. At its Colorado River headgate, each canal's full capacity of water is diverted. There are spillways located along the canal to allow releases of water back to the river if the canal is too full. The size of the canal gradually diminishes throughout its length, roughly in proportion to the amount of water taken out through the various laterals along the way. If all goes according to plan, there is just enough water left in the canal at the last lateral to meet the needs of irrigators along the lateral. Operation is based on the continuous availability of water in the main canal and the laterals from which irrigators can draw at will, up to a maximum rate of diversion. It is a simple and relatively inexpensive system, suitable for areas with senior water rights and good water supplies.

11.1 May 1947: Kenneth Matchett uses siphons to irrigate on his farm near Grand Junction, Colorado (Source: Kenneth Matchett).

Most Grand Valley farmers use flood or furrow irrigation. Almost no sprinklers are in use, partly because water is supplied through open ditches without pressure, and partly because of the saline soils. Kapper Alexander, who grows mostly hay on seventy acres in the western part of the valley with water from the Grand Valley Canal, explained: "I farm the easiest way I can." Ditches carrying water to his lands are concrete, with side cuts at regular intervals covered by sliding metal plates, which he opens to flood-irrigate his fields. The hayfields he is irrigating are covered in standing water.

Back in 1947 Ken Matchett was the first irrigator in the Grand Valley to use siphon tubes to take a controlled amount of water out of his ditches and direct it down carefully prepared furrows between planted crops (Figure 11.1). He also was the first to install gated pipe—metal in those days—in place of ditches through which water can be guided into furrows at measured intervals. "The Soil Conservation Service used my farm as a place to demonstrate gated pipe," he explained.

While on-farm practices have improved over the years, little has been done to improve the main conveyance channels or the laterals, except under the salinity control program. In the systems used in the Grand Valley and throughout much of the West, a large amount of diverted water returns to the river, never having been applied to irrigation use. The water returns through waste or spill ditches, constructed specifically to release excess water from the canal as necessary to regulate supply and demand in the system. It also returns as outflows from laterals with unused water. This is the so-called "carriage water," necessary to ensure that the legally entitled maximum diversion rate of water is available at all laterals and headgates throughout the system. Operation of the system depends on this water; by design large quantities of diverted water inevitably return to the river.

From an irrigation perspective continuous-flow gravity systems make good sense. They are relatively cheap to build and operate, and they serve the needs of the irrigator by making available a supply of water on demand. Water that returns to the river then is available for diversion and use by other irrigators downstream.

In the case of the Grand Valley, however, it so happens that the diversions come out of the Colorado River above the Fifteen-Mile Reach; most of the return flows do not reappear in the river until below this critical stretch. As described in chapter 10, the Fish and Wildlife Service sees potentially great benefits to the fish if irrigation diversions could be reduced and stream flows through the reach increased.

In water-short irrigation systems (such as in the Lower Arkansas Valley) it is common for the water supply to be more actively managed. Actual demand for water is likely to be closely monitored. Irrigators may have to "order" water in advance of use, and use is limited to the time and amount ordered. Deliveries might be carefully measured, and the charges for water delivery tied directly to the quantity used (perhaps using "tiered" pricing by which the unit rate increases as total usage exceeds specified quantities).[66] Water use may have to be "rotated," so as to be available to laterals on different parts of the canal system only at periodic, scheduled intervals. "Check" structures (gates installed in the canal to regulate the flow of water) may be used to hold water in sections of the canal so that there is enough "head" of water (water elevation) in the canal to enable diversions into headgates and laterals. There may be "re-regulating" ponds or reservoirs located at points along the canal so that excess water can be stored and returned to the canal when needed, rather than permanently "spilled" out of the canal through drainage ditches or laterals. Canals can be lined with nonporous material to prevent seepage of water. Laterals can be lined, or even converted into pipes, to enable more efficient delivery of water. And these improvements are all in addition to, and separate from, changes that can be made in the on-farm delivery and water-application systems.

In fact, some of these changes already have been made in the Government Highline Canal and to laterals within the Grand Valley Water Users Association system under the salinity control program. In addition to physical improvements already described, users in that system must order water for delivery; there is also a two-block pricing structure, with water delivered in the second block charged at a higher rate. More, however, could be done to this system to make it possible to reduce diversions at the Roller Dam. And the GVIC system, the valley's other major diverter of Colorado River water, operates in virtually the same manner in which it was designed and built more than one hundred years ago.

The issue is incentives. Who will pay to make the structural and management changes necessary to allow reduced diversions of water from the Colorado River? Federal tax dollars and federal hydroelectric power revenues are paying the costs of making improvements in the Grand Valley Project to reduce salinity loadings to the river. As it happens, many of the changes made to the Government Highline Canal and laterals within the GVWUA are the same or similar to changes that would be made to reduce the amount of water diverted. However, the objective is to reduce salt-laden return flows, not to reduce total diversions from the Colorado River.

Why should the water users in the GVIC or the GVWUA be interested in reducing diversions of water on which they have historically depended to supply their needs? Why should they be interested in changing their traditional irrigation practices, in paying higher operating and maintenance costs for a more costly system, in perhaps having to pay for the water itself?

For one thing, they may be legally required to do so. For example, upstream water users who are junior in priority might seek a judicial or administrative order compelling reduction of diversions on the grounds that the systems are "wasteful" as a matter of Colorado law.[67] Or an action might be brought under the Endangered Species Act on the basis that these diversions are "taking" endangered fish because of their adverse effect on critical habitat during low-flow months.[68]

Alternatively, water users in the Grand Valley might be interested in reducing diversions if the costs of making the changes were paid by those who would benefit from the reduced diversions. Thus, upstream junior appropriators might be interested in helping to pay the cost of the changes if the benefits of a reduced Grand Valley "call," discussed in chapter 9, exceeded the costs. Those desiring additional upstream water development might be willing to provide financial assistance if, either directly or indirectly, the reduced diversions would help to make more development possible. For example, increased flows in the Fifteen-Mile Reach at critical times that would help to assure recovery of the endangered fishes might allow additional upstream water development at other times. The state of Colorado might want to invest state funds in a program that would upgrade irrigated agriculture in the Grand Valley while helping to address the needs of endangered fishes. Finally, the U.S. Congress might be interested in investing federal funds to help remedy the adverse environmental effects of a federal reclamation program by improving valuable habitat for endangered fishes, and the U.S. Fish and Wildlife Service might wish to invest funds from the Upper Colorado River Recovery Program to increase flows through the Fifteen-Mile Reach.

In short, there are many reasons to manage water better in the Grand Valley, and many interests with reason to invest in that objective.[69] The opportunities to make structural and management changes that could reduce the need for the historical levels of water diversions are considerable–opportunities in addition to those possible through retirement of irrigated land and direct transfer of the water. It even seems possible that the money needed to make the changes would be available. A major limitation standing in the way of pursuing these opportunities is legal uncertainty concerning the status of the water that would be "saved" from diversion by making the changes.

It seems ironic that a water-law structure intended to help people use the limited water resources of the West to meet their needs now itself stands as a potential barrier to this purpose. The benefits of irrigating lands in the Grand Valley motivated some remarkable efforts to develop the needed water supply. Now other needs are pressing their claim to this water supply. From an engineering perspective it appears there are means by which water historically diverted from the Colorado River for irrigation use in the Grand Valley can be reduced without eliminating existing irrigation activities. As it happens, the increased flows through the Fifteen-Mile Reach that would result from reducing diversions at the Roller Dam and at the GVIC diversion dam during the summer months are thought to have important benefits for at least two species of endangered fish that inhabit this area. It appears that there are several possible legal bases by which flows through this reach could be improved. None, however, are free from potential legal challenge.

The Grand Valley provides a powerful illustration of one of the perverse consequences of prior-appropriation law that rewards appropriators for diverting their maximum entitlement but gives them little incentive to make their existing use more efficient. Some western states such as Oregon, California, Montana, and Washington have changed their laws to help avoid this undesirable situation.[70] Generally, the approaches are designed to reward, rather than penalize, an appropriator for reducing water use. Saved water can be transferred to a new use, either by the appropriator or by a state agency.

~

If there is a future for irrigated agriculture in the Grand Valley, it will probably be with operations like Gobbo Farms and Orchards. Four Gobbo cousins, now in their fifties and sixties, operate the farm as a partnership. Allen Gobbo graduated from college in 1965 as an aeronautical engineer, working first for Ball Aerospace. In 1972 he came back to the Grand Valley to join his cousins in a business combining the operations of their four fathers. These were the sons of the original Gobbo who bought forty acres of desert land in 1920 capable of being irrigated with water from the recently completed Government Highline Canal. Allen runs the business aspects, while Bob runs the cattle operations, Don the equipment and hay and grain, and Fritz the fruit. Together they operate one of the most diversified operations in the valley.

"We farm about eleven hundred acres, seven hundred of which we own," explained Allen. Just two years before, the cousins sold off fifteen thousand acres of grazing lands they owned in the hills south and east of Grand Junction to actor Ricky Schroeder. They still graze their cattle on the land. On their orchard lands (apparently high elevation enough to avoid frosts, though far from the eastern end of the valley), they produce peaches, pears, plums, and apples. Through their connection with Gerber, providing pears for baby foods, they now also sell a squash that the company uses in its "First Foods" for babies. Gerber tells them that their squash is the highest in solids and sugar content of any squash it buys. They raise pinto beans, hay, and sweet corn. And they began growing onions as a replacement for sugar beets in the 1970s.

In true farmer fashion, however, they are not very optimistic about the future. According to Allen, the cousins are not encouraging their kids to take over the operations. "I don't know who will own or run the farm in ten years," he said. "There is no incentive for younger farmers." Don Gobbo added: "Some farmers think they are getting by until they go to see their banker. Not many people in this valley make their living off of agriculture. Their wives work in some off-farm job, or they work and moonlight on the farm." And, according to Fritz Gobbo: "We in agriculture are just too damn efficient. Fewer and fewer of us are producing for more and more people. I hate to see agriculture go under, but that's what's happening."

Peach grower and shipper Harry Talbott is convinced that the large operations will survive. "Right now," he said, "people in the country have a love-hate relationship with agriculture. People like the idea of farms; they like the idea of open space; they like the idea of cows grazing in open fields. They don't like the idea of big corporate farms–they're scary to a lot of people. But these big farms are here to stay. They can do things to survive, and that is why they got big." To stockman Bruce Currier, "The farms that keep going are the ones with people who just can't imagine doing anything else."

PART 3

THE TRUCKEE AND CARSON BASINS
SHARING WATER IN A DESERT

A harsh expanse of dry desert and high mountains
between the Rockies and the Sierra Nevada, the
Great Basin has always been a land in between, a
region apart, not included in visions of other
western regions, the Rockies, the Colorado
Plateau, the Southwest, or the West Coast.

–Jon Christensen

12

LIFE IN A LAND IN BETWEEN

A visitor to the bustling casinos of Reno might see the Truckee River as it makes its way through the heart of the city, thoroughly channelized to minimize flooding problems, but now with its adjacent pedestrian pathway providing a linear park within the city for joggers and bikers. She might be surprised to learn the degree to which this river has been manipulated to make agriculture possible in the deserts of the Great Basin. But the feeling would be more a curiosity than a concern–trying to understand from an urban perspective how people lived in the West earlier in this century.

Likely more surprised would be a Northern Paiute Indian from the 1800s, alive today, to see the changes in this part of her Great Basin homeland. If she had been of the "Cattail-eaters," she would see that the marshes and ponds that provided her sustenance have shriveled from an area averaging 150,000 acres, including Carson Lake, Carson Sink, and the intervening Stillwater Marsh, to perhaps 10,000 acres (including an all-time low of 20 acres in 1992).[1] If she had been of the "Cui-ui eaters," she would see a Pyramid Lake much reduced in size from the 1800s (its surface elevation down perhaps sixty feet, and its surface area decreased thousands of acres),[2] so altering its connection with the Truckee River that the lake's once-productive native Lahontan cutthroat trout fishery is gone, and the cui-ui, upon which the tribe depended for ceremony and sustenance, are unable to move upriver to spawn except with the assistance of a "fishway" and an elevator. She would see that Lake Winnemucca, a

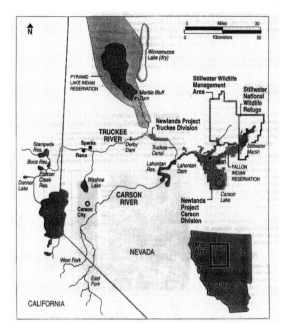

12.1   Truckee-Carson Basin.

water body containing about 3.6 million acre-feet of water around the turn of the century, has disappeared altogether (going dry in the 1930s).[3]

The Northern Paiute once occupied much of the Great Basin, living in small bands in places where they could support themselves, including the desert marshes and lakes formed by water flowing out of the mountains to the west. The Great Basin is a "sink"—that is, a place where surface flows end. Water draining east out of the Sierra Nevada Mountains from Lake Tahoe (the Truckee River) terminates its journey at Pyramid Lake. The next major drainage to the south (Carson River) ends in a series of small lakes and marshes in the Carson Desert (Figure 12.1).

Perhaps only thirteen thousand years earlier this entire area was covered with water. Melting glaciers in the Sierra Nevada formed a vast inland lake, now referred to as Lake Lahontan, with water at an

12.2 Pyramid Lake (Source: Ralph Dunn, Pyramid Lake Fishery).

elevation that reached roughly four hundred feet higher than the present elevation of Pyramid Lake. Tufa deposits–precipitated calcium carbonate–stand today as remnants of this time, as do watermarks high up along cliff sides. Pyramid Lake and the Carson Desert wetlands are vestiges of this once vast inland sea.

Explorer John C. Fremont encountered Pyramid Lake in 1844, naming it for a distinctive triangular rock jutting out of its surface on its east side (Figure 12.2). He was struck by the lake's dark-green color, surmising correctly that it was deep (350 feet). Remarkable for its desert setting, Pyramid Lake was made all the more remarkable by a meal of fish provided by Northern Paiute encountered there. Fremont pronounced this fish–the Lahontan cutthroat trout–superior in flavor to any he had ever eaten. The trout and another fish native to the lake, the cui-ui, provided essential sustenance for the Northern Paiute who lived there. In their own language these Paiute referred to themselves as the "Cui-ui eaters."

To the east and south lived another group of Northern Paiute who called themselves the "Cattail-eaters."[4] They lived in small camps scattered through the shallow lakes and wetlands that represented the terminus of the Carson River. Even in historical times the river has changed course several times as it moves into and through the table-like Carson Desert. A southern branch carries water into Carson Lake, which, in 1882, was described as covering an area of forty square miles with a depth of four feet. Captain James H. Simpson, assigned in 1859 to develop an easier route from Salt Lake City through the Great Basin, remarked: "Carson Lake beautiful blue; lake margined with rushes; the shores are covered with mussel-shells; pelican and other aquatic fowl a characteristic."[5] He noted that "the lake is full of fish. A number of Pi-utes, some two dozen, live near our camp, and I notice they have piles of fish lying about drying, principally chubs and mullet."[6]

Water from the Carson River also moved through the Stillwater Slough into a series of lakes, marshes, and wetlands to the north known as Stillwater Marsh. Described as the "heart" of Cattail-eater territory,[7] the substantial wetlands of the Stillwater Marsh provided a home for "thousands of waterfowl and shorebirds as well as tens of thousands more that migrated seasonally through the area, often stopping to nest and rear young."[8] Waterfowl and fish were important sources of food, as were the cattail, the bulrush, and several other indigenous plants. The presence of these wetlands was made all the more remarkable by the desert in which they existed, an area with an average annual rainfall of five inches—most all of which comes in the winter months. Evaporation in this desert area is extreme: Put a barrel with four feet of water out next to Carson Lake, and it will be completely dry in a year.[9]

Westward emigrants passed through this region beginning in the 1840s, reaching flood proportions following discovery of gold in California in 1848. Discovery of silver near Virginia City in 1859 brought in large numbers of people to the mountains just to the west, creating a demand for food and pasture supplied by settlers moving into the usable lands of the Carson River Basin, including Carson Lake and the Stillwater Marsh, and to the Truckee Meadows at the foot of the Sierras along the Truckee River.

This rapid influx of settlers brought the inevitable conflicts with the resident, largely nomadic Paiute.[10] De facto reservations for the Paiute were established around Pyramid Lake and Walker Lake in 1859, but the tribe stayed in these places only during the fish-harvesting season. By about 1870 the Paiute population in this region had been reduced to a third of its size at the time of first contact with whites.[11] A presidential order in 1874 formally established the Pyramid Lake Indian Reservation, encompassing the lake, lands surrounding the lake, and lands bordering the lower end of the Truckee River.[12]

In 1893 the United States put together an area of about 30,000 acres for distribution to those Native Americans still living in the Stillwater area. Excluded were all the high-quality lands already acquired by nonnative settlers to the region. Lands were distributed under the terms of the Dawes Act, by which each head of an American Indian "household" was given 160 acres of land for farming and grazing uses. Little of the land was suitable for cultivation, and by 1906 the Fallon Indian Reservation had diminished to less than a quarter of its original land area.

13

REDEEMING THE "IRREDEEMABLE"

The reclamation vision of making the desert bloom was put to the test in the Great Basin of Nevada. Here was a land characterized as "irredeemable" by naturalist John Muir, called more Asiatic than American by explorer John C. Fremont–a desolate landscape to be endured before entering into the Promised Land of California.[13] Even a contemporary observer like journalist Jon Christensen writes: "A harsh expanse of dry desert and high mountains between the Rockies and the Sierra Nevada, the Great Basin has always been a land in between, a region apart, not included in visions of the other Western regions, the Rockies, the Colorado Plateau, the Southwest, or the West Coast."[14] He calls the Great Basin "America's wasteland."

Francis G. Newlands, perhaps best known as a principal sponsor of the 1902 Reclamation Act, saw other possibilities.[15] He believed that irrigation could transform unsettled lands in the Truckee and Carson basins of Nevada into valuable farms. Educated at Yale University and Columbia Law School, Newlands arrived in San Francisco in 1870 at the age of twenty-two. Four years later he married the daughter of William Sharon, a man who had made his fortune mining silver from the Comstock Lode in Nevada. In 1885 following Sharon's death, Newlands became trustee of his massive estate in Nevada, including silver mines, mills along the Carson River, and the Virginia and Truckee Railroad. In 1888 Newlands moved to Carson City and then to Reno.

The state of Nevada was in a severe financial crisis. Mining, which had propelled Nevada to statehood in 1864, was in decline. Ranchers controlled most of the readily usable lands in the state, limited as they were, so there was little to draw new settlement to the state. Newlands believed the answer was irrigation: store water in the eastern Sierra Nevada for use on unclaimed but potentially arable desert lands downstream in Nevada. In 1889 he purchased dam sites at Donner Lake and Lake Tahoe in the headwaters of the Truckee River and in Long Valley in the upper Carson River (locations singled out in the irrigation survey directed by John Wesley Powell), together with twenty-eight thousand acres of lands potentially suitable for irrigation in the two basins. In 1890 he proposed "remodeling our present system of irrigation according to some intelligent and scientific plan."[16] He pointed out that "a scientific system of distribution would only require a single dam and a large main canal, with distributing ditches, to control an area now covered by many such canals and dams." The work would pay for itself, he argued, because its cost could be recovered through sale of the additional irrigable lands. In 1892 Newlands became Nevada's representative in Congress.

Irrigated agriculture already existed in those few parts of Nevada lucky enough to have both arable land and readily available water. A small group of Mormons from Salt Lake City planted crops in 1851 in the Carson Valley, a broad expanse of land in Nevada downstream of the point where the East and West Forks of the Carson River join, to sell to California-bound travelers. The Truckee Meadows, a comparable but smaller area along the Truckee River above Reno, attracted the attention of California cattlemen in 1858. Eventually, additional lands were irrigated along the Humboldt River and the lower potions of the Truckee and the Carson (Figure 13.1). To people like Newlands, much more seemed possible.

Eleven days after President Roosevelt enthusiastically signed the Reclamation Act on June 17, 1902, Frederick Newell–soon to be appointed head of the new Reclamation Service–privately submitted six possible projects to the secretary of the interior. One was called the Truckee-Carson Project (later to be called the Newlands Project), and it envisioned over four hundred thousand acres of additional irrigated lands in western Nevada. In July the secretary with-

13.1 Homesteading along the Carson River, 1908 (Source: Churchill County Museum).

drew 2.6 million acres of federal public lands in the Truckee and Carson basins from entry under the homestead acts, while planning for the reclamation project proceeded (Figure 13.2). Newell pressed Newlands to use his influence with the Nevada legislature to get a new water code enacted, with a state engineer empowered to administer water rights. The legislature responded in February 1903, and in March the secretary of the interior approved the Truckee-Carson Project as one of the first five federal reclamation projects.

There were two key factors motivating the project (aside from now-Senator Newlands, of course). One was the availability of large areas of unclaimed public lands downstream on the Carson River and, to a lesser extent, the Truckee River, thought to be suitable for irrigation. The other was Lake Tahoe. This extraordinary mountain lake is essentially the source of the Truckee River. Its brilliant transparency caused Mark Twain to compare boat rides on the lake to balloon voyages because of the sensation of floating on air.[17] Not only did the lake itself contain a massive supply of water, but, Powell's engineers realized, with a relatively small dam at its mouth, the large spring runoff from its high-Sierra drainage area could be captured and held for release later in the summer when natural stream flows could not provide enough water for irrigation. There was, of course,

13.2 The Carson Desert prior to irrigation, 1911 (Source: Churchill County Museum).

13.3 Building the Truckee Canal to carry water to the Carson Watershed, 1905 (Source: Churchill County Museum).

13.4 The dedication of Derby Dam, 1905 (Source: Churchill County Museum).

the minor problem that most of the arable lands existed in the Carson rather than in the Truckee Basin, but that problem could readily be addressed by constructing a canal that would carry Truckee River water through a low divide to the Carson River above the area to be irrigated (Figure 13.3).

Between 1903 and 1915 the Reclamation Service constructed the facilities that would make the Newlands Project a reality. First to be built was Derby Diversion Dam (Figure 13.4) on the Truckee about twenty miles below Reno, together with the 32.5-mile Truckee Canal to bring Truckee River water into the "Truckee Division" near Fernley and the "Carson Division" to the south. In turn, Reclamation constructed a dam on the Carson River to permit diversion of water into two newly constructed canals. This work was completed in 1906.

Attention turned next to making the water supply more secure through the construction of dams that would store water in periods of relative abundance for release during times of need. Construction of an eighteen-foot-high dam at the outlet of Lake Tahoe, completed in 1913, added six feet of lake elevation and an astounding 732,000 acre-feet of water storage. The final piece was the completion

13.5 Lahontan Dam, 1912 (Source: Churchill County Museum).

in 1915 of the Lahontan Reservoir, with a capacity of 314,000 acre-feet, on the Carson River about five miles above the diversion dam used to carry water to project lands (Figure 13.5). Truckee River water carried by the Truckee Canal is stored directly in the reservoir, along with flows from the Carson River, for subsequent irrigation use (Figure 13.6).

Initially, planners for the Reclamation Service estimated that there was enough irrigable land and available water in the area to enable irrigation of more than two hundred thousand acres of land within the Newlands Project. Sale of this public land, it was believed, would readily repay the cost of building the water storage and delivery structures. The Reclamation Service had an obvious interest in seeing these lands sold and dedicated a portion of its effort to advertising and promoting their attractions.

Settlement of lands in the Newlands Project got off to a rocky start. Despite promises to the contrary, the Reclamation Service was unable to deliver water in 1905 to some lands that had already been prepared for planting. Most of the new settlers who "took up their lonely homesteads on the unbroken desert"[18] knew little or nothing about irrigated farming. Reclamation advised them to grow alfalfa

13.6 Truckee Canal emptying into Lahontan Reservoir.

because of the substantial demand for hay for livestock in the area. It turned out, however, that it took three to five years to get good growth from alfalfa plants because the soils lacked humus and required addition of manure or other sources of organic matter (Figure 13.7).

The promise of a virtually unlimited water supply from Lake Tahoe ran into problems when Reclamation was unable to secure rights from the hydroelectric power company then owning the site to take over a small wooden crib dam that existed at the mouth of the lake and to replace it with its own larger facility. A plan to take water out of the lake into Nevada through a tunnel was successfully opposed by the state of California and by property owners on the lake. Not until 1915 did the United States finally obtain legal control of the dam site, and even then it had to agree to operate the dam to ensure minimum year-round flows of water for hydroelectric power

13.7 Flood irrigating alfalfa, 1908 (Source: Churchill County Museum).

generation, measured at a gauge on the Truckee River near the state line.

Despite these problems settlement of the area proceeded rapidly. The number of farms within the Newlands Project jumped from 108 in 1906 to about 415 in 1910, and then to 698 by 1920.[19] The Truckee-Carson Irrigation District (TCID), a governmental unit with taxing authority established under state law, was formed in 1919 to represent the interests of the irrigators in dealings with the Bureau of Reclamation. In 1926 TCID assumed responsibility on behalf of individual irrigators within the district for making the necessary payments to the United States for a share of the construction and operation costs of the Newlands Project, and also took over operation of project facilities (though ownership of the facilities, by law, remained with the United States). Irrigation development within the project never came anywhere close to the two hundred thousand acres optimistically predicted, and is less than sixty thousand acres today.

In the 1930s Reclamation constructed Boca Dam on the Little Truckee River in California to provide a more reliable water supply for irrigators in the Truckee Meadows, largely on lands to the south of Reno. As mentioned, irrigation of these open lands where the Truckee River finally emerges from the Sierra Nevada began in the late 1850s.

More than thirty separate ditches brought water to irrigate about twenty-nine thousand acres.

Then, in 1956, Congress authorized the Washoe Project—originally intended to provide water for the irrigation of fifty thousand acres of land in the Carson and Truckee river basins.[20] The principal features of this project were to be the Stampede Reservoir in the upper Truckee and the Watasheamu Reservoir on the East Fork of the Carson River. Under a modified version of the project, Reclamation constructed instead a dam on Prosser Creek about 1.5 miles above its junction with the Truckee River, and the Stampede Reservoir on the Little Truckee above Boca Reservoir. No dam was ever constructed in the Carson Basin. Nor has any additional irrigation resulted from development under this project, though—as described in chapter 15—project water has been used for other purposes.[21]

Irrigation uses of the Carson River date back at least to 1851. Additional agricultural development in the Carson Valley and in a series of other, smaller mountain valleys in California and Nevada brought over fifty thousand acres of land into irrigation, primarily producing alfalfa and hay. Irrigators constructed small dams at several mountain lakes in the upper Carson to improve their water supply.[22]

As in most of the West, irrigators hold legal rights to use a significant part of the water resources of the Truckee and Carson basins. The federal government took the legal steps necessary to establish water rights for the Newlands Project. It filed "quiet title" actions in federal court in 1913 for the Truckee River and in 1925 for the Carson River to determine these rights. In the 1944 Orr Ditch Decree the court determined that the United States had a right to divert essentially the entire flow of the Truckee River at Derby Dam—up to fifteen hundred cubic feet per second to irrigate 232,800 acres of land within the Newlands Project. Moreover, this right had a "priority" date of July 2, 1902—meaning it could divert and use the full amount of this water in preference to all those with later priority dates. The diversion right, held in the name of the United States, was for the project as a whole, but the decree also established water "duties" for irrigated lands.[23] The federal court set that amount at 3.5 acre-feet of water per acre for "bottom" lands and 4.5 acre-feet per acre for "bench" lands, based on the amount of water thought to be necessary to grow alfalfa on these lands. In other words, each acre of irrigated benchland within the Newlands Project can have as much as fifty-four inches of water placed on it during the irrigation season—land that otherwise receives five inches of precipitation a year.

The 1980 decree for Carson River (known as the Alpine Decree) established identical water duties and also established a "consumptive use" duty of 2.99 acre-feet per acre—the amount of water totally consumed by alfalfa plants during the growing season. The Alpine Decree also confirmed the right of the United States with the 1902 priority date to store the entire flow of the Carson River reaching the Lahontan Reservoir.[24]

14

AN ENVIRONMENTAL RECKONING

The Newlands Project, though modest in size, utterly transformed the Truckee and Carson rivers as they moved to their desert endings. The dam at Lake Tahoe held back much of the spring runoff that once passed unobstructed on its hundred-mile-journey to Pyramid Lake.[25] Derby Dam channeled off perhaps half of the water reaching this point of the Truckee River—more in dry years.[26] In the irrigation season sometimes no water passed the dam. Because virtually all of this water moved into the Carson drainage, almost none ever found its way to Pyramid Lake.

The Lahontan Reservoir totally impounded the flows of the Carson River, holding back its springtime abundance, and releasing water either to meet downstream irrigation demands or—in the nonirrigation season—to generate electricity at a power plant immediately below the dam.[27] The diversion dam, located five miles downstream, moved most or all of the water out of the river into two canals during the irrigation season. Water reaching Carson Lake or Stillwater Marsh came either from hydropower releases or irrigation return flows.

The first visible casualty of Newlands Project water use was Lake Winnemucca. This lake existed largely as an overflow from Pyramid Lake and, at its known peak in the 1880s, was 25 miles long, 3.5 miles wide, contained over 3 million acre-feet of water (compared to about 26 million acre-feet in Pyramid Lake), and created up to twenty-four thousand acres of wetlands.[28] In 1936, even as Lake Winnemucca was rapidly disappearing, President Franklin D.

Roosevelt issued an executive order creating Winnemucca Lake National Wildlife Refuge. Roosevelt, it seemed, had no more power over water than had the Danish King Canute, who, according to legend, placed his throne in the ocean and (unsuccessfully) ordered the tide not to come in: By 1939 Lake Winnemucca was dry.

Then, in the early 1940s, the Lahontan cutthroat trout disappeared altogether from Pyramid Lake. The abundance of this fish and its excellent flavor had encouraged heavy commercial exploitation beginning in the 1880s, but its numbers began to decline as upstream diversions for the Newlands Project reduced the level of the lake.[29] The life cycle of the trout depended on migration out of the lake upstream during the winter months for spawning. These remarkable trout, which grew to as much as twenty pounds, migrated even up to Lake Tahoe and beyond.[30]

Beginning in about 1910, inflows to the lake consistently fell below the four-foot-per-year evaporation rates in this desert area (Figure 14.1). As the lake level steadily declined, the river cut down through the alluvial soils underlying the channel—forming a multi-channeled delta at the river's mouth. Except in years of extremely high flows, fish were unable to pass out of the lake through these shallow channels. Moreover, construction of structures such as the Derby Dam blocked fish passage up the river. Finally, extreme low flows during the drought years of the 1930s made movement out of Pyramid Lake for spawning impossible, and the remnant lake population eventually died out.

Pyramid Lake continued its steady decline, reaching its known low in the mid-1960s.[31] The cui-ui, a species of sucker found only in Pyramid Lake, had so declined in numbers by this point that it had the dubious distinction of being among the first species listed in 1967 as "endangered"—that is, identified by the U.S. Fish and Wildlife Service as on the brink of extinction.[32] Like the Lahontan cutthroat trout, the cui-ui must migrate out of the lake upriver to spawn. Unlike the trout, the cui-ui is exceptionally long-lived, with females reaching up to forty-five years of age.[33] This long life apparently enabled the cui-ui to survive long periods without reproduction, allowing it to maintain at least some population during the many years in which upstream migration out of Pyramid Lake was not possible.

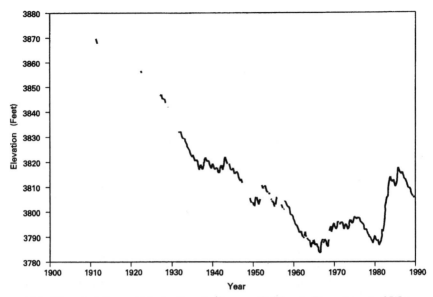

14.1 Historical Pyramid Lake Levels (Source: California Department of Water Resources).

Water development in the Truckee and Carson rivers also has had a profound effect on the natural features of the Carson Desert, the terminus of the Carson River. Even in historical times the course of the river has shifted considerably within the open, flat desert expanse, moving from Carson Lake on the south to Carson Sink on the north to the Stillwater Marsh on the east.[34] In 1862, for example, a flood during the winter carved out a channel directly to the Carson Sink, with the flow of the river splitting between the old channel to Carson Lake and the new channel to Carson Sink.

In the 1890s Carson Lake was a substantial body of water, estimated to be twelve miles long and eight miles wide, covering an area of over twenty-five thousand acres.[35] Overflow from Carson Lake passed through Stillwater Slough into Stillwater Marsh, an extensive wetland area composed of a connected series of shallow ponds. In high-flow years water from both the Carson River and the Stillwater Slough (and even occasionally from the Humboldt Basin to the north) would reach the Carson Sink, described in 1898 as "half shallow lake, half tule swamp which extends for 20 miles along the valley bottom and furnishes enough salt grass, sedges, and tules to winter many thousand head of stock, and a breeding ground for great numbers of water and shore birds."[36] In periods of prolonged drought these wetlands might nearly disappear.

There is something remarkable about wetlands in a desert. Immediately upland from the wetlands, only spare vegetation such as saltbush and greasewood grows. Yet the ponds and marshes of the Lahontan wetlands support a rich mosaic of habitats, ranging from freshwater cattails to salt-tolerant alkali bulrush. They provide particularly valuable habitat for migratory and resident birds such as ducks, geese, black-necked stilts, American avocets, long-billed dowitchers, egrets, and white-face ibises. The wetlands are a primary feeding ground for American white pelicans coming from one of the largest breeding colonies in the United States at Anaho Island in Pyramid Lake. In 1988 the Lahontan Valley wetlands became the fourth site in the United States adopted into the Western Hemispheric Shorebird Reserve; they have been nominated for protection under the Convention on Wetlands of International Importance (the Ramsar Convention).[37]

Diversions of Carson River water into the Newlands Project beginning in the early 1900s diminished spring and summer flows into the desert wetlands, as did other upstream irrigation uses of water in the upper Carson valleys. The effects of these depletions were masked for many years, however, by the additional Truckee River water diverted into the Carson watershed. Wintertime hydroelectric power releases from the Lahontan Reservoir stayed in the Carson River, directly feeding the wetlands with relatively high-quality water.

Then, in 1967, Secretary of the Interior Stewart Udall promulgated the first Operating Criteria and Procedures (OCAP) for the Newlands Project, establishing a limitation of 406,000 acre-feet of water that could be diverted for the Newlands Project each year. This action effectively eliminated diversion of water from the Truckee to run the hydroelectric plant at the Lahontan Dam. In the 1970s, with less water transported from the Truckee, the Lahontan Valley wetlands began to recede noticeably. Between 1972 and 1977 wetland acreage in the area (in the fall) decreased from about forty-eight thousand acres to about twelve thousand acres.[38] A series of wet years between 1983 and 1985 brought the wetlands back to about forty-six thousand acres in 1986, but then a drought period reduced the wetlands area to only twenty acres in 1992 and about eight thousand acres in 1993.

In addition to the dramatic decline in the extent of the wetlands, there has been a related increase in the concentration of total dissolved solids (salts) and in such trace elements of concern as arsenic, boron, and mercury.[39] These water-quality problems reflect both the greatly reduced amounts of dilution water reaching the wetlands and the fact that most of the water supply for the area comes from irrigation drainage. Wastes from long-abandoned mines, tailings, and mineral-processing facilities, located upstream in the vicinity of Virginia City and Dayton, continue to leach mercury and other contaminants into the Carson River. One such area is now a designated Superfund site.

15

THE ONGOING SEARCH FOR REDEMPTION

The driving force behind changes in water use in the Truckee-Carson Basin has been the Pyramid Lake Paiute tribe. The tribe first succeeded in getting the attention of a sympathetic secretary of the interior in 1964 when Stewart Udall appointed a committee to look into water use by the Newlands Project and its effects on Pyramid Lake. Dissatisfied with the Operating Criteria and Procedures issued by Secretary Udall in 1967, the tribe initiated the first of what would become a remarkable, and remarkably successful, process of litigation. Represented by Robert Pelcyger, a young Yale-trained lawyer who started his legal career with the California Indian Legal Services in 1968,[40] the tribe filed a federal suit challenging the 1970 OCAP promulgated by then secretary of the interior Rogers Morton. Simultaneously, the tribe brought suit demanding that the attorney general of the United States seek a tribal-reserved water right for sufficient Truckee River water to maintain the cui-ui fishery.[41] In 1972 Federal District Court Judge Gerhard Gesell found that the OCAP's authorization to divert up to 378,000 acre-feet of water for the Newlands Project failed to meet the secretary's trust responsibility to the tribe. In a subsequent 1973 memorandum Judge Gesell established a maximum diversion of about 288,000 acre-feet.[42]

The tribe found a powerful ally in the cui-ui, protected under the Endangered Species Act. Congress had listed the cui-ui as an endangered species in 1967. The 1973 Endangered Species Act required federal agencies to use all available authority to assist the

recovery of listed species. The Pyramid Lake tribe pointed out to
the secretary of the interior that the Washoe Project had been authorized in 1956 for fish and wildlife purposes as well as for irrigation water supply. The water in the Washoe Project's Prosser Reservoir already had been dedicated to replacing existing deliveries from
Lake Tahoe so the fishery in Truckee River below the reservoir could
be protected. No water-supply contracts existed for the recently completed Stampede Reservoir on the Little Truckee River. Why not
use this water to help provide flows to Pyramid Lake at spawning
times? Pointing to his obligations under the Endangered Species
Act, the secretary of the interior decided to do just this, and the
courts upheld this decision as permitted by the project authorizing
legislation, and fully warranted under the Endangered Species Act.[43]
And in 1976 the Bureau of Reclamation used the authority of the
Washoe Project Act to build Marble Bluff Dam three miles above
Pyramid Lake to stabilize the downcutting of the river's mouth caused
by the declining level of the lake, as well as to establish a fishway, a
channel through which it was hoped the cui-ui would be able to
move upstream out of the lake to spawn. The first cui-ui recovery
plan, issued in 1978, focused on developing a better understanding
of the needs of the fish and on a hatchery program to sustain fish
populations.

　　Lisa Heki is a biologist in charge of the cui-ui recovery program for the U.S. Fish and Wildlife Service. In March 1994 she showed
me around the Marble Bluff facility, where an elevator has been
built to lift migrating cui-ui up over the thirty-five-foot dam structure
(Figure 15.1). The cui-ui were close to spawning time, and she was
facing a difficult decision: how much water to release from the Stampede Reservoir to aid their upstream migration. Water had been
released from Stampede before for this purpose, but never as much
as she wanted to release, and never when there was so little storage
water available in the reservoir. Recreational interests in California
were pressuring her to release as little as possible to maintain reservoir
fishing and boating uses. She went ahead with the planned releases,
and when I saw her next several months later, she was visibly pleased
with the results. Despite the drought, large numbers of cui-ui had
made it up out of Pyramid Lake to spawn in the Truckee River.

15.1 Measuring cui-uis at Marble Bluff Dam.

Administrative regulation of Newlands Project operations through the OCAP remains a contentious and still-unresolved issue. The current OCAP, issued in 1988, establishes provisions for annual determination of allowable water diversions from the Truckee and Carson rivers. That determination is based on the number of acres of project lands with established rights to receive water, the headgate duty of water for those lands (depending on whether they are benchlands or bottomlands), an "efficiency factor" for delivery of water from the rivers to the headgates, and a series of storage "targets" at the Lahontan Reservoir that vary by month.

Broadly stated, the objective of the OCAP is to deliver the legally obligated quantity of water to project irrigators using as little Truckee River water as possible. The tribe, in its ongoing efforts to increase flows into Pyramid Lake by reducing Truckee

River diversions, has aggressively challenged virtually all aspects of project water use, including the substantial losses of water in the conveyance facilities, the validity of water use on some lands, the acreage to be counted in calculating the amount of water obligated to the project, and whether particular lands should be regarded as either bottom or bench for purposes of assigning a water-delivery amount. Since 1967 Truckee River diversions have provided an average of about 40 percent of project water supplies.[44]

In addition to revisions to the OCAP and protective measures for the cui-ui, a third key piece fell into place for the tribe in 1987 when Harry Reid replaced Paul Laxalt as senator from Nevada. Senator Reid comes from northern Nevada and has a strong interest in water matters. He wanted "comprehensive solutions" to the water conflicts in the basin. His active brokering among basin interests led to enactment of Public Law 101–618 in 1990, containing the Fallon Paiute Shoshone Tribal Settlement Act and the Truckee-Carson–Pyramid Lake Water Rights Settlement Act.[45] Among its provisions this law apportions the waters of the Truckee and Carson rivers between California and Nevada, addresses the use of reservoir storage use in the upper Truckee to provide drought protection for Reno and Sparks, establishes a water-rights acquisition program to provide water for the Lahontan Valley wetlands and for Pyramid Lake, and directs measures to reduce water use in the Reno area, at the Fallon Naval Air Station, and within the Newlands Project.

This was an important development. Storage capacity in the seven reservoirs of the upper Truckee Basin exceeds 1 million acre-feet of water, most of which is in Lake Tahoe. There has been little coordination, however, among these facilities in the management of storage and of releases for downstream use. Operation of Lake Tahoe storage has been driven by an agreement reached in 1915 requiring certain minimum flows to be maintained at the California-Nevada state line (known as the Floristan Rates) to serve a series of hydroelectric facilities then in operation. Negotiations between the Pyramid Lake tribe and the Sierra Pacific Power Company (which provides both electricity and water to the Reno-Sparks area) produced the Preliminary Settlement Agreement, which would eliminate the rigidity of the Floristan Rates and, among other things, allow more efficient use of storage in the upstream reservoirs, for enhancing cui-ui spawning conditions and for subsequent urban use.[46] The 1990 act directs the secretary of the interior to negotiate an operating agreement for the Truckee River to carry out the Preliminary Settlement Agreement.

The 1990 Settlement Act encourages market-based reallocation of water from irrigation to environmental uses by establishing a water rights acquisition program. Eventually, the acquisition program may be used to transfer irrigation water to Pyramid Lake, but at present its use is focused on providing water for the Lahontan Valley wetlands. The Nature Conservancy initiated efforts to purchase water rights from users in the Newlands Project for transfer to the wetlands in 1988. Congress provided initial funding support in 1989. Then, in section 206 of the 1990 act, Congress directed the secretary of the interior to acquire water and water rights necessary to support approximately twenty-five thousand acres, on average, of primary wetlands within the Lahontan Valley.

Underlining John Muir's aphorism that pulling on one thread shows how everything is related,[47] the success of the Pyramid Lake tribe in reducing Newlands Project water use had the unforeseen consequence of seriously diminishing the annual quantities of water reaching the wetlands at the terminus of the Carson River. Water released from the Lahontan Reservoir in the nonirrigation season to operate a hydroelectric facility at the dam previously went directly to the wetlands. Water diverted into the irrigation canals but unused for irrigation flowed eventually to the wetland areas. Canal seepage and water stored in re-regulating reservoirs provided wetland and recreational benefits. And, of course, some of the return flows from water applied to lands in the project also eventually made their way to the wetlands. The more efficient the irrigation system of the Newlands Project, the less water reaches the wetlands. Actions to benefit one natural system (Pyramid Lake) were inadvertently hurting another natural system (the Lahontan Valley wetlands). For a time in the 1980s, as this effect became painfully apparent, environmental interests favoring one or the other of these values came into competition.[48]

The 1990 act reaffirmed the OCAP principles promoting greater reliance on Carson River water for the Newlands Project,[49] but authorized a water-acquisition program to help offset the OCAP's impacts on the wetlands. The U.S. Fish and Wildlife Service has proposed acquiring rights to an average annual supply of 125,000 acre-feet of water to be used to sustain about 25,000 acres of wetlands in four areas: Stillwater National Wildlife Refuge, Stillwater Wildlife Management Area, Carson Lake, and Fallon Paiute-Shoshone Indian Reservation wetlands.[50]

Finally, the 1990 act promoted water-use efficiency in meeting water demands in the basin. Thus, the secretary of the navy was directed to study ways to reduce water needs associated with the naval air station near Fallon. Entities providing municipal or industrial water in either California or Nevada must prepare a "water conservation and management plan" evaluating water-conservation measures and considering their implementation.[51] And the secretary of the interior was directed to study ways in which the delivery efficiency of the Newlands Project could be improved to 75 percent within twelve years.[52]

There are no quick fixes for working out the water problems of the Truckee and Carson basins, but there are some promising general approaches and, perhaps, some lessons to be learned from previous experience. If progress is not made in the basin, it will not be from lack of trying. There were perhaps a dozen separate processes (broadly defined) under way in 1994 in the basin addressing water-related issues. These include negotiations to develop a new Truckee River Operating Agreement (and a related environmental-impact statement), the water rights acquisition program (and a related environmental-impact statement), the cui-ui recovery program, the Stillwater Area Remediation Plan (dealing with irrigation drainage issues), restoration efforts along the lower Truckee River, efforts by the Lahontan Valley Environmental Alliance to develop a community consensus on water matters, contracting discussions between the Bureau of Reclamation and the Truckee-Carson Irrigation District for operation of the Newlands Project, and a mediation process established by Senator Reid in late 1994 and concluded unsuccessfully in 1995 in an attempt to revisit the 1990 Settlement Act. There are at least as many major participants in these processes. Yet there is little apparent coordination, either formal or informal, among the processes or participants, despite some efforts by the Department of the Interior to the contrary.

The participants in these processes all are working with a limited and highly variable water supply. As is almost always the case with water, the fundamental issue is control: who determines the amount, timing, and manner of water use. Under western water law, control of the resource is given to those first to put it to use. In the Truckee-Carson, as in most of the West, this means irrigated agriculture.[53] To induce the development of an economy that would support settlement of the West, much of the West's water was dedicated to irrigation, with projects like Newlands built by the Bureau of Reclamation to help make that water available at very low cost.

Much of what has happened since 1967 can be understood as attempts to define more explicitly the legal rights of Newlands Project irrigators and the Truckee-Carson Irrigation District to control and use the water of the Truckee and Carson rivers. In a very real sense, until the institution of the OCAP in 1967 there were essentially no limits on their use of the water in these rivers once it reached either the Derby Dam or the Lahontan Reservoir. Even now there remains considerable uncertainty, as every legal question continues to be litigated aggressively either by the tribe or by the water users.

When the secretary of the interior sought to impose the court-ordered OCAP in 1973, TCID refused to comply, asserting that Interior's action exceeded its authority. It continued to divert water beyond that authorized under the OCAP. The United States then moved to cancel its 1926 contract with TCID and to assume control of project operations. TCID brought an action against the United States, claiming that the OCAP constituted a governmental "taking" of TCID's property rights to water and seeking an injunction against the contract cancellation. The Nevada Federal District Court postponed deciding the case until other legal issues were resolved, but in 1983 held against TCID.[54] TCID has continued to operate the project on a year-to-year basis, but the United States has the authority to award the contract to another entity.

16

WHAT HAPPENS TO IRRIGATION?

Water issues in the West are nothing if not complex. In all the concern about providing for the water-related interests of the Pyramid Lake tribe, the Pyramid Lake fishery, and the Lahontan wetlands, little attention has been given to the consequences for the irrigation-based economy and culture that exists because of the Newlands Project. Towns like Fallon and Fernley depended for much of this century, either directly or indirectly, on irrigated agriculture as an important part of their economic base. Seepage water from the canals and ditches that carried irrigation water to the fields charged the groundwater aquifers from which domestic water supplies come. Efforts to buy out irrigation uses and transfer the water to the wetlands bring further into question the long-term viability of what is already a modest agricultural economy. Efforts to make water-conveyance facilities more efficient threaten the long-term adequacy of traditional drinking-water supplies from groundwater.

What exactly was the commitment made by the United States to Newlands Project irrigators and to the communities that grew up around these irrigators? What does that commitment mean today? At a minimum it seems clear that there was a commitment to provide water determined necessary for growing crops on project lands identified as irrigable and for which a water allotment was obtained. For most irrigated project lands this means, by court decree, providing up to 3.5 or 4.5 acre-feet of water per acre to the irrigator's headgate and, by implication, providing "carriage" water as necessary to get that amount of water to the headgate–limited only by the physical availability of water in the system. In OCAP terminology, this is the maximum allowable delivery.

The policy debate–whether this commitment was only to continued irrigation use on project lands or whether uses of the water can be changed–is now largely settled. It was a difficult debate because the equities argued heavily for keeping the water under individual control only so long as it stayed in its original use. Reclamation projects had been authorized and built in most cases to support the development of an irrigation economy that could in turn support western settlement. The full cost of the projects and, in particular, that part attributable to providing an irrigation-water supply, almost always substantially exceeded the amount of money the irrigators paid to the United States. In short, the reclamation program represented a major public investment in western agriculture, and there was understandable reluctance to allow individual irrigators or irrigation districts to profit from a change of use of the water.

In the end the need to encourage reallocation of water resources in the West, and the conclusion that a market-based approach would best accomplish this objective, seem to have won out. In the Newlands Project individual irrigators now may sell or otherwise transfer their water rights to others with different uses. And, in fact, as of October 1993, Newlands irrigators have sold water rights providing over twelve thousand acre-feet of water for use in the Lahontan wetlands.[55] The price for permanent annual use of an acre-foot of water (without land) has increased from about $170 to about $400 because of the demand for wetlands water.[56]

The U.S. Fish and Wildlife Service estimates that from half to three quarters of the lands presently irrigated within the Newlands Project will eventually go out of production as water rights for the wetlands are purchased and transferred.[57] Agriculture accounts for only about 2-3 percent of the personal income generated in the area (though this understates the importance of related economic activities such as livestock that derive from the modest agricultural base), so the direct economic effects of this change, though significant, probably are manageable. Of perhaps greater concern to those living in the area is the marked change in its character that will result as culti-

vated farmland with its green, open spaces returns to desert range-
land or is subdivided for residential development.

17

WHAT NEXT?

Water development in the Truckee and Carson basins proceeded with little regard for its effects on the environmental values that already depended on that water. There is nothing unique about that statement—the same was true throughout the West. What is somewhat unique about the Truckee-Carson is the degree to which efforts are being made to restore at least some measure of ecological integrity within two important water-based natural systems in the basins. In this respect the efforts in the Truckee-Carson may be something of a model (including a model of what *not* to do) for similar activities now emerging throughout the West as attention turns to undoing some of the unacceptable effects of one-hundred-plus years of generally unconstrained water development.

The Truckee-Carson is especially notable because so much of the restoration effort has centered on redefining control and use of the water resource rather than on the more common preference for structural and technical fixes. To be sure, fish hatcheries have been built to maintain fish populations; dikes, levees, and other structures have been constructed to manage water reaching the wetlands; check structures and other physical improvements are being added to improve the efficiency of the water-conveyance system in the Newlands Project. These actions have been useful—even necessary.

But the real challenge in the Truckee-Carson and across the West is learning how to reconnect the essential ecological functions of water with a system of water use that developed with little concern for, or appreciation of, these functions. In the Truckee-Carson the water rights for irrigation of lands within the Newlands Project have gone through an extensive process of definition and clarification since 1967, through both litigation and administrative action. A number of issues with potential application in other settings have been addressed. Aggressive efforts by the Pyramid Lake Paiute tribe have forced detailed attention to the legal status of lands receiving irrigation water and the amount of water obligated to the lands. Are the lands specifically entitled to receive project water? Involved here are such questions as whether the lands in irrigation use have been classified by Reclamation as irrigable, whether they are individually identified as entitled to receive water in contractual agreements with the district or the United States, and whether water is being used "beneficially" on those specified parcels. In the Newlands Project some irrigators have used project water on lands never authorized to receive water.[58] The tribe asserts that use of water on unauthorized lands is illegal and that water rights based on such use should be forfeited. The irrigators have been seeking a change of place of use with the Nevada state engineer to validate their rights.[59]

Assuming the lands legally entitled to receive water are identified, there is then the issue of the quantity of water they are entitled to receive. Measurement of water use in western irrigation has been crude or nonexistent until fairly recently. There has been little reason to make the investments necessary for measurement. Now, however, with increased pressures on the resource, measurement is becoming important. Equally crude have been estimates of the duty of water. Many irrigators have assumed that more is better and have been inclined to apply water (when available) well in excess of the physical needs of crops. The existence of legally decreed water duties for lands in the Newlands Project, denoting maximum amounts of water to which irrigators are entitled, is not typical in the West. But there is a concept of "beneficial use" of water that establishes a general requirement that the amount and manner of water use are limited to that reasonably necessary to accomplish the purpose of the use.

In the Newlands Project there is a distinction between so-called benchlands and bottomlands in the legally established duty of water. One of the points of controversy has concerned the criteria for classification of lands into these categories developed by the Bureau of Reclamation, and the bureau's application of these criteria in the classification process.[60] Over 75 percent of lands within the Carson Division are classified as bottomlands, whereas virtually all lands in the Truckee Division are benchlands.

In calculating the quantity of water to be supplied to the farmlands, the designated duty of either 3.5 or 4.5 acre-feet per acre is multiplied times the amount of acreage. The tribe successfully argued that the acreage for this calculation should be carefully defined to include only that specific area of land actually irrigated. Thus, land areas dedicated to ditches, structures, and other noncrop uses must be eliminated from these calculations.

Then there is the question of the status of the water rights for lands legally entitled to receive water but that are not being put to irrigation use. Do the landowners have a continued claim to receive project water? In the Newlands Project there may be as many as 17,862 acres of land in this category.[61] The Pyramid Lake Paiute tribe has asserted that these water rights should be regarded as abandoned, forfeited, or never perfected due to nonuse.

In the Newlands Project, as in all irrigation projects in the West, more water is diverted from the river than is used by the crops. A rough rule of thumb is that two acre-feet of water are diverted for every one acre-foot that crops actually consume. Water is lost by evaporation, by seepage from canals, ditches, and laterals, by evapotranspiration of noncrop vegetation, and by return flows through drainage ditches and groundwater percolation. Water delivery and on-farm systems can be made more efficient from an engineering standpoint, but only at considerable cost. Even assuming that irrigators then have a legal right to the use of water saved by making system improvements (doubtful under the water laws of most western states), the economic value of the water to the irrigators rarely equals or exceeds the cost of making it available. Water is essential for irrigated agriculture, but most of irrigated agriculture in the West depends on that water being very cheap. The value of the crops that are produced, for the most part, cannot tolerate high water costs. Certainly this is true in the Newlands

Project, where most of the irrigated land produces alfalfa and hay.

In pursuing its objective of minimizing diversions from the Truckee River, the OCAP establishes a formula for determining "project efficiency," defined as water deliveries at farm headgates divided by total project diversions. TCID is required to meet certain efficiency targets and is penalized for failing to do so. The targets are based, in part, on assumed water savings that would result from implementing identified conservation measures, including instituting a system of ordering water, improved accuracy in measuring water, changes in use of the existing system of regulatory reservoirs, and shortening the irrigation season.

Experience to date with improving project efficiency has been disappointing. TCID has implemented many of the proposed conservation measures, but considerably fewer water savings have resulted than anticipated.[62] Nevertheless, the Bureau of Reclamation believes it is possible to meet the 1990 act's goal of achieving 75 percent efficiency by the year 2002. The agency's proposed least-cost alternative for achieving this result involves acquiring water rights from four project areas totaling about 8,340 acres (identified as requiring the diversion of a relatively large amount of water to meet considerably smaller headgate delivery requirements), installing measuring devices at about half of the farm delivery points throughout the project, and concrete-lining roughly the first six miles of one of the two main canals in the Carson Division.[63] At a capital cost of $62.5 million, the bureau estimates that project diversions would be reduced by 45,700 acre-feet, and 33,690 acre-feet of water would be transferred to the wetlands.

Is this a good public investment? Consider that the total capital investment in the Newlands Project to date is something like $15 million (actual, not adjusted, dollars).[64] Consider also that, at an assumed price of one thousand dollars per acre, the entire area presently irrigated within the Newlands Project could be purchased for approximately the same amount of money that would be expended to achieve the 75 percent efficiency objective. The difference, of course, is that with efficiency improvements irrigated agriculture would still exist in the community.

Are there better alternatives? David Yardas of the Environmental Defense Fund and Graham Chisholm of the Nature Conservancy have developed what they call "Concepts for a Second-Generation Truckee-Carson Settlement." Among these concepts are proposals to move from the convoluted computations of the OCAP to some fixed maximum annual diversion that would be available to Newlands Project water users; to transform project water rights into equivalent shares that would be freely transferable; to move toward "decoupling" the Truckee River supply from the Carson Division by purchasing a large share of the Truckee Division water rights, retiring these lands, and generally limiting use of the Truckee Canal only to those times that would not interfere with cui-ui and Lahontan trout spawning; using storage space in the upper-Truckee reservoirs to hold purchased, leased, or saved project water from the Truckee River, and using storage space in the Lahontan Reservoir for purchased, leased, or saved project water from the Carson River; recovering "recoupment" water—owed because of intentional overdiversions by TCID in violation of the OCAP—through converting a share of Truckee River water stored in the upper-basin reservoirs to water available for release to support the Pyramid Lake fishery; restoring the riparian ecosystem of the lower Truckee River to better facilitate fish passage and to establish improved spawning habitat; establishing a package of water rights for the wetlands that includes a firm base supply and a more variable interruptible supply; creating a Lahontan Valley Restoration Trust with management responsibility for variable water supplies for the wetlands; and developing an assured, long-term domestic water supply for the Fernley and Fallon areas.[65]

Underlying these recommendations is a recognition that significant restructuring of the manner in which water is managed and used in the basins is necessary. The system as it presently exists simply does not meet the needs of the array of basin-water interests. Despite more than twenty-five years of efforts aimed at making the system work, and despite some quite significant changes from practices in existence in 1967, more needs to be done. Perhaps most fundamentally the rigidities in the system need to be overcome.

Just how difficult this process is became painfully clear during the failed negotiation efforts that occurred over five months between late 1994 and 1995. Irrigation interests had not participated in the development of the 1990 Settlement Act, leaving a number of key issues unresolved. By 1994 there was a sense that perhaps the ingredients for a deal were now in place. People in what is referred to as the Lahontan Valley–the lower Carson River including the towns of Fallon and Fernley–were getting organized with the help of an activist University of Nevada extension agent, Mary Reid. A broad-based group of interests including local business people, elected officials, irrigators, and ranchers formed the Lahontan Valley Environmental Alliance. There were some new members on the board of the Truckee-Carson Irrigation District, including Ernie Schank and Bill Shepard. The Nature Conservancy had hired a full-time representative, Graham Chisholm, to live in the area and work on water and community issues. And there was a new chair of the Pyramid Lake Paiute tribe, Norman Henry. Senator Reid convened the negotiations and hired a professional facilitator to run them. He set a deadline of five months to put pressure on the various interests to move toward agreement.

In the end negotiations foundered on how much water the irrigators believed they needed to be able to continue to divert and use, and still have a viable system. As they moved into the final session, Ernie Schank and the other irrigators decided that they just couldn't "give their water away."[66] The Lahontan Valley Environmental Alliance supported the irrigators in this judgment. Participants in the process were disappointed but seemed determined to put as positive a spin on the outcome as possible. Mary Reid called the negotiations a beginning, not an ending.[67] One observer blamed the outcome on the rising fortunes of the Republicans in the 1994 congressional elections and hopes raised by having leadership presumed more sympathetic to agriculture than to environmental interests. "[Senator] Reid's legislative hammer suddenly turned to Jell-O," said Reno journalist Faith Bremner.[68]

Ron Anglin has responsibility for acquiring water rights from irrigators in the Newlands Project for transfer to the wetlands. "The 1990 Settlement Act created a bunch of objectives that conflict. It didn't create more water," he told me. "Reallocation of water is tough. It was tough on the Indians when the Newlands Project shifted the use of so much water and," he added "moving water back to the wetlands and Pyramid Lake is tough on the agricultural community. But," he asserted, "there is enough water."

PART 4

THE YAKIMA BASIN, WASHINGTON
MAKING THE "OLD WEST" WORK

Water is life and belongs to the earth.

–Memorial of the Yakama Tribe of American Indians

Yakima River Basin
(General Reference Map)

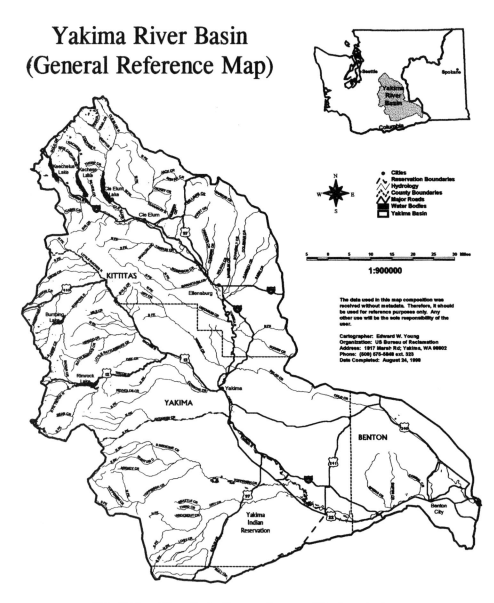

18.1 Yakima River Basin (Source: Bureau of Reclamation).

18

THE PLACE

There is much of the "old" West in the Yakima Basin (Figure 18.1).
Many people live directly off the land and resources of the basin,
and many more have livelihoods that relate in some significant way
to the region's resource-development-based economy. It is a pre-
dominantly open landscape, largely rural, with a scattering of small
to mid-size urban centers. Caught in the rain shadow of the Cascades, the basin has highly variable precipitation—averaging from 80
to 140 inches of moisture annually in the mountains to the north and
west, but less than 10 inches in the south end of the basin.

One does not need to be in the Yakima Basin long, however,
before becoming keenly aware of the transition occurring even here.
One of the first and most striking signs is the large number of espresso
stands found throughout this rural part of Washington—drive-through
stands, converted gas stations, even mobile homes parked along the
road (Figure 18.2). More telling is the large number of second homes
growing up in the northern part of the basin. Seattle, just over the
other side of the mountains, is getting closer by the day as it continues its steady growth. Some people now live in the northern foothills
of the Yakima Basin and commute daily to jobs in the Seattle area.
The old foothills coal-mining town of Roslyn, transformed into the
town of Cicely for the television program *Northern Exposure*, still draws
buses of tourists from Seattle eager to see this local version of Alaska.

Moving south through the basin, out of the pine-covered foothills of the Cascades and the hay meadows in the Kittitas Valley,

18.2 Espresso stand in Ellensburg.

through the gaps in east-west trending ridges, the traveler notes a distinct shift in character. The city of Yakima, largest in the basin with a population of sixty thousand people, serves as a convenient dividing point. As one passes through Union Gap, a break in the last ridge south of Yakima, the basin opens up noticeably. This is farm country, on a scale exceeded by few other places in the West. The rolling terrain gradually becomes more open and flat as it drops slowly but steadily down to the Columbia River. The impressive white expanse of Mount Adams, standing alone in its volcanic splendor off to the west, is a reminder that this is the Pacific Northwest and not—despite the abundant farmland—the Central Valley of California.

The basin is defined by the Yakima River and its many tributaries. Its drainage area is 6,155 square miles, about 3 percent of the full Columbia River Basin. The headwaters of the Yakima begin below Snoqualmie Pass above Keechelus Lake, and the main stem trends generally southeast into the Kittitas Valley. The western border of the Yakima Basin is formed by the Cascade Range, and most of the water in the many streams of the basin originates in the snows or rains of these mountains. The lower but still impressive Wenatchee Mountains form the northern border of the basin and provide a series of streams flowing into the Kittitas Valley. To the east, over the divide, the Columbia River carves its way south through the Columbia Plateau on a course that essentially parallels that of the Yakima at this point. The Kittitas Valley is separated from the city of Yakima by three east-west-trending ridges, and the Yakima turns into a very different river as it cuts its way through these ridges. There is little development in this hilly stretch, which is popular for recreational uses such as rafting, tubing, boating, and fishing.

Roughly midway along its journey to the Columbia River, at the north edge of the city of Yakima, the Yakima River is joined from the west by its major tributary, the Naches River, which, with its own major tributary, the Tieton, increases the flows of the Yakima by about a third. The last significant addition of water to the Yakima occurs ten miles downstream when Ahtanum Creek joins the river just above Union Gap. At this point the river turns more to the east and moves between Rattlesnake Hills on the north and Horse Heaven Hills on the south, through the heavily agricultural Lower Yakima Valley. When the Yakima finally reaches its destination at the Columbia, just above the point where it is joined by the Snake River, there are times when, in the words of a report on the Yakima Basin, "there is little to mark."[1] The modest flows of the Yakima, greatly diminished by uses in the basin, are quickly swallowed up by the much larger Columbia.

The Yakima Valley is one of the most productive agricultural areas in the West. Particularly in the rolling, middle portions, it is orchard country. Yakima is famous for its production of apples: Forty-five percent of the apples grown in the United States come from Washington, and nearly half of the apples produced in Washington come from the Yakima Valley.[2] Increasingly, it is becoming known for its production of high-quality grapes—wineries are sprouting up alongside the vineyards in some locations. Washington is one of only three states where hops are grown, and most of the hops produced in Washington come from the Yakima Valley. The distinctive trellised fields are a common sight in some parts of the valley. Dairies are becoming an important component of the agriculture of the valley—apparently moving here to escape the high costs of California and the coastal Northwest.

There is very little that doesn't grow, and grow well, in the Yakima Valley when water is brought to the land. The value of agricultural production in Yakima County—the agricultural heart of the Yakima Basin—totaled about $690 million in 1992.[3] The average value per acre of irrigated agricultural production in Yakima County in 1992 was $2,600; by comparison, the average annual per acre value of irrigated lands in all federal reclamation projects across the West is about $922.[4] Agriculture directly accounts for more than 20 percent of employment in the county.

The Yakima River and its tributaries once also provided high-quality spawning grounds for five species of salmon as well as for steelhead. Annually, hundreds of thousands of anadromous fish passed through these waters on their way to the Pacific Ocean or returning to spawn. These fish provided an abundant food source for Native Americans living in the area. Today native summer chinook, coho, and sockeye salmon no longer exist in the Yakima. Perhaps less than 1 percent of historical populations of anadromous fish still inhabit the basin. This extraordinary decline is true in other parts of the Columbia Basin as well.

It is perhaps not too serious an oversimplification to say that fish and other in-stream values were traded for agriculture in the drive to settle and develop the Yakima Basin. As the terms of that trade have become better understood, its wisdom is being reassessed.[5] Unlike some other parts of the West, irrigation in the Yakima Basin has created a solid agricultural economy that contributes not only to the support of the local area but also to regional and national demands for agricultural products. Nevertheless, some now question the costs and ask whether there are ways to maintain that agriculture—but in a manner that imposes fewer costs on fish, water quality, and other ecological values.

19

THE FIRST PEOPLE

At the time Lewis and Clark ventured through the Columbia Basin, the American Indians now known as the Yakama[6] followed a nomadic life, centered on harvesting the region's natural wealth. In the spring they sought edible roots such as camas or bitterroot, and in the summer and fall they went into the mountains to pick huckleberries and to hunt wild game. Perhaps most important for sustaining the life of these Native Americans was the harvest of salmon that occurred at certain places along the Columbia River, the Yakima River, and other points.[7] From wooden platforms constructed on the side of rock cliffs, they used dip nets (long handles with nets at the end) to take salmon from the rapids, as well as spears, fish traps, and gill nets (Figure 19.1).

Most of the fish were dried and kept available for later use. One common technique involved pulverizing the fish in a mortar with a pestle to produce pemmican. Pounded strips of fish were packed in baskets lined with fish skin and used as a food supply in the winter months. According to one source, the availability of this high-protein food "may well have made possible a relatively secure economic life throughout most of their [the Yakama's] history."[8]

In 1855 Territorial Governor Isaac F. Stevens assembled leaders from among the many bands of American Indians that lived in the area to sign a treaty ceding to the United States roughly seventeen thousand square miles of territory from the Cascade Mountains on the west to the Columbia River on the south, and including the

19.1 Tribal fishing platforms in the Yakima River.

Columbia Plain and the Snake River on the east. In return the Indians reserved an area of 1,875 square miles in the southwest corner of the Yakima Valley.[9] Fourteen Native Americans affixed their mark to the 1855 treaty, in theory as representatives of fourteen distinct bands of Indians collectively called the Yakama. Today approximately sixty-one hundred American Indians live on the 1.4 million acres of land within the Yakama Reservation.[10]

The transition to life on a reservation—a life that was to be supported by an agriculture the Indians had never practiced—cannot have been easy. American Indians living in this area in the first half of the nineteenth century probably had primary ties only with their families and their villages, rather than with bands or tribes.[11] Although these Indians shared many common customs and activities, three distinct languages were spoken. In 1855 there was no sense among those signing the treaty that they were part of a tribe known as the Yakama; putting them together on one reservation did not likely change this sense overnight.

Unlike the result of many such treaties, the Yakama ended up with productive and livable lands. On the west the reservation reaches up the slopes of Mount Adams and includes well-forested lands in the Cascades. On the east the reservation includes fertile agricultural lands in the Yakima Valley, lands that are included within the Wapato Division of the federal Yakima Project.

In 1887 Congress passed the Dawes Act, seeking to transform reservation lands owned in common into allotments privately owned by individual Native Americans.[12] By the terms of the act, each family head was to receive 160 acres of arable lands or 320 acres of other land (such as for grazing); single individuals over eighteen were to receive 80 acres. For twenty-five years the allotments were to be held in trust by the United States, after which time the holders would be able to sell the lands to others. A later amendment to the act authorized allotment holders to seek patent title to the lands at any time. Once the allotment process was completed, unclaimed lands within the reservation were then to be opened up to entry and purchase by others.

Despite resistance by many tribal members, the first allotments on the Yakama Reservation were made in 1892. By 1914, when the allotments rolls were closed, 4,506 individuals had been granted allotments covering a total of 440,000 acres.[13]

20

RECLAMATION IN THE YAKIMA

An already substantial irrigation economy existed in the Yakima Basin when the Reclamation Service began its investigations in 1903. Perhaps as many as 121,000 acres of land were in irrigation, served by an extensive network of privately constructed ditches. Earlier settlers had constructed very little storage, so irrigation depended on the availability of natural flows in the river.[14] Yet there was much more land in the basin, land sufficiently level for irrigation and with soils like those already producing bountiful crops. All that was needed was a source of funds and some engineering expertise to provide better control of the basin's water supplies, and the irrigated area in the basin readily could be quadrupled.

First, however, some clarity had to be brought to the claims for use of the waters of the Yakima. The state of Washington (at least in this arid part of the state) followed the prior-appropriation doctrine. Water was available on a first-come, first-served basis. The only legal record of the amounts of water claimed and their appropriation dates existed in the form of filings in county records. Such filings were not required, however, for a valid appropriation to exist; and the existence of a filing in no way assured that the claimed amount of water actually was being appropriated and used. To compound the problem, fires in the Yakima County Courthouse in 1882 and 1906 destroyed some early filings.[15]

The Reclamation Service moved first to encourage the state to enact "irrigation laws" that would set out clear rules for establishing water rights. An irrigation commission appointed by the governor in 1904 drafted a bill that the legislature considered in 1905.[16] Though the legislature could not agree on a general water law, it did enact a bill authorizing the United States to withdraw all unappropriated waters in a basin from appropriation by others for some limited period as necessary to develop reclamation projects.[17] Shortly thereafter the United States filed notice of its intention to evaluate the development of unappropriated water resources of the Yakima and Naches rivers, thereby establishing its priority right to any available water.[18]

To determine the extent of unappropriated water, it was necessary to clarify existing claims. This the Reclamation Service set out to accomplish by measuring actual diversions from the river during the month of August 1905 and then entering into contractual "limiting agreements" with the water users, capping the monthly diversion rate during the irrigation season at this August amount and reducing it to two thirds of this rate in September and one half in October. Measured total diversions in August 1905 were 2,095 cubic feet per second (including about 100 cubic feet per second that were "wasted" into the Columbia River).[19] By March 1906 limiting agreements had been signed with virtually all parties claiming water from the Yakima, and the secretary of the interior authorized the expenditure of reclamation funds for work on the Tieton and Sunnyside units of the Yakima Project.

The question of the water rights of the Yakama Indians received considerable attention during the early efforts to develop the Yakima Irrigation Project. The Indian Service had filed a claim for a diversion right of 1,000 cubic feet per second for the reservation irrigation project in 1903. The Reclamation Service measured the August 1905 use of water on the reservation at 147 cubic feet per second. Reclamation estimated at that time that as many as 120,000 acres of irrigable lands existed on the reservation, and that 17,000 acres were already under irrigation.[20] The Interior Department's plan, supported by Congress, was to include the reservation lands as part of the Yakima Project.

In 1904 Congress passed an act specifically providing for the sale of surplus or unallotted lands on the Yakama Reservation.[21] Proceeds either could be used to pay for irrigation facilities for the reservation or could be distributed directly to tribal members. Opposition by tribal members prevented implementation of this law. Washington congressman Wesley Jones then sponsored a bill passed by Congress in 1906 that authorized the secretary of the interior to sell, with the consent of the allottee, irrigable allotment lands in excess of a base unit of twenty acres.[22] Funds from the sale of the lands were to pay the costs of the irrigation works necessary to supply water to the twenty-acre allotments still held by the tribe, and the allottee was to receive a perpetual water right for the land, whether the water was used or not, so long as maintenance charges were paid. In addition, unallotted lands determined to be irrigable within the reservation were to be available for homestead entry under reclamation law.[23]

Once again, however, very few tribal members were interested in selling even part of their allotments, and little progress was made in developing the on-reservation irrigation system. In 1912 the Reclamation Service and the Indian Service submitted a report to Congress on "The Condition of the Yakima Indian Reservation."[24] The accompanying transmittal letter from the secretary of the interior concluded that the 147 cubic feet per second allocation made in 1906 was inadequate and that additional water should be provided from the storage under construction as part of the Yakima Project (without charge for construction costs) sufficient to irrigate an additional thirty-two thousand acres of land (based on twenty acres times sixteen hundred allottees).

A letter in 1912 from the chief judge of the Yakama Tribal Courts and the corresponding secretary of the Indian Councils to the chairman of the House Committee on Indian Affairs objected to a bill before Congress (sponsored by now-Senator Jones) that would contractually provide additional water: "Our riparian rights are older than those of the white man. This reservation we were permitted to hold when the Government took all our other land. Water is life and belongs to the earth. Our land is poor without water. . . . We own half of Yakima River and all water in reservation, but we are not protected in any rights."[25] A 1913 Joint Congressional Commission report concluded that the water rights of the reservation applied to "not less than one-half of the natural flow of the Yakima River and should be sufficient to irrigate one-half of each allotment of irrigable land on said reservation."[26]

In 1914 Congress directed that the reservation receive at least 720 cubic feet per second of water in the "low-water irrigation season," an amount deemed necessary for irrigating forty acres on each allotment.[27] Today about 140,000 acres are irrigated within the Wapato Division. Nearly 40 percent of these lands are owned by non–Native Americans.[28]

The secretary initially approved the Yakima Project in December 1905 but required satisfaction of eight "conditions" before funds could be expended. In addition to the clarification of existing water claims and water supply for the Yakama Reservation just discussed, pending litigation and issues related to purchasing the Washington Irrigation Company and the Sunnyside Canal had to be settled.

The Sunnyside Canal was the inspiration of Thomas Oakes, president of the Northern Pacific Railroad, who saw the agricultural potential of the area and realized the benefits agricultural development could bring to his railroad, which had laid its line through the Yakima Valley in the late 1880s.[29] Through the land-grant program used to encourage the building of railroads, the Northern Pacific acquired substantial acreage along its right-of-way, which it wanted to sell. Carrying locally grown crops to market would provide business for the railroad.

Construction of the canal began in 1890. In 1892 the Northern Pacific's irrigation and land development company filed a claim to divert one thousand cubic feet per second from the Yakima River.[30] In October 1905, to get control of this substantial claim, the United States purchased the Sunnyside Canal from the Washington Irrigation Company, which had taken over the irrigation development in 1900. Purchase of the Sunnyside both resolved the dispute about water rights with this company and made possible the further development of the Sunnyside Canal by the Reclamation Service.

The Sunnyside Canal is the second-largest "division" of the Yakima Project, exceeded only by the Wapato Division within the Yakama Reservation (Figure 20.1). At the time the United States purchased the Sunnyside Canal, it was fifty-six miles long; with a capacity of 650 cubic feet per second, it brought water to about forty

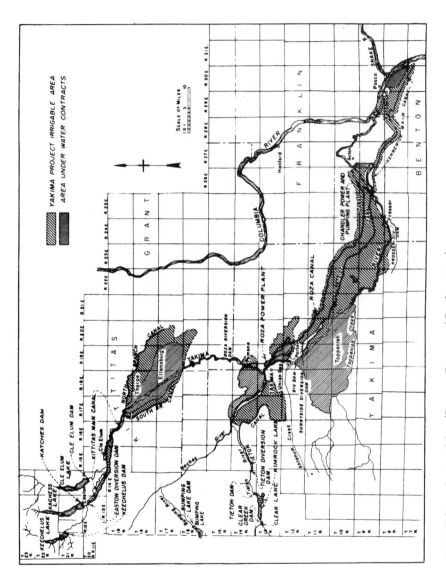

20.1 Yakima Project Map (Source: Bureau of Reclamation).

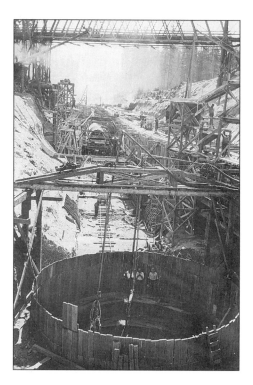

20.2 Building the Tieton Dam, 1915 (Source: Bureau of Reclamation).

thousand acres of land. In the fall of 1906 the Reclamation Service began construction of a new diversion structure with a capacity of 1,015 cubic feet per second, and by 1923 the system was complete. Today the Sunnyside Canal carries water to seven irrigation districts and other organizations serving over 103,000 acres of land.

Federal investment in the Sunnyside Canal, as in other irrigation systems in the West, supported development beyond that possible with private investment alone–thus making large land areas much more valuable. Development of the Sunnyside Canal originally was a business investment, made to increase the value of lands "under" the canal–those able to be irrigated with its water. The investment was expected to be returned with a profit by sales of the land that had been acquired at low (or no) cost. The cost of building and operating the Sunnyside Canal, however, exceeded revenues

20.3 Building the Tieton Canal to carry water to the Naches Watershed, 1916 (Source: Bureau of Reclamation).

earned by land sales or through charges for water delivery. Two private ventures failed to stay in business with the Sunnyside Canal before the United States took it over in 1906.

Federal investment was even more critical for the construction of water-storage facilities, as illustrated by the Tieton Unit (Figure 20.2). By the 1890s the natural flows of the Naches and its major tributary, the Tieton, had been fully appropriated, but there remained substantial areas of uncultivated irrigable lands in the Lower Naches Valley and along Ahtanum Creek. Water storage was needed to enlarge the usable supply, but the cost of constructing this storage and the related delivery facilities could not be financed privately. In 1907 Reclamation began construction of a canal to move water from the Tieton River to lands in the Naches and Ahtanum watersheds (Figure 20.3). Because users on the Naches already claimed these tributary flows, the Reclamation Service constructed Bumping Lake Dam on the Bumping River, an upstream tributary of the Naches. This dam stores unclaimed winter and spring flows and delivers the water to

20.4 Camp at Keechelus Dam Site, 1913 (Source: Bureau of Reclamation).

downstream irrigators as "replacement" for water diverted from the Tieton. About twenty-seven thousand acres of land are irrigated as part of the Tieton Division.

The Yakima Project was built on the assumption that storage of springtime runoff water would permit major expansion of the irrigated acreage in the Yakima Valley. Following Bumping Lake Dam (completed in 1910), Reclamation constructed three large dams in the headwaters of the Yakima River: Kachess Lake, between 1910 and 1912; Keechelus Lake, completed in 1917 (Figures 20.4–5); and, between 1931 and 1933, Cle Elum Dam[31] (Figure 20.6). All told, the reservoirs of the Yakima Project hold about 1 million acre-feet of water.

A lot of water—and yet, not enough. Remarkably, the Bureau of Reclamation holds contracts to supply more than 1.7 million acre-feet of water per year despite the system's capacity to store only about 1 million acre-feet.[32] Apparently to consolidate management of both natural flow and storage-water rights, Reclamation included more than just storage water in its contracts. Problems arise, however, in years of low runoff. These problems become acute when there is a

20.5 Pulling stumps to build dam at Keechelus near headwaters of the Yakima River, 1913 (Source: Bureau of Reclamation).

series of low-water years so that there is no carryover water in storage. And in-stream needs such as those of the salmon and steelhead were neglected altogether.

Between 1937 and 1945 contract commitments were shorted in all but two years. By this time irrigated acreage in the Yakima Valley had more than tripled. In addition to the Sunnyside and Tieton divisions, the Yakima Project now included the Wapato Division on the reservation and the Kittitas Division in the Kittitas Valley. The Roza Division on benchlands north of Sunnyside had been authorized in 1935 and began receiving water in 1941. Plans were in place for what became the Kennewick Division at the bottom end of the basin—to be supplied with return flows only. In an effort to obtain clarity concerning the delivery obligations from the Yakima Project, the United States filed a proceeding in U.S. District Court seeking to quantify the water rights of all users with whom the Bureau of Reclamation had a contractual or legal delivery obligation. The 1945 court decree divided what it called the "total water supply available," defined as "that amount of water available in any year

20.6 Cle Elum Reservoir in the headwaters of the Yakima River.

from natural flow of the Yakima River, and its tributaries, from storage in the various Government reservoirs on the Yakima watershed and from other sources."[33]

In addition to this unusual merging of direct-flow water and contract storage water into a single water supply, the decree also established two classes of water entitlements in the Yakima—proratable and nonproratable.[34] All users whose rights are regarded as nonproratable are treated as senior to all users whose rights are considered proratable. In times of drought proratable users share shortages proportionately; nonproratable users likely receive their full allocation.

Despite this attempt at comprehensive management of the basin's water supply, shortages continue to be a problem. Between 1973 and 1994 supplies were inadequate in eight years—requiring users with junior, proratable rights to cut back their uses.[35] That is, in two of every five years junior rights were rationed. As we will see in the next chapter, being junior has nothing to do with the value of the water use.

21

A TALE OF TWO IRRIGATION DISTRICTS

As the Yakima River flows past the city of Yakima and cuts through Union Gap, it begins arcing to the southeast, reaching the low point of its arc just west of the city of Prosser, then turning back northeast until just before Benton City. Cradled in this arc between the river on one side and Rattlesnake Hills to the north are the Sunnyside and Roza divisions of the Yakima Project served by, respectively, the Sunnyside Valley Irrigation District and the Roza Irrigation District. Physically side by side, these two districts provide a striking contrast in many ways.

The Sunnyside Division is about fifty miles long and ranges from one to eight miles wide. It contains over one hundred thousand irrigable acres of land, served by seven separate irrigation districts and two ditch companies. Generally these are bottomlands, relatively easily serviced from the Sunnyside Canal constructed in a contour above much of the arc (Figure 21.1).

As described in chapter 20, the Reclamation Service purchased the Sunnyside Canal from a private company in 1905, and with the construction of a new diversion dam and headgate, and the extension of the canal, it was the first unit of the new Yakima Project to be approved and built. A Board of Control, with twelve directors representing the fourteen separate entities receiving water from the Sunnyside Canal, generally governs the Sunnyside Division. The Sunnyside Valley Irrigation District, with about 80 percent of the division's land area, acts as the operating agent for the Board of Control.[36]

21.1 The Sunnyside Canal.

The Roza Division encompasses about seventy thousand acres of rolling benchlands, lying in a narrow strip above the Sunnyside Division. Construction of the Roza unit was authorized in 1935, and initial water deliveries occurred in 1941. The Roza Canal is a "highline" canal that takes up to twenty-two hundred cubic feet per second of water out of the Yakima River at the Roza Diversion Dam ten miles above the city of Yakima, moves the water through two tunnels totaling over three miles in length, runs under the river through a siphon, and carries water to the Roza Power Plant about three miles above the city. Roughly half of the water is used at that point to generate electricity and then is returned to the river. The remainder of the water continues on down the canal to provide irrigation uses. The full length of the canal is ninety miles.[37]

Both areas are highly productive agriculturally, but they tend to grow very different crops. The primary crops grown in Sunnyside's bottomlands are forage and grains. By comparison, fruit, hops, and other multiyear plantings dominate in the uplands of the Roza Division. These lands are warmed by the higher air that moves along the hills, and their gentle slopes provide good drainage.

Water supply for irrigators in the Roza Division is based on a contract between the Roza Irrigation District and the United States, which provides a maximum of 375,000 acre-feet of water, to be supplied in prescribed monthly increments.[38] This is a proratable agreement; thus, annual deliveries may be reduced according to the Total Water Supply Available (TWSA).

Water rights relied on by users within the Sunnyside Division are far more complex, but they are regarded as providing a maximum annual delivery of 458,520 acre-feet of water.[39] Much of this water (about 315,000 acre-feet) was at least claimed, if not actually used, prior to the initiation of the Yakima Project. Thus, it is treated as primarily nonproratable.

The Bureau of Reclamation estimates the TWSA on a monthly basis in April, May, and June of each year. This figure is relied on by both the Bureau of Reclamation, in its water-management decisions, and irrigators, in making final cropping decisions. Between 1940 and 1980 the projected TWSA averaged 3.3 million acre-feet per year.[40] In 1993 and 1994, however, the TWSA was about 2 million acre-feet. In below-average water supply years (1993 and 1994 were the worst on record), water users holding proratable rights receive reduced water deliveries. Thus, in 1994, users in the Roza Division received less than 40 percent of their full apportionment. By comparison, users in the Sunnyside Division received about 79 percent of their apportionment.[41]

This is the effect of the priority system whereby shortages are not shared—the senior gets his fill before the junior gets any. But it is a peculiar version in the Yakima because there are two classes of rights, one of which almost always gets its entire delivery amount, and the other which has a highly variable water supply.

Not surprisingly, this difference in the reliability of water supply greatly affects the behavior of water users in the two divisions. The Roza Irrigation District has invested heavily in improvements in its water delivery and use systems in order to take best advantage of the water supply available to it.[42] For example, check structures have been added to the main canal to provide better control of the water supply. Two re-regulation reservoirs have been constructed to allow short-term storage in those times that supply exceeds demand. Open dirt laterals are being converted to pressurized pipelines. These are the same kinds of improvements we encountered in the Grand Valley to reduce salt-loaded return flows to the Colorado River. One additional step taken by farmers in the Roza District is to convert from rill or furrow irrigation to sprinklers and drip systems.

Ron Van Gundy is the manager of the Roza Irrigation District. In August 1994 when he was showing me around the district, project deliveries to his users were only 39 percent of their contract entitlement. The district relies heavily on groundwater to bolster its water supplies.

"We got started on our water-conservation efforts back in the early 1970s," he explained. "We had a drought in 1973 that made us realize we had a water-supply problem. About that same time we started to understand we had a water-quality problem too." Most irrigated lands in the Roza District are on sloping hillsides. Without careful management, soil washes off cultivated fields–adding contaminated sediments to the Yakima River. "We figured out that using our water more carefully could help us with both our quantity and our quality problems," Ron pointed out. In addition to making improvements in the water delivery and application systems, the Roza District encouraged its irrigators to move toward perennial crops requiring less soil cultivation.

Jim Trull is the manager of the Sunnyside Valley Irrigation District. His office is a block from Ron's, in the town of Sunnyside. As manager of the Sunnyside District, he is also manager of the Sunnyside Canal and supervises distribution of water to the fourteen separate entities and other users that are part of the Board of Control. A complex set of agreements developed over the years establishes the water entitlements of the entities and their obligations to pay the costs of operating and maintaining Sunnyside Division facilities. "If the district had formed fifty years later," Jim commented, "it would all have been just one organization. As it is, our job gets a little complicated in a dry year like this."

About two thirds of the division's water rights are senior (pre– May 10, 1905) and thus nonproratable. The remainder, however, are subject to rationing. "We are getting cut back, too," Jim explained. "We're down to about 80 percent of our entitlement." Nevertheless, the kinds of system and on-farm improvements made in the Roza District have not been made in the Sunnyside. In most years the water supply for Sunnyside water users is excellent, and the crops grown on lands in the Sunnyside generally return lower revenues per acre than those grown in the Roza. The motivation to spend the considerable sums of money necessary to upgrade irrigation practices in the Roza simply is not there.

22

ADJUDICATING WATER RIGHTS

In 1977 the Washington Department of Ecology initiated a general adjudication for all surface-water rights in the Yakima Basin.[43] The purpose of an adjudication is to determine existing legal rights to use water, not to establish new rights. It is to give legal certainty to the title of a water right, especially its priority and the amount of water claimed for use.[44] Over twenty-one hundred claims were filed with the Yakima County Superior Court by September 1, 1981.[45]

Judge Walter E. Stauffacher presides over the adjudication proceedings; he has done so virtually since the beginning. A retired superior court judge, he holds a special appointment to sit as judge for the adjudication. Judge Stauffacher holds "water day" the second Thursday of every month in the Yakima County Courthouse. Many of the lawyers representing the large water users in the adjudication have been involved in the proceedings since the 1970s.

Proceedings this complex and multipartied tend to move slowly, gathering momentum as procedures are developed and as issues get better defined and narrowed. Thus, in 1989 (twelve years after the adjudication started) Judge Stauffacher identified four procedural "pathways" on which the adjudication was to proceed: (1) federal reserved rights for American Indian claims; (2) federal reserved rights for non–American Indian claims; (3) state-based rights of major claimants; and (4) state-based rights for other claimants, by subbasin.[46]

As of 1996 only the American Indian claims had been finally decided. In addition to quantifying the tribe's irrigation-water rights (and clarifying which rights are nonproratable and which are proratable),[47] Judge Stauffacher determined that the Yakama held a reserved-water right.[48] In particular he held that the 1855 treaty impliedly reserved Yakima River water to maintain its fishery for the benefit of the tribe. He found, however, that the treaty right had been "substantially diminished" by a settlement reached in 1968 between the Yakama and the United States providing compensation to the tribe of $2.1 million for a number of claims, including damage from loss of fishing rights.[49] He quantified the diminished reserved right as "the minimum instream flow necessary to maintain anadromous fish life in the river, according to annual prevailing conditions."[50] The Bureau of Reclamation's superintendent of the Yakima Project, in consultation with the Yakima River Basin Systems Operation Advisory Committee, irrigation district managers, and others, is to determine the specific quantity of water needed to maintain the fish. The Washington Supreme Court affirmed Judge Stauffacher's decision.[51]

Determination of the water rights held by the so-called major claimants (essentially those with water-delivery commitments from the Yakima Project) is the other major issue in the Yakima adjudication. Prior to taking up the determination of these claims, Judge Stauffacher decided to address a number of what he termed "threshold issues." His opinion and order respecting these issues, rendered in 1992, set out a series of legal interpretations guiding his determination of water-rights claims.[52]

First he had to decide who owns the water rights he was adjudicating. On its face this is a straightforward matter: The United States filed claims under state law for the appropriation of water for the Yakima Project; users predating the Reclamation Project filed claims for these preexisting uses. In practice this issue provides a window into the byzantine nature of western water law, in which things are not necessarily what they seem. The party named as the "appropriator" of water often is acting in a representative capacity for the actual user of water. Irrigation districts claim water on behalf of users within their boundaries; the United States claims water controlled by Yakima Project facilities for delivery to irrigation districts. A basic tenet of prior-appropriation law is that an appropriation consists both of the physical diversion of water *and* its application to beneficial use. In a 1937 decision involving the Yakima Project, the U.S. Supreme Court held that project water rights–though in the name of the United States–are owned by the owners of the land on which the water is used.[53]

Nevertheless, Judge Stauffacher concluded that "even though the water rights are unquestionably appurtenant to the lands upon which they are beneficially used, that in the 'unity and integration' of the Project, the U.S. and the Major Claimants [irrigation districts] do retain some rights in the water for the diversion, distribution and conveyance of water within the Project, albeit in a representative capacity for the landowners."[54]

Judge Stauffacher then turned to the question of quantifying the extent of the water rights. First he considered whether water rights extended only to lands historically irrigated or whether they existed also for lands intended to be irrigated. This is another murky area of western water law. In the Newlands litigation the courts followed the well-established principle that transfers of water rights are limited to their historical (legal) use. An adjudication, however, is different. It is merely a determination that water rights have been established–not necessarily about the manner in which they have been used. Here Judge Stauffacher held that water rights were established to the full extent of the total number of irrigable acres agreed to in the contracts between the United States and the irrigation districts.[55]

In addition to the total land area to be considered in adjudicating water rights, he also discussed his responsibility for evaluating whether the quantities of water allocated by contract or decree are "reasonable."[56] Once again Judge Stauffacher declined the invitation to scrutinize actual water uses, leaving the issue of whether the beneficial-use standard imposes efficiency requirements beyond those historically practiced. Beneficial use for purposes of an adjudication, he concluded, is amply demonstrated by the production of valuable crops.

What, then, has been the result of this twenty-year (so far) adjudication process? With the exception of the "substantially diminished" tribal reserved-water right, it appears there will be no significant changes from the water allocations outlined in the 1945 decree.[57] An expensive way to conclude that what has been decided has been decided.

23

THE SALMON

The American River begins below Chinook Pass in the Cascades, just over the divide from fourteen-thousand-foot Mount Rainier. It joins the Little Naches to form the Naches River. By August of each year, spring chinook salmon have made their way up to the American River to spawn. Bob Tuck, a fish biologist for the Yakama Indian Nation, pays close attention. In particular he is looking for redds, distinctive areas in the gravel beds of the river's channel shaped by the tail of the female salmon into somewhat concave depressions, with a ridge of gravel at the downstream end of the "nest." Redds can be ten to fifteen feet long and are located in areas of good current so that water will move through the gravels, flushing and aerating the eggs during their incubation. In addition to their distinctive concave shape, redds also can be identified by the brightness of their gravels, the normal accumulation of silt having been removed by the scraping action of the fish's tail. Spawning female salmon can be readily identified because their tails are whitish, a product of the considerable effort it takes to shape the redds. Males often are recognizable by scars on their backs, earned in fights to claim the right to be the spawning partner.

Once the redd is prepared, the female is joined by the male; they move back and forth over the redd, the female dropping several thousand eggs while the male adds his milt to fertilize the eggs. Exhausted by these final acts, the fish survive only a short while longer. Seven to nine months later, fry emerge from the fertilized eggs and begin another life cycle for the spring chinook.

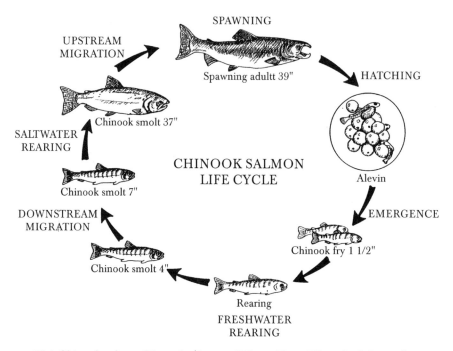

SPAWNING

UPSTREAM
MIGRATION

Spawning adultt 39"   HATCHING

Chinook smolt 37"

SALTWATER
REARING

CHINOOK SALMON
Chinook smolt 7"   LIFE CYCLE   Alevin

DOWNSTREAM   EMERGENCE
MIGRATION

Chinook fry 1 1/2"

Chinook smolt 4"

Rearing
FRESHWATER
REARING

23.1 Chinook salmon life cycle (Source: Yakima Basin Watershed Council).

The life cycle of an American River spring chinook is a tale of survival (Figure 23.1). Of the thousands of eggs that are laid in each redd, perhaps 60 percent will emerge as fry.[58] The fry float quickly away from the redd and find shelter downstream in locations where they can grow. Monitoring of spring chinook smolts in 1988 indicated that fewer than one out of every two fry survive to reach Prosser Dam and, by extrapolation, to the confluence with the Columbia River.[59] Once the young salmon reach the Columbia, they then have to navigate the McNary, John Day, Dalles, and Bonneville dams during their 350-mile journey to the ocean. They spend up to three years in the ocean before once again returning to the Columbia on their way back to the Yakima and the American. Between 1983 and 1987 the estimated survival rate for smolts that made their way out of the Yakima ranged from a high of 5.3 percent to a low of 1.7 percent.[60] Thus, for example, out of more than 135,000 smolts that out migrated in 1983, about 6,000 adult spring chinook eventually returned to the Yakima.

According to the Northwest Power Planning Council, anadromous fish runs in the Yakima in the 1800s may have totaled as many as eight hundred thousand in a year.[61] Between 1981 and 1990 an annual average of about eight thousand anadromous fish found their way back to the Yakima–perhaps as few as 1 percent of the historical run. Native summer chinook, coho, and sockeye are completely gone. Spring chinook, fall chinook, and summer steelhead are severely diminished in number. Their survival is in serious question.

Salmon recovery in the Columbia Basin cannot be solved by actions in the Yakima alone. Even historically, Yakima-spawned salmon have represented only somewhere between 4 and 11 percent of the Columbia River salmon run in any given year.[62] Moreover, most of the life of a salmon born in the Yakima is spent outside of the basin.

But the Yakima Basin is regarded as important by fish biologists, particularly because of the considerable spawning habitat still available. The Yakima joins the Columbia at a point where there are "only" four dams for the fish to find their way through, compared to at least eight for those who spawn in the Snake River Basin in Idaho. Moreover, major progress has been made in installing fish screens throughout the basin to reduce the likelihood that fish will be diverted out of streams into irrigation canals and ditches.

Even with these apparent advantages, Yakima Basin salmon and steelhead face some major problems within the basin. Perhaps most significant is the greatly altered flow of the Yakima and its tributaries, caused primarily by the storage and diversion of water for irrigation use. Each year an average of about 2.4 million acre-feet of water is diverted from the Yakima River for irrigation uses.[63] Considerably smaller amounts are diverted for municipal use and for hydroelectric power generation. Although more than half of the diversions eventually return to the river, critical segments below major diversion points are seriously dewatered.

An example is Prosser Diversion Dam, where much of the water remaining in the river at this point is diverted during the summer months to supply irrigation uses in the Kennewick Division. Water also has been diverted to run a hydroelectric dam in some

23.2 Fish passageway at Roza Diversion Dam.

years. The Bureau of Reclamation has attempted since the late 1950s to maintain a minimum flow of 50 cubic feet per second below Prosser Dam.[64] Studies suggest, however, that a flow of at least 450 cubic feet per second is desired to allow passage of fish, and that flows of 800 to 1,000 cubic feet per second are desirable for fish spawning and rearing.[65] Moreover, the quality of the water below Prosser is "the poorest in the Yakima basin with high water temperatures, high suspended sediment concentrations, and low dissolved oxygen levels in some of the deeper areas. Ammonia concentrations may reach toxic levels in some years and pesticide concentrations are the highest in the subbasin."[66]

Fifty miles upstream at the Sunnyside Diversion Dam, flows are reduced to only three hundred cubic feet per second for much of the irrigation season because of major diversions for the Wapato and Sunnyside divisions. Upstream adult fish passage is difficult at this flow, as is the passage of smolts on their way to the Columbia River. Although return flows make their way back to the Yakima below

Sunnyside Dam, the water quality in this stretch is another problem for the salmon. Water temperatures in this reach may exceed seventy degrees Fahrenheit in the summer—at the upper end of the temperature range regarded as tolerable for salmon.[67]

Salmon and steelhead navigating the lower Naches River encounter a seriously dewatered stretch below the Wapatox Diversion Dam, where diversions for the power plant frequently deplete flows to as low as 125 cubic feet per second throughout the year. In the Yakima above the confluence with the Naches, fish must negotiate the Roza Diversion Dam (Figure 23.2). The Bureau of Reclamation seeks to maintain a target flow of 300 cubic feet per second below Roza, but studies indicate that at least 400 cubic feet per second are desired for adult fish passage, and 700 to 900 cubic feet per second are needed for good rearing conditions below the dam.[68] In addition to these critical points there are numerous more localized flow problems, such as diversions within tributaries that reduce flows below that necessary to permit passage for spawning and to provide suitable habitat for the rearing of fry. If the Yakima is viewed as one of the best places in the Columbia Basin to help bring back the salmon, what, then, are conditions in other areas? It is a chilling thought.

A section of the 1855 treaty entitled "Privileges Secured to Indians" gave the Yakama Indians the "exclusive right" to take fish from all streams within or bordering the reservation, together with a right of taking fish "at all usual and accustomed places." In 1970 the United States brought suit against the state of Washington, seeking to clarify the rights of tribes to take anadromous fish from rivers outside the reservation in the western part of the state. This was an extension of other cases involving a series of arrests made of Native Americans during the 1960s for alleged violation of state fishing regulations. In a landmark decision by Federal District Court Judge George Boldt, the treaty rights of the tribes (based on language identical to that in the treaty with the Yakama) were determined to protect Indian fishing privileges and to entitle the tribes to take up to half of the harvestable yield of fish.[69] Although the Boldt decision dealt directly with fishing rights only in the Puget Sound, its reasoning supports fishing rights for the Yakama (and other Columbia River treaty tribes) outside of their reservation in all "usual and accustomed" places.

The problem, however, is the availability of fish. As the "harvestable yield" of salmon continues to decline, all commercial fishing for salmon in the Columbia Basin has been halted; in 1994 the United States called a stop to commercial fishing for salmon in the ocean off the coasts of Oregon and Washington as well. The cessation of even ceremonial fishing on the Columbia in 1994 caused the Yakama to journey to Willamette Falls on the Willamette River in Oregon to hold the traditional Washat ceremony—part of the First Foods Feasts that the Yakama celebrate before taking salmon and other foods.[70]

The question of whether the right to take fish includes the power to ensure there are fish available presented itself in the Yakima Basin in the early fall of 1980 when fish biologists discovered sixty spring chinook redds in a stretch of the upper Yakima River thought not to be used for spawning. Flows there ran artificially high at this time of the year because of releases upstream from the Cle Elum Dam for downstream irrigation use. Many of the redds had been created in parts of the riverbed that would be without water when irrigation releases ceased. Federal District Court Judge Justin Quackenbush initially ordered the flow in that reach of the river to be maintained at 650 cubic feet per second and, following a hearing in late November, ordered flows to be maintained as necessary through the remainder of the nonirrigation season.[71]

The Ninth Circuit upheld this decision.[72] The court chose not to take on the question of the treaty rights of the Yakama, basing its decision instead on the federal district court's continuing authority over the water resources of the Yakima River from the 1945 consent decree. The court fully recognized the importance of the issue before it: "This appeal involves the collision of two interests: the Yakima Nation's interest in preservation of their fishing rights, and the eastern Washington farmers' interest in preservation of water needed for crops in the dry spring and summer."[73] It chose, however, to leave the question of treaty water rights for the Yakama to the Yakima Basin water adjudication.

The Quackenbush decision in 1980 prompted important changes

in the management of the Yakima Project and broadened the decision-making process to include fisheries considerations. To find ways to protect the spawning needs of the salmon while minimizing dependence on extra releases of water, Judge Quackenbush instigated the creation of a Systems Operation Advisory Committee (SOAC) to advise the superintendent of the Yakima Project. The SOAC consists of four biologists: one from the Washington Department of Fisheries, one from the Yakama Nation, one from the U.S. Fish and Wildlife Service, and one representing the water users. Working with SOAC, the Bureau of Reclamation came up with a water-management plan for the Yakima Project in 1981 known as the "flip-flop."[74]

As already described, spring chinook spawn in the late summer and early fall. Under natural conditions this would be the low-flow period in the river. A redd established in the gravels of the flowing river in that period of time could expect to be flushed and aerated through the winter incubation period by continuing flows. Flows in the Cle Elum Reach of the Yakima River in late summer, however, were considerably higher than they would have been under natural flow conditions because of releases from upstream storage to meet the needs of downstream irrigators. Had the releases been cut back in the usual manner at the end of the irrigation season, many of the redds would have been without water and the eggs would not have survived.

To avoid creating this situation, Reclamation devised an approach designed to draw heavily from the storage in the upper Yakima in the first part of the irrigation season, and then to cut back releases from these sources before the chinook begin spawning in this area. Late-season needs for irrigation water would be met, as much as possible, from storage in the Naches River Basin (the "flip-flop"). Releases from storage in the upper Yakima then would be made during the winter only as necessary to protect the redds that are established during the spawning season.

Reclamation instituted the flip-flop in 1981 and, with some fine-tuning, has used it every year since. Use of this approach apparently has protected salmon propagation in the upper Yakima from at least some of the adverse effects of historical dam operations. The water users have accepted operation of the flip-flop, though with some serious reservations. In particular, they are concerned about the legal status of the water that otherwise would not have been released but for the maintenance of the redds. Is the release of this water legally required by the Yakama's treaty right to the minimum in-stream flow necessary to maintain anadromous fish life in the river? Is this water simply released as part of the management of the Yakima Project by the Bureau of Reclamation? Who should bear the burden of any reduced carryover that might result in the upstream Yakima reservoirs as a result of flip-flop operations? In particular, do the nonproratable water rights bear any of this burden? Who should bear the increased operation and maintenance costs that are associated with management of the flip-flop?

Some guidance came from a 1994 decision by Judge Stauffacher in the context of the ongoing adjudication. The Roza Irrigation District sought an order from the court preventing Reclamation from releasing water from reservoir storage to provide a "flushing flow" intended to help salmon smolts move out of the Yakima River into the Columbia. Judge Stauffacher used the opportunity to amplify the part of his 1992 decision granting the Yakama Nation a treaty-based water right for the minimum flows necessary for maintenance of fish life in the river. In particular he emphasized the process by which the Reclamation manager in charge of the Yakima Project is to determine minimum in-stream flow "in light of the annual prevailing conditions," in consultation with the SOAC. In this instance the SOAC asked for thirty-five hundred acre-feet to be released in May 1994 to help flush smolts out of the Yakima—an amount reduced to fourteen hundred acre-feet because of some timely rainfall. In upholding the decision to release this water, Judge Stauffacher stated: "So long as the Yakima Field Office Manager can show that a good faith decision has been made to maintain fish life, regardless of the life phase, with the sparest amount of water possible, then this Court will defer to their scientific expertise."[75]

Two federal court decisions in 1994 underscore the increasing sense of urgency attached to protecting the anadromous fishes of the Columbia River Basin. In *Idaho Department of Fish and Wildlife v National Marine Fisheries Service,*[76] Judge Malcolm Marsh concluded the time for more aggressive action by the National Marine Fisheries Service has come: "NMFS has clearly made an effort to create a rational, reasoned process for determining how the action agencies are doing in their efforts to save the listed salmon species. But the process is seriously, 'significantly,' flawed," he stated, "because it is too heavily geared toward a status quo that has allowed all forms of river activity to proceed in a deficit situation–that is, relatively small steps, minor improvements and adjustments–when the situation literally cries out for a major overhaul. Instead of looking for what can be done to protect the species from jeopardy, NMFS and the action agencies have narrowly focused their attention on what the establishment is capable of handling with minimal disruption."[77]

Then, in *Northwest Resource Information Center v Northwest Power Planning Council*,[78] the Ninth Circuit Court of Appeals reached the same basic conclusion with respect to the efforts of the Northwest Power Planning Council: "The Council's approach seems largely to have been from the premise that only small steps are possible, in light of entrenched river user claims of economic hardship. Rather than asserting its role as a regional leader, the Council has assumed the role of a consensus builder, sometimes sacrificing the Act's fish and wildlife goals for what is, in essence, the lowest common denominator acceptable to power interests and DSIs."[79]

The opinion lays out a general summary of the efforts since the 1970s to give better protection to the anadromous fishes in the Columbia River Basin, focusing particularly on the considerable efforts of the Northwest Power Planning Council since its inception in 1980. The decision draws at some length from Judge Marsh's opinion, noting that it "is relevant to the instant case not just because it involves, ultimately, the same issue–what to do about preserving and restoring the salmon–but because it urges policy and operations in a direction away from the status quo toward affirmative action."[80]

24

TAKING STOCK

In many respects the Yakima Basin represents a realization of the reclamation ideal. With considerable federal assistance, the water supplies of the basin were more fully developed for economically productive uses, and the irrigated lands in this fertile area expanded fourfold. Highly valuable crops are being produced, and irrigated agriculture remains the base of a healthy economy. Because of the federal project, previously existing agricultural lands receive a more secure water supply, additional irrigable lands have come into production, and irrigable lands within the Yakama Reservation receive a good water supply (Figure 24.1).

At the same time, the Yakima Basin also portrays many of the fundamental flaws of the reclamation vision. Its single-minded focus on irrigation neglected virtually all other values and uses for water. Salmon simply were not a consideration. Water quality was not a concern. Project planners, relying on the ability of a centrally (and presumably rationally) managed water supply to provide for ever-expanding irrigation demands, seriously overcommitted the basin's water supply. The policy decision to make irrigation water available at a fraction of its real cost encouraged expansion of irrigated agriculture in the Yakima Basin beyond a sustainable level.

Transformation of the complex water allocation and use structure in the Yakima Basin to one more reflective of contemporary values and needs is a challenging process. Important initial steps already have occurred. Survival and recovery needs of endangered

24.1 Yakima Project office.

anadromous fish now figure directly in the management and use of
water. Through the Systems Operation Advisory Committee, fish
biologists communicate directly with the Bureau of Reclamation and
the water users about the water-related needs of the fish. Washington
courts have officially recognized that the Yakama Nation holds a
legal right to the water necessary to maintain the anadromous fishery in the Yakima that predates all irrigation rights.

Two important, and complementary, approaches now are being pursued to improve conditions in the Yakima: physical improvements in the water storage, delivery, and use systems; and voluntary
reallocation of water-use entitlements. Both emphasize protection of
anadromous fish, but there are important benefits for existing water
users as well. The Yakima River Basin Water Enhancement Project
Act, enacted in 1993, calls for conservation improvements within the
divisions of the Yakima Project to reduce irrigation and hydropower
diversions of water and improve in-stream flows at critical locations
in the basin.[81] Federal funds (matched by funds from the state) are
being made available to support development of conservation plans
and implementation of conservation measures. "Target" in-stream flows

at Sunnyside and Prosser dams are established and are to be increased by fifty cubic feet per second for every twenty-seven thousand acre-feet of decreased diversions achieved by conservation measures.

Certainly there are plenty of opportunities to use water more efficiently within the Yakima Basin, as illustrated by the efforts of the Roza Irrigation District. To the degree that reduced diversions provide increased flows in reaches of critical importance for the fish, conservation can provide real benefits. But conservation alone is not enough. The Yakima is seriously overappropriated–that is, more water is claimed for out-of-stream use than can be provided in low-flow years. Because of historical peculiarities and inflexibilities in the allocation system, it is also misallocated from an economic perspective.

The Yakima Enhancement Act also authorizes funds to directly purchase or lease water to improve stream flows. The Environmental Defense Fund proposed a water leasing and transfer program for the Yakima that offers the opportunity for more fundamental re-structuring of water usage in the basin.[82] Two entities would be cre-ated: the Yakima Basin Trustees, representing interests in acquiring water for in-stream flows; and the Lease Oversight Committee, rep-resenting water-right holders in the basin. A ten-year test water-leas-ing program would be established. Leased water would come pri-marily from the "fallowing" of irrigated lands. If the lands are within an irrigation district, both the landowner and the irrigation district must agree to the lease. The lease would be treated as a temporary transfer under Washington state law and would have to be approved by the Washington Department of Ecology. The Lease Oversight Committee would verify the amount of leasable water made avail-able by land fallowing and would more generally seek to protect the interests of the water users.

The Bureau of Reclamation has in fact begun a modest effort to lease water on a short-term basis from irrigation uses. This pro-gram focuses on making water available for improved in-stream flows. The first such lease, established in 1996, transferred about one thou-sand acre-feet of irrigation water to maintain in-stream flows in the Teanaway River, a tributary of Yakima in the upper portion of the basin. Increased summertime flows encourage salmon to move up the

Teanaway into high-quality spawning and rearing habitat.[83]

In addition, there are important benefits that could be gained through trades among existing water users–primarily from nonproratable users to proratable users. To this point there has been very limited transfer activity in the basin, constrained at least in part by the uncertainty of water rights during the ongoing adjudication. The need for greater flexibility among water users to shift supplies was underlined by a series of drought years in the early 1990s and the sometimes severe effect of the limited water supply on those users holding proratable water entitlements. For example, in 1994 the proratable water users of the Kittitas Reclamation District stopped receiving Yakima Project water as of early August, and there were only limited opportunities for users in this division to negotiate with users in other divisions holding nonproratable rights to purchase some of this water.

Operation of a water market in the Yakima is complicated by a number of things. There is, of course, the adjudication proceeding and the yet-to-be-finally-decreed quantity of water regarded as legally available to districts and users. Assuming that transferred water would be limited to historic consumptive use, however, and that the adjudication is not likely to alter rights to this amount of water, probably a more serious impediment is simply a lack of clarity concerning how transfers should proceed. The Environmental Defense Fund proposal is helpful in this regard because it lays out a procedure developed with substantial input from the water-user community and the Washington Department of Ecology, as well as from the Bureau of Reclamation. Some kind of broadly agreed to procedure probably would help encourage transfer activity and avoid some disputes during the transfer process.

Still another complication is presented by the highly managed nature of the Yakima River under the "Total Water Supply Available" concept. The availability of water transferred by lease or purchase will be subject to the monthly calculations of the TWSA by the Bureau of Reclamation during the irrigation season. The now decreed but unquantified right of the Yakama to fish-protection flows casts still another cloud of uncertainty over water rights in the basin. Finally, there is the need for a vastly improved capability to measure water diversions for better management of the basin's water resources.

Management of the Yakima Project is centered on centralized administration of Yakima River water by the Bureau of Reclamation, with the goal of providing as full delivery as possible, on a monthly basis, of the full entitlement available to users within the six divisions. Water is allocated in big blocks, appropriate for an irrigation system in which the users are regarded as common beneficiaries with basically common needs. The degree to which such a system could be decentralized–for example, through the institution of a water bank–is an interesting question that warrants investigation.[84]

What other steps can be taken? The Washington Department of Ecology sought to compel the investigation of use of water within districts, to ensure that water was being used beneficially on lands legally entitled to receive the water. Judge Stauffacher refused to require such an investigation for purposes of the adjudication proceeding. Given the trust duty of the secretary of the interior to the Yakama Indian Nation, and to protection of threatened and endangered species, the United States may have a responsibility to ensure that no more than the *minimum* quantity of water legally required to be delivered is provided to off-stream users, and that all reasonable actions are taken to protect the anadromous fishery in the Yakima Basin. Thus the United States may have a legal duty to ensure that project water is not being supplied to lands not legally entitled to use this water–for example, lands outside district boundaries.[85] The United States may have the duty to reexamine land classifications within districts to ensure that only irrigable lands are being serviced with project water. Clearly the United States has the duty to ensure that satisfactory water-conservation plans have been prepared and implemented as required by the 1982 Reclamation Reform Act.[86]

The time and effort involved in implementing these kinds of administrative measures can be substantial. Because such requirements will certainly be viewed by water users as antagonistic to their interests, they are likely to resist or at least only minimally cooperate. Furthermore, the amount of water that would be produced for the stream by such measures is uncertain at best.

There is no shortage of options in the Yakima,[87] and some important progress has in fact been made. But the overcommitment of the water resources of the Yakima Basin is so pronounced, and the environmental harm resulting from that overcommitment so serious, that incremental improvements are simply not enough. More is needed.

To have any real hope for success in the Yakima Basin, such efforts ultimately must come from within the basin. The emergence in 1994 of the Yakima River Watershed Council was especially promising in this regard. Instigated by individuals associated with irrigated agriculture and primarily from the business community in the valley, the council in 1996 had a membership of more than one thousand with a fifty-person board of directors.[88] Funding provided by members, supplemented with grants and other sources, supported four full-time staff. The mission of the council was "[t]o develop and to implement, through consensus, a plan to provide consistent and adequate water to meet all economic, cultural, and natural environmental needs in the Yakima River Basin." Its work was carried out largely through a series of committees.

Mel Wagner led the efforts of the council as its "CEO." A retired small businessman in Yakima, he knew virtually nothing about water when he took on the job. But he had the trust of the people who were promoting the council, and they knew he had the kinds of people skills that would be critical if the council were to work–skills developed not only in his business, but also from many years of civic activities, including United Way campaigns.

Key to the council's efforts was a commitment to include representatives of all of the interests in the valley. One critical piece fell into place when the Yakama Nation agreed to participate in September 1994. Tribal Director Delano Soluskin initially was skeptical. His grandfather, onetime chairman of the tribal council, had prodded Delano to "learn mainstream culture" and become a lawyer in order to watch out for the tribe's interests. Instead he learned accounting and started working for the tribe not long after it was given self-governance in 1978, setting up a centralized accounting system. Now, as tribal director, he likens his responsibilities to that of a city manager.

"How could it be enough for those yet unborn just to be able to see a picture of a salmon?" he asked. "When I caught my first salmon, my family had a feast and a ceremony. A salmon is a living spirit." We were meeting in Delano's office at the Yakama Nation's headquarters in Toppenish. "We look at water differently than the white culture," he explained. "We begin meals with water and we end meals with water. There are seven sacred foods of the Nation and water is essential to all.

"We need to make improvements in the irrigation system that serves the reservation," Delano acknowledged. "But it is just as important to us to develop riparian corridors for wildlife along the streams that flow on the reservation."

Bob Tuck probably played a critical role in persuading the tribe to join with the Watershed Council. A valley native and long-time fisheries consultant to the tribe, Tuck has fought aggressively over the years to restore habitat for the salmon in the Yakima Basin. He has been outspoken about what he regards as wasteful irrigation practices in the basin that, in his view, rob the fish of much-needed water. He represents the Yakama Nation on the Systems Operation Advisory Council and has worked hard through this process to get changes in Bureau of Reclamation operations that would favor the fish.

The irrigation and business interests that initiated the Watershed Council were not natural allies for Tuck. But both he and they knew that there was potentially more to be gained by joining forces than by continuing their historically adversarial relationship. "The old days where everybody could go off on their own and manage any particular resource the way they saw fit are over," says Tuck. "There are strings all over the place. Everyone on the council sees this and has to deal with it firsthand."[89]

Mel Wagner also worked hard to bring environmental interests actively into the council. Katherine Ransel, codirector of the Northwest office of American Rivers in Seattle, was one of his hard-won recruits. She too came to the council with considerable skepticism. How likely was it, she wondered, the interests that initiated the council really wanted to deal with the tough environmental problems presented by irrigation-water use in the Yakima Basin? But she is also an attorney by training, an experienced environmental advocate with a quick mind, unafraid to match ideas with those who have different interests. As an insider to the process, she was an active participant.

Wagner kept these highly disparate interests together with a commitment to consensus that forced people to search for ways to reach an acceptable outcome, getting perhaps less than they wanted but more than they might achieve otherwise. After two years of intensive effort (especially for a largely volunteer organization) the council produced a "Report on the State of the Water Resources of the Yakima River Basin."[90] Then, in June 1998, it produced "A 20/20 Vision for a Viable Future of the Water Resource of the Yakima Basin."[91] In 1998, motivated by new legislation offering state funding to watershed-planning processes, a three-county authority took over from the council.[92]

Prolonged drought in the early 1990s motivated the agricultural business interests in the basin to initiate the council. Frustration with the water-allocation system under drought brought in the irrigation interests. But human nature is human nature. In the words of Mel Wagner, "Everyone's for change as long as they don't have to do anything different." Recent years have been average or above-average years for water supply, and the motivation brought on by drought has dissipated. Among many irrigators attention has returned to ways to build new dams and increase the capacity of existing ones rather than the earlier focus on improvements in system water use efficiency and in some voluntary reallocation of water. Just who in the Yakima Basin could afford the cost of additional storage has not yet been addressed.

This is the kind of thinking that has dominated water use in the West for most of this century. It worked so long as there was someone else to pay for this kind of development in addition to the user of the water, and so long as the ecological consequences of such development could be ignored. But public subsidies for new water development are less and less politically popular, and environmental considerations now weigh heavily in new development decisions. These realities exist in the Yakima just as they do elsewhere in the West. Phil Shelton, the council's thoughtful communication/ research director, mused: "We're not ready for limits yet in the West. The frontier is still deeply ingrained in our culture." Phil is a journalist by training, and prior to working for the council he served for fourteen years as the managing editor of *Good Fruit Growing* magazine. "Some of our members say, 'next time a two-year drought comes along, we'll be ready to do some good things.' But how do you get ahead of the curve? How do you get people to act instead of react?"

In 1995 the Roza and Sunnyside districts did just that–they acted. After years of unsuccessful discussions about possible mergers of the two organizations, they agreed to form a Board of Joint Control. Under this structure they remain independent entities but share some functions and some employees. Initially they focused on ways that the Roza District could fund improvements in the Sunnyside in return for a share of the conserved water. Water-quality concerns, however, soon emerged as a more immediate need for coordinated action.

The federal Clean Water Act includes a provision requiring states to identify streams not meeting water-quality standards and to establish the total maximum daily loading of pollutants to the stream consistent with meeting the standards.[93] The Washington State Department of Ecology concluded in 1994 that the lower Yakima River was not meeting water-quality standards, identifying problems including DDT, ammonia, bacteria, sediment, and water temperature.[94] Fearing a regulatorily imposed "solution," the Roza and Sunnyside boards decided to develop their own cooperative program.[95]

The irrigator-initiated program is startling. Adopted by the Roza-Sunnyside Board of Joint Control on December 16, 1997, the program establishes a permit system for all discharges into project-operated waterways including canals, laterals, drains, and wasteways.[96] A primary purpose is to ensure that discharges are piped to avoid soil erosion. Water-quality parameters are established for irrigation runoff, focusing primarily on turbidity. Runoff not meeting standards will be subjected to a compliance plan. Failure to achieve compliance can result in loss of irrigation water. Buffer zones with no cultivation and no cattle grazing are required alongside project waterways.

This aggressive action by these entities sets a new standard within the irrigated agricultural community. It reflects a determination to take the initiative for making necessary changes rather than fighting change. It allows the irrigators to manage the process instead of responding to requirements imposed by others.

Will the program work? It's too soon to know. The challenge is considerable: According to the state's water-quality coordinator in the Yakima Basin, Chris Coffin, sediment reductions coming from drains into the river will probably have to reach from 75 to 95 percent.[97] But Jim Trull explains: "We have too much at stake to hold our ground and wait until it comes."[98]

~

Watershed-focused public/private collaboratives are emerging across the western states.[99] The Yakima River Watershed Council was unusual because of its genesis in the business community. Businesses tend to be flexible and adaptive because it helps them to survive. Irrigators tend to be cautious and conservative because it helps *them* to survive. In this situation, however, adaptability is called for—searching for a level and manner of water use that is compatible with fish-friendly streams. The present use of water by irrigation in the Yakima Basin cannot be sustained. More efficient, better-managed use of irrigation water is essential but, by itself, is not enough. Some water-use entitlements from less productive lands will be reallocated to lands capable of yielding higher returns from their use. Some presently irrigated acreage will be retired. The only real question is, Who will make these decisions?

PART 5

FROM RECLAMATION TO SUSTAINABILITY

25

FROM RECLAMATION TO SUSTAINABILITY

The reclamation movement that emerged in the late nineteenth century and came to full flower in the twentieth century viewed the West as a place of possibility, of opportunity. Here the human hunger for land could be satisfied if only that land could yield a livelihood. Thus were dry lands in the Lower Arkansas Valley, the Grand Valley, the Truckee and Carson basins, and the Yakima Valley transformed into productive agricultural lands. Thus was a means for widespread human settlement of parts of the West provided. Driving through these areas of the West today, we can clearly see the fruits of that vision.

Now at the threshold of the twenty-first century, however, the West is a very different place. Populating the land is no longer a priority. As mentioned in the introduction, the West now is the fastest-growing region in the United States. Between 1970 and 1995 the seventeen-state western region grew by 32 percent, compared to 19 percent in the rest of the country.[1] Nearly a third of the nation's population lives in the West, an area projected to have another 28 million residents by the year 2025. The question today is not how to attract people to the West but how to maintain the quality of life that is attracting them.

The West grew, in part, by turning its limited supplies of water into working resources. It transformed something that originally appeared to be a limitation to its growth into one of the important engines driving growth. It achieved this rather remarkable result through two primary means: First, it effectively gave control of its water resources to those who would put them to economic use; and second, it provided a broad array of public assistance, ranging from the enormous subsidies of the federal reclamation and flood-control programs to the creation of state bureaucracies designed primarily to provide legal certainty to water users and state laws authorizing water districts to assess property taxes.

Although the benefits of this approach in terms of water development have long been apparent, many of its costs are only now becoming clear. One is the rigidity of the system that has been established. Everything from the water rights themselves to the physical structures that make their use possible were designed for a particular purpose—little, if any, thought was given to accommodating other uses. This physical and legal structure has been struggling to keep pace with changing water-use preferences.

Another cost is the extent to which water appropriations control the sources from which they come. Water within a stream is a public resource, but the need to control stream flows to satisfy claims to their use has had the effect of turning over a public resource to private users. A major consequence has been the widespread loss of what might be regarded as public values of water: certain kinds of recreational uses, for example, and—in particular—the ecological values of water.

The Pacific Institute defines sustainable use of water as "the use of water that supports the ability of human society to endure and flourish into the indefinite future without undermining the integrity of the hydrological cycle or the ecological systems that depend on it."[2] From an ecological perspective it seems clear that western water resources are not being used sustainably. During the last century, for example, more than twenty species of fish have gone extinct west of the Continental Divide, and at least one hundred more are considered threatened, endangered, or of special concern.[3] River-basin studies performed for the Western Water Policy Review Advisory Commission made it clear that native fish and other water-dependent species are in trouble in river systems throughout the West.[4]

Consider the implications for native fish species of more than a century of unrestricted river development: "As rivers were beheaded by dams and natural variation in flow disappeared, so did the resilient species and biological communities adapted to these inherently transient systems. Streams became inhospitable both above and below high dams. Hydroelectric generators killed fish moving downstream; tailwaters are too cold for warm-adapted species to reproduce. Loss of current or substrates types eliminated those requiring riffles. Reservoirs filled with nonnative predators reduced survival of young. Channels directly flooded by reservoirs support few if any native fishes in systems west of the Continental Divide."[5] In addition to widespread loss of in-stream habitat, large portions of the West's wetland and riparian areas have been lost. For example, only 7 percent of the floodplain wetlands that existed in 1918 along the Rio Grande still remain.[6] Moreover, because of water-quality impairment, perhaps a third or more of western lakes and streams are unable to support one or more uses for which they have been designated by the state in which they are located.[7]

Particularly if ecological needs are to be met, direct human demands for water already exceed the supply capacity of western water resources in many parts of the West. In its second national water assessment in the 1970s, the U.S. Water Resources Council found the water resources of most western river basins overextended.[8] The California Department of Water Resources reached a similar conclusion for that state in 1994, at least in drought conditions, and projected significant shortages of water even in normal years by the year 2020.[9] If indirect human demands such as those for recreation are included, the shortfall becomes even more pronounced.

Since the 1960s Congress has been enacting legislation pushing us in the direction of environmental sustainability. The first (and perhaps still best) articulation of this policy objective is found in the 1969 National Environmental Policy Act:

> The Congress, recognizing the profound impact of man's activity on the interrelations of all components of the natural environment, particularly the profound influences of population growth, high-density urbanization, industrial expansion, resource exploitation, and new and expanding technological advances and recognizing further the critical importance of restoring and

maintaining environmental quality to the overall welfare and development of man, declares that it is the continuing policy of the Federal Government, in cooperation with State and local governments, and other concerned public and private organizations, to use all practicable means and measures, including financial and
technical assistance, in a manner calculated to foster and
promote the general welfare, to create and maintain conditions under which man and nature can exist in productive harmony, and fulfill the social, economic, and
other requirements of present and future generations of
Americans.[10]

This remarkable statement heralded a changing attitude about economic development and marked the emergence of a substantial array of new federal laws aimed at supervising many aspects of new
development to reduce their "profound impact" on the environment
and to promote a more "productive harmony" between humankind
and nature.

In the Wild and Scenic Rivers Act, Congress made it clear that
not all rivers should be developed.[11] The NEPA established that–at
least where federal actions are involved–agencies and citizens should
be fully informed about the adverse environmental consequences of
these actions, and that alternatives should be fully explored.[12] In the
Clean Water Act, Congress implicitly stated that we should not use
our rivers to dispose of wastes, except after they have been treated
through a technologically specified process, and that we should not
develop in our wetlands if possible.[13] The act set as goals restoring
and maintaining the chemical, physical, and biological integrity of
the nation's waters. In the Endangered Species Act, Congress said
that proposed federal actions should not jeopardize protected species, and that individual actions should not kill or harm endangered
animal species.[14] It set out a national commitment to conserve plant
and animal species and the ecosystems upon which they depend.
With changes to the Federal Power Act, Congress required that environmental values be given equal consideration with economic values in hydropower licensing decisions.[15] In these and other laws
Congress began the process of articulating a different kind of rela-

tionship between humans and their environment. Congress acknowledged with these laws the value and importance of natural resources as part of the natural environment in which humans live, not just as inputs for production.[16]

These are things that now *must* be done, as a matter of federal law. Substantial as they are, they fall well short of assuring achievement of the broad goals to which they aspire. Preparation of an environmental-impact statement will not by itself create conditions under which humankind and nature can exist in productive harmony. Nor can the restoration and maintenance of the biological, physical, and chemical integrity of water be achieved simply by requiring treatment of discharges from point sources.

The federal environmental laws enacted in the past thirty years represent a kind of consensus baseline of how certain human actions may affect the natural environment. They are directed primarily at actions requiring federal support or approval, however, and at large primarily business-based sources of pollution. Much of what we do as individuals remains (properly, I think) beyond the reach of such rules.

Although there appears to be considerable agreement about the goals of environmental law, much less consensus exists regarding some of the specific approaches set out in these laws for accomplishment of their particular objectives. Few seem to like regulatory approaches, but most acknowledge that, without forcing requirements of some kind, most of us are unlikely to change what we are doing. Federal statutory and regulatory requirements often are highly detailed and prescriptive—sometimes requiring actions that may be less productive or effective than other possible approaches.[17] Within the understanding that the outcomes of alternative approaches must be at least as environmentally beneficial as would be the required approaches, there is considerable interest in providing greater flexibility in the manner in which federal environmental requirements are achieved.

Imagine federal laws that required states to achieve their stated water quality standards *within some time certain* but left the means by which these standards are achieved up to the states and interests within the states. Imagine federal laws that charged states with the responsibility of assuring no net loss of wetlands, but left the manner in which this is achieved to the states and the affected interests. Imagine federal laws that *rewarded* states (and landowners) for actions taken to recover listed threatened and endangered plant and animal species through, for example, protection of critical habitat areas.[18]

The centralization of natural-resources management that began with the Progressives may well have reached its end.[19] What seems likely to remain at the national level is this kind of definition of goals and objectives, and the determination of whether meeting specific goals and objectives requires establishing some national-level responsibilities. More and more the trend seems to be toward cooperative management processes in which the affected interests actively participate. There may still be federal-level decisions that must be made, but in practice these decisions increasingly are shaped through the process.

We may in fact choose to modify and expand the legal requirements relating to environmental protection in the years ahead, but the real challenge is to extend from this legal baseline in ways that move us closer to our goals: to find ways to satisfy direct human needs for water while more fully respecting the other valuable functions of the hydrologic cycle;[20] to find ways that we *want* (or that we can live with), in addition to ways that are required. Although circumstances in the West have changed greatly, the work ahead to make human uses of water sustainable is no less important, no less difficult, than that facing westerners a century or more ago to make water usable. It will require an equivalent commitment, both human and financial, to achieve.

The work of making western water uses sustainable will be driven by the water users themselves, just as reclamation was a century ago, but the makeup of those water users will be considerably different. There will be irrigators, to be sure, and their representative organizations. There will be water-using industries and, of course, urban water suppliers. But there will also be representatives of Native American tribes like Bob Pelcyger in Nevada and Bob Tuck in Washington. There will be recreational representatives—for example, owners of whitewater rafting companies. There will be fishing and hunting groups like Trout Unlimited and Ducks Unlimited. There will be a variety of environmental interests represented by people like Graham Chisholm of the Nature Conservancy and Katherine Ransel of American Rivers. There will be participants with interests in their riparian lands, such as cities like Grand Junction and Reno and federal and state land-management agencies. There will be people from affected communities like Mel Wagner in the Yakima and Mary Reid in the Truckee-Carson. They all will be seeking to advance their own interests in relation to the use of water.

It will be an effort driven, in part, by federal regulatory requirements. As the stories illustrate, federal agencies are key participants in virtually all aspects of western water development and use. People like John Hamill and Lisa Heki now directly participate in water-management decisions to implement the Endangered Species Act in the basins in which they work. It will be an effort involving federally constructed facilities, supported in part with federally provided funds and technical and information assistance, though almost certainly less so than in the past. States will be essential participants, both in their traditional role of setting the basic rules under which water is allocated and used, and in their more recent role representing state interests in federally required environmental processes.

For the most part, however, sustainable uses of water will emerge from a shared sense within a given watershed that the desired values and uses of the water-based resources of the watershed are not being realized, and that there are ways in which real improvements in these uses can be made that are legally, financially, and technically feasible, broadly supported, and achievable.

There is an increasingly widely shared sense that more is possible, that the West's watersheds and water resources can be managed in ways that will provide increased benefits to those living within those watersheds without necessarily diminishing the benefits enjoyed by traditional users of water. Not, however, if we continue to do business as usual. Not if we assert absolutely that any changes must necessarily harm existing interests so that no change is possible. Not if we continue to exclude valid interests from decision-making processes. Not if we force people to comply with unproductive requirements. Not if we continue to fail to work cooperatively where possible to achieve shared interests.

We now better understand and appreciate the value and importance of natural systems, including those that are water based. Given our wonderful human faculty for adaptation, we are making real efforts to integrate environmental values into human activities. Humans need to use natural resources for their sustenance, and humans know how to use resources to enhance and improve their lives. I find it difficult to imagine that humans will not continue to develop and use natural resources to generate as much human benefit as we are capable of. But I also expect and believe that humans can learn and change. We have made remarkable strides in a relatively short period of time in this country dealing with the problems of human-generated pollution. We are struggling mightily with the mysteries of ecology and the atmosphere to learn how to moderate harmful human-caused effects on biological and climate systems. If we come to understand that more human benefit can result from a river operated and used differently from the way it is presently used, surely we will find a way to change our uses of that river. We have, I believe, already reached general agreement that new economic development, including water development, must occur in a manner that minimizes or avoids environmental losses. I believe we are headed in the direction of agreeing that development should and must be a source of environmental gain.[21]

The following four chapters explore several areas in which substantial gains are possible. First is the matter of how direct human uses can be satisfied with less water—described as reducing the gap between diversion and consumption. Second concerns how we can satisfy human water needs in a manner more compatible with other hydrologic and ecologic functions that sources of water provide. Third addresses how already-developed water can meet new and changing needs. Fourth is the process of governance through which these matters can be decided and implemented.

26

REDUCING THE GAP BETWEEN DIVERSION AND CONSUMPTION

Human diversions of water resources from their sources in the American West have been determined as much by cost and the availability of water as by the direct need they are meeting. Thus, for example, senior irrigators are likely to divert more water from a stream than are junior irrigators for an equivalent use. Senior irrigators are likely to have lower-cost, less efficient delivery and use systems. Until people like Elwood Mead started pointing out that these cheap systems often deprived others of the opportunity to develop and use water,[22] states paid no attention to these practices. New appropriators soon found it necessary to begin building storage dams to gain control of water not already claimed. Thus proceeded what might be called the "extensive" development of western water resources–a process by which new demands were satisfied by extending control over more of the resource, rather than by more careful and efficient "intensive" development and use of water.[23]

This was a strategy that worked reasonably well so long as federal subsidies were available to pay much of the cost of this development, and environmental concerns remained in the background. It is a strategy we can no longer afford. Instead, a primary objective of water policy should be to encourage actions that help reduce the considerable gap that presently exists between the diversion or withdrawal of water from its source and the use of water necessary to accomplish the purposes for which it was diverted. According to the U.S. Geological Survey, of the 178.9 million acre-feet of water taken out of surface-water and groundwater sources in 1990 in the nineteen western states for domestic, industrial, thermoelectric power, and irrigation uses, 81.7 million acre-feet were consumed–46 percent.[24]

The place to begin thinking about reducing this gap is with the West's major water diverter: irrigation. Statistics on irrigation-water use over this century suggest that irrigators themselves are using water more efficiently.[25] Indeed, we encountered such examples in all four of our stories. Irrigators in the Lower Arkansas Valley, for example, have made on-farm changes to utilize their diversions more fully. The Roza Irrigation District in the Yakima Basin made improvements to its water-delivery system. In both cases changes were initiated because of the direct economic gains made possible–measured in terms of increased irrigated acreage, a more reliable water supply for existing irrigated lands, the cultivation of more water-intensive crops, and reduced labor.

The lower Arkansas is a chronically overappropriated river, however, and the Roza is a junior water-right holder in the supply-limited Yakima River. Many irrigators (particularly those with senior water rights) are satisfied with their existing irrigation systems and see little reason to make costly changes for uncertain benefits. Unless they are forced to make changes (as have been irrigators in the Newlands Project) or someone pays the full cost of making the changes (as does the Bureau of Reclamation for the Grand Valley Project), the motivation simply does not now exist.

Moreover, real problems of interdependence have developed over the years that make change both physically and legally difficult. The inefficiencies of traditional surface-water irrigation systems long ago were simply built into other water uses, both upstream and downstream. Upstream users seeking to appropriate water were subject to the full diversion right of senior downstream users. They developed their rights in recognition of this downstream use. Downstream users developed their appropriations on the basis of the water available in the stream, much of which may have included return flows from more senior upstream appropriators. Even within a single irrigation system, the original methods of irrigation are the ones on which water-use patterns were established. Unused water, both surface and subsurface, from higher lands often provides water to users within the system on lower lands. Expectations, sometimes with a legal basis, have developed around these patterns of water use.

It is this reliance on what some would call wasteful or inefficient use of water that causes irrigators to resist calls for water conservation. And they are right to resist conservation that would not account for and protect these reliances. For the most part, however, the debate about irrigation-water conservation has been far too simplistic. Water conservation that works cannot be implemented without a broad, system-wide understanding of how water presently is being used, how existing uses can continue to be met, and whether changes are possible that can produce desired additional benefits while meeting existing uses.

Making more efficient use of water, measured in terms of reducing the gap between the amount of water diverted and the amount usefully consumed, is not an end in itself. It is a means, potentially, of achieving other desired objectives. The most easily achieved of these objectives will be to reduce the amount of direct diversions from surface-water sources, thereby increasing flows that remain in the stream channel between the original point of diversion and the point where unused water returns to the stream. Thus, if a desired objective is to improve stream flows in this particular segment,and the value of that improvement is worth the investment necessary to make a reduction in diversions possible, conservation can be beneficial. This is the primary objective of water-conservation planning in the Yakima Basin. It is also a benefit of reducing diversions in the Grand Valley.

Similarly, if an objective is to reduce the amount of contaminants that return to a water body with irrigation return flows, and the value of that reduction is worth the value of the investment necessary to achieve that reduction, there are ways to make that objective work. This is the sort of effort ongoing in the Newlands Project to address water-quality concerns in the Lahontan wetlands and, in the Grand Valley, to reduce salinity in the Colorado River.

If, however, the objective is to increase the amount of water available for new consumptive uses, conservation alone is unlikely to help. In a stream system wherein uses of water already are fully committed, new consumptive uses are likely to have to replace existing consumptive uses. Water conservation can reduce consumptive use to some degree, but rarely will these conservation improvements produce substantial *additional* water in the system unless the historical uses have taken water permanently out of a water basin.[26]

Uses of water legally established under the laws of the state in which water is diverted or withdrawn are protected from impairment or harm as a consequence of others changing their use of water. Not all patterns of dependence among water users enjoy legal protection—for example, a user relying on water that leaks from a poorly constructed storage or conveyance system probably does not have a legal right to require that unintended leakage to continue. Moreover, a downstream user enjoying the benefits of return flows of "imported" water (water from another basin) cannot require the importer to continue to make that water available. In general, however, the laws of the states following prior appropriation require that water legally available to an appropriator remain available in the same amount and timing under which the appropriation was established.

Several states have begun making clarifications of their water laws that should help encourage water conservation. One approach, taken by California, assures appropriators that conservation of water (defined as the use of less water to accomplish the same purpose) is itself a beneficial use.[27] Other states, such as Oregon and Montana, have attempted to define statutorily the legal status of water that is conserved. Oregon authorizes appropriators who have installed conservation measures that reduce existing water uses to make other use, of up to 75 percent, of the conserved water.[28] Montana authorizes appropriators who "salvage" historically diverted water to lease or sell the water, or to change its use.[29]

These statutes alter the traditional assumption of prior appropriation that water no longer diverted and used by an appropriator simply becomes available to the next junior appropriator. Instead they offer an important incentive to existing users to consider whether they can make changes reducing historical uses that produce benefits exceeding the cost of the changes, either through additional use of the conserved water or by selling or leasing that water to another. Such an approach recognizes the need to encourage the conservation and reallocation of water and the importance of providing incentives to existing users for this purpose. It provides a means by which existing users may continue their activities, but with more efficient water delivery and use systems.

The broad policy objective of water conservation is to reduce unneeded uses of water where there are more benefits that can be produced by other uses of the water. In some respects this long has been an objective of water law: Appropriations are understood to be limited to the *minimum* amount of water necessary to accomplish the purposes of the appropriation. In practice, however, there has been virtually no effort to apply this so-called "beneficial use" standard to reduce the amount of water diverted under existing water rights. Nor is there much interest today in some kind of across-the-board administrative or regulatory process requiring appropriators to upgrade their practices so that more water is available for other uses.

In some respects it is surprising that there has been so little political support for such an approach. Water is a common resource, shared by many uses and users. The appropriation and private use of a portion of the water are considered necessary and important because of the benefits provided by those uses. Legally, an appropriator holds a "right" to use water to accomplish the beneficial purposes of the appropriation, which is regarded as a property right. The property interest, however, is not to some fixed quantity of water but to a priority date for using an amount of water *necessary* to accomplish a stated purpose or purposes. The amount of water necessary might very well be viewed as changeable over time as new practices and technologies make it economically feasible to reduce total water use to accomplish the same purpose. What is necessary might even be viewed as dependent on other demands on the water resource.[30] As an analogy, consider the widespread use of zoning to direct and limit land uses in urban areas. Just as such laws have greatly altered traditional uses and expectation of uses of private property, so too might water uses in highly competitive or sensitive places become subject to specified use standards.

One explanation for the limited interest to date in such an approach is the costs it would impose, both for government to administer and for users to comply with, relative to the benefits that

would be gained. Experience in the lower Truckee and Carson basins emphasizes this point. Many years and many millions of dollars
have been spent in an attempt to improve irrigation efficiency of a
relatively small irrigated area (roughly sixty thousand acres). It is
inconceivable that funding could be found to make possible this
kind of effort for the roughly 46 million acres of land irrigated in the
western states.

One possible approach might be to combine the carrot and
the stick. A carrot could follow the Montana model and make it
clear that any appropriator reducing historical diversion and use of
water can apply that water to another use, or transfer the water, so
long as other water users are not harmed. Appropriators thus would
be given a clear incentive to consider making such changes. To reduce unnecessary transaction costs, such an approach should be
implemented through processes that simplify determinations of historical diversion and use, and evaluations of injury to other water
users. Possible options are discussed in chapter 28 addressing water transfers.

A stick might be a beneficial-use requirement setting a duty of
water for existing uses and then applying a gradually increasing efficiency factor to promote water delivery and use improvements—the
kind of thing happening in the Newlands Project in Nevada.[31] Alternatively, irrigation practices could be required to meet some technologically or economically based standards within a specified time—in
the manner of the Clean Air Act and the Clean Water Act. Irrigators
would be put on notice that their water-use practices will be expected to meet these standards or requirements at some known time
in the future. Irrigators whose practices do not meet such standards
would be encouraged to search for alternatives that would warrant
the investment necessary to meet beneficial-use (or water-quality)
requirements. Failure to make improvements within the required
time would subject irrigators to possible litigation in which the issue
of the legal sufficiency of their practices would be at question—litigation likely driven by junior appropriators or in-stream interests hop-
ing to benefit.[32]

To survive as a viable activity in the next century, irrigated
agriculture must bring its practices more closely in line with the in-

terests and needs of other water users in the West. There is no compelling policy reason why irrigation should somehow be insulated from the changes taking place in this region.

Many in irrigated agriculture do not believe that the problems caused by their water uses are their problems. In their view they were first to establish such practices; others must adjust to them. If others want certain practices to change, they will have to pay the full costs of doing so. Moreover, irrigators should be able to decide whether or not to make the changes—even if others do pay for them.

In my view this is wishful thinking. Sooner or later changes are going to occur—in fact, they are already occurring. Irrigators in the Newlands Project discovered that they controlled far less water than they had originally believed. A similar fate struck irrigators using water from the Central Valley Project of California when Congress unilaterally allocated eight hundred thousand acre-feet of project storage to fish and wildlife uses in 1992.[33] Irrigators in the Grand Valley face the possibility that their water-use practices will be determined to be wasteful, shifting a portion of their historically controlled water to upstream junior appropriators such as cities on the Front Range of Colorado.

At one time I hoped irrigators would themselves take more of the initiative in finding ways to modernize and improve their systems, using funding from others who would benefit from use of the conserved water. The arrangement between the Imperial Irrigation District and the Metropolitan Water District of Southern California seemed to offer a model—urban users providing funding for irrigators to improve their systems in return for the use of conserved water. Now I am less certain. Very likely this deal would not have occurred had IID not been threatened with the loss of a portion of its water right.[34]

Thus I now believe that general standards or requirements regarding irrigation practices will have to be publicly determined and generally applied so that irrigators will have a clear understanding of what is expected of them. I favor requirements that are proportionate to benefits, that reflect local needs and interests, that provide opportunities irrigators can meet through their own initiatives to the degree possible, that are phased in over time. I favor giving irrigators clear control over conserved water so they will have the incentive necessary to make these changes without being forced to do so. I favor providing public funding to encourage these improvements where other incentives are not sufficient and where there would be real benefits. There are a number of possible approaches, with different advantages and disadvantages. For example, tiered pricing of water has proved to be an effective means of encouraging more efficient water use in the Broadview Water District in the Central Valley of California.[35] The critical thing is to move this process ahead.[36]

The general understanding under which western water development occurred was that appropriators should take as much water as they could use. Today that should be understood to mean that appropriators should take only as much as they need. Reducing the gap between these two measures for existing appropriators will require a mix of incentives and standards. All new appropriations should already be subject to a heightened standard of need and of efficient use, but state water laws continue only to require the more general "beneficial use" standard. Reducing the gap between diversion and consumption is a slow and difficult process, but one that is essential if western water uses are to be sustainable.

27

ALLOWING OUR RIVERS TO FUNCTION LIKE RIVERS

Virtually all western rivers of any significant size have been altered to enable human control and use of their water. The result is a complex network of diversion dams, storage dams, water-delivery canals, ditches, laterals, siphons, and drainage systems. On the Arkansas River in Colorado, for example, there are tunnels carrying water from streams on the west side of the Continental Divide into the Arkansas Basin, storage dams on the tributaries in the headwaters, a pumped storage hydroelectric plant using water from two of these storage facilities, two large storage and flood-control dams on the main stem, and numerous diversion dams and other structures for every ditch taking water from the river. The river has been channelized into a large concrete trough for flood-control purposes as it passes through the city of Pueblo.[37]

As with most western rivers, operation of this sizable physical infrastructure is driven primarily by irrigation-water needs. At times of high runoff (primarily during the spring) unoccupied space in reservoirs is filled as much as possible. In a system like that in the Arkansas, this can mean bringing water from other, less developed water basins as well. As runoff from snowmelt declines, reducing natural stream flows, stored water is released from reservoirs to meet downstream demands–primarily for irrigation but also for urban and other uses. Thus, springtime peak flows are considerably reduced, while late-summer and early-fall flows are increased. At many dams reservoir releases are run through hydroelectric power facilities in quantities and at times designed to meet demands for electric power. Revenues from the electricity generated often help pay the costs of constructing and operating dams, thus reducing the cost of water to other water users such as irrigators.

Rivers are dynamic systems.[38] The size and shape of their channels reflect the volumes of water and sediment they carry and the geology through which they move. Unregulated, river flows vary widely during the year, and from year to year—especially in the West. The banks of the channel generally reflect the "average" high-flow level. The floodplain represents the land area periodically inundated when flows exceed the bank-level channel capacity.

Rivers transport sediments and dissolved solids such as salt and minerals. In very high flows even coarse materials like stones can be moved. Suspended sediments such as silt and fine sand can be carried in any kind of flow, but if a river is slowed by a blockage, these sediments tend to drop out, causing the stream bed to aggrade. Water with little suspended sediment, on the other hand, picks up such materials as it moves and carries them downstream.

The manner in which a river functions determines more than just its size and shape. It determines the nature of its aquatic environment and the life-forms that can be viable there—whether, for example, it is suitable habitat for trout, and if so, what kinds of trout. It also determines the vegetation that can grow in the riparian zones along the river or stream. Cottonwood seeds, for example, require overbank inundation to germinate, and then groundwater levels within reach of plant roots during the initial growing season, to develop into trees.

In turn, these various physical attributes of river systems yield a wide range of benefits and values that have gained increased recognition in recent years. A well-functioning river is likely to have good-quality water: water that supports healthy fisheries, water that people can swim in, water that people can drink with only a modest amount of treatment. A well-functioning river is designed to accommodate floods and even benefits from periodic flooding. A well-functioning river supports healthy riparian areas, which in turn provide a major portion of the habitat on which plant and animal species in the West depend.

A dam alters a river in many ways.[39] By its physical presence it obstructs or blocks the movement of fish and other migratory aquatic biota. Water stored behind a dam forms a reservoir, changing the stream environment to a lake or pool environment. Sediments carried in river water tend to settle out when the water is arrested. Outlet works, typically placed as low as possible in the reservoir to take full advantage of storage capacity, release water downstream often colder than natural stream flows. The more dams in a river, the more altered that river is likely to be.

Human habitation of the West as we know it would not be possible without this kind of active control and use of its surface-water resources. Though vilified by many for the environmental damage they have caused, dams provide important, essential functions now relied upon to some degree by virtually every person who lives in the West. Although water regulation and control structures are absolutely necessary, some existing facilities may no longer be necessary, and most existing facilities likely require modification to make their operation more environmentally compatible.

New water-regulation structures now must meet demanding environmental-protection requirements and are designed to provide multiple benefits. And there has been considerable effort, particularly over the past twenty years, to consider ways that existing facilities might be operated in a manner that provides benefits in addition to those they were originally designed and built to provide. In many cases changes have been made in dam operations with little or no effect on traditional beneficiaries, while mitigating some of their environmentally harmful effects or providing other benefits. In some cases dam operations have been forced to change to meet environmental requirements, such as recovery of endangered fish.

Our stories provided good examples of such changes. Diversions of water from the Truckee River at Derby Dam for the Newlands Project have declined by perhaps a third or more to help recover the endangered cui-ui in Pyramid Lake. Stampede Reservoir in the upper Truckee Basin is operated primarily to provide flows for cui-ui spawning and for in-place recreation uses. The timing of water releases from dams in the Yakima Project has been "flip-flopped" to better match the spawning needs of salmon, and water is being

released for the sole purpose of flushing salmon smolts out of the
Yakima into the Columbia. Water diversions in the Grand Valley are
managed in part to provide water for endangered fish in a key segment of the Colorado River.

These are not isolated examples. In a Natural Resources Law
Center study funded by the Bureau of Reclamation and the U.S.
Environmental Protection Agency, we looked at sixteen Bureau of
Reclamation water projects around the West at which changes in
operation either had been made or were proposed to be made because of serious environmental problems.[40] I was struck by a couple
of things. One was the number of places in which such problems
were prompting changes—it's happening all across the West. A second was the ability to find acceptable ways to make these changes.
In some cases the changes were fairly straightforward and seemed to
cause little or no concern. There *are* things that can be done, and
many are widely agreed to be for the better. These were all federal
facilities, and for the most part the affected federal agencies (largely
the Bureau of Reclamation and the Western Area Power Administration, the federal entity marketing electricity generated at federally
owned dams) absorbed the losses or paid the costs. Rarely were irrigators or their representative organizations expected to pay more
than a token share of any costs. In no cases did the changes require
any lands to be taken out of irrigation, though the water supply dedicated to irrigation use decreased in several instances.

This study suggests that there are opportunities to increase the
benefits provided by existing water-control structures, to reduce their
negative effects, and to do so in ways acceptable to traditional beneficiaries of the projects.

The best opportunities probably exist with federal facilities,
including dams and other structures operated and maintained by the
Army Corps of Engineers and the Natural Resources Conservation
Service. The operation of such facilities is directly subject to congressional directives such as the National Environmental Policy Act (requiring federal actions to be evaluated for their environmental consequences) and the Endangered Species Act (directing agencies to
use all available authority to help recover endangered species and
not to take actions that might jeopardize the existence of such spe-

cies). Indeed, these requirements drove some of the changes we identified in our study of Bureau of Reclamation projects.

Scientists have begun developing an environmental baseline
to help guide future dam operations. In the spring of 1996 the Interior Department conducted an experiment in controlled flooding on
the Colorado River. For a week Reclamation opened the gates at
Glen Canyon Dam to allow 1,270 cubic meters per second of water
through—considerably more than the approximately five hundred
cubic meters per second that ordinarily would have been released,
but far below the predam flood peak of about thirty-five hundred
cubic meters per second that occurred in 1957.[41] Results indicate considerable success picking up sands from the channel bottom and depositing these sands above the normal high waterline, and some
success in moving coarser, rocky materials in areas of rapids at this
level of flow. Riparian vegetation, including exotic vegetation such
as tamarisk, which now covers much of the floodplain, appeared to
be unaffected, suggesting the need for much higher flows to reduce
such vegetation. Effects on biological values are uncertain, but concerns such as disturbing the invertebrate food supply for fish proved
unfounded.

For the most part changes that have occurred to date have
taken advantage of the "slack" existing in the system—the fact that
sometimes stored water can be found that is not legally committed
to a user, that coordinating operation of dams within the same system
may make possible some additional uses of the water, that users
themselves sometimes have flexibility in the timing or manner of
their use that can make other uses possible. When there is some
good reason to change, there seems to be room for that change.

In some cases operational changes mean real economic losses.
For example, some of the water diverted from the Truckee River
generated electricity in the wintertime at the Lahontan Power Plant,
with revenues going to the Truckee-Carson Irrigation District. Because this water use had not been legally authorized, these diversions
were the first to go when Secretary Udall instituted limits in 1967.

Some hydroelectric peaking power operations have been cur-
tailed because of the harmful environmental effects of rapid changes
in amounts of water released. For example, after many years of study,

the Interior Department decided to curtail much of the peaking power use of water released from the Glen Canyon Dam and to moderate the rate at which releases are increased and decreased. Curtailing this inexpensive generation of electricity has meant increased costs for consumers in some cases and losses of revenues for generators.

In virtually all cases these changes cost money. Studies are required to evaluate the effects of any proposed changes. Sometimes changes are required in the physical structures themselves—for example, new outlet works, bypass structures, fish ladders, and fish screens. The question of who pays for these changes can be highly controversial. Costs can be surprisingly high: more than $80 million, for example, to install a new outlet works for water-temperature control at Shasta Dam on the Sacramento River in California.

Our work in building and operating these federal water projects is not yet complete. It will not be complete until these projects can operate in an environmentally acceptable manner. Sustainable use of water means making necessary changes. It means finding ways to pay the associated costs.

There are many who believe that the water users who are the current beneficiaries of these facilities should pay some or all of the costs of making them operate in an environmentally acceptable manner. With respect to irrigators in particular, they point to the subsidized cost of the water supply that irrigators have been enjoying—and the fact that, if irrigators had been required to pay the full costs of building and operating these facilities, many would not have been built—at least not at their present scale—and would not be operated the way they are. Moreover, they argue that the artificially low cost of their water supply encourages irrigators to use more water than is economically (and environmentally) warranted. Requiring these users to pay for mitigating the harmful environmental effects of their water use—in the jargon of economists, to internalize their externalities—would be the best way to encourage more efficient use of water. To require water users to pay these costs is simply to treat them in the same manner as industries and businesses that are required to install expensive equipment to clean up their air and water discharges.

I am sympathetic with this thinking. There is no doubt in my mind that full-cost pricing is the most effective way to allocate limited resources. Natural-resources policies, until recently, consistently violated this principle in the belief that subsidies would encourage development, with total benefits greater than costs.[42] Until we became aware of the ecological costs of this development, such encouragement appeared to make good sense.

I am persuaded, however, that redressing the shortcomings of federal water projects is more properly a national responsibility. The investment in these projects was not a business decision. It was a policy decision to encourage the development of the West. Perhaps, at the beginning, some really believed that reclamation-project beneficiaries would be able to pay the full costs of the project. Certainly by the 1920s no one still held on to that belief. Yet the great boom in project development occurred between the 1930s and 1960s, rationalized initially by a depression-era interest in public-works projects and, later, by revenues from hydroelectric power and by finding more and more public benefits that could be treated as nonreimbursable.

Even aware as I am of the damage caused by federal water-project development, I find myself more impressed by its original vision and purpose and by the benefits it has provided and continues to provide. I would not feel this way if I were a salmon or a Colorado pikeminnow, but I am not a salmon or a pikeminnow. At the same time I feel a clear sense of responsibility for the harm caused by these projects. It simply is not acceptable to me that my ability to live and work in the West is made possible only by eliminating species of fish that have thrived in western rivers for millions of years.

Irrigators *have* benefited from federal water projects throughout the West. They *do* use water made available at well below full cost. They *do* use more water than is necessary to grow their crops. As illustrated in our stories, however, much of this irrigation would never have existed if it weren't for federal reclamation projects. In the Grand Valley likely only those lands closest to the river, mostly developed in the 1880s and 1890s, would now be irrigated. The same is true in the Truckee and Carson basins and in the Yakima Valley.

Reclamation water projects brought lands into irrigation that would not otherwise have been irrigated. They did this by building facilities on a scale that would have been impossible had they been paid for by the water users. In part it is the scale of these facilities that explains their environmental effects–huge main-stem dams capable of storing large amounts of a river's flow, hydroelectric power generators at the dams, transmountain diversion works moving water from one river basin to another, large water-delivery canals tunneled through hillsides. Urban-water suppliers have constructed such facilities, but rarely have irrigators–unsupported by public funds–been able to do so.

This question of how to make the operation of water projects more compatible with environmental values has been one of the West's most contentious resource issues in recent years. Many water managers and some state officials believe federal environmental requirements are excessive and impose burdensome and unnecessary costs on states.[43] They resent being forced to make changes in the manner in which rivers and their water are used, a matter traditionally under their control. They resist having to pay for these changes. In some cases they believe that legal rights are being unconstitutionally infringed upon. The result often is protracted confrontation, endless studies, even more endless negotiations–with little real incentive to reach resolution short of a court order to do so.

At least with respect to federal facilities, making this issue a national-level responsibility rather than the responsibility of direct project beneficiaries would likely reduce resistance to these changes in the West. The issue of who pays would be removed. The question of who decides would be eliminated. The real work of figuring out what changes are needed and how best to implement them could at least move forward. Perhaps, with respect to nonfederal water projects, states might choose to take on a similar role. From my perspective there would be much wisdom in their doing so.

This is not a one-way process, however. While I believe existing contractual project beneficiaries should be freed from responsibility for paying for the changes needed to make these facilities operate in an environmentally acceptable manner, I also believe future project uses should be more market driven. Thus, as contracts are renewed, I believe they should include escalating charges that gradually move toward at least full-cost recovery, if not actual market value. Consideration should be given to ways to open up the use of projects to others, compatible with the legal rights of existing beneficiaries. Our goal for the twenty-first century should be to ensure that uses of federal water projects are potentially available to anyone, that existing users are faced with the "opportunity cost"–what they could gain if someone else paid them to acquire their use of the project–as they make their decision to continue their use, and that users appreciate the value of what they have because they are paying at least its full cost.

The purpose of changes to the water regulation infrastructure is to allow us to move closer to what is called "the natural flow regime."[44] The scientific community seems to be reaching agreement that the key to maintaining and restoring the integrity of river ecosystems is to mimic their natural dynamic character as much as possible. The complex, interrelated processes that form a riverine ecosystem begin with the movement of water and sediment. The flow regime creates a physical environment within which life-supporting habitats develop. Human alteration of the natural flow regime affects the physical and ecological functions of the system.

Western rivers are highly modified. Not only does the natural flow regime no longer exist, in many cases its predevelopment critical variables–magnitude, frequency, duration, timing, and rate of change–are unknown. Nevertheless, "[j]ust as rivers have been incrementally modified, they can be incrementally restored, with resulting improvements to many physical and biological processes."[45] The objective is to allow the river to act more like a river–ideally, as the river worked before development, but at least more like a natural system, with all of its variability as well as its cycles.

In sum, our water-development infrastructure in the West provides important benefits, but sometimes at unnecessary–even unacceptable–costs from an environmental perspective. Traditional project beneficiaries resist responsibility for the environmental damage caused by these projects and by the use of water that river development makes possible. I have suggested using federal financial resources for federal water projects, and encouraging states to take on this responsibility for nonfederal water projects in return for opening up use of these facilities to those willing and able to pay their full costs. We need to move ahead with the critical work of making these projects environmentally compatible and with allowing our rivers to act like rivers.

28

WATER THAT CHANGES USE
TO MEET DEMAND

Paralleling the need for changes in the manner of operation and use of our water-development infrastructure is our need to make it easier to change our uses of developed water. By "developed" water I mean that portion of the natural supply that is regulated or controlled by human actions and legally committed to human uses. The use of developed water is governed by water rights established under state laws. The primary purpose of these legally defined allocations of water is to provide certainty and security to existing users and to provide a means to sort out disputes among these users. Typically, water rights are described in relation to a specific use and based on the assumption that this use will not change, at least not in location, unless the water use simply ceases and the legal entitlement is abandoned. If uses do change, they are constrained by the rule that the change not cause injury or impairment to other legally protected water uses.

Here again culture and tradition play an important role. Many water users believe that water, though it can be appropriated and taken out of a stream for use, should not be bought and sold like a commodity. This view is strongest in those states in which, by law, a water right is regarded as "appurtenant" to the land (and the use) for which the water was appropriated. It is also most likely to prevail among agricultural irrigators, whose present and future livelihoods are most directly linked to keeping appropriated water within the irrigation systems that they use and on which they depend.

In my experience most irrigators believe their water rights—no matter how substantial—do not assure them enough water: Who knows when a drought is coming or how long it might last?[46] Irrigators with junior water rights such as those in the Lower Arkansas Valley and proratable users in the Yakima Basin often lack adequate supplies.

Most irrigators believe, rightfully in many cases, that they cannot compete economically with other new demands for water that would generate higher returns than their irrigation use. Water that leaves an agricultural irrigation system to go to some urban use almost certainly will not return to agriculture. As illustrated in the Lower Arkansas Valley, the permanent sale of irrigation-water rights has meant permanently lost irrigated agriculture. Even if the farm is not sold with the water rights, irrigated agriculture no longer is possible. To those remaining in agriculture, the sale and transfer of water rights often have meant the downward spiral of their water systems and their communities.

Yet, with the ability to further develop water supplies increasingly limited, some already developed and used water must meet growing demands for consumptive uses. It is not so much a question of *whether* such transfers should occur but *how* they should occur.[47]

Much of the transfer of water use from agricultural to urban purposes has occurred through the process of changing the underlying land use. Cities have expanded into adjacent farming areas. Subdivisions with irrigated lawns and parks have replaced irrigated croplands. This process of transition has not been uncontroversial or without its problems, but it has happened in a more or less gradual fashion, driven by the growth patterns of an area. Water taken out of agricultural use provided at least some of the supplies needed to support this new urban growth.

For the most part, however, urban-water demands have been met through large-scale development of water, comparable in some respects to that which supported irrigated agriculture. Cities like Los Angeles and Denver constructed major water storage and conveyance facilities in remote locations where water was available and had not yet been claimed by others. Los Angeles went a step further in the Owens Valley, buying up irrigated lands and the associated water.[48] This more aggressive approach of shutting down a portion of an existing water-dependent economy in a distant place to move the water to a city provoked a strong reaction in California. Even today the Owens Valley image remains a powerful symbol characterizing the single-minded pursuit of water for growth without concern for its consequences to others.

With undeveloped sources of water less and less available, however, urban areas are turning to more distant agricultural areas looking for supplies of water. In Colorado, cities have taken advantage of the strong property-rights tradition in state water law that makes it relatively easy to purchase irrigation-water rights, transfer the place of use to the urban area, and change the use from agricultural to urban purposes.[49] Beginning in the 1950s and 1960s Denver and other cities in the metropolitan area began buying water rights used to irrigate high alpine meadows in South Park, a mountain valley near the headwaters of the South Platte River that flowed down through the Denver metropolitan area. Ranching has now disappeared almost altogether from this valley. As described in part 1, in the Arkansas River drainage to the south, upstream cities like Colorado Springs and Pueblo began buying up water rights used to irrigate agricultural lands in the Lower Valley in this same period. Even the city of Aurora, located in the South Platte Basin, got involved in buying agricultural water rights in the Arkansas. In the most heavily affected part of the Lower Arkansas Valley, Crowley County, irrigated agriculture will in the foreseeable future shrink to a land area only about 10 percent of its former size. This trend of large-scale purchases of water rights used in distant agricultural areas, usually in rural areas with few other sources of economic activity, has produced growing resistance to water transfers in Colorado.

Historically, water transfers have occurred through one-of-a-kind negotiated agreements involving the permanent sale of irrigation-water rights to another user. Then the actual transfer of water and change of use are subjected to a state-level review, primarily to ensure that there will be no harm to other existing water rights. Because of the substantial expense involved in reaching agreement and acquiring state approval, buyers understandably wanted to purchase the water rights permanently and transfer as much water as they could to their use.

The nature of agricultural-to-urban water transfers has been changing in recent years. More creative approaches are being developed, approaches that (a) provide existing water users with more flexibility in defining the terms under which water is to be transferred, (b) may not involve the permanent transfer of ownership of water rights, and (c) bring capital into an irrigation system that can be used for upgrading the system and for strengthening the continued agricultural viability of the area rather than shutting it down.[50] I have already referred to the agreement between the Imperial Irrigation District and the Metropolitan Water District of Southern California, under which the MWD provided funding to the IID for making improvements in its irrigation delivery system in return for the use of one hundred thousand acre-feet of water. Since then the MWD has entered into several other innovative, one-time transfer agreements with irrigators in California that demonstrate other ways some agricultural water might shift to urban use without undermining the existing agricultural economy.

One particularly promising strategy, tested in California in the drought years of the early 1990s, falls under the general heading of water banking. Water banking is an institutionalized process for facilitating the transfer of use of already developed water.[51] It is a process designed to make already-utilized water available for different uses, but in a manner that specifically meets the needs and interests of the historical users.

With a well-structured water bank, a well-defined transfer procedure already would be in place, transferable water would be identified, and questions of injury would be resolved within the procedure. The bank serves as the entity legally authorized to manage the process. The holders of existing water rights are given the continuing option of placing their rights in the bank for rental, lease, or sale under terms and conditions known in advance. Would-be buyers also know in advance the rules governing purchase of water or water rights from the bank. Within this structure a true market for water can develop, allowing price to adjust to the supply and demand for already developed water—at least that portion voluntarily placed into the market by water-right owners.

There are a number of important potential advantages to such a general approach. One is that it allows the irrigation community to think more carefully about the circumstances, if any, under which it might be willing to voluntarily relinquish use of a portion of the water it now uses. Individual irrigation districts and mutual ditch companies could begin internal discussions about whether there are procedures and conditions, supported by their members, under which water they have historically diverted and used might be made available for use by another. If the board of directors of an entity is not able to agree on acceptable terms, the irrigation system would not participate in the bank.

A water bank could provide irrigators, now focused almost exclusively on simply maintaining their system, with opportunities for improving that system as well as individual on-farm water-use practices. It could continue the process—begun in many cases long ago—of creating and supporting a viable agricultural economy. It could serve as a vehicle through which members of the irrigated agricultural community could take positive steps to maintain and protect their irrigation systems, as well as nearby communities that may depend on this economic activity.

As illustrated by the Fort Lyon Canal experience in the Arkansas Basin, water transfers are a difficult and emotionally charged issue for many irrigators. In many instances the most economically valuable thing possessed by irrigators is their water rights. As described, some farmers in the Lower Arkansas Valley are ready to quit farming; others might be ready if they can leave with enough money. Others wouldn't live any other place doing any other thing, but they worry about how they are going to survive. Until recently irrigators have been presented with an unhappy choice: Sell out everything or stay and take your chances.

Water banks provide another option. Users need not permanently sell their water rights if they choose not to. Nor do they need to stop irrigating altogether. They could choose simply to irrigate less land, or to grow less water-intensive crops, or to forgo the irrigation necessary to grow that third cutting of hay, if they found that they could earn more money by selling that portion of water through the bank.

From a buyer's perspective an important advantage is that water banks might reduce resistance to agricultural-to-urban water transfers. Banks might open up supplies of water that simply would not be available under other approaches. The transaction costs associated with banking transfers should be considerably less than those now encountered. And if, in fact, it turns out that there is a considerable amount of water that might be available through a water bank, its per-unit purchase price is likely to be less than it otherwise would be.

One important question from a buyer's perspective is the security and reliability of a water supply that is not permanently purchased. Urban-water utilities are highly risk averse, typically holding a reliable yield from their water-supply systems that is well in excess of their expected maximum demand. Such utilities tend to plan in long time horizons (for example, fifty years), anticipating high levels of growth and establishing in advance a water supply that can fully meet this projected growth. It seems likely that the desire for long-term commitments of water could be met through a combination of some permanent sales of water rights and leases of pools of water that could be assembled from a large, and even changing, number of sources. Moreover, it may be less important for a city to own permanently a water supply that is needed only periodically for droughts or for other relatively short-term needs. This water need might more efficiently and cheaply be supplied through a water bank in such circumstances.

Banks can be operated at the ditch or district level, at the subbasin or basin level, or even statewide. They can be established by an irrigation organization just for transactions involving its members or users. A bank operating within a single district or water-delivery system can provide a user-driven mechanism for allocating water available for use within a system, rather than existing formulaic approaches typically allocating a fixed share on an acreage basis irrespective of need or value. In fact, many irrigation systems already accommodate some intradistrict seasonal transfers or exchanges. A bank would simply further facilitate and encourage such arrangements.

Two or more neighboring irrigation systems might create a bank that would facilitate short- or long-term transfers between their users. By effectively pooling their water supplies they might discover opportunities for more efficient uses. Irrigation systems with underutilized water-storage facilities might want to offer units of storage capacity for lease or sale to others. The possibilities are considerable.

In my view banks will be most effective if they are specially sanctioned under state law, operated at the basin or subbasin level, and given the authority to fully manage the transactions within statutory guidelines. They will be most effective if the procedures and rules under which they operate are developed in close coordination with water users and with the active participation of other interests in the basin. They will be most effective if the rules and procedures are simple and straightforward, easily understood and easily administered. Regional operation offers the advantages of developing a shared understanding of water supplies, river operations, and water uses that will make analysis of injury problems easier. It also potentially allows consideration of transfer options that might involve more than one irrigation system, taking advantage of opportunities for coordinating the management and use of these systems in ways that could make more water available for use.

Whatever the particular approach, the objective is the same: to increase the beneficial uses of water through voluntary, market-driven arrangements that provide value to new users (through use of the water) and to traditional users (through direct payments for relinquishing use of the water); to water-supply systems for their improvement (through revenues earned from operation of the bank); and possibly to communities and the environment (through creation of funds for their benefit). That the aggregate amount of water used in irrigated agriculture must and will decline is not to say that irrigated agriculture should cease or even that it should shrink markedly. Far from it. From my perspective irrigated agriculture has been, is, and should remain one of the core parts of the American West. But it can remain viable and functional with the use of less water only so long as the shift of water happens in a manner that supports and encourages, not undermines, the viability of irrigated agriculture on those lands and in those areas where it is sustainable. That should be a fundamental goal of water policy in the American West.

29

GETTING THERE

The physical and legal infrastructure guiding and enabling human use of western water resources has developed over a period of about 150 years. During this time it has served the interests of its intended beneficiaries well. With the loss of public support for additional large-scale water development, however, and the growing interest in such things as the recreational and ecological values of water, this system is struggling to maintain its traditional control of western rivers and aquifers. Changes are occurring within the traditional framework, and they are being generated from outside. Whether these changes will amount to simply a modified version of the existing infrastructure or something more fundamentally different remains uncertain. Business as usual, however, is not an option.

How the western water infrastructure is responding to and accommodating needed changes is the subject of this chapter. Considered first are water-rights holders and their organizations. These are the parties with the most control of the resource itself and the ones with the most at stake. Next are states, the titular owners (on behalf of the public) of the water resources within their boundaries, and the public representatives setting rules respecting water allocation and use. Third is the federal government in its roles as river developer and manager, as landowner and manager, as tribal trustee, and as implementer of national legal requirements, largely related to environmental protection. Fourth is a relatively new player: so-called watershed-based "partnerships" involving an array of public and private parties with some interest in a particular watershed and its water resources. All are essential participants in the process of "getting there."

WATER-RIGHTS HOLDERS

All living things use water. In this sense all water users are the same. In the American West, however, only one class of users enjoys the recognition and protection of law—those holding water rights. Water rights exist under state law to protect investments made by human users to develop and use water. They exist to ensure that those who have made an economic commitment to some water-dependent activity do not lose that investment because of other human water uses. Water rights are regarded as property rights because of the economic investment they protect.

Water rights also are a public grant. They provide public sanction for individual use of a common resource. They offer public protection for this use, subject to several significant conditions. One is that the claim to water must be "perfected" through actual use. Another is that the use must be "beneficial." A third is that the use must continue ("use it or lose it"), or the grant will be regarded as abandoned.

Control of western water resources rests largely with water-right holders and their representative organizations.[52] It is they who determine how much stream flow will be stored in reservoirs and when that water will be released for downstream use. It is they who determine how much stream flow will be diverted and groundwater withdrawn. It is they who control how much of this water returns to streams and aquifers and the condition of the return flows. It is they who control western water.

There is nothing malevolent about this fact. It is the outcome of a nineteenth-century bargain: Political leaders wanted rapid, economically viable human settlement of an arid region—possible only with large-scale development of the West's limited water resources—and developers wanted a low-cost, secure supply of water to support their economic activities. States protected that development with generous water rights, and the federal government supported it with equally generous subsidies. From an economic perspective the results were spectacular–unmatched in any other arid part of the world. From an environmental perspective the results were disastrous in many locations.

By and large those with water rights fiercely resist the intrusion of other interests into the water arena. They point, legitimately, to their economic dependence on water and on the essential nature of their water uses for the purposes they support (primarily irrigation and human use). They point to their sometimes considerable investment in the facilities necessary to capture and carry water to the place of use (while often neglecting or mischaracterizing the degree of public investment in many of these facilities). They emphasize their knowledge about water and their longstanding involvement in its management and use. They rely heavily on their water rights as evidence of their superior claim to its control and use, and on (as they see it) their immunity from responsibility for adverse effects of their water uses on other values and uses of water.

There is, of course, nothing untoward about watching out for one's own interests. Indeed, most water-right holders take their responsibilities as stewards of the water resource very seriously. What is perhaps unfortunate is the manner in which this watching out has manifested itself. For the most part the water-right holders of the West have devoted far more effort to resisting change than to shaping it to their benefit. Many continue to believe that concerns about water quality, ecosystems, recreational water uses, water-dependent endangered species, and other similar values have no place in decisions about water or in its management and use. Aware as they are about the limited water supply, their needs for water, the costs of providing water, and the benefits produced by these uses, they see these other values as less important and as potentially interfering with more essential needs and interests–the ones they supply.

Our stories support these general characterizations of the role played by organizations that were created by traditional water users to provide their water. The Truckee-Carson Irrigation District, for example, vigorously opposed every effort to improve the Pyramid Lake fishery because its members believed they held considerably greater control over water from the Truckee River than did the Pyramid Lake Paiute tribe and the Interior Department. The district and the tribe engaged in a protracted war of litigation for many years, which still continues at a reduced level today. By refusing to comply with an order to reduce their diversions of Truckee River water, the TCID ended up subjecting itself to heightened federal supervision of its water uses. By refusing to participate in negotiations that produced congressional settlement legislation for the tribes, the irrigators caused several issues to remain unresolved. In subsequent negotiations the irrigators were unable to come to agreement. After thirty years of fighting, irrigators dependent on water from the Newlands Project have seen their supply decrease, their costs increase–and, still, there is no resolution.

In the Grand Valley of Colorado, the Bureau of Reclamation was unsuccessful in persuading water users in the private Grand Valley Irrigation Company to participate in the salinity control project. Investment in system improvements would have been considerably more cost-effective for the Grand Ditch than in the Grand Valley Water Users' Association Highline system–the one built as part of the Reclamation project. GVIC irrigators distrusted Reclamation– and, it turned out, their own water-supply organization–to alter their main canal and laterals, even though the costs would have been fully paid.

There are, of course, many good examples around the West of irrigation districts taking creative steps to strengthen their members' positions. In our stories, for example, was the work of Tommy Thomson of the Southeastern Colorado Water Conservancy District to convince irrigators in the Lower Arkansas Valley to stop irrigating in the wintertime and to store that water for summer use. There was the work of Vern Gundy in the Roza Irrigation District to improve control over delivery of system water for better efficiency, and the joint efforts of the Roza and Sunnyside districts to deal directly with their sediment problems.

By and large, however, most of the water-rights community fears it will lose more than it will gain by attempting to participate collaboratively in–perhaps even lead and guide–the process of change. Water-right holders benefit enormously from the status quo. They have many powerful allies, particularly in western state legislatures and among western congressional representatives. Most prefer to use their influence to attempt to stop, or at least slow down, the process of change.

Still, the water-rights community is far from monolithic. Gridlock in California over additional water development caused a far-reaching rift between agricultural-water users and urban-water suppliers, making it possible for Congress in 1992 to reallocate up to eight hundred thousand acre-feet of water in the Central Valley Project to environmental uses.[53] Urban-water suppliers, industrial/business users, and agricultural irrigators needing additional supplies are less likely simply to oppose change, and more likely to search for ways to work with change to achieve their needs. They are likely to favor markets. They may well support development of water use efficiency standards–initially for themselves and then for others. They may well be sensitive to growing public support for watershed restoration.

THE STATES

Historically, states concerned themselves almost exclusively with encouraging human development of water in support of settlement and economic growth. Users developed basic allocation rules later codified by state legislatures. Courts sorted out disputes between competing appropriators.

As conflicts among users grew, and as claims for water exceeded the available supply in many rivers and streams, states began to develop more refined allocation and administration systems.[54] They created a new position, usually called the state engineer, with responsibility for water matters. Beginning with Wyoming in the 1890s, they instituted permit systems for obtaining new water rights. In addition to setting out the all-important priority date, permits identified point of diversion, place of use, purpose of use, and rate of diversion associated with the water right. Although the laws of most western states give the supervising body the authority to evaluate appropriations on a "public interest" basis, in fact little use has been made of this authority to reject or condition claims.[55] States have been concerned primarily with assuring that claimants are capable of putting water to the proposed use, and that claims are roughly proportionate to the use.

For the most part the surface-water resources of the West are now fully allocated among a large number of appropriators and users. Legally recognized claims by these appropriators equal, or even exceed, the physical water supply from most sources. Except in a few locations, new claimants are unlikely to be able to divert and use reliably any significant additional amount of water. This is especially true if the ecological needs of these sources are taken into account.

Groundwater development is at or beyond its limit in many places.[56] The legal rules governing groundwater are considerably more rudimentary than those related to surface water. In general, states have focused on groundwater only where high levels of development have prompted conflicts. The physical linkages between surface water and groundwater remain unacknowledged in the laws of most states.

Thus, except perhaps for groundwater, states, in their capacity as supervisors of the initial allocations of water within their borders for economic uses, have little left to do. Indeed, many states are now engaged in complicated, expensive, and time-consuming adjudications attempting to sort out more clearly just what allocations of water already have been made. As illustrated in the Yakima Basin, the result of an adjudication is likely to be little more than a ratification of the status quo.

In their larger capacity as guardians and trustees of the water resource for the benefit of their citizens, however, states have much to do. They have more to do, I believe, by way of providing legal protection for unappropriated water for ecological or other valuable in-stream uses. They have much more to do by way of clarifying the conditions upon which existing uses can take place—in particular, the amount of water a user may control and use, and the effects the use may have on other uses of the water. And they have much to do in developing more effective means by which some existing uses can be changed to new uses while safeguarding other valuable interests.

State in-stream laws and programs are still in their infancy.[57] The notion that water has value in-stream continues to be treated with skepticism or even hostility by many traditional water interests. States have moved cautiously, generally setting aside water only in areas with limited development potential (such as in high mountain settings) and quantifying the amount of water as the minimum possible. Typically, they have restricted the process of claiming in-stream water to a state agency, sometimes subject to approval by the legislature itself, on the basis that supporters of in-stream flows would attempt to tie up all unappropriated water. They have limited the purposes for which in-stream flows may be preserved, most commonly to preserve a sports fishery, neglecting other ecological values of rivers.

As westerners become more and more interested in the uses and values of water that are served by maintaining in-stream flows, these restrictions seem likely to drop away. First, there is no sound basis in my view for prejudging the purposes for which in-stream flows might be protected. As with appropriations generally, any valuable (beneficial) use should potentially be considered. Second, as methods for quantifying the timing and amounts of water associated with achieving a particular in-stream water use are established and refined, the matter of quantification should be resolved according to the objective of the use. Third, instead of excluding interested groups and individuals from establishing such claims, appropriate requirements should be established that would ensure that their participation fits within the existing water-rights system.

Fourth, because there is little unappropriated water remaining, states are likely to open up their water right transfer rules to allow transfers of water from out-of-stream to in-stream uses. A few states already allow existing rights to be transferred to the state program, but there will be more incentive for groups to acquire and transfer out-of-stream rights if they can hold and manage these rights themselves. More states are likely to follow Montana's lead in allowing the temporary leasing of water rights for use in-stream.

Several western states have asserted a leadership role in attempting to meet their citizens' legal obligations under the Endangered Species Act so that existing water uses can continue. Thus, for example, the states of Colorado, Utah, and Wyoming have been working with the U.S. Fish and Wildlife Service, the Bureau of Reclamation, water users, and environmentalists to develop a successful recovery program for endangered native fish in the upper Colorado River Basin, including the Fifteen-Mile Reach adjacent to the Grand

Valley. And, under the 1997 Platte River agreement establishing a coordinated program for dealing with endangered species issues in the Platte River, the states of Colorado, Nebraska, and Wyoming have joined with the Fish and Wildlife Service and Reclamation as well as other interests to define and implement measures that will protect several listed species residing in and along the Platte in central Nebraska.

As more and more pressure is placed on the West's essentially fixed (but highly variable) water supply, states are likely to consider ways to spell out more carefully the nature and extent of water rights so that additional valuable uses will be possible. Considering their importance in the arid West, water rights are remarkably ill defined in some respects. They are clear about the source of water (for example, the river or stream), the point of diversion, and—generally—the place of use. They tend to be vague about the purpose of use, the timing of use, and especially the amount of water that can be diverted and used within a given period of time. They say little or nothing about the manner of use. This is especially true for water rights established some time ago (as most were), but it remains largely true today for new appropriations. Indeed, even highly expensive and lengthy adjudication processes such as the one in the Yakima Basin have done little to clarify many key elements related to actual use. As suggested earlier, states may begin to set up standards governing the efficiency with which water is used. They could place limits on diversions or on return flows. They could do this statewide or in designated areas where conflicts are especially great. They could provide standards by which waste or unreasonable use could be determined, making it easier for junior appropriators to challenge seniors. They could establish water quality protection requirements for water-rights holders independent of the Clean Water Act.

In addition to possible state legislative efforts, water rights are likely to become more clearly defined through administrative or judicial processes. For example, when a water right goes through a state change-of-use process, the matter of historical use generally is closely scrutinized. In Colorado, at least, it is customary for the changed water right to carry specific conditions related to the timing with which water may be diverted and the amount of water that may be used consumptively. The traditional description of an appropriation based simply on a maximum rate of diversion is converted into a considerably more precise volumetric amount, with a limitation placed on consumptive use in some period of time (usually annually). It is thus conceivable that more careful definition of water rights could be an outcome of state adjudication processes in general.

Perhaps the single most important water-related task facing states concerns the manner in which the reallocation of developed supplies occurs.[58] At present state laws related to water transfers are not designed to facilitate transfers. They are intended to protect existing water rights. Thus they place emphasis on the "no injury" rule, the effect of which is to ask the proponent of the transfer to prove a negative—a difficult thing to do. As already discussed, water banking offers a general mechanism by which transfers might be facilitated while problems such as third-party effects can be successfully managed. States could greatly aid this process by establishing clear rules under which water banks could operate. There might be a role for a water bank at the state level, perhaps to supplement others that would operate at more regional or local levels. Even if water banking is not used, there is a need for states to develop rules and procedures explicitly designed to manage water transfers. Some portion of already developed and used supplies must shift to new uses. Existing procedures are cumbersome, expensive, and produce some undesired results. They need to be changed.

THE FEDERAL ROLE

While, ostensibly, use of water resources is a matter of state law, the federal government has played a central role in western water development and use.

In this century the federal government has served as an important agent of change in western water—first, through the large-scale development of rivers for economic benefits and, more recently, through legal regulation of river uses to accomplish environmental objectives. In its role as developer, the United States (largely through the Bureau of Reclamation and the Army Corps of Engineers) acted primarily as a partner—providing funding and technical expertise—and a broker—bringing together sometimes competing interests to

share in the increased river benefits that its projects provided. As in
the Yakima, Reclamation actively encouraged states to improve their
water laws so that project water rights were more secure, and so that
it could contract with users more efficiently. Reclamation continues
to operate many of the projects it built, working closely with traditional project users. The Corps of Engineers remains responsible for
river regulation, including flood control, on many western rivers.
The Western Area Power Administration and the Bonneville Power
Authority market electricity generated at federal dams.

Federal involvement began modestly. Congress made the practical judgment back in the 1800s that the territories and states should
have primary responsibility for making decisions directly allocating
the use of water within their boundaries.[59] Through efforts such as the
Powell and Hayden surveys, the federal government sought to assist
western settlement and development by identifying and mapping the
lands and resources, including water, that would support settlement.
With the 1902 Reclamation Act, Congress greatly elevated the federal
role in river development to support settlement of the West, initially
through making water available to small family farms for irrigation.

The Progressive Movement, espoused by Teddy Roosevelt and
Gifford Pinchot, envisioned an even larger role for the federal government in managing the use of natural resources. Private enterprise
had demonstrated itself to be a remarkable engine for the development of the abundant natural resources on the American continent,
but its fixation on short-term profit maximization disregarded effects
on the availability of resources for future generations and neglected
opportunities for more coordinated development and use of resources
that might in fact yield greater public benefits, if fewer individual
profits. Here was a role for government: to guide private development in a manner that produced greater total benefits to society.

In the water-resources context the Progressive Movement
embraced the need for comprehensive river-basin development in
the early 1900s. As first articulated in the 1908 report of the Inland
Water Commission, river systems provide multiple benefits, including navigation, flood control, water supply, and hydroelectric power.[60]
Government supervision is required to ensure that these different
uses are coordinated and fully developed. In the 1920 Federal Power

Act, Congress established the Federal Power Commission (now the Federal Energy Regulatory Commission) to provide for the "comprehensive development" of the nation's navigable rivers.[61] In practice, however, it gave this body licensing control only over the construction of private hydroelectric power generation facilities.

It was in the evolving role of the federal government as constructor and operator of large dams on major rivers that the notion of governmentally supervised, comprehensive river-basin development really manifested itself. With the construction in the 1930s of what became the Hoover Dam on the Colorado River, the Bureau of Reclamation became the operator of the first true "multiple purpose" dam—specifically constructed to provide navigation, flood control, water supply, and hydroelectric benefits. Given the interstate (and international) character of the river and the fact that federal funds were used to build the facilities, it made sense that a federal agency should be the operator. This same pattern was repeated all across the West over the next forty years, with the Army Corps of Engineers also playing an active role in constructing and operating multiple-purpose river-development facilities.

The fundamental federal role was the financing, construction, operation, and maintenance of the physical structures necessary to comprehensively develop river systems (as opposed to water) for their multiple economic uses. Without federal financing such large-scale, multipurpose river development would likely not have been possible. This remarkable development of western rivers played an important, even defining, role in the growth of the American West.

To some the logical corollary of comprehensive river-basin development was comprehensive river-basin management. If the federal government owns the major water-development facilities, and these facilities are managed by federal agencies, why shouldn't their operation be still further integrated and enhanced by placing river-basin planning and management under the direction of a single entity, capable of comprehensively running the river basin for its greatest benefits? Such was, in fact, the thrust of the Water Resources Planning Act of 1965.[62] In the Yakima Basin the Bureau of Reclamation's development and management of essentially the entire water supply approximated this model in some respects.

Events, however, had overtaken this idea. Many federal water projects were being built as much for political as for economic reasons, and the cost of constructing these facilities was becoming its own issue. Attention increasingly was focused on the need for more rigorous cost/benefit analysis before federal funds were committed to water projects.[63] This analysis revealed the degree to which these projects were being federally subsidized–those directly benefiting from the projects were paying back only a fraction of the costs incurred to provide these benefits.[64]

Attention also focused increasingly on the environmental costs of river development. The Sierra Club's John Muir could not rally sufficient political support in opposition to the building of Hetch Hetchy Dam in Yosemite National Park early in the century, but the Sierra Club's David Brower had greater success blocking the proposed Echo Park Dam in Dinosaur National Monument in the 1950s.[65] From that point forward large main-stem dams have faced a heavy burden of proof that their economic benefits outweigh their economic costs *and* the costs imposed on the natural environment.

The federal government has invested nearly $22 billion (unadjusted for inflation) through the Bureau of Reclamation to construct water projects to provide water for irrigation and other uses in the seventeen western states since 1902.[66] Additional funds have been invested through Reclamation construction of water projects not involving irrigation, and by the Army Corps of Engineers. To date irrigation-water users have paid slightly less than $1 billion of the $7.1 billion they are committed under contract to pay. Hydroelectric power revenues are projected to pay $3.7 billion of this $7.1 billion amount. Nearly $5 billion of the total federal outlays are regarded as "nonreimbursable"–that is, they will never be returned to the federal treasury.[67]

Federal interests have shifted from comprehensive river-basin development to more focused concerns about uses of water. This interest emerged first in an important way in federal efforts to assure that some water was available to meet the needs of Native American tribes who had agreed to settle within specified reservations of land, ceding their claims to much larger areas of land that could then be opened to non–Native American settlement and development. Interestingly, it was the U.S. Supreme Court and not Congress that determined that a reservation of public land—initially reservations for tribal homelands, and later for other federal purposes—carried with it an *implied* reservation of water necessary to fulfill the purposes for which the reservation was established.[68] The nature and scope of these federal reserved water rights, rights regarded as holding a priority date of the creation of the reservation of land, evolved slowly from their first official recognition in 1908.[69] Even today their validity is challenged by some thoughtful observers, and the courts have generally narrowed and restricted their application since the late 1970s.[70] To help resolve American Indian reserved right claims, Congress increasingly has gotten involved in ratifying negotiated settlements quantifying the extent of such reserved water rights and in providing funding needed to make the settlements work.[71]

Federal representation of tribal interests in western water matters has had a decidedly mixed history. Few federal water projects (the Yakima is an exception; the Newlands Project is more typical) benefited Native American reservations. Reserved water rights for American Indians, though legally determined to exist early in this century, have only been established, quantified, and brought into use for a small number of tribes. Responsibility for this limited record of accomplishments does not rest solely with the United States, however. The tribes themselves have been slow to assert their interests in many cases, and some tribes still are unsettled about pursuing property interests in a resource they don't believe can be owned.

Nevertheless, progress has been made since the U.S. Supreme Court in 1963 provided a basis on which to quantify Native American reserved water rights.[72] Some tribes have resolved their reserved water rights claims through litigation. For example, in the Yakima Adjudication, the court recognized that the Yakama Nation holds a treaty-based right to Yakima River flows necessary to preserve salmon. Others such as the Pyramid Lake Paiute tribe have used negotiated settlements, supported by congressional legislation. In the process many tribes have become far more skilled at representing their own interests. They are considerably less dependent on the Department of the Interior and less likely to expect the United States to take care of their interests, in water or anything else.

As "domestic dependent nations" (in the words of Chief Justice John Marshall), tribes hold considerable sovereignty over matters within their reservations–authority on a par with that held by states. Although nations, they are also regarded as dependent on the United States, with whom they treated for land. The power and authority of tribal governments exist awkwardly within the political and constitutional framework that governs the United States.

Congress could do much to clarify tribal rights to water. Just as Congress has largely abdicated its responsibilities in this matter with respect to federal public lands, so too has it chosen not to provide general guidance for tribes and states respecting tribal water rights. That is unfortunate, though perhaps understandable politically.

Then there are the large areas of the West still in federal ownership and management: national forests, national parks, public-domain lands, wildlife refuges, military bases. The uses for which these lands are managed require water, and, as the proprietors of these lands, the responsible federal agencies have become increasingly involved in providing for water-related needs. For those lands specifically set aside as reservations, the primary tool has been the reserved water right. In some cases federal agencies have gone through the procedures required under state water law to obtain state water rights for specific uses on federal public lands, either based on their reserved-rights claims or simply as appropriators.

For the most part federal reserved-rights claims converted into state water rights have been modest in size and limited in scope. Efforts, for example, to claim reserved-water rights in national forests for protection of fish and wildlife values failed to gain judicial support, as did claims for flows needed to maintain the physical integrity of stream channels in national forests for water-supply purposes (so-called channel-maintenance flows).[73] Reserved-rights claims for some national parks and wildlife refuges have been successfully made for large proportions of their water because of the clearly related purposes of these reservations. For lands not specifically reserved, including most of the public-domain lands managed by the Bureau of Land Management, there are no reserved-water rights.[74]

Lacking clear congressional direction regarding how they should address the water-based needs of the federal lands, the agencies have attempted to utilize a variety of approaches and tools.[75] In situations where unappropriated water still exists, they have sometimes sought appropriations under state law. They have sought Wild and Scenic River status or other protective land-management designations to preclude or limit additional water development. They have used their authority to condition certain uses of the public lands in a manner they believe provides benefits for the water-related values for which they are responsible.

In addition to primary responsibilities for American Indian tribes and federal public lands, federal agencies have been made subject to, and given a dominant role in the implementation of, a series of environmental-protection laws enacted by Congress since the 1960s. As described in chapter 25, many of these laws bear directly or indirectly on water resources, typically intended to prevent or ameliorate the adverse effects of human land or water uses on the public health and environmental values supported by that water.

Here the federal government, operating primarily through the Environmental Protection Agency, the Army Corps of Engineers, and the Fish and Wildlife Service, has emerged as a major regulatory presence, conditioning and limiting many of the river-development activities it committed so much effort to supporting over most of this century. There is no small irony in the role of the Army Corps of Engineers now administering the section 404 program of the Clean Water Act that restricts development in wetlands—a responsibility that causes it occasionally to deny a permit for the very kind of water-development project that historically it has itself been ready to build. Similarly, the Federal Energy Regulatory Commission, historically the champion of hydroelectric power generation, is struggling with its new responsibility in its licensing and relicensing of hydroelectric facilities to give "equal consideration" to the fish and wildlife values of the river.

Federal interests in western water have never been single-dimensional, but they are now far more diffuse and, in some respects, contradictory than they have been in the past. No longer the ready source of financial largess, no longer the willing helpmate of economic-development interests, more likely to represent interests regarded as adverse to those of their traditional constituencies, federal agencies administering water-related (and other land and resource management) programs in the West find themselves more and more just another participant in the West's ongoing water wars–albeit one with considerable financial and other resources, and with strong regulatory authority in some instances.

As discussed, Congress has shifted the focus of federal water programs from water development to environmental protection. Armed with a mix of regulatory requirements and financial incentives, federal agencies now concern themselves with matters of water quality and species protection more than with water supply. The strong public-participation processes built into federal-agency decision making have opened up western water issues to a much broader set of interests. Increasingly, federal agencies find themselves in the role of advocate rather than broker and helpmate. In this context they often find themselves operating in multiple-interest processes in which they are representing one or more of the interests competing for particular uses of water. Sometimes agencies themselves initiate the process–as a mechanism for attempting to reach agreement among competing interests or for working out acceptable ways to implement legal requirements. Sometimes agencies are drawn into processes set in motion by others.

In either event these processes are beginning to define a new means by which western rivers and their water are being governed. They are emerging to fit the circumstances and needs of the resource, as it becomes clear that existing mechanisms are incapable of effectively governing that resource. To a considerable degree they are processes "owned" and shaped by the participants. And the participants extend beyond just those with water rights and federal and state agencies. Tribes are likely to be key players, as are major environmental groups. Particularly at the watershed level they are likely to include newly emergent partnerships of interests existing under the generic name of watershed initiatives. I turn next to the remarkable growth of place-focused watershed partnerships and the role they may play in "getting us there."

Watershed Partnerships

The water-development consensus binding together water-rights holders, states, and the federal government (including Congress)[76] began unraveling in the 1960s, and by the 1980s gridlock had set in, with newly instituted environmental requirements now used to block most new water projects and even to challenge some existing water uses. Tribal water claims appeared poised to displace the senior rights of appropriators in many parts of the West. Anglers and white-water boaters started pressing their claims for river management more favorable to their interests (which were themselves likely to be conflicting). Cities began turning to irrigated agriculture as their next supply source. The world of western water as it had existed for most of this century was in turmoil.

Out of this growing chaos emerged watershed initiatives[77]—ad hoc efforts to find mutually acceptable solutions to specific water-related concerns. Typically spearheaded initially by one of the particular interests in the watershed (such as an agency faced with making a regulatory decision, an environmental group interested in some environmental enhancement, or a land or water developer), watershed initiatives sought to break through the gridlock by bringing in other interests in a shared search for mutually acceptable solutions. The emergence of watershed initiatives reflected both the increasingly divergent interests in the manner in which water is used and the increasingly diffused power to make such choices.

A few states have moved to formalize watershed initiatives,[78] but most initiatives are informal and ad hoc. They have taken many organizational directions, ranging from loose confederations whose participants are simply those that show up at meetings, to formal, structured entities with clearly defined objectives, ground rules for participation, and well-established decision-making processes.

Watershed initiatives represent an attempt to transcend the limits of their individual parts. They reflect the increasingly fractionalized nature of water-resources decision making and management in the West. They search for approaches that will provide increased benefits and/or reduced losses for those involved. They better fit the nature of ecological problems that do not lend themselves to single interests or artificially established boundaries. Water, the quintessential shared resource upon which so many things depend, is especially incapable of being adequately dealt with by individuals, institutions, and rules with a narrow or limited focus.

The emergence of watershed partnerships is less a reflection of the fundamental wisdom of "local control" than the necessity of making natural-resources decisions in the physical, social, and economic context of which the resources are a part. It is a recognition that places are the sum of their parts, and that when these places are altered by, for example, the removal of certain of their parts, there are consequences that must be considered. Watershed-oriented initiatives reflect the increasingly complex nature of the demands placed on our land and water resources. They are an attempt to organize ourselves in a manner better suited to make the kinds of tough choices that lie ahead, choices that more often will present themselves as trading one benefit for another rather than as choices about who gets to benefit.

Organizations like the Yakima River Watershed Council are emerging in many parts of the West in response to this growing focus on the watershed. Typically they are coalitions of the wide array of interests concerned with uses of a shared source of water. At this point they are voluntary associations, formed primarily to address some immediate problem in the watershed not being managed satisfactorily under existing processes. They make it possible to approach issues without the jurisdictional constraints faced by governmental entities. They provide a mechanism for dialogue among interests that often don't otherwise commonly talk.

They generally operate, however, without the force of government. Any agreements must be implemented through actions of the participants, not by the watershed organization itself. They have no reliable source of funding. They tend to be minimally staffed, depending heavily on the goodwill of participants to provide time and effort. For technical support they are dependent on staff made available by participating agencies and other entities with sufficient resources. As organizations dependent on the continued support of their participants, they must operate by consensus—a challenging standard in issues as controversial as water.

It is too early to say for sure where these watershed partnerships are headed— whether they represent a transition to something else, or whether they themselves will in fact become key institutions in future governance of water matters in the West. Either way, I suspect that they represent a development of lasting importance as well as a widely felt dissatisfaction with existing water-governance institutions, and that, either directly or indirectly, they will become an important, even primary, mechanism for water and watershed governance in many parts of the West–providing a means by which the many interests in a watershed can reach some accommodation.

I believe that the full range of water and other interests can potentially be represented within the context of the geographically-based management and decision-making processes emerging in many parts of the West. Federal lands, for example, all exist within watersheds and water basins. The water-based needs of these lands are not isolated from the full range of interests in the water of that watershed or water basin. There are legitimate water-related needs that in some cases are not necessarily provided for under federal law. These interests can and should be pursued in open processes that include and consider others with interests in the relevant water sources and their watersheds. If forums for this purpose do not now exist, federal agencies could take the initiative in starting such efforts.[79]

Watershed partnerships will not, however, replace the important role of existing organizations in attending directly to the needs and interests of their constituencies. Here it will be important for these organizations to evolve as well, providing more active and positive representation of their members in such watershed-based decision-making and implementation processes. Irrigators and urban-water users need advocates who understand their needs and interests and their importance, just as do environmental groups.

Nor will watershed partnerships take the place of governmental entities with explicit legal obligations. Such agencies will continue to bear ultimate responsibility for ensuring that legal requirements are met and that decisions under their authority are made.

The western-water playing field, however, is likely to be different. It is likely to be larger for one thing, encompassing far more players than before. The game will focus less on maintaining the status quo and more on searching for new approaches that enlarge the benefits provided by water for more and different interests while respecting the needs of traditional users. Playing skills are likely to be somewhat different as well. Communication will be even more important, as will be creativity and inventiveness. Progress will be made cooperatively, for the most part, or not at all.

Environmentalists sometimes express deep reservations about watershed processes because they may not be well represented in the local area and they fear being closed out of more locally-based decisions.[80] To the degree that such processes are designed to exclude or isolate environmental or other legitimate and important interests, they are likely to be self-defeating in the long run. As Bob Tuck pointed out in the context of the Yakima Basin, there are just too many strings now attached to significant natural-resource development and use activities. Process manipulation may postpone, but not avoid, the day of reckoning.

Some local interests, on the other hand, doubt the value of watershed-based processes where decisions reached in the process risk veto by federal and state regulators who may not even have been involved in the process. Why, they ask, should the Corps of Engineers—or the Environmental Protection Agency—or the U.S. Fish and Wildlife Service—be able to tell a water district or a city that it cannot build a dam—particularly if that entity has been able to get support of a local watershed council?

Jack Robertson, deputy director of the Bonneville Power Administration, has suggested empowering watershed partnerships by giving their decisions a *presumption of validity* with federal and state law. He suggests that interested federal and state agencies, including those with regulatory responsibilities, be full participants in watershed partnerships. Such agency participants would be charged first and foremost with ensuring that watershed decisions fully comply with the statutes they are directed to implement. But they would also be charged with making every effort, consistent with their legal responsibilities, to help the watershed process reach mutually satisfactory outcomes. Because final decisions by such entities would carry a presumption of validity, participating agency representatives would be on the line to ensure that such decisions meet legal requirements. At the same time, other participants in the process can proceed with confidence that, if acceptable measures are developed within the process, final decisions would carry a presumption of legal validity. Anyone attempting to challenge their validity would carry the burden of rebutting that presumption.

Such an approach is appealing for a number of reasons. Without in any way changing legal requirements (for example, that no federal action jeopardize the continued existence of a protected species), it has the potential to encourage the development of ways to meet these legal requirements that may be more supportive of interests within the watershed as well. It transforms some of the adversarial dimensions of regulation into a process of joint problem solving. It makes more clear to all participants the basic rules within which their deliberations must operate. It gives participants a higher expectation that their agreements (assuming they are able to make them) will go forward.

There are also some potentially troublesome aspects to this proposal. It would potentially place federal and state regulators in a difficult relationship with other watershed participants. They are certain to be heavily criticized by some for legal requirements viewed as unnecessary, and by others for legal requirements viewed as too weak. They will carry a heavier than normal burden for interpreting the legal mandates they are representing, especially as issues arise that are not clearly addressed in existing law and regulation. Likely, agencies would need to develop procedures by which such representatives could get necessary policy and legal guidance, and under which their decisions could gain the support of the agency. There will be the difficult question of the discretion to give such representatives, particularly regarding some requirements that may indeed be counterproductive in such processes. There will be the challenge of finding the numbers of qualified people that such participation will require.

Nevertheless, for watershed-based partnerships to reach their potential, such an approach may be necessary. Almost certainly, placing this kind of potential power in watershed entities would do much to encourage their development and use.

I am amazed by the vitality of watershed partnerships at this early stage of development, particularly given their extremely limited structure and authority. This vitality suggests to me their potential value which, in some places, has already produced important results. At the same time, collaborative processes are extraordinarily difficult and time-consuming. They test our commitment to truly participatory decision making.

PUTTING THIS TOGETHER

In sum, the processes guiding human use of water resources in the West and the roles of traditional participants could look very different in the future from the way they look today. The task occupying our attention for the past 150 years—establishing human control over water resources to meet human needs—is now largely complete. The primary task ahead is to integrate changing human water needs and interests and to restore and maintain ecological functionality of water-dependent natural systems.

The emergence of watershed partnerships and the increased use of problem-specific, place-specific collaborative processes reflect the changed nature of western water decision making. They reflect the declining control of traditional water users, particularly irrigators, over the sources from which they draw their water. They reflect the shifting role of the federal government from water development partner to implementer (or at least arbiter) of environmental-protection requirements. They reflect the growing number of interests dissatisfied with the benefits they receive from western water resources. They reflect a recognition that, in many settings, emergent interests in water can best be served through the difficult work of accommodation.

Epilogue

A FAUSTIAN BARGAIN?

We all live in the city. We all live in the country.

—William Cronon, *Nature's Metropolis*

Wilford Gardner, retired dean of the College of Natural Resources at the University of California, Berkeley, asked a National Research Council Committee on the Future of Irrigation in 1995 whether the use of irrigation to help settle the American West was a Faustian bargain.[81] Were the costs, he asked, in terms of our commitment of the lion's share of the region's limited water resources to irrigation, in terms of the massive alteration of the sources of water to make it usable for irrigation, in terms of the environmental degradation resulting from irrigated agriculture, of the decline in those parts of the West unable to sustain an irrigated agricultural economy, of the unreimbursed public funds expended to make much of this irrigated agriculture possible—were these costs too great a price to pay for what they produced? The response of this group, of which I was a member, was a unanimous no. It was not a conclusion I might have reached ten years earlier.

The West, I suspect, is not doomed to eternal damnation just because of its twentieth-century embrace of large-scale water development. From this comfortable vantage point it is easy to criticize the unsustainable overexpansion of western irrigated agriculture that occurred during this century, and the overdevelopment of water resources that supported it. Yet in 1902 passage of the Reclamation Act was a bold and progressive action. Making lands productive at a cost that average people could afford surely seemed like the right thing to do. And then, demonstrating that human ingenuity could harness a powerful resource like the Colorado River with the Hoover Dam–*just the fact that we could do it*–must have seemed extraordinary to most people in the desperate times of the 1930s. At the heart of the reclamation movement was an understandable desire for human betterment. But now, at the end of the twentieth century, those good intentions have long since been lost. Family farms turned into Cadillacs in the desert, to use Reisner's image. Human betterment turned into human greed and folly.

In parts of the West it seems there are two different worlds and two apparently irreconcilable views regarding water. One is rooted in the tradition of the American West in which economic existence is possible only with active human control and use of water. This is a highly utilitarian tradition, in which the highest and best use of water is to make it possible for humans to live and thrive in an arid environment–to make the desert bloom.[82] In this view water exists for humans to control and use as necessary for their needs. Frank Milenski spoke for this perspective in the Lower Arkansas Valley.

The other sees water more as an amenity, essential in modest amounts for human survival, to be sure, but otherwise more valuable in the stream, the wetland, the lake, than in a ditch going to irrigate alfalfa or grow corn. It is a world concerned more about water as a source of recreation, as a source of aesthetic enjoyment, as a necessary ingredient supporting natural plant and animal life.

This apparent schism is exacerbated by the propensity of the adherents of either view to denigrate the other and to question the motives and intentions of those with whom they disagree. Traditional water users and their representatives become water "buffaloes." Environmentalists become socialists or communists. Responsible, moderate voices searching for accommodation of interests are lost in the rhetoric.

It has been my experience that many agricultural water users genuinely fear some of the changes that are occurring in the West:

the region's increasing urbanization and agriculture's consequent loss of political power, the indifference or even antipathy some urban westerners express (especially in time of drought) toward irrigation use of water, the implications of increasing environmental values for their traditional way of life. They have long lived with an awareness of their vulnerability to the next natural disaster–drought, floods, tornadoes, hailstorms. They have lived in uneasy dependence on an agricultural economy that can be highly fickle and that is largely outside their ability to control. Understandably, they are unwilling to fall victim, as perhaps they see it, to other outside forces that seem to threaten their way of life. In reaction, perhaps, there is both a defensiveness and an aggressiveness that often serve to deepen the division with other water interests.

There is, of course, another way. Who knows better than the irrigators themselves and the organizations that provide them water what can be done to improve their water uses? Who better understands how the rivers are operated than the organizations that control and operate the dams, hydroelectric facilities, diversion structures, and water uses? Who better understands the legal agreements under which they store, deliver, and use water? *Who is the most economically at risk?*

This is hardly a golden age for irrigated agriculture, and many members of this sector find themselves largely on the defensive, trying to hold on to what they have against seeming attacks from all directions. For people accustomed to thinking of themselves as good citizens, providing an unmatched supply and variety of foods at equally unmatched prices, it is a time of deep frustration and confusion.

As the stories illustrate, irrigation added considerable value to those lands where water was made available. In some places, such as in the Yakima Valley of Washington, irrigated agriculture remains a vital economic activity with a bright future. In other places, such as the Lower Arkansas Valley of Colorado, it remains an important element of a modest rural economy. Its continued viability is important locally, but it may not be economically sustainable in its present form. In still other places, like the Grand Valley of Colorado, irrigated agriculture is slowly but surely being displaced by growing urbanization, while other interests compete actively for the water it has controlled and used. And in places like the lower Truckee and Carson basins of Nevada, irrigated agriculture is struggling to remain viable in the face of overwhelming pressures for its effective elimination. There is no single "future" for irrigated agriculture but many futures, dependent on a large number of factors—local, national, even global—that will play out differently in different locations.[83]

As I have come to better understand the role of irrigated agriculture in the West, I have developed a conviction that the changes that are necessary as we move into the twenty-first century should not come at the expense of this sector. Irrigated agriculture remains important to the West, as are ranching, dryland agriculture, logging, and mining. These roots of the modern West still serve as the core of the West's economy in many locations. They return a living from vast land areas that otherwise could not support human habitation. They provide the raw materials that are essential to the way we all live. They make possible a diversity of lifestyles, cultures, and landscapes that are as much a part of the West as its mountains and its bright blue skies.

Development of the West proceeded on the basis of an understanding: control of resources for economic growth. It was a social contract that capitalized on individual initiative, the power of opportunity, and the value of public subsidies. As the West has changed, the need and value of this contract have largely disappeared. Yet its effects can still be seen. Charles Wilkinson included in his "the lords of yesterday" the control over western water given to its early economic users.[84]

Irrigated agriculture cannot continue to be practiced in the manner in which it has been. We cannot afford to continue to use the amount of water now used for irrigation. We cannot continue the operation of our rivers based largely on the needs of irrigators. We cannot continue to avoid facing the water-quality problems resulting from irrigated agriculture.

The transition from traditional irrigation to irrigation in the twenty-first century promises to be painfully difficult. Irrigators, after all, are in the business of growing crops, a business constantly buffeted by economic and policy forces largely outside their control. For better or for worse, they have the added factor of having to provide their own supply of water. Anything that affects the cost or the availability of that supply has the potential of affecting their livelihood. Understandably, they are suspicious of any such changes. Traditionally they have flatly resisted changes affecting water, preferring the devil they know to the one they don't.

On balance, however, irrigated agriculture in the West has been remarkably resilient over the past hundred years. The current challenges facing this sector, particularly related to competition for water and to environmental impacts, represent today's problems to be solved more than enemies to be defeated. They are real problems, to be sure, and they do in fact represent real threats to the traditional manner in which much of irrigated agriculture has operated. It is not surprising that many irrigators fear these threats to their way of life and resist changes with unknown consequences for their future.

Just as irrigators are faced with some difficult choices about changing how they do business, so too are the rest of us faced with choices about the kind of West we want to live in. Is a viable agricultural sector an important part of that future—one that includes irrigation? If so, what does that mean for our own water uses and the manner in which we provide for these uses? Is it enough that we have water available from our taps whenever we want it? Does the price we pay for that water matter? What does it mean in an arid region to have sufficient water left in streams and rivers to allow desired recreational uses? What does it mean to have enough water in-stream to support a river's ecological integrity? Should we be concerned about how these needs and interests are met? I suspect that those who read this book, particularly if they have gotten this far, believe with me that this process of change is important—that the manner in which it happens is as important as the outcome it seeks.

William Cronon uses the story of the emergence of Chicago as one of the major cities in the United States to explore the relationship between rural and urban America.[85] Chicago grew from a small trading post to the country's second-largest city in the 1800s by selling the products of rural America (grain, lumber, meat) to urban

America. It not only returned income to the producers of these products but also made available to rural residents the products of the cities, especially manufactured goods. As Cronon points out, the rhetoric most often emphasizes the dichotomies between rural and urban areas, of which there are many. His remarkable scholarship, though, provides a deeper insight about the fundamental inseparability of these two places. In Cronon's words: "We all live in the city. We all live in the country."[86] Peel away the rhetorical veneer and "[w]hat often seem separate narratives finally converge in a larger tale of people reshaping the land to match their collective vision of its destiny."[87]

The relationship Cronon describes is largely a commercial one. Today that commercial linkage is perhaps less central—encompassed increasingly by a growing regional identity, fathered in significant part by Wallace Stegner, and championed today by people like Charles Wilkinson and by a changing economy and demography that blur the traditional separation of rural and urban. Cities grow to meet other cities, as along the Front Range of Colorado and the Wasatch Front of Utah. And cities spread out farther and farther into rural areas. People living in the western states increasingly tend to view themselves as westerners rather than as, say, Coloradans. People move to "the West," not just to Phoenix or Las Vegas, where they end up living. And, like me, many discover a West with a proud ranching and agricultural heritage they had thought little about. Some learn that this heritage could not have developed without a wholesale commitment of the region's water resources.

Growth in the West no longer is linked directly to the use of water. As much as anything, it is linked to quality of life. The Faustian bargain we face today is whether we are willing to sell that quality of life for the next one hundred years of economic development, or whether we might have learned something from our experience with water.

It is still possible to restore parts of the water-based West that were readily sacrificed in this century to "development." It is possible to reclaim at least portions of western waterways for the rivers they once were: to restore and protect their native fisheries and aquatic life, their wetlands, their riparian areas. It is possible to remove dams, probably far more than we now realize, and to make those that we need operate in ways that better support essential river functions. It is still possible to meet direct human needs, today and in the foreseeable future, with far less water than we are using today.

If an important part of the history of the West can be told through the development and use of its water over the past 150 years, then much of the West of the future will be reflected in what it now chooses to do with its water. What is offered in this book is an approach to water issues intended to create a deliberate process for reshaping the manner in which water is used and enjoyed. Just as the reclamation vision of 1902 foresaw a West of irrigated family farms supported by the damming and diversion of its rivers, so too a reclamation vision of today might foresee a West with its rivers reshaped anew to meet the desires and needs of today's West.

There is nothing inevitable about the trends toward sustainability suggested here. Indeed, it is far more likely that we will continue to use water in pretty much the same manner that we do now, that we will continue to manage and use rivers as we do now, that we will continue to make decisions about these matters in the manner we do now. Those who established these approaches believed they made sense. They may not be happy with the way things are working, but at least they know how things are working. At the same time, change *is* occurring. Irrigation water uses *are* getting more efficient. Water-based environmental values *are* getting more protection. Uses of water *are* shifting. Our stories illustrate well the adjustments that are occurring across the West.

This is not a book preaching the existence of a "water crisis" and offering a path to salvation. Rather, it is intended to be a book that says the choices we make about water matter. They matter not because we are all about to die of thirst or from drinking poisoned water or because our water-based ecological systems are about to collapse—though these are all evils clearly to be avoided. They matter because the manner in which we use water says so much about who we are as a society. The future of the Lower Arkansas Valley in Colorado turns in no small part on decisions that are made about use of the Arkansas River and its connected alluvial aquifer. These are the decisions of traditional users—agricultural irrigators and cities.

They are the decisions of new users–those in growing urban areas and in recreation. They are the decisions of those now empowered to protect the ecological values of water–the Corps of Engineers and the Fish and Wildlife Service. The same is true in the Grand Valley, the Lahontan Valley, and the Yakima Valley.

The approaches suggested are directions, not quick fixes. I characterized them as "for the twenty-first century," and by that I mean the century–not just the year 2000. The particulars are less important than is an acknowledgment that they should be shaped by a clear view of our objectives. If we are to have in the West, as Wallace Stegner has urged, a "society to match its scenery,"[88] we must use our rivers, our aquifers, and their water wisely.

Notes

PREFACE

1. See, for example, E. Walter Coward, Jr., "Indigenous Organization, Bureau-cracy, and Development," *The Journal of Development Studies* 13, no. 1 (Oct. 1976): 92–105; E. Walter Coward, Jr., "Principles of Social Organization in an Indigenous Irrigation System," *Human Organization* 38, no. 4 (Winter 1979): 395–400. For a good overview of issues concerning irrigation organization and development in Asia, including sociological observations by Walt Cow-ard, see E. Walter Coward, Jr., ed., *Irrigation and Agricultural Development in Asia: Perspectives from the Social Sciences,* (Ithaca, N.Y.: Cornell University Press, 1980).
2. Sarah F. Bates et al., *Searching Out the Headwaters: Change and Rediscovery in Western Water Policy* (Washington D.C.: Island Press, 1993).
3. James N. Corbridge, Jr., ed., *Special Water Districts: Challenge for the Future* (Boulder, Colo.: Natural Resources Law Center, in cooperation with the Center for Natural Resource Studies, [1984]).

INTRODUCTION

1. Sixty years ago fewer than 50 percent of all Westerners were city dwellers; today 86 percent reside in urban areas. According to historian Richard White, the West has been the nation's most urbanized region since the 1890s. *"It's Your Misfortune and None of My Own:" A History of the American West* (Norman: University of Oklahoma Press, 1991), 184.
2. Plants evolved in the ocean. Viewed in evolutionary terms, their existence on land has been brief. Plant growth (photosynthesis) depends on water, carbon dioxide, and solar radiation. In the sea, plants were immersed in water, and carbon dioxide was readily available. On land, radiation is much more available, but water and carbon dioxide are less available.

    To utilize carbon dioxide out of the atmosphere, plant cells must dissolve the gas in water—a process that requires wet cell walls to be exposed to the atmosphere. Large amounts of water are evapotranspired during this process, perhaps as much as one hundred times as much water as is retained in the plant. It is primarily this water that must be replaced through irrigation in areas with little rainfall.

    Land plants have made some remarkable adaptations. Perhaps most obvious is the development of a root system capable of drawing in water from relatively large areas of soil. In addition, land plants have developed a vascular system capable of moving water rapidly within the plant. Land plants also have developed an epidermis, a covering that allows in carbon dioxide while reducing water loss. (Dr. John S. Boyer, written communication to members of Committee on the Future of Irrigation in the Face of Competing Demands, 1994.)

3. Indeed, there is a religious-like fervor that characterizes the writings of irrigation promoters in the late 1800s and early 1900s. Perhaps most prominent are the books of William B. Smythe such as *The Conquest of Arid America* (New York: Macmillan, 1905).

4. Total freshwater withdrawals for the western United States, including Alaska and Hawaii, were estimated at 179 million acre-feet in 1990—an increase of 30 percent over 1960 estimates. Of this, agriculture continues to be the largest use category in the western States at an estimated 140 million acre-feet in 1990. At the same time, human population in the West increased by 75 percent between 1960 and 1990, at nearly double the national population growth rate, leading to increased domestic use of freshwater supplies. Although total withdrawals increased by 35 percent and population increased by 29 percent between 1960 and 1975, from 1975 to 1990 total withdrawals actually decreased 2 percent while population increased by another 35 percent. And withdrawals for irrigation and livestock increased by 28 percent between 1960 and 1975, but decreased by 7 percent from 1975 to 1990. However, the general declines in groundwater withdrawals since 1975 and agricultural withdrawals since 1980 have been largely because of the use of more water-efficient irrigation systems and less water-intensive crops, and because fewer acres are being irrigated by groundwater due to declining water levels in some areas. Thus, these figures demonstrate that the rate of change in total water withdrawal patterns in the West is due more to changes in irrigation, the dominant use, than to population change. Of note, between 1960 and 1990 domestic per-capita use increased from 129 gallons per day in 1960 to 160 gallons per day in 1990. The following table illustrates comparative water use by category in 1960 and 1990 as a percentage of total withdrawals.

Water Use Category	1960	1990
Agriculture	86%	78%
Domestic	5%	8%
Thermoelectric Power Generation	4%	9%
Hydroelectric Power Generation (in-stream use)	752*	1,730*

*million acre-feet

    See Department of the Interior, *Estimates of Water Use in the Western United States in 1990, and Water Use Trends, 1960–1990*, by Wayne B. Solley, open-file report, U.S. Geological Survey, 97–176 (Washington, D.C.: 1997).

5. Leslie F. Sheffield, *Economic Impact of Irrigated Agriculture* (Arlington, Va: Irrigation Association Educational Foundation, 1985). See also Kenneth D. Frederick with James C. Hanson, *Water for Western Agriculture* (Washington, D.C.: Resources for the Future, 1982); National Research Council, *A New Era for Irrigation* (Washington, D.C.: National Academy Press, 1996).

6. According to the Department of Agriculture, nationwide the average value of irrigated cropland in 1988 was $1,573 per acre compared to $726 per acre for dry cropland and $316 per acre for grazing land. Department of Agriculture, *Agricultural Irrigation and Water Use*, by Rajinder S. Bajwa et al., Agriculture Information Bulletin 638, Jan. 1992, 3. This same report concluded that the average irrigated farm produces 4.5 times the value of crops as does the average nonirrigated farm (p. 2). See also Frederick, *Water for Western Agriculture*. According to the National Research Council, "Irrigated agriculture occurs on just 14.8 percent of the harvested cropland and yet produces 37.8 percent of the value of crops" (*New Era for Irrigation*, 47).

7. According to the 1992 Agricultural Census, 279,357 farms irrigated 49,401,030 acres in the United States as a whole. Of this, the seventeen western states of California, Oregon, Washington, Idaho, Utah, Nevada, Arizona, Colorado, New Mexico, Wyoming, Montana, North Dakota, South Dakota, Nebraska, Kansas, Oklahoma, and Texas accounted for 204,329 farms, which irrigated 39,076,240 acres of farmland. See Department of Commerce, Bureau of the Census, *1992 Census of Agriculture: Farm and Ranch Irrigation Survey (1994),* vol. 3 of Related Surveys, pt. 1 (Washington, D.C.: Government Printing Office, 1996), 1 (table 1). The Department of the Interior calculates the total acreage of these seventeen western states at 1,160,129,920 acres. See Department of the Interior, Bureau of Land Management, *Public Land Statistics 1996* (Washington, D.C.: Government Printing Office, 1997), 6 (table 1.3). (This publication is now available on-line at <http://www.blm.gov/nhp/pubs/PLS>.) Thus, 3.4 percent of the total land area of these seventeen western states is irrigated.

Moreover, large areas of formerly irrigated lands already have shifted out of agricultural use. Although data on the amount of irrigated lands that have been permanently retired from agricultural use are sparse, the 1992 Census of Agriculture published the results of a follow-up farm irrigation survey, which shows that between 1992 and 1994 an estimated 18,787 farms, which had irrigated a total of 1.6 million acres, had discontinued irrigation. However, the majority–80 percent–of these farm operators reported that their discontinuance was not permanent, citing reasons such as sufficient soil moisture, a shortage of surface or groundwater, uneconomical conditions, equipment failure, and loss or sale of water rights as the cause of irrigation discontinuance. Therefore, the remaining 20 percent of farmers reporting permanent discontinuance of irrigation amounted to 3,747 farms retiring 152,055 acres of irrigated farmland in the United States.

In the seventeen western states this amounted to a total of 9,179 farms discontinuing irrigation on 684,616 acres of farmland, with 2,493 farms reportedly permanently retiring 80,248 acres of irrigated farmland. In addition, it is noteworthy that *all* of the 77 farms reportedly selling their water rights in the entire United States between 1992 and 1994 were from the seventeen western states. This amounted to a total of 7,370 acres retired due to a sale of irrigation-water rights in the West. See U.S. Department of Commerce, *1992 Census of Agriculture,* 141 (table 35).

8. Sam Bingham, *The Last Ranch: A Colorado Community and the Coming Desert* (New York: Pantheon Books, 1996), 6.

9. Contemporary western historians and writers point out the almost warlike mentality often prevalent in the thinking of those settling and developing the West in the nineteenth and much of the twentieth century. Thus historian Patricia Nelson Limerick focuses on "conquest" in *The Legacy of Conquest* (New York: W.W. Norton, 1987); Donald Worster identifies "empire" in *Rivers of Empire: Water, Aridity, and the Growth of the American West* (New York: Pantheon Books, 1985).

10. These statistics are taken from Western Water Policy Review Advisory Commission, *Water in the West: Challenge for the Next Century* (Denver: 1998), 2-14.

11. For some journalistic impressions of recent western growth see Timothy Egan, "Urban Sprawl Strains Western States," *New York Times,* Dec. 29, 1996. *See also* Timothy Egan, "The Mild West: Tourists Ride Into Town, Cowboys Ride Into the Sunset," *New York Times,* July 5, 1992 (discussing the loss— indeed, the colonization—of western heritage as a result of urban growth: "The West as a home for dust-chewing cowboys, lonely ranchers and strong-willed miners and loggers has all but disappeared. But the West as a theme park built around its legends is stronger than ever."); Timothy Egan, "Boomtown U.S.A.," *New York Times,* Nov. 14, 1993 (discussing the transformation of Boise, Idaho, a national leader in job growth, from a farming community to a diversified, high-tech economy); Timothy Egan, "Las Vegas Stakes Claim in Nineties Water War," *New York Times,* April 10, 1994 (discussing Las Vegas's attempt to appropriate additional portions of the Colorado River to meet its growing population); Timothy Egan, "Portland's Hard Line on Managing Growth," *New York Times,* Dec. 30, 1996.

12. Center for the American West, *Atlas of the New West: Portrait of a Changing Region* (New York: W.W. Norton, 1997).

13. See, for example, Wallace Stegner, *Where the Bluebird Sings to the Lemonade Springs: Living and Writing in the West* (New York: Random House, 1992). ("Aridity, more than anything else, gives the western landscape its character," p. 46.)

14. Marc Reisner, *Cadillac Desert: The American West and Its Disappearing Water* (New York: Penguin Books, 1993); Philip L. Fradkin, *A River No More: The Colorado River and the West* (Berkeley: University of California Press, 1996); Worster, *Rivers of Empire;* William L. Kahrl, *Water and Power: The Conflict Over Los Angeles' Water Supply in the Owens Valley* (Berkeley: University of California Press, 1982); Russell Martin, *A Story That Stands Like a Dam: Glen Canyon and the Struggle for the Soul of the West* (New York: Holt, 1989).

15. Wallace Earle Stegner, *Beyond the Hundredth Meridian: John Wesley Powell and the Second Opening of the West* (Boston: Houghton Mifflin, 1954); Wallace Stegner, *Angle of Repose* (New York: Penguin Books, 1991); Mary Hunter Austin, *The Land of Little Rain* (Gloucester: P. Smith, 1969); Marie Sandoz, *Old Jules* (Lincoln: University of Nebraska Press, 1985); Stanley G. Crawford,

Mayordomo: Chronicle of an Acequia in Northern New Mexico (Albuquerque: University of New Mexico Press, 1980); William deBuys and Alex Harris, *River of Traps: A Village Life* (Albuquerque: University of New Mexico Press, in association with the Center for Documentary Studies at Duke University, 1990); Arthur Maass and Raymond L. Anderson, . . . *And the Desert Shall Rejoice: Conflict, Growth, and Justice in Arid Environments* (Cambridge, Mass.: MIT Press, 1978); Charles F. Wilkinson, *Crossing the Next Meridian: Land, Water, and the Future of the West* (Washington D.C.: Island Press, 1992).

16. National Environmental Policy Act, U.S. Code, vol. 42, sec. 4331(a) (1994).

PART 1

1. David H.Getches, "Meeting Colorado's Water Requirements: An Overview of the Issues," in *Tradition, Innovation, and Conflict: Perspectives on Colorado Water Law,* ed. L.MacDonnell (Boulder, Colo.: Natural Resources Law Center, 1985). This amounts to roughly half the amount of water produced annually in the South Platte drainage to the north, or in the Rio Grande drainage to the west.

2. Zebulon Montgomery Pike, *Zebulon Pike's Arkansaw Journal: In Search of the Southern Louisiana Purchase Boundary Line,* ed. Stephen Harding Hart and Archer Butler Hulbert (Westport: Greenwood Press, 1972).

3. David Lavender, *Bent's Fort* (Lincoln: University of Nebraska Press, 1954), 141–42.

4. The State Historical Society of Colorado has authored and published a good set of essays entitled *Bent's Old Fort* (Denver: 1979). An excellent account of travel on the Santa Fe Trail that includes a stop at Bent's Fort is Susan Shelby Magoffin, *Down the Santa Fe Trail and into Mexico:The Diary of Susan Shelby Magoffin,* ed. Stella M. Drumm (Lincoln: University of Nebraska Press, 1982).

5. Lewis H. Garrard, *Wah-to-Yah and the Taos Trail* (Palo Alto, Calif.: American West Publishing, 1968), 15.

6. Ibid., 31.

7. Ibid., 32.

8. Ibid.

9. Carl Abbott, Stephen J. Leonard, and David McComb, *Colorado: A History of the Centennial State,* rev. ed. (Boulder: Colorado Associated University Press, 1982).

10. Quoted in Stan Hoig, *The Sand Creek Massacre* (Norman: University of Oklahoma Press, 1961), 7–8.

11. Quoted in Hoig, *Sand Creek Massacre,* 68–69.

12. Dena S. Markoff, "The Beet Sugar Industry in Microcosm: The National Sugar Manufacturing Company, 1899 to 1967" (Ph.D. diss., University of Colorado, Boulder, 1980), 33–41. James E. Sherow, *Watering the Valley: Development Along the High Plains Arkansas River, 1870–1950* (Lawrence: University Press of Kansas, 1990), 12.

13. Sherow, *Watering the Valley,* 17.

14. William E. Pabor, *Colorado as an Agricultural State* (New York: Orange Judd, 1883), 112–13. Pabor attributed this unsatisfactory state of affairs to control of the land base by a few large cattle ranchers. One of these ranches, for

example, derived from a Mexican land grant and included essentially the entire Purgatoire River Basin to near its confluence with the Arkansas River.

15. Abbott, Leonard, and McComb, *Colorado: A History*. Boosters like Gilpin were actively recasting the image of the plains as desert to encourage settlement and development of Colorado.

16. Stephen Harriman Long, "A General Description of the Country Traversed by the Exploring Expedition," in *Early Western Travels: 1748–1846*, vol. 17, ed. Reuben Gold Thwaites (Cleveland: Arthur C. Clark, 1905), 94, 147.

17. One observer reported irrigation on lowlands along the Arkansas five miles above Bent's Fort in 1839. Farnham, *Travels on the Great Western Prairies*, cited in Alvin T. Steinel, *History of Agriculture in Colorado* (Fort Collins: Colorado State Board of Agriculture, 1926), 16.

18. Steinel, *History of Agriculture*, 20.

19. Pabor, *Colorado*, 13.

20. For a complete list of all major water rights in the Arkansas River Basin by date of decree as of 1984, see Alan W. Burns, *Selected Hydrographs and Statistical Analyses Characterizing the Water Resources of the Arkansas River Basin, Colorado*, U.S. Geological Survey, Water-Resources Investigation Report 85–4092 (Denver: 1985).

21. Percy S. Fritz, *Colorado: The Centennial State* (New York: Prentice-Hall, 1941), 275.

22. Ibid., 275–76.

23. Ibid., 276.

24. James E. Sherow, "Utopia, Reality, and Irrigation: The Plight of the Fort Lyon Canal Company in the Arkansas River Valley," *Western Historical Quarterly* 20, no. 2 (May 1989): 168.

25. "Water: The Sustainer of Life" and "A Champion Promoter: Theodore C. Henry," folder #453 in the manuscript collection of Michael Creed Hinderlider, Colorado State Historical Society. James E. Sherow, "Marketplace Agricultural Reform: T. C. Henry and the Irrigation Crusade in Colorado, 1883–1914," *Journal of the West* 31, no. 4 (October 1992): 51–58.

26. Sherow, "Utopia," 170–71.

27. *LaJunta and Lamar Canal Co. v Hess*, 25 Colo. 513 (1898); *LaJunta and Lamar Canal Co. v Hess, and La Junta and Lamar Canal Co. v Fort Lyon Canal Co.*, 31 Colo. 1 (1903); *Blakely v Fort Lyon Canal Co.*, 31 Colo. 224 (1903).

28. John Wesley Powell et al., *Report on the Lands of the Arid Region of the United States, With a More Detailed Account of the Lands of Utah*, 2d ed. (Washington D.C.: Government Printing Office, 1879).

29. Department of the Interior, Census Office, *Report on Agriculture by Irrigation in the Western Part of the United States at the Eleventh Census: 1890*, by F. H. Newell (Washington D.C.: Government Printing Office, 1894), 123.

30. *Irrigation and Reclamation of Arid Lands*, 51st Cong., 1st sess., 1890, S. Rept. 928, serial 2708.

31. Regional Director's Report on Initial Development Gunnison-Arkansas Project, Roaring Fork Diversion, Colorado, January 1950 at 23 in Fryingpan-Arkansas Project, *Letter from Acting Secretary of the Interior Transmitting Report on the Fryingpan-Arkansas Project, Colorado, Pursuant to Section 9 (A) of the Reclamation Project Act of 1939* (53 Stat. 1187), June 18, 1953, Committee Print.

32. Markoff, *Beet Sugar Industry*, 55

33. Ibid., 64.

34. Ibid., 69.

35. This story is related in chap. 3 of Markoff, *Beet Sugar Industry*.

36. Ibid., 106.

37. Imported sugar comprised roughly 90 percent of the domestic U.S. sugar supply at that time. This "duty" was therefore more rightly considered an import tax, from which customs revenues for raw sugar averaged $55 million for the years immediately preceding 1890. During this time period the United States was realizing a large surplus in customs revenue, and sugar was the single largest contributing revenue item. Because only one tenth of the sugar was produced domestically—almost entirely from the sugar-cane districts of Louisiana—this protective duty was politically criticized as lacking connection to widespread economic need for specific market protection. As a result bills were introduced in the House and the Senate in 1888 proposing a reduction in the sugar duty, and there was widespread political agreement among both Democrats and Republicans that a reduction was needed.

   However, the Republican-sponsored McKinley Tariff Act of 1890 went further than these previous proposals, for it allowed *all raw sugar* to be imported free of charge. In place of the repealed duty, the act instituted a duty of one half cent per pound on *refined sugar* to protect domestic sugar refineries. This provision was open to political criticism on the grounds that it merely served (as it did) the dominant market position of the "Sugar Trust," which had attained a virtual monopoly in domestic sugar refining just prior to the passage of the act. Furthermore, the act bestowed a "bounty" (i.e., subsidy) of two cents per pound—the rate of the former duty simply inverted—on domestic raw sugar to protect the nominal market position of domestic sugar producers.

   The act passed in October of 1890; congressional elections were held immediately thereafter in November. Politically, public outrage at what was perceived to be a monopolistic and protectionist measure led to an overwhelming ouster of the Republican party at the polls. Republicans were beaten as they had never been beaten before, losing their majority position in both the House and the Senate. The shift in political power to the Democrats resulted in passage of a new Tariff Act in 1894, which repealed the bounty provision and replaced it with an ad valorem duty on imported raw sugar while retaining the duty on imported refined sugar. F. W. Taussig, *The Tariff History of the United States*, 8th ed. (New York: G. P. Putnam's Sons, 1931), 275–77, 284.

38. Markoff, *Beet Sugar Industry*, 124.

39. According to Sherow (*Watering the Valley*, 103): "By 1900 Coloradans, through the prior appropriation system, had put to use nearly all of the surface water in the Arkansas River Valley. Nearly 100 ditch systems irrigated more than 7,000 farms on more than 300,000 acres. Pueblo and Colorado Springs had built elaborate public waterworks serving approximately 50,000 people. The Colorado Fuel and Iron Company, which employed about 16,000 people and supplied the High Plains region with coal, managed a complex water system for manufacturing steel and mining coal."

40. The Colorado Fuel and Iron Company (CF&I), Colorado's most important corporation around the turn of the century, was an outgrowth of the spread of western railroad enterprises. CF&I evolved from the Colorado Coal and Iron Company, a conglomerate of three smaller firms from William Jackson Palmer's Rio Grande empire. This enterprise was originally intended to perform many functions: the sale of town lots and agricultural lands, the mining and marketing of coal, the manufacturing of coke, and the production of iron and steel at Pueblo. However, for the decade after its opening in 1882, the Colorado Coal and Iron Company struggled to compete with larger eastern suppliers of steel for the business of western railroads in need of rails. During this time the $2 million steel-works venture was kept alive largely by the sale of domestic and railroad coal and the production of coke for Colorado smelters, rather than the sale of steel products.

    Although Colorado Coal and Iron enjoyed a relatively strong overall market position, entrepreneur John C. Osgood organized the Colorado Fuel Company in 1884 to compete with Colorado Coal and Iron in the coal market. Due to important contracts with major western railroads, aggressive acquisitions of coal lands in Colorado, and strategic alliances with key Denver businessmen, Osgood's corporation emerged between 1888 and 1892 as the largest coal producer in the Rocky Mountain West region. The result of this market dominance was a merger of the two companies, at Osgood's behest, in 1892. The new Colorado Fuel and Iron Company emerged with 45 percent of the state's output of coal and possessed the only integrated steel plant in the entire West. And over the next decade CF&I merged with numerous smaller outfits to raise its market share of Colorado coal production to 75 percent. CF&I then retooled the Bessemer works at Pueblo between 1899 and 1903, at a cost of $20 million , and was able to triple its output through a national pooling agreement, which granted CF&I 7 percent of the national market for steel rails. At its height CF&I employed an "army" of over 15,000 people, from clerical help to coal miners, stretching its empire from Wyoming south to New Mexico. Abbott, Leonard, and McComb, *Colorado*, 135–36.

41. Sherow, *Watering the Valley*, 71. A company study in 1905 determined that, at full operation, the plant would need a "daily supply of 48 to 50 million gallons."

42. *Kansas v Colorado,* 206 U.S. 46 (1906). Under art. 3, sec. 2, cl. 2 of the United States Constitution, the Supreme Court has original jurisdiction in "all cases . . . in which a state shall be a party." This original jurisdiction has been invoked to resolve interstate water use disputes on the Arkansas, Colorado, Connecticut, Delaware, Laramie, Mississippi, North Platte, Rio Grande, Vermejo, and Walla Walla rivers. See A. Dan Tarlock, James N. Corbridge, Jr., and David H. Getches, *Water Resources Management: A Casebook in Law and Policy*, 4th ed. (New York: Foundation Press, 1993), 832.

43. Sherow, *Watering the Valley*, provides a lengthy discussion of this irrigation development in chap. 5.

44. The Supreme Court explained that, in balancing the prior-appropriation doctrine of Colorado with the riparian doctrine of Kansas, equitable apportionment required that the Court "consider the effect of what has been done upon the conditions in the respective States and so adjust the dispute

upon the basis of *equality of rights* as to secure as far as possible to Colorado the benefits of irrigation without depriving Kansas of the like beneficial effects of a flowing stream." *Kansas v Colorado,* 206 U.S. at 100 (emphasis added).

For an excellent discussion of the *Kansas v Colorado* case and some of the subsequent developments in the equitable apportionment doctrine, *see* A. Dan Tarlock, "The Law of Equitable Apportionment Revisited, Updated, and Revised," *University of Colorado Law Review* 56, no. 3 (1985): 381.

45. *Kansas v Colorado,* 206 U.S. at 117.

46. Despite a series of "relief to water users" acts in 1922, 1923, and 1924 extending the time in which payments must be made, see *Relief to Water Users Act,* U.S. Statutes at Large 42 (1922): 489 ("An Act to authorize the Secretary of Interior to extend the time for payment of charges due on reclamation projects"); *Extend Relief to Water Users Act,* U.S. Statutes at Large 43 (1923): 1324 ("An act to extend the time for repayment of charges due on reclamation projects"); *1924 Relief Act,* U.S. Statutes at Large 43 (1924): 116 ("An act to authorize the deferring of payments of reclamation charges").

47. Sherow, *Watering the Valley,* 131.

48. E. Louise Peffer, *The Closing of the Public Domain: Disposal and Reservation Policies 1900–50* (Stanford, Calif.: Stanford University Press, 1951), 220. Senator Gore of Oklahoma was moved to comment that the dust storms were the "most impressive lobbyist that have ever come to this Capitol."

49. Stats. at Large of USA 4 (1846): 22-23.

50. Department of Agriculture, Economic Research Service, *A History of Federal Water Resources Programs, 1800–1960,* by Beatrice Hort Holmes, Miscellaneous Publication No. 1233 (1972), 3.

51. Sherow, *Watering the Valley,* 138.

52. According to Commissioner of Reclamation Michael Strauss: "This development would provide (a) about 185,000 acre-feet of supplemental irrigation water at canal headgates in the Arkansas Valley through transmountain diversion, conservation of flood flows, re-regulation of winter flow, and reuse of return flows for water-thirsty lands which, even with this additional supply, will experience an average annual headgate shortage of about 16 percent; (b) about 15,000 acre-feet of municipal water to supplement the municipal water supply for Colorado Springs, Pueblo, and several Arkansas Valley towns where additional quantity and better quality water is critically needed; (c) about 467 million kilowatt-hours of electric energy to help meet the critical need for electric power in the project service area and permit expansion in the normal uses of electric energy; (d) flood protection which would eliminate 66 percent of the probable annual flood damages between Pueblo and the John Martin Reservoir, estimated to be about $890,000; (e) sediment control, stream-pollution abatement, and preservation and propagation of fish and wildlife in certain areas; all of which are important and valuable contributions of the project." Proposed Report of the Commissioner of Reclamation to the Secretary of the Interior, April 16, 1951, reprinted in *Fryingpan-Arkansas Project,* House Document No. 187, Government Printing Office, 1953, 11.

53. U.S. Statutes at Large 76 (1962): 389. The project cost more than a half billion dollars to build and was completed in 1982. In addition to structures

on the West Slope that divert and move water through the mountains to the Arkansas Basin, the project added greatly increased storage space in the Arkansas Basin, including the Pueblo Reservoir located just upstream of the city with more than 350,000 acre-feet of capacity. Designed to bring about 70,000 acre-feet of Colorado River Basin water into the Arkansas Basin annually, actual transmountain diversions have averaged about 53,500 acre-feet. (Bureau of Reclamation, *Water Management of the Arkansas River,* by Roger Weidelman, revised draft, Oct. 5, 1993, p.2.)

Water made available by the Fryingpan-Arkansas Project is allocated to municipal and irrigation users by the Southeastern Colorado Water Conservancy District, the entity that is responsible for paying a total of about $195 million to the United States over a fifty-year period that began in 1982. Conservancy districts are a form of special government initially authorized in Colorado in 1937. See *Water Conservancy Act,* Colorado Revised Statutes sec. 37–45–101 to sec. 37–45–148 (1990 and supp. 1996). They hold considerable governmental authority, including the power to assess a tax on all property within their boundaries. Under "allocation principles" adopted by Southeastern's board of directors in 1979, at least 51 percent of the annual project water supply is allocated initially to municipal and domestic use. Water for irrigation uses must supplement other supplies already available to the users. Ditch companies within the boundaries of the district make requests for project water in the spring of each year, which are acted on by the board according to the amount of water expected to be available. The district pays the United States eight dollars for every acre-foot of water the project makes available for urban or irrigation use (amended contract, sec. 11). Actual demand for project water between 1982 and 1989 averaged about 45,400 acre-feet, with a high of about 108,700 and a low of about 12,500 (Bureau of Reclamation, Review of Operations, Fryingpan-Arkansas Project, Colorado, Sept. 1990, table 8, p. 37).

54. W. W. Wheeler and Associates and Woodward-Clyde Associates, *Water Legislation Investigations for the Arkansas River Basin in Colorado,* vol. 2 of *Comprehensive Report* (Denver: 1968), 9; see also *Fellhauer v People of the State of Colorado,* 447 P.2d 986, 989 (Colo. 1968).

55. Gordon McCurry reviewed and improved this lay description of groundwater hydrology. His comments are greatly appreciated.

56. Doug Cain, "Water Facts and Figures: Quantity and Quality," in *Arkansas River Basin Water Forum: "A River of Dreams and Realities,"* Colorado Water Resources Research Institute Information Series No. 82 (Fort Collins: Colorado State University, 1995), 62. Roughly 13 million acre-feet of groundwater is estimated to be contained in the entire basin in Colorado.

57. Office of the State Engineer, *Stream Depletion by Wells in the Arkansas River Basin–Colorado, March 1975* (Denver: Colorado Department of Natural Resources: 1975), 19, table 6.

58. Ibid., 22, table 7.

59. *Fellhauer v People,* 447 P.2d 986, 988 (Colo. 1968).

60. *Safronek v Lemon,* 123 Colo. 330, 228 P.2d 975 (1951). A discussion of Colorado groundwater law and its efforts to integrate groundwater pumping with surface water diversions is provided in MacDonnell, "Colorado's Law of

'Underground Water': The South Platte River and Beyond," *University of Colorado Law Review* 59 (1988): 579–625. Unused water percolating into the ground from ditches, laterals, and cultivated fields eventually finds its way back to the river. In the late 1800s a few people noticed that these return flows actually increased the flow of the Poudre during the mid to late irrigation season, making more water available for diversion by downstream irrigators. The importance of this fortuitous event was not lost on those observers, and the legal system adopted the more general principle that groundwater in Colorado is presumed to be connected to surface water. R. L. Parshall, "The Importance of Return Flow to Colorado Irrigators," in *A Hundred Years of Irrigation in Colorado . . . 1852* (Denver: Colorado Water Conservation Board, 1952), 58.

61. In 1969 the General Assembly responded with changes in water law that made it possible for groundwater pumping to continue, so long as any water actually taken from another user was replaced from some other source. Additional litigation in the 1970s resulted in a system under which wells already in operation prior to the 1969 statute were permitted to pump unregulated for three of out every seven days. New wells had to replace any water they depleted from the river. In practice little changed respecting existing groundwater use in the Arkansas Valley, but new development effectively stopped.

62. "Arkansas River Compact," Colorado Revised Statutes (1990), sec. 37–69–101 to sec. 37–69–106 (1990); Kansas Statutes, Annotated (1989), sec. 82a–520. The U.S. Congress subsequently ratified the compact reached between Colorado and Kansas in U.S. Statutes at Large 63 (1949): 145

In 1928 Colorado had filed an action against Kansas seeking a decree that would bring certainty to the two states' respective claims to the water of the Arkansas River. The John Martin Reservoir became the vehicle through which this resolution would be accomplished. A stipulation in 1933 allocated water users in Colorado below the dam 160,000 acre-feet of water annually (Sherow, *Watering the Valley,* 136). Finally, in 1944, the U.S. Supreme Court rendered its decision. *Colorado v Kansas,* 320 U.S. 383 (1944). Reminiscent of its earlier decision, the Court found no convincing evidence that water uses in Colorado had clearly harmed users in Kansas and urged the states to work out an agreement for allocation of the river's water. Colorado agreed to deliver to the Kansas line 52,000 acre-feet in the irrigation season and 25,000 acre-feet in the winter. If less than 237,000 acre-feet of water were available in any year, 32.5 percent would go to Kansas and 67.5 percent to Colorado. If more than 237,000 acre-feet were available, the excess would be split fifty-fifty between the two states.

63. Generally, all flows of the Arkansas River reaching the reservoir between November 1 and March 31 are stored. Under an agreement reached in 1980, 40 percent of the stored water goes into a "Kansas account," and 60 percent into a "Colorado account," which is divided among the nine canal companies in Colorado diverting Arkansas River water below the dam. Inflows during the summer are passed through up to 750 cubic feet per second. Flows above 750 cubic feet per second are added to storage. To respond to the Bureau of Reclamation's proposed Gunnison-Arkansas Project and other upstream development interests, the compact included a provision recognizing that additional development would occur, but requiring that any such

development not "materially deplete" waters of the Arkansas River used at the time of the compact.

64. *Kansas v Colorado,* 524 U.S. 675 (1995).

65. Department of the Interior, Bureau of Reclamation, *Review of Operations, Fryingpan-Arkansas Project,* final draft (Colorado, July 1990), 16–22.

66. M. F. Hockemeyer, "Winter Storage Is New Irrigation Tool," *Arkansas Valley Journal,* July 9, 1983.

67. Donald L. Miles, *Salinity in the Arkansas Valley of Colorado* (Denver: Colorado State University Extension Service, 1977), 10. Taylor O. Miller, Gary D. Weatherford, and John E. Thorson, *The Salty Colorado* (Washington, D.C.: Conservation Foundation, 1986).

68. The term "concentration" generally denotes how much of one material (chemical mass) is in a specified quantity (volume) of an environmental medium such as air, water, soil, or food. In particular, concentrations of contaminants in water are phrased either as the mass of a contaminant per given volume of water (usually 1 liter) or as the mass of a contaminant per given mass of water. To illustrate, the former "mass/volume" concentration method is expressed as the number of milligrams of chemical X per liter of water. Now, because we know that 1 liter of water at 4°C has a mass of 1,000 grams, we can also express the mass of chemical X in milligrams per liter as being equivalent to the mass of chemical X in milligrams/1,000 grams–in other words, as the latter "mass/mass" expression. To quantify, there are 1 million milligrams in 1,000 grams, or 1 milligram is equal to one millionth of 1,000 grams. Thus, a *concentration of 1 milligram per liter is equal to one part per million.* Extrapolating, this means that 1 microgram per liter is equal to one part per billion, and so on. The following table reveals how the different units for measuring water pollution concentrations can be used interchangeably.

Mass/Volume	Mass/Mass	Dimensionless
Milligrams/Liter =	Milligrams/1,000 grams =	Parts per Million (PPM)
Micrograms/Liter =	Micrograms/1,000 grams =	Parts per Billion (PPB)
Nanograms/Liter =	Nanograms/1,000 grams =	Parts per Trillion (PPT)

See L. Harold Stevenson and Bruce Wyman, *The Facts on File: Dictionary of Environmental Science* (New York: Facts on File, 1991), 290 (app.).

69. Miles, *Salinity in the Arkansas Valley*, 30

70. Ibid., 1. In total about 85 percent of the total quantity of surface water generated within the basin is consumed before it leaves Colorado.

71. Ibid., 3.

72. *Arkansas Valley Journal,* Jan. 6, March 31, May 5, 1955, cited in Markoff, *Beet Sugar Industry*, 328, n. 2.

73. The Otero is still another T. C. Henry creation. Initiated in 1890 with an appropriation of 123 cubic feet per second, the canal proved unable to provide water to the lands it served. In 1909, now organized as an irrigation district, the Otero constructed Clear Creek Reservoir with a storage capacity of 10,000 acre-feet. With the sale of its storage system in 1955, approximately 5,000 acres of irrigated lands were retired. M. F. Hockemeyer, "T. C. Henry's Magnificent Dream," *Arkansas Valley Journal,* Jan. 2, 1984; M. F.

Hockemeyer, "La Junta Called Garden Spot of Nation," *Arkansas Valley Journal,* Jan. 9, 1984; M. F. Hockemeyer, "Struggle Characterizes Otero District," *Arkansas Valley Journal,* Jan. 16, 1984; "The Otero Reorganizes Twice," *Arkansas Valley Journal,* Jan. 23, 1984.

74. M. F. Hockemeyer, "Water Sale Births 'Colo. Canal Co.,'" *Arkansas Valley Journal,* September 12, 1983.

75. Markoff, *Beet Sugar Industry,* 359.

76. Kenneth R. Weber, "What Becomes of Farmers Who Sell Their Irrigation Water? The Case of Water Sales in Crowley County, Colorado" (Institute for Behavioral Sciences, University of Colorado, Boulder, November 16, 1989, photocopy), 8. See also Jake Gaffigan, "Sundown on a Jewel," *Colorado Farmer and Rancher,* August 1, 1989, pp. 16–17, 22,33.

77. Weber, "What Becomes," tables 6 and 7.

78. Bruce Yoder, "Canadian Interests Control R.F. Water," *Arkansas Valley Journal,* June 18, 1983.

79. Kenneth R. Weber, "Irrigation, Sugar Beets, Water Sales, and NIMBY Industries: Agricultural Development and Decline in Crowley County, Colorado" (Institute for Behavorial Sciences, University of Colorado, Boulder, April 23, 1990, photocopy), 7.

80. By 1990 Crowley County's population had increased slightly to 3,946 people. Department of Commerce, Bureau of the Census, *1990 Census of Population and Housing: Population and Housing Characteristics for Census Tracts and Block Numbering Areas: Colorado (Outside Metropolitan Areas)* (Washington D.C.: Government Printing Office, 1993), 2.

81. "Water Production of Components of Twin Lakes Reservoir and Canal Company" (provided by John U. Carlson, photocopy), appendix G, Twin Lakes Exhibit K.

82. Kenneth R. Weber, "Irrigation Water Sales from the Sellers' Perspective: The Crowley County, Colorado Case" (Institute for Behavioral Sciences, University of Colorado, Boulder, May 1990, photocopy), 3.

83. Ibid., 4.

84. Weber, "What Becomes," 12.

85. Gaffigan, "Sundown," 22.

86. Weber, "What Becomes," table 13.

87. Weber, "Irrigation, Sugar Beets," 20.

88. Kenneth R. Weber, Irrigation Water Transfers and Communities in Decline: The Marginality of Marginal Analysis (Institute for Behavioral Sciences, University of Colorado, Boulder, June 5, 1990, photocopy), 11.

89. Robert A. Young and R. Garth Taylor, "Some Measures of the Economic Impacts of a Large-Scale Rural to Urban Water Transfer" (paper presented at Seminar on Water Allocation and Transfer Systems in a Maturing Water Economy, University of New England, Armidale, NSW, Australia, July 1990).

90. Charles W. Howe, Jeffrey K. Lazo, and Kenneth R. Weber, "The Economic Impacts of Agriculture-to-Urban Water Transfers on the Area of Origin: A Case Study of the Arkansas River Valley in Colorado," *American Journal of Agricultural Economics* (December 1990), 1200–04.

91. Ibid., 1203

92. Department of Commerce, Bureau of the Census, *1987 Census of Agriculture,*

vol. 1, pt. 6 (Washington, D.C.: Government Printing Office, 1989).

93. Forty thousand acres of land have been removed from the tax base as irrigated lands in Crowley County, dropping the tax assessment from six dollars per acre to twenty-five cents per acre for unused dryland. As of 1994 Olney Springs had only two businesses remaining. A medium security prison at Ordway, the Arkansas Valley Correctional Facility, has been in operation since the late 1980s. The facility was built to house five hundred inmates but has in fact been holding around nine hundred. Employees at prison have not chosen to live in the area. Most commute from Pueblo. Unless something happens to turn things around, Crowley County may be dissolved and rejoined with Otero County as it was at the turn of the century.

94. The Two Forks Dam was to be the biggest water project in the history of Colorado, creating a thirty-one-mile-long, 7,300-acre reservoir in Cheesman Canyon along the South Platte River, with total costs for the undertaking projected to be as high as $1 billion. The 615-foot-high dam would have stored over 358 billion gallons of water, most of the water coming from Colorado River diversions west of the Continental Divide. The project's name, Two Forks, was a reflection of the fact that it was to be located near the confluence of the South Platte and its North Fork and would involve two dams, the Two Forks and Turkshead dams. If Two Forks had been built, the project would have compared in scale with Arizona's Glen Canyon Dam, California's Hetch Hetchy Dam, Nevada's Hoover Dam, and Wyoming's Flaming Gorge Dam. The proposed double curvature, thin-arched Two Forks dam–located twenty-five miles south of metropolitan Denver near the Foothills treatment facility–would have spanned seventeen hundred feet across Cheesman Canyon at the crest, rising more than six hundred feet from the floor of the canyon. Originally, in the 1940s, the dam was envisioned as a much smaller project, with a storage capacity of approximately three hundred thousand acre feet. However, by the time the Denver Water Department attempted to push the project to fruition in the 1980s, the Two Forks Dam would have impounded 1.1 million acre-feet of water in storage, with a capacity to deliver ninety-eight thousand acre-feet, or almost thirty-two billion gallons, of water each year–enough water to satisfy growing water demands in the Denver area for thirty-five years, assuming a population increase of 392,000 new residents. See Elise Jones and Steven L. Yaffee, "The Two Forks Project (A)" (School of Natural Resources, University of Michigan, 1992, discussion draft), 1, 11–12; Daniel F. Luecke, "Controversy Over the Two Forks Dam," *Environment* 32, no. 4 (May 1990): 42.

95. *1991, Annual Reports of the Officers of the Fort Lyon Canal Company* (Las Animas, Colo.: Fort Lyon Canal Company, 1991), 20.

96. Gronning Engineering Company, *Fort Lyon Canal Company Water Transfer Alternatives Study, Final Report* (Denver: Colorado Water Conservation Board, February 1994), 1–3.

97. Chris Woodka, "Farmer Favors Selling, but Not to These Guys," *Pueblo Chieftain,* Jan. 26, 1992.

98. Dean Preston, "Board Trades Words with Water Developers," *Pueblo Chieftain,* Feb. 21, 1992.

99. Gronning Engineering, *Fort Lyon Canal*, 2–3.

100. Chris Woodka, "Canal Shareholders Face Dilemma," *Pueblo Chieftain*, Jan. 26, 1996; Jana Mazanec, "Farmers Consider Selling Water to Thirsty Denver," *USA Today*, Jan. 29, 1992.

101. *Arkansas Valley Journal*, March 5, 1992.

102. For a discussion of Colorado water transfer law see MacDonnell, "Changing Uses of Water in Colorado: Law and Policy," *Arizona Law Review* 31, no. 4 (1989): 783–816.

103. Gronning Engineering, *Fort Lyon Canal*, 2–4.

104. Ibid., 2–5.

105. MacDonnell et al., *The Water Transfer Process as a Management Option for Meeting Changing Water Demand*, vol. 1 (Boulder, Colo.: Natural Resources Law Center, 1990).

106. Gronning Engineering, *Fort Lyon Canal*, 4–16. In fact, in 1990 Fort Lyon farmers grew alfalfa on over 57,000 acres–63 percent of all lands. Alfalfa production in that year totaled nearly 220,000 tons with an estimated value of more than $16 million. Corn, sorghum, wheat, and barley accounted for the remainder of the Fort Lyon lands planted with crops.

107. Ibid., 3–7.

108. Ibid., 3–8.

109. Gronning Engineering, *Fort Lyon Canal*, 2–13.

110. MacDonnell, "Marketing Water Rights: A New Trading System Is Developing in the American West to Accommodate Increasing Demands on This Scarce Resource," *Forum for Applied Research and Public Policy* 13 (3): 52-55.

111. Demographic changes in the eight westernmost contiguous states were dramatic during the 1980s and show no sign of letting up in the near future. The population increase during this period for these eight states illustrates this migration pattern, largely to the inland or intermountain West: for example, the population of Arizona increased by 34.8 percent, California by 25.7 percent, Idaho by 6.7 percent, Montana by 1.6 percent, Nevada by 50.1 percent, Oregon by 7.9 percent, Utah by 17.9 percent, and Washington by 17.8 percent. Although largely an outgrowth of economic depression and postindustrial discontent in California–over a half million people left California in 1990 alone–this out-migration to adjacent western states is part and parcel of a larger social movement away from industrial centers and toward rural landscapes–a movement that defines the "New West." William G. Robbins, *Colony and Empire: The Capitalist Transformation of the American West* (Lawrence: University of Kansas Press, 1994), 189, 193 (in particular, see chap. 10, "Epilogue: Recycling the Old West").

In the aggregate, very few regions in the world have experienced the same level of population growth as the American West, which grew from 250,000 people in the latter half of the nineteenth century to a population total of fifty million people today–an increase of 20,000 percent! To put this explosive growth in perspective, if the rest of the world had experienced similar growth rates for this same time period, the global population would now stand at two hundred billion people. Although the western United States is the most urbanized region of the country, this migration trend to the inland West can be characterized as a "lifestyle-driven boom," in which urbanites seek to escape the stresses of modern megalopoli. Nevertheless, major metropolitan centers of the interior West–such as Denver, Salt Lake City, and Phoenix–possess the most sustained growth rates of the region, and this trend shows no sign of waning. Dennis Brownridge, "The Rural West Is Actually Very Urban," in *Reopening the Western Frontier,* ed. Ed Marston (Washington, D.C.: Island Press, 1989), 7–15. (This book is a compilation of four special issues of *High Country News* originally published in fall 1988 dedicated to examining the phenomenon of the resettling of the West.)

112. Dan Hyatt, "Task Force Looks at Single Ownership of Valley Water," *Arkansas Valley Journal,* April 2, 1992.

113. Gronning Engineering, *Fort Lyon Canal,* 6–10 and chap. 7. The water-bank design outlined in the Fort Lyon study would establish a nonprofit organization with a full-time manager and a board of directors. All shareholders within the Fort Lyon Canal Company would be eligible to lease their shares to the bank. Lands irrigated with water available under these shares would have to be "fallowed." Any water user located below the Pueblo Dam in Colorado could rent water from the bank. Sealed lease and rental offers would be accepted by the bank until March 5 of each year. Apparently the bank would "acquire" leased water from the lowest-cost bidders up to some "goal" for acquisitions determined as of February 15. Presumably the goal would be established through prior discussion with potential renters of bank water. Apparently, the bank would then rent the water to those submitting the highest-price bids, up to the amount of water leased. A second bid opening would occur on July 20. Renters from previous years would have a right of first refusal "at the highest bid price." Renters may hold multiyear contracts for water at an established price.

Transactions are based on "transferable yield," essentially the consumptive use of the leased water minus any adjustments necessary to account for losses incurred in storing and delivering the banked water. There is considerable discussion in the proposal regarding the manner in which the bank would be operated to avoid injury to other water users–both within the Fort Lyon Canal and elsewhere in the lower Arkansas River. Apparently there would be detailed case-by-case analysis of all transactions each year to protect against possible injury. Based on an analysis of the Fort Lyon system, factors for return flows, main canal losses, and lateral losses are presented. It is not clear whether these factors will operate as working assumptions for all water to be leased out of the Fort Lyon, or whether there will need to be a site-specific analysis for each transaction. The proposal concludes that about 1.5 units of consumptive-use water must be leased by the bank to provide one unit of rented water.

The Fort Lyon water-bank proposal is tailored to fit a particular situation. It contains considerable detail regarding operational issues in using particular storage systems, and in using exchanges to move Fort Lyon water to other users in the lower Arkansas. At this stage it is simply a consultant's proposal in a report. A substantial number of actions need to be taken before it actually becomes operational, assuming there is support for the proposal from the shareholders of the Fort Lyon Canal Company.

Because it is a canal-specific bank, only shareholders of the Fort Lyon

Canal Company are eligible to lease water to the bank. Furthermore, the water available for the bank may be rented only to users in the Lower Arkansas Valley of Colorado below the Pueblo Reservoir. Some shareholders in the Fort Lyon system have expressed interest in permanently selling their company shares, whereas others have aggressively resisted such sales because of fears about detrimental effects to their water rights and to the irrigated agricultural community in the area. A well-crafted bank could provide alternative economic uses of some of the water (and thus benefits to those shareholders wanting to lease water), while limiting the place of use to the Lower Arkansas Valley helps to assure that the economy of this area would continue to benefit from the use of the water.

Generally, the proposed bank would follow a market approach and would utilize a sealed-bid process twice a year to rent banked water. The proposed approach, however, apparently would attempt to predetermine demand for rental water and would acquire leased water accordingly. It would not simply allow supply and demand to match up. Although bidders would be free to indicate their leasing and renting price, the proposal contains prices, assumed for purposes of analysis, of $60 per acre-foot of consumptive use (leased) and $140 per acre-foot of consumptive use (rented). The difference would be used by the bank to cover its operating expenses and to ensure that there is no injury to other water rights. Thus there is no direct fee, but the implicit cost of the transaction is $80 per acre-foot. The single largest part of the cost is the .5 acre-foot of consumptive-use water assumed to be necessary for release to avoid possible injury to other water rights. The major bank expense is the fixed cost of staff and office. Fees for water storage are the next-largest category of expenses. After some initial substantial start-up losses the bank is projected to generate "profits" in most years.

Considerable attention is given to ensuring that water users will not be injured because of operation of the water bank. Such attention probably reflects the extraordinary sensitivities of many water users in the Arkansas River Basin (and other parts of Colorado) that the long-established return-flow interdependencies among users be protected. For example, even though the transferable yield is restricted to consumptive use, the new use would not be credited with any return flows without a special showing of the existence of such return flows. Protecting water rights is important, but the extremely conservative approach recommended here may impose an unnecessarily high cost on possible water-bank transactions.

The proposed bank will require either the approval of a substitute supply plan by the state engineer or a court decree authorizing its operation. No legislative approval would be necessary.

114. Gronning Engineering, *Fort Lyon Canal,* 6–23.
115. Frank Milenski, *Water: The Answer to a Desert's Prayer* (Swink, Colo.: Milenski Agriculture Consulting Service, 1990).
116. Frank Milenski, *In Quest of Water: A History of the Southeastern Colorado Water Conservancy District and the Fryingpan-Arkansas Project* (Swink, Colo.: Milenski Agricultural Consulting Service, 1993).
117. First acknowledged in *Model Land and Irrigation Co. v Madsen,* 87 Colo. 166,

285 P. 1100 (1930), this principle was supported in *Fort Lyon Canal Co. v Catlin Canal Co.*, 642 P.2d 501 (Colo. 1982).

118. Frank Milenski, *Frank's Ditties* (Swink, Colo.: Milenski Agricultural Consulting Service, 1994).

119. Lower Arkansas River Commission, *Implementation Plan for Water Resources and State Park Development in Southeastern Colorado* (Denver: Lower Arkansas River Commission, 1993).

120. F. N. Beil, *The Great Plains Reservoirs* (Denver: Colorado Water Conservation Board, 1971), 4.

121. Boyle Engineering Corporation, *Engineering Hydrology Study of the Great Plains Reservoirs, Final Report for Colorado Division of Wildlife* (Denver: Boyle Engineering Corporation, 1993).

PART 2

1. William E. Pabor, *Wedding Bells: A Colorado Idyll* (Denver: W. E. Pabor's Sons, 1900), 118.

2. Department of the Interior, Bureau of Land Management, *The Valley of Opportunity: A History of West-Central Colorado,* by Steven F. Mehls (Grand Junction, Colo.: Bureau of Land Management, 1988), 145. We encountered Pabor in part 1 as a promoter of agriculture in the Arkansas Valley. He came to Colorado in the 1870s to become part of the Union Colony, a settlement encouraged by Horace Greeley and based on an idealized model of community-centered agricultural development. Donald J. Pisani, *To Reclaim a Divided West: Water, Law, and Public Policy* (Albuquerque: University of New Mexico Press, 1992), 79–81.

3. Colorado was the name given in 1602 by an Oñate expedition to the stream today known as the Little Colorado. This river was named "Colorado"– which means "red" or "reddish colored" in Spanish–because, as the Oñate expedition put it, "the water is almost red." Over time the name gradually became associated with the lower reach of the main Colorado River.

Because the upper branches of the Colorado were explored and mapped separately in the nineteenth century, the name of the lower river, for many years, extended only to the junction of the Green and Grand rivers. However, at the insistence of the Colorado Legislature in 1921, Congress officially declared that the name of the Grand River would be changed to that of the Colorado River so that some portion of the river would flow through the state of the same name. Earlier, in 1861, when Colorado was organized as a territory, Congress had selected the name Colorado largely on the basis that the headwaters of the main Colorado originated in the territory. This move may have been justified geographically, but it was an unwarranted break from the perspective of established nomenclature. See George R. Stewart, *American Place-Names: A Concise and Selective Dictionary for the Continental United States of America* (New York: Oxford University Press, 1970), 107.

4. Michael Eastin, "The Little Empire of the Western Slope: Boosterism in the Early Grand Valley," *Journal of the Western Slope* 3 (Spring 1988): 28.

5. The Gunnison-Beckwith expedition of 1853 and 1854 traced a course from the San Luis Valley over Cochetopa Pass to the present-day Gunnison River. Fol-

lowing a diversion south around the treacherous Black Canyon of the Gunnison, the expedition traversed to the Uncompaghre River near what is today Montrose, Colorado, and descended the Uncompahgre River Valley down to the Colorado River. The party then shadowed the Colorado River for a short while before cutting west to the Green River. James Schiel, *The Land Between: Dr. James Schiel's Account of the Gunnison-Beckwith Expedition Into the West, 1853–1854*, ed. and trans. Frederick W. Bachmann and William Swilling Wallace (Los Angeles: Westmore Press, 1957), 21–22.

In describing the Gunnison-Beckwith expedition's emergence from the Western Slope of Colorado into the Great Basin in late 1853, Dr. James Schiel observed: "It is a remarkable feature of the character of the whole country between the Rocky Mountains and the Sierra Nevada of California that whole formations disappear, as it were, before our eyes. The washing away of mountains takes place here on an immense scale and is the more easily observed as no vegetation of any account is present to hide the destruction from the eye. Nature seems here only to demolish without developing any compensatory creative activity." Jacob H. Schiel, *Journey Through the Rocky Mountains and the Humboldt Mountains to the Pacific Ocean* (Norman: University of Oklahoma Press, 1959), 57.

Dr. Schiel traced the expedition's path down the Gunnison River Valley, where "[g]rass grows abundantly . . . and the banks of the river are clothed in willow bushes and cottonwoods," to the "valley of the Uncompahgra." Here the expedition encountered "great difficulties" in cutting "through cactus and thick fields of artemisia" (sage) peppered with "thick oak bushes." Schiel found the region to consist largely of "light argillaceous soil" and to be almost "completely without vegetation." The expedition then turned up the "valley of the Grand River," where the "steep slopes of the mountains are covered with a crumbling green sandstone and a red slate giving them an unusually bright coloring whose charm is nevertheless lessened by the desolate barrenness of the entire region and the complete absence of all vegetation" (44, 52).

As Schiel himself described this geologic transformation:

> From the day we climbed down into the valley of the Uncompahgra to the hour we pitched our tents at the foot of the Wasatch Mountains about the middle of October, every agreeable characteristic of the landscape had disappeared with the exception of the view toward these mountains.
>
> The route led chiefly over argillaceous soil, sand or sandstone, which comprises several of the smaller mountain chains. . . . From there washes down the dry, infertile soil of the lowlands along the Grand and Green Rivers. (55–56)

Similarly, the expedition of Colonel John C. Fremont in late 1853 and early 1854 traced a path up the San Luis Valley, across Saguache Creek and into the Saguache Valley, from which the expedition crossed the Continental Divide at Cochetopa Pass and, following the Cochetopa Creek down to Tomichi Creek, descended into the present-day Gunnison River Valley. From there the expedition had to detour south around the impassable Black Canyon of the Gunnison. Then, descending the Uncompahgre River, the party again reached the Gunnison River and followed it down to the Grand (Colorado) River, where they made a difficult crossing near present-day Grand Junction, Colorado.

     After pursuing the Grand River Valley for almost a hundred miles, the expedition then cut southwestward toward the Green River and eventually crossed near the present-day town of Green River, Utah. Solomon Nunes Carvalho described the plateaued expanse between the Colorado and Green rivers as "barren and sterile to a degree" with almost "no water between the two rivers, a distance of about forty miles." Carvalho went on to describe the arid landscape as dominated by "dangerous projections of different strata of rock, thrown into its present state by some convulsion of nature," and inhabited by "[d]warf artemisia," which "grows sparsely in this sandstone" vista. "With Fremont: Solomon Nunes Carvalho's Account of the Fifth Expedition, 27 Nov. 1853–21 Feb. 1854," in *The Expeditions of John Charles Fremont: Travels From 1848 to 1854*, vol. 3, ed. Mary Lee Spence (Urbana: University of Illinois Press, 1984), 423, 428–443, 466 (n. 7–16).

6. F. V. Hayden, *Annual Report of the United States Geological and Geographical Survey of the Territories Embracing Colorado and Parts of the Adjacent Territories; Being a Report of Progress of the Exploration for the Year 1874* (Washington, D.C.: Government Printing Office, 1876).

7. To be fair, Crawford then went on to say: "And yet, there was something in it which, at once, appealed to the senses, and told one that this would one day be a most fruitful and luxuriant valley." Quoted in Kathleen Underwood, *Town Building on the Colorado Frontier* (Albuquerque: University of New Mexico Press, 1987), 9, 11.

8. By treaty ratified by the U.S. Senate in 1863, the Ute Indians in Colorado ceded to the United States their claims to lands east of the Continental Divide but were given dominant rights in the western part of the territory. A subsequent treaty in 1868 established a reservation for the Ute in western Colorado that was to be their exclusive territory. See "Treaty with the Tabeguache Indians," Oct. 7, 1863, Stats. at Large of USA 13 (1863): 673; "Treaty with the Ute Indians," March 2, 1868, Stats. at Large of USA 15 (1868): 619.

     The 1863 treaty with the Ute gave them all the land west of the Continental Divide. At that time the white people were too preoccupied with mining gold and settling the Eastern Slope to be concerned with the lands west of the Divide. However, the rapid settlement of Colorado quickly infringed upon these Ute lands. Therefore, the 1868 treaty united all the Ute bands and demarcated the boundaries of the Ute reservation more precisely than the vague boundaries established by the 1863 treaty. The Ute Indians were shocked, however, to discover that much of their prime hunting territory–high alpine meadows near the Continental Divide–had been excluded from the boundaries of their new reservation. This was only the beginning of tensions between the federal government and the Ute, and these tensions were further exacerbated by the failure of the federal government to prohibit settlers, prospectors, and miners from crossing the reservation boundaries. See Robert Emmitt, *The Last War Trail: The Utes and the Settle-*

ment of Colorado (Norman: University of Oklahoma Press, 1954), 24–25.

Tensions between the federal government's paternalism and the Ute Indians' fierce independence came to a head in the so-called White River Massacre. At the center of this historical drama was Nathan Cook Meeker, who ascended to a position of national prominence by founding the town of Greeley in 1869 as an agricultural "Union colony" in eastern Colorado. Despite the predictions of many naysayers that this area was an agriculturally infertile "Great Desert," Meeker's community on the eastern plains of Colorado became the first large-scale western irrigation success outside of Mormon Utah. Then, in 1877, Meeker was appointed as the federal agent to the White River Ute. His appointment was largely based upon his theory that, in order to assimilate the native peoples into American culture, it was necessary to found an agricultural colony for the Ute modeled upon the accomplishments of Greeley. Meeker envisioned a productive and economically self-sustaining community that would enable the Ute Indians to ascend from a hunting to an agricultural lifestyle more befitting civilized individuals. Emmitt, *Last War Trail,* 44–50.

Although relations between Meeker and the Ute started out favorably, the Ute proved difficult to convert fully to an agricultural way of life. Meeker nonetheless remained optimistic about his project. By 1879, despite significant successes at converting some pasture to farmlands, Meeker began to express concern that some of the Ute were incorrigible and likely to engage in violence against his efforts. Tribal opposition to farming gradually increased until Meeker was assaulted by a leading Ute chief in September of 1879. Meeker began to fear for the well-being of the white settlers under his direction on the reservation and sent telegrams to Washington, D.C., requesting military protection from the federal government. Emmitt, *Last War Trail,* 134–35, 155–57.

Then, on the morning of September 29, 1879, a small band of Ute ambushed a force of soldiers en route to answer Meeker's request for assistance. That very same afternoon Ute murdered Meeker and all his employees at the White River Agency. In all, thirty white men were killed and forty-four were injured. See Marshall Sprague, *Massacre: The Tragedy at White River* (Boston: Little, Brown, 1957), forward. The killing of Meeker prompted widespread coverage by the alarmist media of the day—the news even reaching the East Coast—and was, for example, labeled "a scene of slaughter" by a headline in the *Denver Daily News.* The attack was widely regarded as unprovoked, and calls for the extermination of the Ute became frequent as the towns and settlements of Colorado formed militia units and prepared for battle. The conditions of unrest led then-Governor Pitkin to proclaim that "[t]he barbarities practiced by the Utes have inflamed our people almost beyond the possibility of control." See Emmitt, *Last War Trail,* 233–38.

9. The Grand Valley was considered as a site for a reservation but, according to one source, was viewed as more valuable for settlement by the United States: "Mr. Mears [one of the U.S. commissioners sent to survey the valley as a possible reservation location] at once saw that, for the benefit of Colorado, it would be better to keep the Indians out of the state, as the land in the

Uncompahgre and at Grand Junction would become very valuable, if settled by whites." Jerome G. Smiley, ed., *Semi-Centennial History of the State of Colorado,* vol. 2 (Chicago: Lewis Publishing, 1913), 441.

10. According to one account, "In the early days of September 1881, a bugler for the U.S. Army issued a series of shrill blasts signaling that the land that had once belonged to the Ute Indians was now open for settlement by the whites. The bugle had barely silenced when the stampede began: a flood of settlers entered the Grand Valley. This multitude soon demanded a supply of water to transform the barren land into towns, farms, ranches, and orchards." Don Davidson, "The Grand River Ditch," *Journal of the Western Slope* 1 (Winter 1986): 1.

11. Mary Rait, "Development of Grand Junction and the Colorado River Valley to Palisade from 1881 to 1931, Part 1," *Journal of the Western Slope* 3 (Summer 1988): 8 (hereafter Rait, "Part 1").

12. Davidson, "Grand River Ditch," 1.

13. The court-appointed receiver determined that ditch expenses were ten thousand dollars per year, whereas revenues were thirty-five hundred dollars. Davidson, "Grand River Ditch," 21.

14. Joyce Sexton, "History of the Fruit Industry in Mesa County," in *Western Colorado Horticultural Society Proceedings* (Grand Junction: Western Colorado Horticultural Society, 1987), 92–98.

15. Ibid., 93. Cross Orchards, now operated as an outdoor museum by the Museum of Western Colorado, provides an opportunity today to revisit that period of time. The land originally was purchased in 1896 by Isabelle Cross, heiress to a family fortune made manufacturing shoes in Massachusetts. Neither she nor other members of the Cross family ever lived on the 243-acre farm. Rather, it was operated "as a showplace of Western Colorado agricultural and economic potential."

16. Ed Currier, grandson of Edwin J. Currier, graciously provided a family history he prepared as well as some correspondence that is used here.

17. Despite assurances by valley interests in 1907 that the cost of the system would be paid to the United States within three years after completion, irrigators within the Water Users Association did not begin payments until the contract had been renegotiated in 1928. The renegotiated contract extended the payment period to forty years, deducted $812,000 from the original repayment cost, and established a reduced annual charge for the first five years.

18. Markoff, *Beet Sugar Industry,* 15.

19. A portion of the flow is siphoned off to the Orchard Mesa system under the river between the second and third tunnels. At the Price-Stubb Pumping Plant, water is made available to the Palisade Irrigation District (6,000 irrigable acres) and the Mesa County Irrigation District (2,000 irrigable acres). The Highline Canal, completed in 1917, extends fifty-five miles and carries water to about 23,300 acres of land within the Grand Valley Water Users Association. Today water from the Grand Valley Project is provided to about 33,000 acres of land.

20. The canal also provided water to lands within the Palisade Irrigation District and the Mesa County Irrigation District, both of which previously had depended on unreliable pumping systems out of the Colorado River.

21. Rait, "Development of Grand Junction and the Colorado River Valley to Pali-
    sade from 1881 to 1931, Part 2," *Journal of the Western Slope* 3 (Autumn 1988):
    38–41 (hereafter Rait, "Part 2").
22. J. H. Miner and C. C. Smith, "Report on Orchard Mesa Irrigation District"
    (U.S. Reclamation Service, January 30, 1917, memorandum to chief of con-
    struction).
23. Nolan J. Doesken et al., "A Climatological Assessment of the Utility of Wind
    Machines for Freeze Protection in Mountain Valleys," *Journal of Applied Me-
    teorology* 28 (March 1989): 194, 195–96.
24. Salinity problems in agriculture occur most frequently in arid or semiarid
    regions where there is insufficient rainfall to transport salts from the plant
    root zone. These arid regions compose roughly one quarter of the earth's
    surface. In the western United States salinity is an agricultural problem in
    about one half of the irrigated areas. This amounts to approximately eight
    million acres of salt-impacted soils in the seventeen western states. As a
    whole, millions of hectares of land around the world are too saline to pro-
    duce economically viable crop yields, and more land becomes unproductive
    each year as a result of salt accumulation from irrigation.
        Salts and other residues are left behind in the soils and accumulate
    over time because water evaporates from the ground in a pure state. This
    process of evapotranspiration tends to leave a salt concentration in the
    remaining soil solution four to ten times greater than the concentration in
    the irrigation water. Moreover, each successive irrigation contributes salt to
    the soil, the relative contribution varying according to the amount of water
    entering the soil and the salinity of the incoming water. And this salt concen-
    tration will remain in the soil unless water in excess of crop requirements
    leaches away this salt buildup. However, in the arid West there is essentially
    no leaching, as each irrigation replaces approximately the same amount of
    water removed from the soil by evapotranspiration.
        Furthermore, irrigation runoff—water that has passed through the
    soil or "drainage"—has a higher salt concentration than pure irrigation wa-
    ter and contributes to salinity problems along rivers and streams. A large
    proportion of this drainage water returns to the natural river channel down-
    stream of the irrigated lands. As a result of this process the salt concentra-
    tion in rivers and streams, especially in arid and semiarid regions, tends to
    increase from the headwaters to the mouth of the waterway. Sometimes the
    cumulative effect of multiple irrigators along a water body can thus render
    the downstream salt concentration so great that the water cannot be used
    for irrigation. D. L. Carter, "Problems of Salinity in Agriculture," in *Plants in
    Saline Environments,* ed. A. Poljakoff-Mayber and J. Gale (Berlin-Heidleberg:
    Springer-Verlag, 1975), 25, 25–27.
        Salinity affects many metabolic components of plants and tends to
    induce adaptive changes in plant anatomy and morphology. Most plants
    and almost all crops have difficulty growing in highly saline soils because
    conditions of "salt stress" can inhibit root growth, induce root decay, cause
    wilting by undercutting normal turgid conditions, prevent development of
    leaf mass necessary for effective photosynthesis, and interfere with flowering
    processes or cause the production of nonviable seeds. Certain species of natu-

rally salt-tolerant desert plants, like the ice plant, have evolved mechanisms to minimize salt stress. For example, the ice plant first excludes salt during water uptake by storing the excess salt out of harm's way in its root tissue. Second, it accumulates sugar alcohols (polyols) as a means of salt resistance. These polyols function, in higher concentrations, to counteract the common inhibitory effects of salt on water uptake and retention by plants. See Department of Agriculture, Cooperative State Research Service, *Plant Tolerance to Salt and Drought Stress*, no. 2, by Hans J. Bohnert, Richard G. Jensen, and Mitchell C. Tarczynski (Washington, D.C.: Government Printing Office, 1994).

When a salt dissolves in water, it separates into cations and anions. The primary cations are calcium, magnesium, sodium, and potassium; the major anions are chloride, sulfate, carbonate, and bicarbonate. Many of these salt ions are essential as major and minor nutrients for effective plant growth. However, excessive salinity inhibits plant growth either because of the toxic effects of a specific ion or because of the general effects of high ion concentrations. Plant growth is further inhibited by a decrease in the water potential of the soil as a result of high salinity. In other words, high salt concentrations limit the osmotic potential of the soil. Those terrestrial plants that are naturally salt tolerant are called halophytes and are environmentally characterized by high concentrations of soluble salts around their root zones. Although halophytes are dependent upon high soil-water salt concentrations, most terrestrial plants—and nearly all irrigated crops—are not similarly adapted and are known as glycophytes. See also *McGraw-Hill Encyclopedia of Science & Technology*, vol. 16, 7th ed. (New York: McGraw Hill, 1992), 562–64.

25. Department of Agriculture, *The Seepage and Alkali Problem in the Grand Valley, Colorado,* by Dalton G. Miller (Washington, D.C.: Department of Agriculture, Office of Public Roads and Rural Engineering, 1916), 15.

26. Rait, "Part 1," 44–45.

27. Merton N. Bergner, "The Development of Fruita and the Lower Valley of the Colorado River from 1884 to 1937" (master's thesis, University of Colorado, Boulder, 1937), 33.

28. Rait, "Part 1," 45.

29. Ibid., 46.

30. Sexton, "History," 96.

31. Halka Chronic, *Roadside Geology of Colorado* (Missoula, Mont.: Mountain Press, 1980), 256.

32. Miller, Weatherford, and Thorson, *Salty Colorado,* 5.

33. Ibid., 24. See also Joseph F. Friedkin, "The International Problem with Mexico Over the Salinity of the Lower Colorado River," in *Water and the West: Essays in Honor of Raphael J. Moses*, ed. David H. Getches (Boulder, Colo.: Natural Resources Law Center, 1988).

34. U.S. Code, vol. 43, sec. 1571 (1994).

35. During the late 1970s the U.S. Environmental Protection Agency funded a number of case studies of the Grand Valley. These studies were carried out in conjunction with the Department of Agricultural and Chemical Engineering at Colorado State University and investigated irrigation practices in the valley, looking in particular at the effects of existing irrigation practices on crop yields, irrigation return flows, and salinity levels, as well as exploring various agricul-

tural salinity-control measures to mitigate future salinity concentrations. First, they summarized the results of applied research on agricultural return flow salinity-control measures for the period 1969 to 1976, in particular evaluating implementation of the Grand Valley Salinity Control Demonstration Project for both salinity and economic impacts on existing agricultural practices in the region. See, generally, Robert G. Evans et al., *Implementation of Agricultural Salinity Control Technology in Grand Valley* (Ada, Okla.: Robert S. Kerr Environmental Research Laboratory, Office of Research and Development, U.S. Environmental Protection Agency, July 1978). Second, they evaluated furrow, border, sprinkler, and trickle irrigation methods for their potential usefulness as salinity-control measures necessary to offset the heavy salt loads naturally occurring in the Grand Valley as a result of saline soils and the marine-derived geologic substratum of the region. See, generally, Robert G. Evans et al., *Evaluation of Irrigation Methods for Salinity Control in Grand Valley* (Ada, Okla.: Robert S. Kerr Environmental Research Laboratory, Office of Research and Development, U.S. Environmental Protection Agency, July 1978). Third, they analyzed alternative means of reducing salt loads in the valley as a result of irrigation return flows, including conveyance channel linings, field relief drainage, on-farm improvements (such as irrigation scheduling, head ditch linings, and sprinkler and trickle irrigation methods), economic control measures like taxation or land retirement, modified legal regulations, and treatment of return flows via desalting systems. See, generally, Wynn R. Walker, Gaylord V. Skogerboe, and Robert G. Evans, *"Best Management Practices" for Salinity Control Measures in Grand Valley* (Ada, Okla.: Robert S. Kerr Environmental Research Laboratory, Office of Research and Development, U.S. Environmental Protection Agency, July 1978). Fourth, they used the Grand Valley as a case-study area for development of technical and institutional solutions to the problem of irrigation return flow pollution, finding that the most cost-effective technologies for reducing excessive salt loads and freeing surplus water supplies for selling, renting, or leasing to water users upstream from the Grand Valley are a combination of lateral lining and on-farm improvements. See, generally, Gaylord V. Skogerboe et al., *Socio-economic and Institutional Factors in Irrigation Return Flow Quality Control, Volume 4: Grand Valley Case Study* (Ada, Okla.: Robert S. Kerr Environmental Research Laboratory, Office of Research and Development, U.S. Environmental Protection Agency, August 1978). Fifth, they used a numerical model of salt transport to evaluate water-flow modeling and total dissolved solids (TDS) concentrations for the Grand Valley under various scenarios, finding that reductions in salt loading are directly proportional to reductions in the volume of return flow. See, generally, Gaylord V. Skogerboe et al., *Irrigation Practices and Return Flow Salinity in Grand Valley* (Ada, Okla.: Robert S. Kerr Environmental Research Laboratory, Office of Research and Development, U.S. Environmental Protection Agency, August 1979). And, finally, they analyzed the economically optimal seasonal depth of irrigation water to apply under conditions of both limited and surplus water supply, with a view to developing general guidelines that might have practical significance for various irrigation regimes under all water-supply scenarios. The results of field experiments involving corn and wheat showed that irrigation can be terminated earlier than is the common practice in the Grand Valley, resulting in both increased crop yields for farmers and reduced saline return flows reaching water users downstream on the Colorado River. See, generally, Gaylord V. Skogerboe et al., *Potential Effects of Irrigation Practices on Crop Yields in Grand Valley* (Ada, Okla.: Robert S. Kerr Environmental Research Laboratory, Office of Research and Development, U.S. Environmental Protection Agency, August 1979).

36. Department of the Interior, *Quality of Water, Colorado River Basin,* Progress Report No. 17, January 1995, 63, table 9. Even when stage two is completed, the total annual reductions are expected to be only 122,347 tons per year.

37. Personal communication from Brent Uilenberg, Bureau of Reclamation, May 25, 1995. This includes $5 million for wetlands and wildlife mitigation.

38. Thus, if the sum total of the flow rights held by users on a lateral is x cubic feet per second, then a constant flow of x cubic feet per second is diverted from the main canal to the lateral so long as sufficient water is available to do so.

39. Department of the Interior, *Quality of Water,* 55–56, tables 6, 7. This total includes expenditures by Reclamation and by the Department of Agriculture.

40. See, for example, Loretta C. Lohman et al., *Estimating Economic Impacts of Salinity of the Colorado River,* Bureau of Reclamation report, February 1988. This report cites total damages of $310 to $831 million per year, p. 5.

41. Richard L. Gardner and Robert A. Young, "An Economic Evaluation of the Colorado River Basin Salinity Control Program," *Western Journal of Agricultural Economics* 10 (1985): 1; Richard L. Gardner and Robert A. Young, "Assessing Strategies for Control of Irrigation-Induced Salinity in the Upper Colorado River Basin," *American Journal of Agricultural Economics* 70 (1988): 37. In March 1994 the Bureau of Reclamation requested comments from the public about the salinity control program. Most of these comments were supportive of continuing the program, but several raised questions about a number of aspects of the program, including the Grand Valley Unit.

42. Daniel Tyler, *The Last Water Hole in the West: The Colorado–Big Thompson Project and the Northern Colorado Water Conservancy District* (Niwot, Colo.: University Press of Colorado, 1992).

43. See Lawrence J. MacDonnell and David H. Getches, "Colorado River Basin," in *Waters and Water Rights,* vol. 7, ed. R. Beck (Baltimore: Michie, 1994) for an overview of Colorado River issues.

44. This call was in effect an average of fifty-nine days per year during the irrigation season between 1987 and 1990. Resource Engineering, "Analysis of the Orchard Mesa Check Operation Under Current and Historic Stream Administration Practices"(Glenwood Springs, Colo., August 11, 1993, photocopy), 10, table 1.

45. Personal communication from John Gierard, Bureau of Reclamation, February 20, 1995. Another source places total diversions at about 880,000 acre-feet per year (Bishop-Brogden Associates, "An Analysis of Potential Irrigation Water Savings in the Grand Valley of Colorado" [Denver, February 1994, photocopy], 3). Irrigation diversions are estimated to total 630,000 acre-feet. An additional 250,000 acre-feet of water is diverted during the irrigation season (April to October) for power purposes.

46. Robert Follansbee, "Upper Colorado River and Its Utilization" (United States Geological Survey, Water Supply Paper 617, 1929), 49.

47. James L. Cox, *Metropolitan Water Supply: The Denver Experience* (Boulder, Colo.: University of Colorado, Bureau of Governmental Research and Services, 1967).

48. Tyler, *Last Water*, 104.

49. In the debate surrounding construction of the Colorado–Big Thompson Project, West Slope interests demanded "compensatory storage" to protect existing and future consumptive water uses in their area (Tyler, *Last Water*, 51). Green Mountain Reservoir, constructed on the Blue River near Kremmling, was added to the project to meet this demand. Senate Document 80, prepared in 1937 to accompany legislation authorizing the Colorado–Big Thompson Project, called for Green Mountain Reservoir to have a capacity of 152,000 acre-feet, with 52,000 acre-feet dedicated to provide "replacement" of water diverted out of the basin and 100,000 acre-feet for "power purposes" (to operate a hydroelectric power plant at the dam with the revenues going to help pay the cost of the project). Senate Document 80 specifically directed use of the 52,000 acre-feet as necessary to meet the 1,250 cubic feet per second diversion right of the Shoshone Power Plant as against diversions out of the basin for the C-BT Project; the 100,000 acre-foot pool also was to be available for meeting "existing irrigation and domestic appropriations of water, including the Grand Valley Reclamation project," as well as future domestic and irrigation uses in western Colorado (U.S. Senate, *Synopsis of Report on Colorado–Big Thompson Project, Plan of Development and Cost Estimate Prepared by the Bureau of Reclamation, Department of the Interior,* 75th Cong., 1st sess., June 15, 1937.), 3.

50. Roger Weidelman, "Water Management of the Arkansas River" (Loveland, Colo., Bureau of Reclamation, preliminary draft, October 5, 1993), 2.

51. Personal communication from Philip C. Saletta, Supervising Resource Engineer, Colorado Springs Utilities, November 2, 1994.

52. Ibid.

53. The energy boom of the 1970s was more intense in some respects than any of the other mining booms—from the California and Nevada gold rushes of the nineteenth century through the later mining frenzies in Idaho, Montana, Colorado, Arizona, and New Mexico—which have played an important role in shaping the contours of the American West. Western Colorado was a focal point of this most recent boom, which, driven by the international demand for oil, stretched the length of the Rocky Mountains through New Mexico, Colorado, Utah, Wyoming, Idaho, and Montana, and even to the extraction of strippable coal reserves in the Dakotas. According to 1974 estimates, western Colorado contains the richest oil-shale deposits in the world in the small area of the Piceance Creek Basin—an estimated 500 billion barrels of recoverable oil in seams at least five feet thick. Fueled by the energy crisis of the mid-1970s, the Rocky Mountain region saw over two hundred small boomtowns spring up through the early 1980s, including twenty-five in Colorado alone. These boomtowns were generally located adjacent to various energy minerals, ranging from oil shale to coal, uranium, oil, natural gas, and even subterranean reservoirs of carbon dioxide. The massive oil-shale depos-

its of western Colorado became the "epicenter" of this boom. The United States's most valuable oil-shale deposits lie in Colorado, Utah, and Wyoming, and their development was assisted by the fact that most of these deposits are on federal lands and available for long-term leasing under the Mineral Leasing Act of 1920. Sizable federal subsidies during the energy crisis only served to intensify the rate of development so that, in 1974 alone, oil companies bought oil-shale leases worth $210 million.

However, "the limitless West is a land of limitations," and water scarcity became a major limiting factor in water-intensive oil-shale production, which requires a barrel of water to produce each barrel of oil. Oil companies thus set out on large campaigns to purchase senior water rights from ranchers and farmers. However, community polarization was inevitable, for the oil companies failed to understand that water is the essential unifying medium in western economics, politics, and culture.

These small boomtowns were characterized by a boom-bust economic cycle involving geographic isolation, swift urbanization, economic dependence on energy mineral extraction, and a rapid community decline when the price of the natural resource inevitably dropped. The late-twentieth-century boomtowns had evolved from quiet, rural farming and ranching communities, which were ill prepared from the standpoint of infrastructure, to handle the massive influx of newcomers. This rapid transformation invariably upset the relative stability of farming and ranching economies, creating massive friction between locals and newcomers, and the negative social consequences were observed as widespread "drunkenness, depression, delinquency, and divorce." Then, just as many of these communities adapted municipally to the population influx, the economy shifted, and these boomtowns became bust towns: The thousands of immigrants left almost as quickly as they had arrived.

The social impact of this regional economic downswing, flowing from the greatest local mining boom and quickest resulting bust in the history of the West, was devastating. Towns in the Colorado River Valley—like New Castle, Silt, Rifle, Parachute, and Grand Junction—were hardest hit by this rapid devolution. Shrinking city budgets, a dead housing market, rampant unemployment, and sweeping bank closures were all part and parcel of this quick downswing. One characteristic of these western Colorado bust towns that set them apart from the previous experiences of eastern industrial cities like Akron, Detroit, and Youngstown was that they lacked the occupational infrastructure akin to that in the East to mitigate the pangs of widespread unemployment.

Although the "black gold mine[s]" of western Colorado enabled these towns to remain vibrant throughout a decade characterized by inflation in the double digits and escalating unemployment rates, this ultimately set these towns up for a harder fall. Ironically, this boom-bust cycle has today left many of these western towns with a well-developed municipal infrastructure—new city halls, schools, churches, sewer systems, and paved streets—but very few permanent residents and a faltering local economy. Similar to the nineteenth-century West, rural westerners in these towns have discovered the hard way that outside forces dictating economic development can render locals powerless and irrevocably change the face of their rural lifestyle. Andrew Gulliford, *Boomtown Blues: Colorado Oil Shale, 1885–1985* (Niwot, Colo.: University Press of Colorado, 1989), 1–14.

54. [The Orchard Mesa Check: Read this if you want an example of why western water issues can be so complicated.] The importance of this downstream demand to upstream users became apparent in the early 1990s when the Orchard Mesa Irrigation District sought a water-court decree for operation of what is called "the check." Water for lands within OMID is diverted at the Roller Dam, siphoned under the river, and moved through the Power Canal to a pumping plant, where it is lifted up onto the mesa. The power water used to lift the irrigation water originally returned directly to the Colorado River through the plant tailrace. Robert E. Norman, "Grand Valley Water Management Study: A Carrot or a Hammer?" (Grand Junction, Colo., Bureau of Reclamation, 1993, photocopy). Four hydraulically driven pumps use about 272 cubic feet per second of water to pump the 171 cubic feet per second of water used for irrigation. In addition, water used to operate a hydroelectric plant constructed at this location in 1933 by the Public Service Company of Colorado returns to the river through this tailrace.

In 1926 the Bureau of Reclamation installed a radial "check" (a movable gate) at the point where the tailrace enters the river and built a bypass channel allowing water blocked by the closed gate to enter the Colorado River at a point about twelve hundred yards farther upstream (Figure 31.1). Using the check made it possible for the Grand Valley Project to take advantage of the Grand Valley Irrigation Company's senior rights to supply its more junior power water rights (for Orchard Mesa and the power plant) in times of shortage. In effect, GVIC water could be diverted at the Roller Dam, used to pump water up onto Orchard Mesa and generate electricity, and then released back to the river through the check structure above the GVIC diversion dam. Bureau of Reclamation, "Grand Valley Water Management Study Flow Protection Plan" (Grand Junction, Colo., Dec. 19, 1994, photocopy), 11. Orchard Mesa wanted to gain clear legal sanction for its continued use of the check.

Releases of Green Mountain water provide a critical part of the late-season irrigation supply for the Grand Valley in many years. Operation of the check reduces the amount of water that must be released from Green Mountain for irrigation use in the Grand Valley. Even so, in the drought year of 1977, sixty-six thousand acre-feet of water was released from Green Mountain to meet existing West Slope uses. In the four-year period from 1987 to 1990, replacement releases from Green Mountain averaged about fifty-four thousand acre-feet per year.

For many years the Denver Water Board contested operation of Green Mountain Reservoir because it was perceived to threaten the yield from Dillon Reservoir. As the consequence of a long series of court cases and negotiations, Green Mountain is recognized to hold a 1935 priority to store 152,000 acre-feet plus a refill right while Dillon Reservoir and the Roberts Tunnel hold a 1946 priority (a storage right of 252,678 acre-feet and a direct-flow right of 788 cubic feet per second). Thus Green Mountain has a better

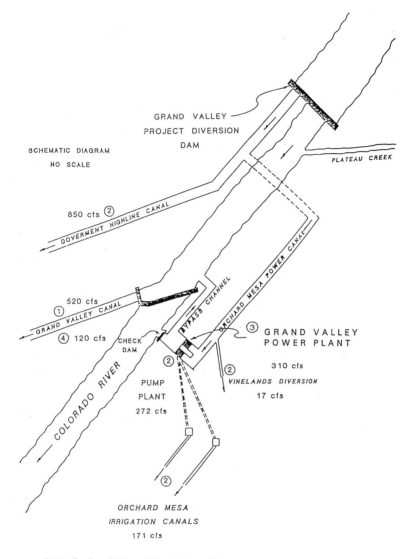

GRAND VALLEY
PROJECT DIVERSION
DAM

SCHEMATIC DIAGRAM
NO SCALE

PLATEAU CREEK

850 cfs ②
GOVERMENT HIGHLINE CANAL

520 cfs
①
GRAND VALLEY CANAL

④ 120 cfs
CHECK
DAM

BYPASS CHANNEL

ORCHARD MESA POWER CANAL

③ GRAND VALLEY
POWER PLANT

COLORADO RIVER

②

②

310 cfs
VINELANDS DIVERSION
17 cfs

PUMP
PLANT
272 cfs

②

ORCHARD MESA
IRRIGATION CANALS
171 cfs

31.1 Orchard Mesa Check Dam (Source: Bureau of Reclamation).

legal right to Blue River water than does Dillon. The parties also agreed, how-
ever, that Denver could use its storage on Williams Fork to release water to the
Colorado River to meet demand that would otherwise be supplied by Green
Mountain in exchange for Blue River water it could store in Dillon. More
recently, Denver helped finance construction of the Colorado River Water
Conservation District's Wolford Mountain Reservoir on Muddy Creek, north

of Kremmling. Denver will use its share of the yield of Wolford Mountain as releases to substitute for Green Mountain water it stores in Dillon Reservoir and transports to the Front Range.

In the Orchard Mesa check case, four interests emerged as those potentially most affected: the so-called "preferred beneficiaries" of Green Mountain water, the Green Mountain contract water users, the oil-shale interests, and the transmountain diverters. Preferred beneficiaries are those West Slope users with municipal and irrigation-water rights that were diverting water by 1977–considered to total sixty-six thousand acre-feet of water. Contract users are those holding contract rights for delivery of water out of Green Mountain. About ten thousand acre-feet of water has been committed to date out of a designated pool of twenty thousand acre-feet in Green Mountain. Oil-shale interests generally hold junior conditional water rights with an appropriation date of 1955 or later.

Orchard Mesa wanted to legally decree its practice of operating the check only as necessary to meet the senior GVIC right of 520 cubic feet per second, not GVIC's more junior right of 120 cubic feet per second. In the 1980s Orchard Mesa determined that the added expenses of operating the check made sense only when it was legally required to do so, and the Colorado state engineer agreed that Orchard Mesa was not obligated to operate the check in other circumstances. Studies indicate, however, that the check could be operated to reduce the need for releases from Green Mountain Reservoir by as much as thirty thousand acre-feet in a normal year and 56,600 in a dry year.

Thus, water uses in the Grand Valley affect upstream uses in the Colorado River Basin. Compensatory storage facilities for two Bureau of Reclamation projects, Green Mountain Reservoir and Ruedi Reservoir, help offset the depletive effects of the transmountain diversions out of the Colorado River Basin by these projects. The depletive effects of Denver's large-scale transmountain diversions are offset somewhat by releases from Williams Fork and, now, Wolford Mountain. Nevertheless, even in a river with a native yield that still exceeds existing consumptive uses, many holding water rights believe they would benefit from a reduced call from the Grand Valley. These interests favor reduced diversions in the Grand Valley but prefer that the reduced diversions simply return to the river and become available to help supply the rights of junior appropriators.

After six years in water court, in a proceeding involving more than one hundred separate parties, a settlement was reached.

55. Fradkin, *River No More.*
56. Department of the Interior, Bureau of Reclamation, *Colorado River System Consumptive Uses and Losses Report, 1981–1985* (Washington, D.C.: Bureau of Reclamation, 1991), 22, table C–6.
57. For a good overview of these effects, see Michael Collier, Robert H. Webb, and John C. Schmidt, "Dams and Rivers: Primer on the Downstream Effects of Dams," (U.S. Geological Survey, Circular 1126, June 1996).
58. A good summary is provided in U.S. Fish and Wildlife Service, *Biological Opinion for the Muddy Creek Reservoir Project, Grand County, Colorado* (Denver: U.S. Fish and Wildlife Service, 1990). A more detailed treatment can be found

in U.S. Fish and Wildlife Service, *Colorado River Endangered Fishes Critical Habitat,* by Henry R. Maddux, Lesley A. Fitzpatrick, and William R. Noonan, draft Biological Support Document, Sept. 3, 1993. See also U.S. Fish and Wildlife Service, Colorado River Fishes Recovery Team, *Colorado Squawfish, Revised Recovery Plan* (Denver: U.S. Fish and Wildlife Service, 1991).

59. U.S. Code, vol. 16, sec. 1537(f) (1994).

60. Richard S. Wydoski and John Hamill, "Evolution of a Cooperative Recovery Program for Endangered Fishes in the Upper Colorado River Basin," in *Battle Against Extinction, Native Fish Management in the American West,* ed. W.L. Minckley and J.E. Deacon (Tucson: University of Arizona Press, 1991), 132.

61. Ibid., 133.

62. As revised in 1993, the program contains seven elements, estimated to require funding of as much as $134 million between 1994 and 2004. First, the in-stream flow needs of the fishes are to be identified and protected. Second, important habitat areas are to be restored and managed. Third, the adverse effects of nonnative fishes are to be reduced. Fourth, the genetic resources of the species are to be protected and managed. Fifth, monitoring and research are to be conducted as necessary to support recovery efforts. Sixth, public education is to be pursued through an active program of information dissemination. And seventh, overall planning and coordination of recovery-program activities are to be pursued, as is obtaining adequate funding support. Participation in the Recovery Implementation Program includes, in addition to the Fish and Wildlife Service, representatives from the Bureau of Reclamation, the states of Colorado, Utah, and Wyoming, the Western Area Power Administration, the water-user community, and the environmental community. (U.S. Fish and Wildlife Service, *Recovery Implementation Program for Endangered Fish Species in the Upper Colorado River Basin* [Denver: Department of the Interior, 1993]).

63. See note 54.

64. Fish ladders now have been added at a cost of over $1 million. Pikeminnow have in fact moved through the ladders upstream into the Gunnison.

65. U.S. Fish and Wildlife Service, Colorado River Fishery Project, *Biological Defensible Flow Recommendations for the Maintenance and Enhancement of Colorado Squawfish Habitat in the "Fifteen-Mile" Reach of the Upper Colorado River During July, August, and September* (Salt Lake City: U.S. Fish and Wildlife Service, 1989).

66. The first increment of water to meet this need came from Ruedi Reservoir, a feature of the Fryingpan-Arkansas Project constructed by the Bureau of Reclamation on the Fryingpan River. This reservoir provides compensatory storage to offset the depletive effects of water removed from the West Slope of Colorado for use in the Arkansas Valley on the Front Range. Water stored in Ruedi is not yet fully contracted to users on the West Slope. The Bureau of Reclamation agreed in 1990 to release five thousand acre-feet per year to enhance flows in the Fifteen-Mile Reach, and committed an additional five thousand acre-feet in four years out of five based on changes made in the operation of the reservoir. In 1991 the bureau committed an additional ten thousand acre-feet from Ruedi. (Department of the Interior, Bureau of Reclamation, *Study of Alternative Water Supplies for Endangered Fishes in the "Fifteen-Mile Reach" of the Colorado River* (Grand Junction, Colo.: Bureau of Reclama-

tion, 1992).

67. Hydrosphere Resource Consultants, *Incentive Pricing Handbook for Agricultural Water Districts,* a special report prepared for Bureau of Reclamation, April 1997.

68. MacDonnell, "Colorado Water Law Discourages Irrigation Water Conservation: The Grand Valley Example," *Water Court Reporter* (University of Denver College of Law) Special Supplement, Issue 17 (Fall/Winter 1995/96): 7–14.

69. For a thorough discussion of the takings provisions of the Endangered Species Act, see Federico Cheever, "An Introduction to the Prohibition Against Takings in Section 9 of the Endangered Species Act of 1973: Learning to Live with a Powerful Species Protection Law," *University of Colorado Law Review* 62 (1991): 109. Arguably, so long as the fish-recovery program is in place and meeting its objectives, such a claim would fail.

70. In January 1994 the state of Colorado through its Colorado Water Conservation Board approved a Memorandum of Understanding involving the Bureau of Reclamation, the Colorado River Water Conservation District, the Grand Valley Water Users Association, the Denver Water Board, and the Northern Colorado Water Conservancy District, launching a three-phase Grand Valley Water Management Study. Phase 1 focuses on the technical aspects of saving water in the GVWUA system. Phase 2 addresses the legal issues associated with using saved water in the Fifteen-Mile Reach. Phase 3 involves a feasibility study and NEPA compliance for implementing conservation measures.

71. These laws are discussed in MacDonnell and Teresa A. Rice, "Moving Agricultural Water to Cities: The Search for Smarter Approaches," *West-Northwest Journal of Environmental Law and Policy* 2, no. 1 (Fall 1994): 41–45.

PART 3

1. Robert J. Hallock and Linda L. Hallock, ed., *Detailed Study of Irrigation Drainage in and Near Wildlife Management Areas, West-Central Nevada, 1987–90, Part B. Effect on Biota in Stillwater and Fernley Wildlife Management Areas and Other Nearby Wetlands,* U.S. Geological Survey, Water-Resources Investigations Report 92–4024B (1993), 11, table 1 (hereinafter *Irrigation Drainage*); Department of the Interior, *Final Report of the Secretary of the Interior to the Congress of the United States on the Newlands Project Efficiency Study, Public Law 101–618* (Washington, D.C.: December 1993), 10, 55 [hereinafter *Efficiency Study*].

2. California Department of Water Resources, *Truckee River Atlas* (Sacramento: California Department of Water Resources, 1991), 25, fig. 4.

3. Ibid., 24.

4. U.S. Fish and Wildlife Service, Region 1, *In the Shadow of Fox Peak: An Ethnography of the Cattail-Eater Northern Paiute People of Stillwater Marsh,* by Catherine S. Fowler, Cultural Resource Series No. 5 (Washington, D.C.: Government Printing Office, 1992).

5. Quoted in Steven P. Thompson and Kenneth L. Merritt, "Western Nevada Wetlands: History and Current Status," *Nevada Public Affairs Review* 1 (1988): 44.

6. Quoted in U.S. Fish and Wildlife Service, *In the Shadow,* 18.

7. Ibid., 11.

8. Ibid..

9. California Department of Water Resources, *Truckee River Atlas,* 24, n. 1.

10. Martha C. Knack and Omer C. Stewart, *As Long as the River Shall Run: An Ethnohistory of Pyramid Lake Indian Reservation* (Berkeley: University of California Press, 1984), chap. 3.

11. Ibid., 83.

12. Ibid., 91, fig. 3.

13. John C. Fremont observed of the Great Basin: "Mountain is the predominating structure of the interior of the Basin, with plains between–the mountains wooded and watered, the plains arid and sterile. . . . Between these mountains are the arid plains which receive and deserve the name of the desert. Such is the general structure of the interior of the Great Basin, *more Asiatic than American in its character,* and much resembling the elevated region between the Caspian Sea and northern Persia." John Charles Fremont, *Narratives of Exploration and Adventure,* ed. Allan Nevins (New York: Longmans, Green, 1956), 514 (emphasis added).

Fremont added that the Great Basin "is peopled, we know; but miserably and sparsely. From all that I heard and saw, I should say that humanity here appeared in its lowest form, and in its most elementary state." Fremont went on: "The whole idea of such a desert, and such a people, is a novelty in our country, and excites Asiatic, *not American ideas.* Interior basins, with their own system of lakes and rivers, and often sterile, are common enough in Asia; people still in the elementary state of families, living in deserts, with no occupation than the mere animal search for food, may still be seen in the ancient quarter of the globe; but in America such things are new and strange, unknown and unsuspected." Donald Jackson and Mary Lee Spence, ed., *The Expeditions of John Charles Fremont: Travels from 1838 to 1844,* vol. 1 (Urbana: University of Illinois Press, 1970), 702 (emphasis added). John Muir too explored the Great Basin of Nevada, reveling in its stark, vapid beauty on three different visits. Muir poetically described the Great Basin as a land of "volcanic sands and dry sky." John Muir, *The Mountains of California* (New York: Century Company, 1894), 55. He, like Fremont, thought the Great Basin was an American anomaly, although in a different sense. "To the farmer who comes to this land from beneath rainy skies," Muir noted, "Nevada seems one vast desert, all sage and sand, *hopelessly irredeemable,* now and forever. And this, under present conditions, is severely true." Muir went on to observe that "[s]oil, climate topographical conditions, all that the most exacting could demand, are present, but one thing, water, is wanting. The present rainfall would be wholly inadequate for agriculture, even if it were advantageously distributed over the lowlands" instead of occurring primarily in high elevation "cloud-bursts" with little downhill runoff.

Then, epitomizing his penchant for preservationism while belying Nevada's irrigated future, Muir concluded that the Great Basin was indeed different from most of the United States, but not in the negative sense that Colonel Fremont expressed: "Whether any considerable area of these sage plains will ever thus be made to blossom in grass and wheat, experience will show. But in the mean time, Nevada is beautiful in her wildness, and if tillers of the soil can thus be brought to see that possibly Nature may have other uses even for rich soil besides the feeding of human beings, then will these floodless 'deserts' have taught a fine lesson" (John Muir, "Nevada Farms," *Daily Evening Bulletin,* Oct. 5, 1878) (emphasis added). Because this dated source is difficult to obtain, Muir's book *Steep Trails* (Boston: Houghton Mifflin, 1918) provides a rare collection of his observations on Nevada and the Great Basin. See, for example, pages 154–203 (the above-quoted "Nevada Farms" article is reproduced on pages 154–63).

14. Jon Christensen, "The Great Basin, America's Wasteland Seeks a New Identity," *High Country News,* April 3, 1995.

15. Pisani, *To Reclaim,* 299.

16. Francis G. Newlands, "An Address to the People of Nevada on Water Storage and Irrigation," *Reno Evening Gazette,* Oct. 7–13, 1890, cited in Pisani, *To Reclaim,* at 199.

17. Mark Twain, *Roughing It* (New York: Harper and Brothers, 1913), quoted in California Department of Water Resources, *Truckee River Atlas,* 17.

18. John M. Townley, *Turn This Water Into Gold: The Story of the Newlands Project,* 2d ed. (Reno: Nevada Historical Society, 1998), 24.

19. Department of the Interior, *Tenth Annual Report of the Reclamation Service 1910–11* (Washington, D.C.: 1912), 166; Department of the Interior, *Nineteenth Annual Report of the Reclamation Service 1919–20* (Washington, D.C.: 1920), 253.

20. U.S. Statutes at Large 70 (1956): 775. For a summary description of the project see Water and Power Resources Service, *Project Data* (Denver: U.S. Government Printing Office, 1981), 1217.

21. The now renamed Bureau of Reclamation constructed Boca Reservoir on the Little Truckee River in the 1930s as part of the Truckee Storage Project to provide irrigation water for users in the Truckee Meadows, located on the eastern edge of the Sierras above Reno; as this area has urbanized with the growth of Reno, water has shifted from irrigation to urban use. In 1970 Reclamation completed the Stampede Reservoir as part of the Washoe Project. Originally the storage was intended to be used for irrigation purposes. With the growth in urban demand, it was expected that storage water would be sold instead to Reno; but no contracts for this purpose had been executed. Instead, as described in Chapter 14 in more detail, the secretary of the interior dedicated use of the storage water in Stampede Reservoir to recovery of the cui-ui in Pyramid Lake.

22. The largest of these reservoirs holds under three thousand acre-feet of water. California Department of Water Resources, *Carson River Atlas* (Sacramento: California Department of Water Resources, 1991), 91. Total annual consumption of water from agricultural uses in the upper Carson is estimated to be about 140,000 acre-feet. Halleck and Halleck, *Irrigation Drainage,* 9. By comparison, annual consumptive use in the Carson Division of the Newlands Project averages about 180,000 acre-feet per year. Perhaps a third of this water is supplied from the Truckee River.

23. The duty of water generally refers to the amount of water believed to be reasonably necessary to grow crops on irrigated lands.

24. Because the decree segmented the Carson into several sections for purposes of administering priorities, this priority applies only to competing uses in the lower Carson and apparently has little effect as against uses in upstream seg-

ments of the river.

25. Spring snowmelt first was captured at Lake Tahoe in 1913. With the ability to hold more than seven hundred thousand additional acre-feet of water, the dam at Lake Tahoe stored runoff that previously escaped the lake in high spring flows and ran downstream to feed Pyramid Lake. This stored water became available for other uses. The need to maintain a consistent flow of water to spin the turbines in a series of hydroelectric facilities built in the early 1900s along the Truckee River above Reno led to the construction of dams in the 1930s at two other natural lakes in the Sierras: Donner and Independence.

26. Department of the Interior, *Efficiency Study*, 11. Even with the significant cutbacks in project diversions through the Truckee Canal beginning in 1967, discussed in chapter 14, about one third of the river continued to be taken on an average annual basis between 1967 and 1992 (13).

27. The Lahontan Reservoir captures essentially the entire available flow of the Carson River behind its 162-foot-high dam. Between 1912 and 1992 the average annual inflow to the Lahontan Reservoir from the Carson River was 263,200 acre-feet, less than the storage capacity of the reservoir. Water brought from the Truckee River also is stored in Lahontan. Until 1967 approximately forty thousand acre-feet of water was released from the reservoir during each winter to generate hydroelectric power. Because this water was not diverted for irrigation, it found its way to Carson Lake and Stillwater Marsh. Now water stored in the Lahontan Reservoir is released only during the irrigation season for diversion into the farmlands of the Carson Division. In most years the only water reaching the Lahontan Valley wetlands is drainage from these irrigated lands.

28. California Department of Water Resources, *Truckee River Atlas*, 24.

29. Ibid., 26–27.

30. Knack and Stewart, *As Long as the River*, 8.

31. California Department of Water Resources, *Truckee River Atlas*, 25, fig. 4.

32. U.S. Fish and Wildlife Service, Region 1, Cui-ui Recovery Team, *Cui-ui Recovery Plan, Second Revision* (May 15, 1992), 1.

33. California Department of Water Resources, *Truckee River Atlas*, 27.

34. U.S. Fish and Wildlife Service, *In the Shadow*, 11.

35. California Department of Water Resources, *Carson River Atlas*, 32.

36. Thompson and Merritt, "Western Nevada," 42.

37. U.S. Fish and Wildlife Service, *Stillwater National Wildlife Refuge and Stillwater Wildlife Management Area, Lahontan Valley Wetland: An Introduction to the Issues* (Fallon, Nevada, 1990), sec. 1.

38. "Wetlands Analysis: Executive Summary," in U.S. Fish and Wildlife Service, *Stillwater*, sec. 4.

39. Halleck and Halleck, *Irrigation Drainage*, 14 (table 1), 16–18, 58.

40. "An Interview with Robert Pelcyger," in *Resource Law Notes* (Natural Resources Law Center, School of Law, University of Colorado at Boulder) no. 28 (April 1993): 5.

41. The United States decided to file this action in 1973, but the claim was ultimately denied by the U.S. Supreme Court in *Nevada v U.S.*, 463 U.S. 110 (1983). The United States Supreme Court first found such a water right in

1908 in a case involving the Fort Belknap Reservation in Montana (*Winters v U.S.*, 207 U.S. 564 [1908]). Even though the treaty did not specifically set aside water from the Milk River for Native American use, the Court held that there had been an *implied* reservation of water necessary to fulfill the purposes for which the reservation was established—in that case determined to be for agricultural purposes.

42. *Pyramid Lake Paiute Tribe of Indians v Morton*, 354 F.Supp. 252 (D.D.C. 1973).

43. *Truckee-Carson Irrigation District v Secretary of Department of Interior*, 742 F.2d 527 (9th Cir.1984).

44. Department of the Interior, *Efficiency Study*, 6.

45. Truckee-Carson-Pyramid Lake Water Rights Settlement Act, U.S. Statutes at Large 104 (1990): 3294.

46. A copy of the Preliminary Settlement Agreement can be found in California Department of Water Resources, *Truckee River Atlas*.

47. John Muir has been credited as an early proponent of ecology, the study of the holistic interconnectedness of biotic communities. Stephen Fox has, for example, labeled Muir an "intuitive ecologist" because his primary concern was for nature as a whole, not for individual species. Hence, long before ecology became a well-defined specialization in the general field of biology, Muir was writing of natural harmony without artificial categories and with an awareness of the human dimension in this totality.

To illustrate this nascent ecological philosophy, Muir observed during his first summer in the Sierra Nevada mountain range that: "When we try to pick out anything by itself, we find that it is bound fast by a thousand invisible cords that cannot be broken to anything in the universe. I fancy that I can hear a heart beating in every crystal, in every grain of sand and see a wise plan in the making and shaping and placing of every one of them. All seems to be dancing in time to the divine music." John Muir, *Journal*, July 27, 1869, quoted in Stephen Fox, *The American Conservation Movement: John Muir and His Legacy* (Madison: University of Wisconsin Press, 1981), 291.

48. Lindsey Gruson, "The Dilemma: Save a Fish or a Wetland?" *New York Times*, April 26, 1988.

49. Truckee-Carson–Pyramid Lake Water Rights Settlement Act. The Act removed court jurisdiction to review the OCAP until 1997.

50. U.S. Fish and Wildlife Department, Department of the Interior, *Truckee Carson Pyramid Lake Water Rights Settlement Act, Report to the United States Congress* 3,4 (November 1993).

51. Truckee-Carson-Pyramid Lake Water Rights Settlement Act.

52. Ibid.

53. Mining uses preceded irrigation in many parts of the West, but for the most part these uses were transitory. Irrigated agricultural uses were early, extensive, and still continue. Thus these uses generally represent the dominant senior water rights in most rivers of the West.

54. *Truckee-Carson Irrigation District v Secretary of Department of Interior*, 742 F.2d 527 (9th Cir. 1984).

55. Water Rights Report, 11.

56. The price is based on a transferrable quantity of 2.99 acre-feet per acre, the consumptive-use duty established by the Alpine Decree.

57. Water Rights Report, 8.

58. This situation exists in many other reclamation projects around the West (Department of the Interior, Office of Inspector General, *Irrigation of Ineligible Lands, Bureau of Reclamation*, Audit Report No. 94-I-930 (July 1994); Reed D. Benson and Kimberly J. Priestley, "Making a Wrong Thing Right: Ending the 'Spread' of Reclamation Project Water," *Journal of Environmental Law and Litigation* 9 (1994): 89.

59. *United States v Alpine Land and Reservoir Co.*, 878 F.2d 1217 (9th Cir. 1989) ("Alpine II") (reversing in part the district court's upholding of the Nevada state engineer's approval of the irrigator's applications to transfer water rights); *United States v Alpine Land and Reservoir Co.*, 983 F.2d 1487 (9th Cir. 1992) ("Alpine III") (reversing for the second time the district court's approval of the state engineer's decision to transfer the water rights on the grounds that the state engineer improperly decided the issues of abandonment and forfeiture of the water rights to be transferred); after Alpine III the Bureau of Reclamation directed the Truckee-Carson Irrigation District to withhold water deliveries connected with the transfers, and the irrigators sought a preliminary injunction enjoining them from doing so, but it was denied. *United States v Alpine Land and Reservoir Co.*, No. D-184-HDM (D. Nev. June 9, 1994).

60. *United States v Alpine Land and Reservoir Co.*, 887 F.2d 207 (9th Cir. 1989) (deciding that the Department of the Interior [DOI] does have the authority to set basic guidelines for classifying project land as "bench" or "bottom" and district court could review DOI's decision only under an arbitrary and capricious standard*); United States v Alpine Land and Reservoir Co.*, No. D-185-HDM (D. Nev. Aug. 8, 1994) (on remand the district court held that the secretary of the interior did not act arbitrarily or capriciously in classifying the land as "bench or "bottom").

    TCID objected to the classification of some of the lands in the final OCAP and initially was successful in persuading the federal district court to its view. On appeal, however, the Ninth Circuit supported the position of the United States, and in 1994 the federal district court upheld the Department of the Interior's classification scheme.

61. Personal communication from Robert Wigington, August 5, 1994.

62. Department of the Interior, *Efficiency Study*, 21.

63. Ibid., 173.

64. Department of the Interior, Bureau of Reclamation, *Summary Statistics, Vol. 2, Finances and Physical Features* (Denver: Bureau of Reclamation, 1984), 34.

65. Concepts for a Second Generation Truckee-Carson Settlement, Testimony of David Yardas, Environmental Defense Fund, before the United States Senate Energy and Natural Resources Committee, Subcommittee on Water and Power, Reno, Nevada, December 11, 1993.

66. The week before the final session, TCID's newsletter carried an interview with Schank in which he related a dream. He was driving toward his home when he saw spray-painted in red across the road: "Schank is a traitor. He gave our water away." Quoted in Jon Christensen, "No Final Solutions for Farmers," *High Country News*, April 3, 1995.

67. "Community Can Be Proud of Negotiations," letter to the editor, *Reno*

Gazette-Journal, March 6, 1995.

68. Faith Bremner, "Fight, GOP Rise Linked. Analysis: Fallon Farmers React to Key Shift in Congress," *Reno Gazette-Journal,* March 6, 1995.

PART 4

1. State of Washington Water Research Center, *The Yakima Basin and Its Water: At the End, There Is Little to Mark* (Pullman: State of Washington Water Research Center, 1975).

2. Washington Agricultural Statistics Service, *Washington Agricultural Statistics, 1992–1993* (Olympia: 1993), 79.

3. Department of Agriculture, *Washington Agricultural Statistics, Yakima County, 1994* (Washington, D.C.: Department of Agriculture, 1994), 83.

4. Department of the Interior, Bureau of Reclamation, *Water, Land, and Related Data, 1988 Summary Statistics* (Denver: Department of the Interior, 1988), 45.

5. For a discussion of changes being made in other Reclamation projects see MacDonnell, "Managing Reclamation Facilities for Ecosystem Benefits," *University of Colorado Law Review* 67 (Spring 1996), 197-257.

6. In 1994 the Yakama Nation decided to return the spelling of its name to the way it was spelled in the 1859 treaty. Where the spelling of a published document uses "Yakima," it is followed here. Otherwise, this book uses the current spelling preferred by the tribe–Yakama.

7. Richard D. Daugherty, *The Yakima People* (Phoenix: Indian Tribal Series, 1973), 42.

8. Ibid., 46. One source suggests that the name Yakama comes from the Indian word "eyakama" meaning "well-fed people" (Department of Agriculture, *Washington Agricultural Statistics, Yakima County* (Washington, D.C.: Department of Agriculture, 1994), 82. Another source translates the name as "growing family" or "tribal expansion" or even "fertile land" Yakima Indian Agency, *A Primer of the Yakimas* (Toppenish, Wash.: Yakima Indian Agency, 1962), 8.

9. Darlene A. Townsend-Moller and Roger G. Dunham, *Social Assessment of the Yakima Indian Nation* (Pullman: Washington State University, 1975), 11.

10. According to the 1990 census there are 6,136 American Indians living on the Yakama reservation itself and 6,198 on the reservation plus Yakama trust lands. Department of Commerce, Economics and Statistics Administration, Bureau of the Census, *1990 Census of Population, Social and Economic Characteristics: American Indian and Alaskan Native Areas,* sec. 1 (Washington, D.C.: Government Printing Office, 1993), 44. About 1.2 million acres of the reservation are considered tribal trust lands. Townsend-Moller and Dunham, *Social Assessment,* 2.

11. Daugherty, *Yakima People,* 31.

12. U.S. Code, vol. 25, sec. 348 (1994).

13. H. G. Barnett, *The Yakima Indians in 1942* (Eugene: University of Oregon, 1969), 6.

14. Department of the Interior, Bureau of Reclamation, *C. R. Lentz Review, Yakima Project Water Rights and Related Data,* by C. R. Lentz (Yakima: Bureau of Reclamation, 1974; reprint March 1977) (hereafter *Lentz Review*)..

15. *Lentz Review,* 2.

16. Referenced in *United States v Anderson,* 109 F. Supp. 755, 758 (E.D. Wash.

1953).

17. Act of March 4, 1905 (L. 1905, Chapter 88, page 180), State of Washington; Revised Code of Wash., ch. 90.40.
18. *Lentz Review*, 48. The United States apparently kept this claim in place until 1951.
19. *Lentz Review*, 3.
20. Department of the Interior, *Fifth Annual Report of the Reclamation Service 1907* (Washington, D.C.: 1907), 288-89.
21. An Act to Authorize the Sale and Disposition of Surplus or Unallotted Lands of the Yakima Indian Reservation in the State of Washington, U.S. Statutes at Large 33 (1904): 595.
22. An Act Authorizing the Disposition of Surplus and Unallotted Lands on the Yakima Indian Reservation in the State of Washington, U.S. Statutes at Large 34 (1906): 53.
23. This act was deemed to satisfy the condition of the secretary of the interior that a sufficient water supply be secured for the American Indians on the Yakama reservation before there could be expenditures for the Yakima Irrigation Project.
24. 62d Cong., 3d sess., 1913, H. Doc. 1299, serial 6500.
25. Memorial of the Yakima Indians in Washington, 62d Cong., 3d sess., 1913, H. Doc. 1304, serial 6500.
26. Indian Tuberculosis Sanitarium in New Mexico and Yakima Reservation Project in Washington, 63d Cong., 2d sess., 1913, H. Doc. 505, serial 6754.
27. U.S. Statutes at Large 39 (1914): sec. 22, 582. A total of 72,000 acres, soon designated as "A" lands, were eligible to receive water on the reservation without payment of storage construction charges. Additional irrigable lands on the reservation, "B" lands, subsequently received service under so-called Warren Act contracts. In 1921 the Indian Service and the Reclamation Service entered a joint agreement providing 250,000 acre-feet of water for the "B" lands; a 1936 agreement provided an additional 100,000 acre-feet for the "A" lands.
28. Townsend-Moller and Dunham, *Social Assessment*, 59.
29. Louis Tuck Renz, *The History of Northern Pacific Railroad* (Fairfield, Wash.: Ye Galleon Press, 1980), 120.
30. *Lentz Review*, 114.
31. Bumping Lake Reservoir provided 33,700 acre-feet of storage capacity. Kachess Lake created a reservoir with a capacity of 239,000 acre-feet. Kechelus Lake added 158,000 acre-feet of storage. Cle Elum Dam added storage capacity of 436,900 acre-feet. Storage on the Tieton became available with the construction of Clear Creek (completed in 1918) and Tieton (completed in 1925) dams.
32. *Lentz Review*, 50–51.
33. *Kittitas Reclamation District et al. v Sunnyside Valley Irrigation District et al.,* Civil Action No. 21, United States District Court, Eastern District of Washington, Jan. 31, 1945. Thus, for example, the Sunnyside Canal is authorized to divert 449,520 acre-feet of water per year under the decree; since only about 175,000 acre-feet of water is delivered on the basis of water-supply contracts, however, water delivery is based primarily on direct-flow rights. For the Wapato Divi-

sion the decree recognizes a direct-flow right of 720 cubic feet per second (147 cubic feet per second originally recognized in 1906, and an additional 573 cubic feet per second provided for in the 1914 Indian Appropriation Act) as well as contract rights for an additional 350,000 acre-feet. Bureau of Reclamation commitments to water users in the Tieton, Kittitas, and Roza divisions were based on the amounts provided for in the water-supply contracts. The agreements Reclamation entered into with other Yakima River users, known as the "Limiting Agreements," generally were reaffirmed.

34. First the decree declares that all parties whose allocations have been quantified in the decree "have equal rights with respect to the priority" with which deliveries are to be made. In times of insufficient water supply they are to share shortages proportionately. It then excepts a number of water rights from this prorated status, stating that the water obligated under these rights should be "deducted" from the total water supply available. Nonproratable rights include the 720 cubic feet per second right for the Wapato Project, a 250 cubic feet per second right for lands within the Tieton Division, and a total of 791 cubic feet per second for users within the Sunnyside Division. In effect, then, those water users in the Yakima with some kind of legal relationship to the Yakima Project have two priorities–senior (nonproratable) or junior (proratable). It turns out to be an important difference.

35. Yakima River Watershed Council, "A 20/20 Vision for a Viable Future of the Water Resource of the Yakima River Basin" (Yakima, Wash., October 1997, draft), 69. David Lester, "Store More Water and Suffer Fewer Economic Losses, Study Concludes," *Yakima Herald-Republic,* April 20, 1997.

36. Sunnyside Valley Irrigation District, *Annual Report* (Sunnyside, Wash.: 1990).

37. Water and Power Resources Service, *Project Data,* 1346–47.

38. The contract specifies deliveries of 15 percent in April; 19 percent in June, July, and August; 12 percent in September; and 6 percent in October.

39. *Lentz Review,* 119.

40. Personal communication from Don Schramm, Bureau of Reclamation, Dec. 14, 1994.

41. Personal Communication from Jim Trull, Sunnyside Valley Irrigation District, Dec. 16, 1994.

42. Roza Irrigation District, *Comprehensive Water Conservation Plan, Final Document,* prepared for Washington Department of Ecology (December 1992).

43. In the words of the Washington Supreme Court, a general adjudication is "a process whereby all those claiming the right to use waters of a river or stream are joined in a single action to determine water rights and priorities between claimants." *State Department of Ecology v Aquavella,* 674 P.2d 160, 161 (Wash. 1983).

44. A brief summary of the stream adjudication process, prepared by John Thorson, is provided in Western Water Policy Review Advisory Commission, *Water in the West: The Challenge for the Next Century* (Denver, Colo.: 1998), 5: 7.

45. *State Department of Ecology v Aquavella,* 162.

46. *State Department of Ecology v Yakima Reservation Irrigation District,* 850 P.2d 1306, 1309 (Wash. 1993).

47. Judge Stauffacher found that the tribe's irrigation-water rights consist of 720

cubic feet per second (the 147 cubic feet per second recognized by the secretary of the interior in 1906 and 573 cubic feet per second provided by Congress in 1914), which is nonproratable and has a priority date of 1855 (the date of the treaty); 250,000 acre-feet per year under the 1921 Warren Act contract, which is proratable and has a 1905 priority; and 100,000 acre-feet per year under the 1936 Warren Act contract, which is also proratable and has a 1905 priority. *State Department of Ecology v Yakima Reservation Irrigation District,* 1309–10.

48. Reserved-water rights are discussed in chap. 29.

49. *State Department of Ecology v Yakima Reservation Irrigation District,* 1323.

50. Ibid., 1310.

51. Ibid.

52. "Memorandum Opinion Re: Threshold Issues," May 12, 1992, *State Department of Ecology v Aquavella,* No. 77-2-01484-5, in the Superior Court of the State of Washington in and for Yakima County.

53. *Ickes v Fox,* 300 U.S. 82, 95 (1937). The 1945 consent decree, on the other hand, defines delivery obligations of the United States in relation to the Sunnyside, Wapato, Tieton, Kittitas, and Roza divisions and to the water districts and canal companies providing water to users within their service areas (*Kittitas Reclamation District v Sunnyside Valley Irrigation District,* District Court of the United States for the Eastern District of Washington, Southern Division, Civil Action No. 21, Judgment Jan. 31, 1945). Beginning in 1905 the United States had entered into agreements with entities and individuals representing about 95 percent of the claims to water from the Yakima and its tributaries existing as of 1905 (*Lentz Review,* 9). Thereafter the United States entered into water-supply contracts with water districts within the Sunnyside Division, the Yakima Tieton Irrigation District, the Kittitas Reclamation District, the Kennewick Irrigation District, and the Roza Irrigation District, with the Wapato Project (through the Bureau of Indian Affairs), as well as with eighteen other smaller users (*Lentz Review,* 50–51). Supply of water under the contracts is not limited to storage water in Reclamation facilities, but is to come from the "total water supply available" under the 1945 consent decree. In short, legal control over the appropriation and use of the waters of the Yakima River and its tributaries is shared among a large number of different entities, including the United States, the water districts, and the water users/landowners.

54. "Memorandum Opinion," 7.

55. Judge Stauffacher stated the issue as: "Are the irrigation districts limited by the number of acres that have been historically irrigated, rather than the lands capable of irrigation?" (Ibid.) Thus, despite having confirmed that the water rights are "appurtenant to the lands on which they are beneficially used," he focused instead on the rights of the *irrigation districts,* which he determined are based on the total amount of *irrigable* land within their service areas, as determined by the secretary of the interior in the water-supply contracts. In this sense he places ownership of unused water rights in the legal ownership of the district "in its representative capacity for the landowners." Moreover, he ruled that, at least for purposes of the adjudication, specific land areas regarded as irrigable or irrigated need not be individually identified. The general records

of the United States and the districts are adequate.

56. Dispute over the land area to be used for determining water rights is critical because the quantity of water presumed to be allocated under the rights is determined by multiplying the "duty" of water–an amount of water determined to be "reasonably required" to be applied to a unit of land (an acre) during the irrigation season to maximize the production of crops ordinarily grown on such land. The classic statement is from *Farmers Highline Canal and Reservoir Co. v City of Golden*, 272 P.2d 629, 634 (Colo. 1954): "It is that measure of water, which, by careful management and use, without wastage is reasonably required to be applied to any given tract of land for such period of time as may be adequate to produce therefrom a maximum amount of such crops as are ordinarily grown thereon." Thus the total quantity of water allocated to each of the districts under the water supply contracts and the 1945 consent decree is based on the total number of acres within each district regarded as irrigable and the per-acre duty of water established in the contract. Such an approach is a common way in which water allocations for irrigation use were established historically. Presumably it represents the *maximum* commitment of water to some use with a specified priority date; it does not, of course, represent actual use. Nor can it be regarded as establishing a completed or perfected water right to this amount of water; that amount is measured in terms of actual, beneficial use of water.

Thus, in addition to specifying particular acreage regarded as holding a water right, the other ways to evaluate the quantity of water legally controlled by a water right is to determine the duty of water for particular lands, to determine whether no more than this amount of water historically has been applied to the lands, to determine whether the efficiency of the water-delivery system that provides water to farm headgates is "reasonable," and to determine that water use on appurtenant lands has not been abandoned or forfeited. For a discussion of the way these issues have been treated in the context of the Newlands Project in the Truckee-Carson Basin of Nevada, see MacDonnell, "Managing Reclamation Facilities for Ecosystem Benefits," *University of Colorado Law Review* 67, issue 2 (Spring 1996): 197–257. Judge Stauffacher appears to have taken the position that these are not issues to be determined in an adjudication. Rather, he is intent on determining the maximum quantity of water that might be legally obligated to the districts. Beneficial use, then, is amply demonstrated by the fact that valuable crops are grown within the districts. In the words of Judge Stauffacher: "On Saturday, February 29, 1992, the *Yakima Herald Republic* published the 'Yakima Irrigation Project Crop Report' for the years 1988, 1989, and 1990, as furnished by the Bureau of Reclamation. The Project Report lists 20 crops, the acreage of each crop and the dollar value thereof for each of the three years. In 1990, 321,647 acres of the 20 crops reported produced $634,952,886.00 of value. Thus we can clearly see that the yearly reports compiled by the diverting and supplying entities in the aggregate can constitute proof of the "beneficial use" of the water by the landowners within the boundaries of the districts" ("Memorandum Opinion," 28).

Reasonable efficiency is simply one of the considerations in determining water duties. Ordinarily, the duty of water is measured at the field or at the farm headgate. Thus, in *Farmers Highline Canal* the court speaks of the measure of water "applied to any given tract of land." Efficiency then refers to the difference between the amount of water that must be diverted from the water source and the amount of water applied to the land. See Andrew A. Keller and Jack Keller, "Effective Efficiency: A Water Use Efficiency Concept for Allocating Freshwater Resources" (discussion paper no. 22, Winrock International Center for Economic Policy Studies, Washington, D.C., 1995). Judge Stauffacher's ruling in this case appears to include system delivery losses within the measure of water duty. Abandonment or forfeiture is determined not on the basis of failing to use water on specific tracts of land for five or more consecutive years, but on whether the *district* intended to give up some of its water rights because it did not divert the maximum amount to which it is entitled during any five-year period. Again, to quote Judge Stauffacher: "when the district does not receive their *[sic]* full contractual amount of water, can it be said that they have 'abandoned' or 'voluntarily failed' to use that portion of the water right that they do not receive? This would be a very difficult proposition for the state to prove" ("Memorandum Opinion," 24). Moreover, Judge Stauffacher made it clear that he was likely to uphold the water-right quantifications established in the 1945 consent decree.

57. In all likelihood the allocations established in the 1945 consent decree are not going to change in any significant way. Water deliveries based on Reclamation contracts will be fine-tuned to take into account the land area within each entity presently regarded as irrigable, and the duty of water will be based on historical practices. The proratable/nonproratable distinction is virtually certain to be maintained on the same basis as it presently exists. The Bureau of Reclamation will continue to have substantial discretion in the administration of the waters of Yakima Basin that are controlled by the Yakima Project. The one notable outcome of the adjudication is the determination of a water right for the Yakama Nation based on maintaining the anadromous fishery in the river. In practice this water right appears primarily to increase Reclamation's discretion in managing flows of water to be maintained in-stream to protect the fishery. Adjudication of rights in the subbasins should give the state the ability to administer water uses not directly controlled by the project. Groundwater usage unfortunately will not be addressed as part of the adjudication. In short, after nearly two decades of legal proceedings, relatively little will have changed in the water-rights structure of the Yakima Basin.

58. Bonneville Power Administration, *Yakima River Basin Fisheries Project, Draft Environmental Impact Statement* (Portland: Bonneville Power Administration, Oct. 1992), 3.16 [hereafter Yakima EIS].

59. Yakima Indian Nation Fisheries Resource Management, *Yakima River Spring Chinook Enhancement Study, Annual Report FY 1989,* by David E. Fast, Michael S. Kohn, and Bruce D. Watson (Portland: Bonneville Power Administration, Dec. 1989), 49.

60. Ibid., 62-66, tables 20 to 24.

61. Yakima EIS, 1.7. Estimates range down to 300,000 on the low end. Another source places the range at from 600,000 to 960,000 (Yakima EIS, 1.6).

62. Karen E. Kreeger and William J. McNeil, *Summary and Estimation of the Historic Run-Sizes of Anadromous Salmonids in the Columbia and Yakima Rivers*, report prepared for the Yakima River Basin Coalition (Washington, D.C.: Government Printing Office, 1993), reprinted in *Yakima River Basin and Canyon Ferry, Hearings before the Subcommittee on Oversight and Investigations of the Committee on Natural Resources*, House of Representatives on H.R. 1690 and H.R. 1477, Serial No. 103–53 (1994), 330.

63. Yakima EIS, 3.3.

64. Ibid., app. B, p.2–1. Under a 1958 agreement with the U.S. Fish and Wildlife Service, Reclamation attempted to maintain a minimum flow level of two hundred cubic feet per second, except during the peak of the irrigation season, when it could go as low as fifty cubic feet per second. The 1994 Yakima River Basin Water Enhancement Project Act sets "target" flows at three hundred cubic feet per second. *Yakima River Basin Water Enhancement Project Act*, Title XII, P.C. 104–434, U.S. Statutes at Large 108 (1994): sec. 1205.

65. Department of the Interior, Bureau of Reclamation, *Yakima/Klickitat Production Preliminary Design Report, 1990,* prepared for Bonneville Power Administration, Portland, app. B, p. 3–2.

66. Ibid.

67. Bonneville Power Administration, Washington Department of Fish and Wildlife, Yakama Indian Nation, *Yakima Fisheries Project, Final Environmental Impact Statement,* Department of Energy EIS-0169, January 1996, p. 67.

68. Yakima/Klickitat Production Preliminary Design Report, 3–4.

69. *United States v State of Washington,* 384 F.Supp. 312 (W.D. Wash. 1974), aff'd 520 F.2d 676 (9th Cir. 1976), cert. denied, 423 U.S. 1086 (1976). In support of his holding, Judge Boldt found that the Yakama consumed five hundred pounds of salmon per person each year at the time of the treaty, and that they commonly fished for salmon in many places outside the reservation, including in the Puget Sound, the particular focus of the litigation.

70. Carol Craig, "Reawakening the Spirit–Yakama Tribe Leads Rededication of Willamette Falls Fishery," *Wana Chinook Tymoo* (Columbia River Inter-Tribal Fish Commission), nos. 2, 3 (1994): 13.

71. *Kittitas Reclamation District v Sunnyside Valley Irrigation District,* 763 F.2d 1032 (9th Cir. 1985). He approved other physical actions to protect the redds and established a technical advisory group of fish biologists.

72. Ibid.

73. Ibid., 1033.

74. For a more detailed discussion of this situation see MacDonnell et al., *Restoring the West's Waters: Opportunities for the Bureau of Reclamation,* Natural Resources Law Center Research Report, vol. 2 (Boulder, Colo.: Natural Resources Law Center, 1995), chap. 1.

75. "Memorandum Opinion Re: Flushing Flows," Dec. 22, 1994, p. 6, *Washington Department of Ecology v Acquavella,* Superior Court of the State of Washington in and for Yakima County, No. 77-2-01484-5.

76. 850 F. Supp. 866 (D. Or. 1994).

77. Ibid., 900.

78. 35 F.3d 1371 (9th Cir. 1994).

79. Ibid., 1395. DSIs are "Direct Service Industries," companies purchasing power from the Bonneville Power Authority.

80. *Ibid.*, 1391.

81. *Yakima Enhancement Act,* secs. 1201-1212, 4550-4565.The bill includes many more provisions than described here. For example, funds are provided to enlarge the storage capacity of Cle Elum Reservoir and to study the enlargement of Kachess Reservoir; water no longer will be diverted to run the turbines used to pump water to the Kennewick Irrigation District; the project purposes are expanded to include fish, wildlife, and recreation specifically; federal funding will be used to make improvements to the Wapato Irrigation Project with the water savings available for irrigation or for fish and wildlife enhancement; and funds will be provided to study improvements that could be made to Taneum Creek and other tributaries to improve flows and habitat for fish.

82. Environmental Defense Fund, *Water Marketing and Instream Flow Enhancement in Washington's Yakima River Basin–Procedures for Dry Year Leasing and Transfer of Water,* draft Final Report, May 28, 1993.

83. David Lester, "Fish Win Out in First Lease of Water Rights," *Yakima Herald-Republic,* May 17, 1996.

84. For a discussion of water banking in general and a proposed approach for setting up a water bank, see MacDonnell, "Water Banks: Untangling the Gordian Knot of Western Water," *Rocky Mountain Mineral Law Institute* 41 (1995): chap. 22.

85. The situation in the Yakima Basin parallels in many respects the Truckee-Carson Basin. In the Truckee-Carson the Pyramid Lake Paiute Tribe has succeeded in getting the secretary of the interior to take actions reducing diversions for irrigation into the Newlands Project to protect the endangered cui-ui fish in Pyramid Lake. This situation is described in MacDonnell, "Managing Reclamation Facilities."

86. U.S. Code, vol. 43, sec. 390aa (1994).

87. For example, still another option might be to buy back some portion of contract commitments from each of the water districts and other water users as necessary to bring the project commitments into line with a more sustainable supply of water, a supply that factors in the needs of fish and other values. Perhaps an equal percentage of the total contract commitments could be targeted for purchase from each division as a means of equitably sharing the effects of the buy-back. Ideally this approach would be implemented on a voluntary basis. Because many users are likely to object, and market negotiations may be exceptionally difficult, condemnation authority (not presently available) might be needed. In any case, the advantage of such a buy-back approach is that it avoids the need for the United States to engage in detailed investigations of water use within the districts and allows the districts themselves to work out their own approaches for coming up with the water that is to be acquired. Alternatively, a more incremental approach would be to negotiate with districts and users individually in an effort to buy back as much allocated water as would be forthcoming voluntarily at an acceptable price to the United States. In either case Congress would need to provide the considerable funds necessary to restore a more sustainable use of water in the

Yakima Basin.

88. A good description of the council is provided in Farm Credit Service, "Yakima Water Users Team Up to Resolve Water Issues," *Yields*, Second Quarter Report (August 1995): 5–7.

89. Quoted in Bill Dunbar, "Putting (Not Knocking) Heads Together: Can the Yakima River Watershed Council Fix the Yakima Basin's Water Problems?" *Northwest Energy News* 15, no. 1 (Winter 1996): 23.

90. Yakima River Watershed Council, *Report on the State of the Water Resources of the Yakima River Basin* (Yakima: July 1996). The report established a goal of a full water supply for nonproratable users and a 70 percent supply for proratables in a dry year such as 1994. It set a goal of a seven hundred cubic feet per second minimum flow at Sunnyside and Prosser dams, fifty thousand acre-feet dedicated to protecting fish egg incubation, and thirty thousand acre-feet for flushing flows. It also identified several strategies for water conservation to be pursued. And it committed to continuing study of water storage opportunities.

91. Yakima River Watershed Council, "A 20/20 Vision for a Viable Future of the Water Resource of the Yakima River Basin" (Yakima, Wash., June 1998, draft). This report established a goal of as much as 655,000 acre-feet of water that can be used in water-short years to address needs of proratable users, in-stream needs, and municipal water demands.

92. Known as HB 2514, the legislation authorizes voluntary watershed planning in water resources inventory areas. The planning process must be initiated by all counties within the planning area, the largest town or city, and the largest water-supply utility. Tribes with reservation lands within the area also must be invited to be an initiator. Such efforts must evaluate water supply and use within the area, including needs for in-stream flows. Water quality and habitat issues may be included as well. Grants are available to help with initial organizing, assessment work, and the development of management plans.

93. U.S. Code, vol. 33, sec. 1313(d) (1994).

94. Washington State Department of Ecology, *Watershed Briefing Paper for the Upper and Lower Yakima Watersheds,* Publication No. 96–336 (Olympia: Washington State Department of Ecology, 1996). See also Joseph F. Rinella, Pixie A. Hamilton, and Stuart W. McKenzie, *Persistence of the DDT Pesticide in the Yakima River Basin, Washington,* U.S. Geological Survey Circular 1090 (Denver: Government Printing Office, 1993). The Tri-City Herald ran a series of articles in 1997 and 1998 detailing water-quality problems with the Yakima River ("The Yakima: A River Wasted"). These articles can be found on the Internet at *http://www.tri-cityherald.com/yakima/*.

95. The State Department of Ecology has in fact produced a TMDL for several pollutants in the lower Yakima that details the amount and sources of pollution and prescribes limits and a schedule for reducing pollutants to improve water quality to state standards. Joe Jay and Barbara Patterson, *A Suspended Sediment and DDT Total Maximum Daily Load Evaluation Report for the Yakima River,* Publication No. 97–321 (Olympia: Washington State Department of Ecology, 1997). Ecology hopes to be able to achieve its scheduled reductions through voluntary programs such as the one initiated by the Roza

and Sunnyside districts.

96. Roza-Sunnyside Board of Joint Control, *Policies and Programs to Improve Water Quality and the Use of Water,* (Sunnyside, Wash.: 1997).

97. David Lester, "It Runs Through a River," *Yakima Herald-Republic,* March 1, 1998.

98. Ibid.

99. Natural Resources Law Center, *The Watershed Source Book: Watershed-Based Solutions to Natural Resource Problems* (Boulder: Natural Resources Law Center, 1996).

PART 5

1. Western Water Policy Review Advisory Commission, *Water in the West,* 2:14.

2. Peter H.Gleick et al., *California Water 2020: A Sustainable Vision* (Oakland: Pacific Institute for Studies in Development, Environment, and Security, 1995).

3. W. L. Minckley et al., "Sustainability of Western Native Fish Resources," *Aquatic Ecosystems Symposium,* Report to the Western Water Policy Review Advisory Commission (September 1997), 65.

4. River basin reports to the commission: Leo Eisel and J. David Aiken, *Platte River Basin Study;* Sue McClurg, *Sacramento-San Joaquin River Basin Study;* Ernie Niemi, *Water Management Study:Upper Rio Grande Basin;* Dale Pontius, *Colorado River Basin Study;* Jeremy Pratt, *Truckee-Carson River Basin Study;* John M.Volkman, *A River in Common: The Columbia River, The Salmon Ecosystem, and Water Policy* (all cited in Western Water Policy Review Advisory Commission, *Water in the West,* vii).

5. Minckley et al., "Sustainability," 67–68.

6. Nancy B. Grimm et al., "Sustainability of Western Watersheds: Nutrients and Productivity," Aquatic Ecosystems Symposium, Report to the Western Water Policy Review Advisory Commission (September 1997), 39.

7. "Based on surveys conducted by the States, this report indicates that, while most of the Nation's surveyed waters are of good quality, about 40 percent of the Nation's surveyed rivers, lakes, and estuaries are too polluted for basic uses, such as fishing and swimming." Statement of the administrator of the Environmental Protection Agency, Carol Browner, quoted in United States Environmental Protection Agency, Office of Water, *National Water Quality Inventory: 1994 Report to Congress* (Washington, D.C.: Government Printing Office, 1995) (written statement of Carol M. Browner to the President of the Senate and Speaker of the House). For the particular percentage breakdown of water quality for state rivers and streams according to good or degraded status, see pages 25–28.

   The Region VIII Office of the EPA prepared a general summary of water-quality conditions in the western states for the Western Water Policy Review Advisory Commission. EPA Region VIII, *Water Quality in the West* (Denver: May 1997). While finding western water quality to be generally good, it pointed out the continuing concerns with impairment from nonpoint sources.

8. U.S. Water Resources Council, *The Nation's Water Resources, 1975–2000: The Second National Water Assessment* (Washington, D.C.: Government Printing Office, 1978).

9. California Department of Water Resources, *California Water Plan Update:*

Executive Summary, Bulletin 160–93 (October 1994).

10. U.S. Code, vol. 42, sec. 4331(a) (1994).

11. U.S. Code, vol. 16, secs. 1271-1287 (1994). The Wild and Scenic Rivers Act, passed into law in 1968, created a national system of rivers and river segments classified as wild, scenic, or recreational, with levels of protection according to their designation.

12. U.S. Code, vol. 42, sec. 4331(a) (1994).

13. The Clean Water Act prohibits in section 301 the "discharge of any pollutant by any person" without a permit (U.S. Code, vol. 33, sec. 1311[a [1994]); see also sec. 402, found at U.S. Code, vol. 33, sec. 1342 (1994) (laying out the provisions for the "national pollutant discharge elimination system" [NPDES], which requires an effluent permit for any point source pollution discharge). The term "discharge of any pollutant" is defined in sec. 502 as the "addition of any pollutant to navigable waters from any point source" or the "addition of any pollutant to the waters of the contiguous zone or the ocean from any point source other than a vessel or other floating craft.". In addition to a broad definition of "pollutant," "point source" is in turn defined expansively as "any discernible, confined and discrete conveyance, including but not limited to any pipe, ditch, channel, tunnel, conduit, well, discrete fissure, container, rolling stock, concentrated animal feeding operation, or vessel or other floating craft, from which pollutants are or may be discharged." U.S. Code, vol. 33, sec. 1362 [14] (1994).

In evaluating a dredge-and-fill permit application, the Army Corps of Engineers is required to assess the "probable impact including cumulative impacts of the proposed activity on the public interest," including the weighing of factors such as "conservation, economics, aesthetics, [and] general environmental concerns" among other considerations. Code of Fed. Reg., vol. 33, sec. 325.3(c)(1) (1996). Environmental Protection Agency permit guidelines specify in addition that a permit shall be issued only if: (1) there is no practicable alternative "which would have less adverse impact on the aquatic ecosystem;" (2) there will be no violation of applicable statutes, including state water-quality standards, toxic effluent standards, and the Endangered Species Act, caused by the proposed discharge; (3) there will be no contribution to "degradation of the waters of the United States," including impacts upon "human health or welfare . . . [,] aquatic life and other wildlife dependent on aquatic ecosystems . . . [,] aquatic ecosystem diversity, productivity, and stability . . . [, and] recreational, aesthetic and economic values;" and (4) "appropriate and practicable steps have been taken which will minimize potential adverse impacts of the discharge on the aquatic ecosystem." Code of Fed. Reg., vol. 40, sec. 230.10(a)–(d) (1996). In general, the EPA's section 404 regulations can be found at Code of Fed. Reg., vol. 40, secs. 230–233, and the Army Corps of Engineers section 404 and ocean dumping regulations can be found at Code of Fed. Reg., vol. 33, secs. 323–330.

14. Sec. 7 of the Endangered Species Act requires that all federal agencies must insure, in consultation with the secretary of the interior, that any agency actions are "not likely to jeopardize the continued existence of any endangered species or threatened species or result in the destruction or adverse modification of [designated critical] habitat of such species." U.S. Code, vol. 16, sec.

1536[a][2] (1994). Furthermore, the Endangered Species Act makes it unlawful in sec. 9 for any person to "take" any endangered animal species–that is, to sell, import, export, or transport any of the species listed by the secretaries of commerce or the interior pursuant to sec. 4. See U.S. Code, vol. 16, sec. 1538(a)(1)(A)-(G) (1994). A "take" is defined stringently by sec. 3 to mean any attempt by a private party to "harass, harm, pursue, hunt, shoot, wound, kill, trap, capture, or collect, or to attempt to engage in any such conduct" with respect to endangered species (U.S. Code, vol. 16, sec. 1532[19] [1994]).

15. Electric Consumers Protection Act of 1986, U.S. Code, vol. 16, sec. 797(e), 803(a) (1994).

16. For a more complete discussion of this point see MacDonnell and Bates, "Rethinking Resources: Reflections on a New Generation of Natural Resources Policy and Law,"in *Natural Resources Policy and Law: Trends and Directions* (Washington, D.C.: Island Press, 1993), chap. 1

17. In the elegant words of Philip Howard: "Rules preclude initiative. Regimentation precludes evolution. Letting accidents happen, mistakes be made, results in new ideas. Trial and error is the key to all progress. . . . No one should ever, never ever [sic], be allowed to exercise discretion: In matters of regulation, law itself will provide the answer. Sentence by sentence, it prescribes every eventuality that countless rule writers can imagine. But words, even millions of them, are finite. The range of possible future circumstances is infinite. One slip-up, one unforeseen event, and all those logical words turn into dictates of illogic." Philip K. Howard, *The Death of Common Sense: How Law is Suffocating America* (New York: Random House, 1994), 50–51.
And: "Principles are like trees in open fields. We can know where we are and where to go. But the path we take is our own. . . . The sunlight of common sense shines high above us whenever principles control: What is right and reasonable, not the parsing of legal language, dominates the discussion. . . . Law has a lasting stature, as a beacon for common goals and a wise forum in times of trouble, and no longer meddles in our daily affairs. Law would be law again" (177).

18. David Wilcove, Michael J. Bean, Robert Bonnie, and Margaret McMillan, *Rebuilding the Ark: Toward a More Effective Endangered Species Act for Private Land*, Environmental Defense Fund (Washington, D.C.: 1997). In fact, this is increasingly the strategy of programs under the farm bills that pay landowners not to use lands more valuable for habitat or water quality protection. Economic Research Service, *Conservation and the 1996 Farm Act, Agricultural Outlook*, U.S. Department of Agriculture, (Washington, D.C.: Nov. 1996), 1–8 (Special Article).

19. Compare Samuel P. Hays, *Conservation and the Gospel of Efficiency: The Progressive Conservation Movement, 1890–1920* (Cambridge, Mass: Harvard University Press, 1959) with Robert H. Nelson, *Public Lands and Private Rights: The Failure of Scientific Management* (Lanham, Md.: Rowman and Littlefield, 1995).

20. I remember being introduced to the hydrologic cycle at the very beginning of the water-law course I took many years ago, but it really didn't mean much to me then. The notion that water is in a constant state of motion, following gravity out of the atmosphere to lands and oceans, some seeping into the ground,

some used by plants, some filling streams and rivers, returning once again to the atmosphere through evaporation, seemed obvious enough. So what?

What I didn't appreciate then is that this cycling of water links together everything that water touches in its cycle. Every human action altering the hydrologic cycle has consequences for other functions that water already is performing as it moves through the cycle. From the perspective of the hydrologic cycle all water is committed. It is being used and used and used again as it moves through this cycle: allowing plants to fix carbon, providing oxygen and nutrients to fish and other aquatic species, transporting sediments, assimilating wastes, moving heat through the atmosphere, and so on. There is nothing static or fixed about the manner in which molecules of water are used. But they *are* continually in use.

Humans need water too, of course—about two gallons a day just for basic consumption, more than that for normal household uses such as bathing, washing, and cooking. We divert water out of the hydrologic cycle to satisfy these uses. Perhaps more accurately, we become part of the hydrologic cycle as we move water out of the ground or from streams into our houses and onto our lands, make our uses of water, and then return what remains back to the cycle. We redirect the hydrologic cycle to meet our needs and desires.

Water law, as I now see it, can be understood to be the rules that govern human participation in the hydrologic cycle. In particular, water law is primarily intended to sort out conflicts between and among *human* users of water as it moves through the cycle. If I act to alter the cycle (by, for example, diverting water out of a river) I affect the opportunity for others to use that water. Water law sets out the rules under which I may or may not act to alter the hydrologic cycle for my benefit in relation to others who also want to use that same water. Such rules are concerned primarily with human actions affecting the physical availability of water.

Environmental law (related to water) also sets out rules governing human participation in the hydrologic cycle. Water-quality law, for example, focuses primarily on the extent to which human uses may alter the physical, chemical, and biological characteristics of water to the detriment of other uses. Thus, for example, use of water to carry away human-generated wastes is restricted to assimilation of discharges that meet technologically based standards of treatment. It is the assimilative capacity of water that is being allocated, rather than its physical availability.

More controversial are the efforts under some environmental laws to govern human uses of water in relation to their adverse effects on the many uses of water that only indirectly benefit humans. Thus, for example, the filling of wetlands is regulated because such areas are now understood to provide valuable water quality, flood control, and habitat functions. Minimum stream flows are maintained in some river segments to preserve fish populations. Proposed new water uses may be modified in some instances to protect endangered plant or animal species.

These laws and their implementation reflect judgments about the rules that should apply to human uses of water. Initially we were concerned primarily with sorting out disputes respecting physical control of the resource between competing human users. We developed legal rules concerning who could use water and under what circumstances that use could occur. Later, as we began to better understand some of the consequences of human uses on other important water values, we started to develop other kinds of limitations to protect these values. These rules are constantly evolving as needs and interests change.

Thinking about the hydrologic cycle also points out the interdependencies that exist. Water links together everything and everybody that depends on its use. Few water uses totally exclude any other uses of the water. Most simply piggyback on water as it moves through the cycle, taking advantage of its availability for a period and then passing it on. Some uses may transform water physically—for example, from a liquid to a vapor (as when a plant uses water for photosynthesis or when water evaporates to carry away heat), but the effect is to move water into other parts of the hydrologic cycle—not to make it unusable.

Human decisions to use water implicate other uses of water. It is the consciousness itself that humans bring to water uses that separates human uses from other uses. The knowledge that humans have choices and, to some degree at least, understand the possible consequences of those choices imposes a responsibility to make those choices carefully. Because humans have the ability to transform so totally the hydrologic cycle, this responsibility is important. Because water truly is a shared resource, in which one manner of use can impoverish so many other uses, human water use decisions should continually be evaluated.

I had an opportunity in 1996 to spend some time with a three-person delegation from South Africa that had come to the United States to examine American water law. South Africa is engaged in a process of wholesale civil transformation, including its system of water law. As an initial step in water-law reformation a working group developed a set of principles to serve as guidance for their new system. The very first principle concerns "the water cycle" and provides: "*In a relatively arid country such as South Africa, it is necessary to recognise the unity of the water cycle and the interdependence of its elements, where evaporation, clouds and rainfall are linked to underground water, rivers, lakes, wetlands, estuaries and the sea.*" Department of Water Affairs and Forestry, Republic of South Africa, "Water Law Principles," Johannesburg, April 1996, 1. We would do well in the American West to evaluate our existing system of water law in view of the teachings of the hydrologic cycle.

21. For more on the use of incentives to encourage environmentally compatible development in the West, see MacDonnell, "Thinking About Environmentally Sustainable Development in the American West," *Journal of Land, Resources, and Environmental Law* 18, no. 1 (1998), 131-136.

22. Elwood Mead, *Irrigation Institutions: A Discussion of the Economic and Legal Questions Raised by the Growth of Irrigated Agriculture in the West* (1903; New York: Arno Press, 1972).

23. Gilbert White brought this distinction to my attention when we were working together on a study of western water policy in the 1980s.

24. Western Water Policy Review Advisory Commission, *Water in the West*, 2–23, fig. 2–9.

25. The U.S. Department of Agriculture estimates that irrigators reduced water-application rates from a national average of about 25 inches per season during the late 1960s and early 1970s to about 20.5 inches in 1994, nearly a 20 percent decrease. Department of Agriculture, "Water and Water-Related Programs, Accomplishments and Challenges," Report to the WesternWater Policy Review Advisory Commission (May 1997), 28. Reclamation reports that water deliveries from its facilities declined from an average of 3.03 acre-feet per acre in 1970 to an average of 2.88 acre-feet per acre in 1990. Department of the Interior, *Acreage Limitations and Water Conservation Rules and Regulations, Final Environmental Impact Statement,* (Bureau of Reclamation, Feb. 1996), 3.53.

26. This is the reason that conservation investments in the Imperial Valley, where water diverted from the Colorado River never returns to the system, can produce an improved water supply for urban users on the south coast of California.

27. California Water Code, sec. 1011: "When any person entitled to the use of water under an appropriative right fails to use all or any part of the water because of water conservation efforts, any cessation or reduction in the use of such appropriated water shall be deemed equivalent to a reasonable beneficial use of water to the extent of such cessation or reduction in use. No forfeiture of the appropriative right to the water conserved shall occur upon the lapse of the forfeiture period applicable to water appropriated." Subsequent amendments to this section made it explicit that conserved water could be "sold, leased, exchanged, or otherwise transferred."

28. The Oregon Water Resources Code defines "conservation" as the "reduction of the amount of water consumed or irretrievably lost in the process of satisfying an existing beneficial use achieved either by improving the technology or method for diverting, transporting, applying or recovering the water or by implementing other approved conservation measures." Conserved water is "that amount of water, previously unavailable to subsequent appropriators, that results from conservation measures." Oregon Revised Statutes, Annotated, (1988), sec. 537.455(1)(2).

   Upon receipt of an acceptable conservation plan, the Oregon Water Resources Commission shall, "[a]fter determining the quantity of conserved water, if any, required to mitigate the effects on other water rights, . . . allocate 25 percent to the state and *75 percent to the applicant*" unless the water-rights holder wishes to allocate voluntarily more to the state, or more than 25 percent of the funding for the conservation measures comes from state or federal sources. Oregon Revised Statutes, Annotated (1988 & Supp. 1996), sec. 537.470 (emphasis added).

29. According to Montana's Water Resources Code, " 'salvage' means to make water available for beneficial use from an existing valid appropriation through application of water-saving methods." Montana Code, Annotated (1995), sec. 85–2–102 (14). In order "to encourage the conservation and full use of water . . . [,] holders of appropriation rights who salvage water . . . may retain the right to the salvaged water for beneficial *use*" (although any change in the original use or place of use must be approved as a change in appropriation right), or may make a "*sale* of the salvaged water" or a "*lease* of the salvaged water for instream flow purposes." Montana Code, Annotated (1995),

sec. 85–2–419 (emphasis added).

30. California's constitutional provision requiring "reasonable use" of water has, in fact, been interpreted in just this manner. In *Tulare Irrigation District v Lindsay-Strathmore Irrigation District*, 3 Cal. 2d 567 (1935), the California Supreme Court stated: "What is a beneficial use, of course, depends upon the facts and circumstances of each case. What may be a reasonable beneficial use, where water is present in excess of all needs, would not be a reasonable beneficial use in an area of great scarcity and great need. *What is a beneficial use at one time may, because of changed conditions, become a waste of water at a later time'*[emphasis added].

In litigation involving administrative action by the State Water Resources Control Board against the Imperial Irrigation District for alleged waste of water, the California Court of Appeals rejected IID's arguments that their water rights were immune from such examination:

> Our conclusion that the Board Decision substantially impacted the practical use and administration by IID of its water does not, however, result in our acceptance of IID's contention of unconstitutional interference with 'vested' rights. Historic concepts of water 'rights' in California were dramatically altered by the adoption in 1928 of the above referenced constitutional amendment.
>
> Put simply, IID does not have the vested rights which it alleges. It has only vested rights to the 'reasonable' use of water. It has no right to waste or misuse water. *Imperial Irrigation District v State Water Resources Control Board*, 225 Cal. App. 3d 548, 563–64 (1990).

31. Arizona has established such requirements for groundwater users in Active Management Areas. In 1980 Arizona adopted the Arizona Groundwater Management Act to remedy a serious groundwater "overdraft" of nearly 2.2 million acre-feet per year as a result of "nonmanagement" of groundwater resources. Arizona essentially suffered from groundwater mining–withdrawals rates from aquifers were far in excess of net recharge by natural processes–and the 1980 act sought to integrate the management of ground and surface water resources so as to limit this skewed rate of groundwater extraction and equitably allocate the use of groundwater resources among competing users. Tarlock, Corbridge, and Getches, *Water Resources Management* (Westburg, N.Y.: The Foundation Press, 1993), 545. See generally Arizona Revised Statutes, Annotated (1994 and Supp. 1996), sec. 45–401 to 45–704.

The act established four initial "Active Management Areas"–Tucson, Phoenix, Prescott, and Pinal (southeast of Phoenix)–where integrated, "active" management of groundwater withdrawals with surface-water use was prescribed. Preexisting agricultural groundwater users were granted "grandfathered" rights, calculated by an "irrigation water duty," the "amount of water in acre-feet per acre that is reasonable to apply to irrigated land in a farm unit" during three specified "accounting period[s]" Arizona Revised Statutes, Annotated (1994 and Supp. 1996), sec. 45–402[24]. A grandfathered irrigation right, once established, is deemed to be "owned by the owner of the land to which it is appurtenant" and is allowed to be "leased for an irrigation use with the land to which it was appurtenant." Sec. 45–465.

This approach recognizes the vested rights of irrigators who are dependent upon previously unregulated groundwater resources. However, the progressive scheme established by the act for irrigation use of groundwater is designed to impose increasingly stringent water-conservation requirements on the agricultural use of groundwater. The intent is to correct the overdraft problem and ideally make groundwater use in Arizona sustainable over the long run by balancing withdrawal rates with rates of aquifer recharge. At the same time, the amortized scheme is designed to be sensitive to the equities of imposing conservation measures in a wholesale manner on agricultural groundwater users.

During the "first management period" of 1980 to 1990, the irrigation-water duty "shall be calculated as the quantity of water reasonably required to irrigate the crops historically grown in a farm unit and shall assume conservation methods being used in the state which would be reasonable for the farm unit including lined ditches, pump-back systems, land leveling and efficient application practices, but not including a change from flood irrigation to drip or sprinkler irrigation." Sec. 45–564(A)(1) (1994). For the "second management period" from 1990 to 2000 "a new water irrigation duty" is established, to be achieved by the end of the accounting period, with increasingly stringent "intermediate water duties to be achieved at specified intervals" during this management period. The new irrigation water duty "shall be calculated as the quantity of water reasonably required to irrigate the crops historically grown in the farm unit and shall assume the maximum conservation consistent with prudent long-term farm management practices within areas of similar farming conditions, considering the time required to amortize conservation investments and financing costs." Sec. 45–565(A)(1) (1994 and Supp. 1996).

And lastly, the water duty for the "third management period" from 2000 to 2010 is calculated in a manner similar to the second management period and requires yet another "new irrigation water duty" to be achieved by the end of the accounting period, with specified intermediate water duties to be achieved at "intervals during the third management period." In addition, after computing such intermediate water duties, the Arizona water-resources director is allowed to "adjust the highest twenty-five percent of the water duties within an area of similar farming conditions by reducing each water duty in an amount up to ten percent, except that in making the adjustment, no water duty may be reduced to an amount less than the highest water duty within the lowest seventy-five percent of the water duties compared within the areas of similar farming conditions." Sec. 45–566(A)(1) (1994 and Supp. 1996). This scheme illustrates a sensitivity to the economic importance of large-scale irrigation farming in Arizona and its dependence on groundwater reserves, and to the equities of forcing such farmers to adopt costly conservation measures. At the same time, it also recognizes the pressing—and indeed imperative—need to provide for the long-term, sustainable use of Arizona's groundwater resources in the public interest.

32. Still another possible stick, this one related to water quality, could come in the

form of establishing water quality improvement districts along river segments and making them responsible for achieving water-quality standards determined to be impaired by activities within their boundaries. States are now being required to identify sources of impairment on streams not meeting state-established water-quality standards. Most of these sources are likely to be what are called "nonpoint"–that is, they do not discharge pollutants from a discrete source such as a pipe. Irrigation return flows, even if they enter streams through well-defined drainage ditches, are treated as nonpoint. Thus they are not subject to any well-defined responsibility for the pollutants they carry to the stream. Perhaps by making a district responsible for meeting water-quality standards, nonpoint sources such as agricultural water pollution can be more effectively managed.

33. Section 3406(b)(2) of the Reclamation Projects Authorization and Adjustment Act of 1992 requires the secretary of the interior to "dedicate and manage annually eight hundred thousand acre-feet of Central Valley Project yield for the primary purpose" of fish, wildlife, and habitat restoration. *Reclamations Project Authorization Act of 1992,* U.S. Statutes at Large 106 (1992): 4715. The Central Valley Project Improvement Act (CVPIA), of which section 3406 is a part, is included within the Reclamation Projects Authorization and Adjustment Act of 1992, U.S. Statutes at Large 106 (1992): 4706–4731 (codified as amended in scattered sections of U.S. Code, vol. 16).

In theory the CVPIA merely dedicated the uncontracted-for portion of the total Central Valley Project (CVP) yield to environmental purposes. However, in reality, existing project beneficiaries profited from the availability of this surplus capacity even though they were not regarded as directly paying its costs. In particular, this storage water was made available to project water users in dry years, although the severe and prolonged drought that began in 1988 had caused CVP users already to suffer sharp curtailments in supply. See MacDonnell, "Managing Reclamation Benefits," 197, 226–227.

34. Brian E. Gray, "Water Transfers in California: 1981–1989," in *The Water Transfer Process as a Management Option for Meeting New Demands,* vol. 2 (Boulder, Colo.: Natural Resources Law Center, 1990).

35. David G. Cone and David Wichelns, "Responding to Water Quality Problems Through Improved Management of Agricultural Water," Symposium on *Water Organizations in a Changing West,* Natural Resources Law Center, Boulder, Colo., June 1993.

36. Much more also can be done to reduce the gap between diversions and withdrawals for urban uses and the amount of water actually needed. Once again, it is irrigation that is the dominant use of urban-water supplies–now to grow lawns, trees, and gardens rather than crops. The difficulty most people have accepting the fundamental aridity of the West is nowhere more evident than in the urban oases they have created. Urban-water suppliers understand their job as making sure that sufficient water is available to meet demands at all times and at the lowest possible cost. Only relatively recently has that understanding broadened to include water-conservation measures as a way of dampening demand. Only recently have urban-water users begun to understand that their water uses have consequences–that these uses

may be drawing down groundwater levels or reducing stream flows or requiring the construction of dams.

Domestic and commercial uses account for only 10 percent of the withdrawals of surface and groundwater in the seventeen western states, but they are growing as the urbanization of the West continues. States have been more willing to require their public urban water suppliers to demonstrate efficient use of water than their irrigators. Colorado, for example, gave its large public-water suppliers five years to go through a process evaluating their management of water. California urban-water suppliers voluntarily agreed to comply with a publicly developed set of best-management practices. Nevertheless, the disparity between per-capita amounts of water use among western cities remains high, and the degree of commitment to water conservation varies widely as well.

37. The city of Pueblo is now restoring the old channel as part of an effort to attract businesses and people to the area. Called the Riverwalk, the project includes a small lake at its west end, an urban waterfront in the central area, and a "natural area" just downstream. Jim Munch, "The Historic Arkansas Riverwalk Project in Pueblo," *the green line* (Colorado Riparian Association) 8, no. 4 (1997): 1.

38. Dave Rosgen, *Applied River Morphology* (Pagosa Springs, Colo.: Wildland Hydrology, 1996).

39. Department of the Interior, *Dams and Rivers: A Primer on the Downstream Effects of Dams*, by Michael Collier, Robert H. Webb, and John C. Schmidt, U.S. Geological Survey, Circular 1126 (Tucson, 1996), 1–2. Edward Goldsmith and Nicholas Hildyard, *The Social and Environmental Effects of Large Dams*, San Francisco: Sierra Club Books, 1984), 51–138. Geoffrey E. Petts, *Impounded Rivers: Perspectives for Ecological Management* (London: John Wiley and Sons, 1984), 239–241.

40. MacDonnell, "Managing Reclamation Benefits for Ecosystem Benefits," *University of Colorado Law Review* 67, no. 2 (Spring 1996), 197-257.

41. Michael P. Collier, Robert H. Webb, and Edmund D. Andrews, "Experimental Flooding in Grand Canyon," *Scientific American* 276, no. 1 (Jan. 1997), 82–89.

42. Richard Munson, ed., *Reforming Natural Resource Subsidies: Saving Money and the Environment* (Washington, D.C.: Northeast-Midwest Institute, 1994).

43. D. Craig Bell, *Water in the West Today: A State's Perspective*, Report to the Western Water Policy Review Advisory Commission (July 1997), 46–55.

44. N. LeRoy Poff et al., "The Natural Flow Regime," *Bioscience* 47, no. 11 (December 1997): 769–84.

45. Ibid., 780.

46. This attitude is well depicted in de Buys and Harris's wonderful story of living in a small village in northern New Mexico, *River of Traps*. Their neighbor and mentor, Jacobo Romero, urged them constantly, "never give holiday to the water." Up before dawn to go with Romero to irrigate their lands the night after a soaking thunderstorm, de Buys asks: "Jacobo, why do we irrigate even when there is plenty of rain?" Jacobo responds: "[B]ecause Anne [who lives with deBuys and Harris] don't know when it will rain again, and you and me don't know as much as Anne."

47. MacDonnell, "Marketing Water Rights," *Forum for Applied Research and Public*

Policy 13, no. 3 (Fall 1998): 52-55.

48. Kahrl, *Water and Power.*

49. MacDonnell, "Transfers of Water Use in Colorado," in *The Water Transfer Process,* vol. 2 (Boulder, Colo.: Natural Resources Law Center, 1990), chap. 3.

50. MacDonnell and Rice, "Moving Agricultural."

51. MacDonnell, "Water Banks," 22–1 to 22–63.

52. For a thorough discussion of organizations providing water to irrigation users, see Department of Agriculture, *Summary of Irrigation District Statutes of Western States,* by Wells A. Hutchins, U.S. Miscellaneous Publication No. 103 (Washington, D.C.: Jan. 1931); Department of Agriculture, *Irrigation Districts, Their Organization, Operation, and Financing,* by Wells A. Hutchins, Technical Bulletin No. 254 (Washington, D.C.: June 1931); Department of Agriculture, *Irrigation-Enterprise Organizations,* by Hutchins et al., Circular No. 934 (Washington, D.C.: October 1953).

53. Carl Boronkay and Warren J. Abbott, "Water Conflicts in the Western United States," *Studies in Conflict and Terrorism* 20 (1997):137–66.

54. Robert G. Dunbar, *Forging New Rights in Western Waters* (Lincoln: University of Nebraska Press, 1983).

55. MacDonnell and Rice, "Moving Agricultural," 31–35. David H. Getches et al., *Controlling Water Use: The Unfinished Business of Water Quality Protection* (Boulder, Colo.: Natural Resources Law Center, 1991), 104–07.

56. Perhaps the single most important remaining state water allocation issue concerns groundwater. Even this resource has been fully allocated in many areas such as the Ogallala Aquifer and in large parts of Arizona, but in other places new groundwater development continues. Despite the now well understood linkage between groundwater and surface water, states continue to struggle with ways to assure that groundwater withdrawals do not impair other water uses, both surface and subsurface. States like Texas, Nebraska, and Arizona historically have not recognized any connection between groundwater and surface water and now are having difficulty resolving conflicts that inevitably arise when groundwater withdrawals affect surface-water uses. Even states like Colorado and New Mexico, which have long acknowledged the physical relationship between surface water and groundwater, find that the approaches they have relied on to account for this relationship are inadequate.

57. MacDonnell, Teresa A. Rice, and Steven Shupe, ed., *Instream Flow Protection in the West* (Boulder, Colo.: Natural Resources Law Center, 1989); *Instream Flow Protection in the West,* rev. ed. (1993).

58. MacDonnell, "Transferring Water Uses in the West," *Oklahoma Law Review* 43 (1990): 119–30. MacDonnell et al., *The Water Transfer Process as a Management Option for Meeting Changing Water Demands* (Boulder, Colo.: Natural Resources Law Center, 1990).

59. For example, the 1866 Lode Mining Law asserts that vested water rights by "priority of possession" for "mining, agricultural, manufacturing, or other purposes" shall be "acknowledged by the local customs, laws, and decisions of courts." Act of July 26, 1866, ch. 262, 14 Stat. 251, 253 (codified at U.S. Code, vol. 30, sec. 43, 46, 51 [1994]). And, similarly, the Desert Lands Act of 1877

states that "the right to the use of water . . . on or to any tract of desert land of six hundred and forty acres shall depend upon bona fide prior appropriation [at the state level]: and such right shall not exceed the amount of water actually appropriated, and necessary for the purpose of irrigation and reclamation." Act of March 3, 1877, ch. 107, 19 Stat. 377, 377 (codified at U.S. Code, vol. 43, sec. 321–339 [1988]). In reviewing this federal policy, the Supreme Court of the United States said "[we] approve and confirm the policy of appropriation for a beneficial use, as recognized by local rules and customs, and the legislation and judicial decision of the arid-land states, as the test and measure of private rights in and to the non-navigable waters on the public domain." *California Oregon Power Co. v Beaver Portland Cement Co.*, 295 U.S. 142, 155 (1935).

A good summary of the history of federal involvement can be found in Department of Agriculture, *History of Federal Water.*

60. Inland Waterways Commission, *Preliminary Report*, 60th Congress, 1st sess., 1908, S. Doc. 325, serial 5250.

61. "It has always been understood that the principal purpose of the Federal Water Power Act of 1920 was to establish a national policy to promote the *comprehensive development* of water power on government lands and navigable waters other than by the government itself, and that such policy would be administered by abolishing the piecemeal authorities of the Secretaries of the Interior, Agriculture and War over the nation's hydro-electric resources and centralizing them in the Federal Power Commission." *State of California v FERC*, 966 F.2d 1541, 1556 (9th Cir. 1991) (emphasis added). See also *Pacific Gas & Electric Co. v FERC,* 720 F.2d 78, 82 (D.C. Cir. 1983) ("The FPA was enacted to establish a systematic, orderly process for promoting the *comprehensive development* and full use of the nation's navigable waters") (emphasis added). The powers originally vested in the Federal Power Commission were transferred to the Federal Energy Regulatory Commission (FERC) in 1977. See U.S. Code, vol. 42, sec. 7172(a)(1)(A) (1994). The general congressional statement of the Federal Power Act's policy purpose is found in sec. 10(a), which requires projects licensed by FERC to be "best adapted to a *comprehensive plan for improving or developing a waterway* . . . for the use or benefit of interstate or foreign commerce, for the improvement and utilization of water-power development, and for other beneficial public uses, including recreational purposes; and if necessary in order to secure such plan the Commission [now FERC] shall have authority to require the modification of any such project and of the plans and specifications of the project works before approval." U.S. Code, vol. 16, sec. 803(a)(1) (1994) (emphasis added).

62. The congressional statement of policy for the Water Resources Planning Act declares: "In order to meet the rapidly expanding demands for water throughout the Nation, it is hereby declared to be the policy of the Congress to encourage the conservation, development, and utilization of water and related land resources of the United States on a comprehensive and coordinated basis by the Federal Government, States, localities, and private enterprise with the cooperation of all affected Federal agencies, States, local governments, individuals, corporations, business enterprises, and others concerned." Water Resources Planning Act (WRPA) of 1965 (U.S. Code, vol. 42, sec. 1962

(1994); sec. 1962 contains the above-quoted general congressional statement of policy underlying the WRPA.

    See also Robert W. Adler, "Addressing Barriers to Watershed Protection," *Environmental Law* 25 (1995): 973–1106

63. Perhaps the seminal treatment of this issue was provided by Jack Hirshleifer, James C. DeHaven, and Jerome W. Milliman, *Water Supply: Economics, Technology, and Policy* (Chicago: University of Chicago Press, 1960).

64. The most thorough treatment of the federal reclamation subsidy is provided by Richard W. Wahl, *Markets for Federal Water: Subsidies, Property Rights, and the Bureau of Reclamation* (Washington, D.C.: Resources for the Future, 1989).

65. The Echo Park story is well told in Russell Martin's *A Story That Stands Like a Dam: Glen Canyon and the Struggle for the Soul of the West* (New York: Henry Holt, 1985).

66. U.S. General Accounting Office, *Bureau of Reclamation: Information on Allocation and Repayment of Costs of Constructing Water Projects* (Washington, D.C.: July 1996), 2.

67. This is a sizable investment that has produced an enormous array of physical assets such as dams, powerhouses, canals, and recreational facilities legally owned by the United States. The current dollar value of these assets greatly exceeds the outstanding repayment obligations. There has been a flurry of interest in selling off at least some of these facilities to the irrigation districts, water suppliers, and power companies that derive direct economic benefits from their use. The Bureau of Reclamation has developed procedures for reviewing proposed transfers. Congress has been actively considering bills that would transfer ownership of particular Reclamation projects to their primary users.

    There is no compelling reason for permanent federal ownership of all Reclamation water projects and their associated facilities. Neither, however, is there any compelling reason to sell most of these facilities to their traditional beneficiaries–especially if the price is only the remaining repayment obligation. I would except from this statement water delivery facilities (canals, tunnels, ditches, and so on) and drainage facilities that serve only the user or users. Such facilities probably can and should be sold (or given) to their users. There was never any explicit or implied understanding that these facilities were to pass to those who agreed to pay to the United States a portion of the costs of their construction. Rather, it was understood that continued federal ownership was the basis upon which the United States was willing to front the sometimes enormous costs of these projects, to declare portions of their cost nonreimbursable, to reduce repayment obligations in many cases in the face of persuasive evidence of inability to pay, to spread payment out over fifty years, and to forgo assessing interest on the outstanding debt. It is fantasy to argue that immediate project beneficiaries (usually irrigators) have paid for these projects and should now own them. These projects provide valuable benefits to their users at substantially discounted costs. I see no legal and little equitable basis to argue that these users should now be able to own facilities by paying an amount that is considerably below their actual cost (and far below their actual value) when there was never a contractual understanding that this would happen.

With the notion of federally directed comprehensive river-basin management no longer viable, it may be time to consider other kinds of arrangements
that can more effectively accomplish the benefits that true comprehensive
management might provide, but in a structure or form that works better for the
range of interests concerned with water uses–principally, the states and the
interests they most directly represent.

One option is to make it possible for the states themselves to take over
ownership and management of projects within their boundaries, particularly on rivers not shared with tribes or other states. Thus, for example,
considerable attention has been given to moving ownership of the Central
Valley Project to the state of California. This project and its many facilities
operate totally within the state. The state already operates a parallel state-
built water project.

Another interesting candidate is the Central Arizona Project. Just recently completed, this project takes water from the Colorado River but
otherwise operates totally within the state of Arizona. Except for the depletion of water from the Colorado River, there are relatively few major environmental concerns associated with operation of the project. There are
outstanding questions about the manner in which tribes within Arizona will
participate in the project, but, assuming these could be resolved, permanent federal ownership of this project seems unnecessary.

With the possible exception of the Central Utah Project, however,
there are few other federal water projects that seem logically to call for
state-level ownership and management. Most are relatively small in scale,
concern only a limited area of any state, and are important primarily to
interests within the water basins from and in which they draw and deliver
water. Such projects seem like good candidates for ownership and management by some kind of regional organization, with representation by the federal
government, state, tribes (if any) in the basin, the historical water users and
their organizations, and others. For a discussion of such an approach in the
context of the Colorado River, see MacDonnell and Bruce Driver, "Rethinking Colorado River Governance," in *The Colorado River Workshop: Ideas, Issues
and Directions* (Flagstaff: Grand Canyon Trust, 1996), 181–212.

68. *Winters v United States*, 207 U.S. 564 (1908). The U.S. Supreme Court in *Winters* enjoined construction of off-reservation dams and reservoirs that would
have deprived the Fort Belknap Indian Reservation of sufficient water for irrigation purposes. In particular, the Court found that the reservation was created to give the Gros Ventre and Assiniboine Indians living on Montana's Fort
Belknap Reservation a "permanent home and abiding place," but that the "lands
were arid and, without irrigation, were practically valueless" (565, 576). The
Court also noted that adequate reserved water was necessary to realize the
federal government's policy goal of changing Native Americans from a "nomadic and uncivilized people" into a "pastoral and civilized people" (576).

69. Perhaps the most contentious issue in American Indian reserved rights under
the Winters Doctrine has been their actual quantification. Recognition of reserved rights in and of itself is relatively unproblematic. However, converting
a reserved water right into actual acre-feet has been an emotionally charged
issue–particularly where existing appropriators feel they are being cheated by

"super-senior" federal water rights that trump state appropriation law, and where Native Americans feel that they are not being given enough water to satisfy the federal government's trust obligations and allow for tribal economic development.

A majority of Native American reserved water rights remain unquantified because, until relatively recently, there was no single jurisdictional forum for resolving the tension between federal water rights and state prior-appropriation rights. However, in 1952 Congress enacted the McCarran Amendment, which provides for a limited waiver of federal sovereign immunity for purposes of determining federal reserved water rights in state court general adjudications of all water rights within a river basin. The amendment was enacted as sec. 208 of the Department of Justice Appropriation Act, Act of July 10, 1952, ch. 495, 66 Statutes at Large 556, 560 (codified at U.S. Code, vol. 43, sec. 666 [1994]). The McCarran Amendment has allowed state courts to quantify reserved federal water rights, and thereby to remove some of the uncertainty underlying unquantified American Indian water rights and their integration with state prior-appropriation systems. While applying federal law standards, tribal reserved rights may be adjudicated in state-court proceedings under the McCarran Amendment. *Arizona v San Carlos Apache Tribe of Arizona*, 463 U.S. 565 (1983).

In *Arizona v. California* the Supreme Court upheld the special master's determination that the United States intended to reserve for the Colorado River Indian Reservation ample water to make the reservation lands useful, and that this reserved water right could be quantified on the basis of "all the potentially irrigable acreage on the reservations." *Arizona v California*, 373 U.S. 546, 600 (1963). After observing that "most of the lands were of the desert kind–hot, scorching sands–and that water from the [Colorado] river would be essential to the Indian people and to the animals they hunted and the crops they raised," the Court concluded that the potentially irrigable acreage quantification standard was "the only feasible and fair way by which reserved water for the reservations can be measured." Secs. 599, 601.

After years of debate concerning the propriety of the PIA standard, in 1989 the Supreme Court had the momentous opportunity to assess the adequacy of the PIA standard for purposes of quantifying reserved Native American water rights in a Wyoming court general adjudication of all water rights in the Wind River Basin. At issue was the Wyoming Supreme Court's holding that the federal government established the Wind River Indian Reservation "with a sole agricultural purpose"–which included surface-water quantities necessary for agricultural, livestock, municipal, and domestic uses– but that this did not include water quantities for fishery flow, mineral and industrial development, wildlife, or aesthetic uses. The court also found that the Wind River Indian Reservation did not include reserved groundwater rights, but, rather, only surface water in quantities necessary for agricultural needs. *In re the General Adjudication of All Rights to Use Water in the Big Horn River System and All Other Sources, State of Wyoming*, 753 P.2d 76, 96–99 (Wyo. 1988). The U.S. Supreme Court split 4–4 without opinion, essentially affirming the use of the PIA standard and upholding the Wyoming Supreme Court's narrow ruling. See generally *Wyoming v United States*, 492

U.S. 406 (1989). However, noted Native American legal scholar David Getches views the Supreme Court's decision in *Wyoming* as positive in that it settles the PIA standard of *Winters* as the accepted judicial method of quantifying American Indian reserved water rights, and therefore ends the continued quibbling over the appropriate quantification standard and paves the way for negotiating settlements of Native American water rights. See David H. Getches, "Indian Water Rights Perspectives in Conflict," in *Indian Water in the New West*, ed. Thomas R. McGuire, William B. Lord, and Mary G. Wallace (Tucson: University of Arizona Press, 1993), 7, 19.

Based on the intention expressed in establishing the reservation in treaty or other documents, tribal reserved rights may exist for water uses other than irrigation. See, for example, *Colville Confederated Tribes v Walton*, 647 F. 2d 42 (9th Cir. 1981), cert. denied, 454 U.S. 1092 (reserved water right includes sufficient in-stream flows to develop and maintain traditional fishing grounds); *United States v Adair*, 723 F.2d 1394 (9th Cir. 1983) (reservation of water for tribal purposes includes sufficient in-stream flows both to support agriculture and to maintain hunting and fishing).

70. The doctrine of implied federal reserved water rights has spawned ongoing controversy among western water users and policy makers. For example, longtime California water lawyer, Northcutt Ely, criticized the doctrine " 'as a first mortgage of undetermined and undeterminable magnitude,' as a 'sword of Damocles' suspended over 'every title to water rights to every stream which touches a federal reservation.' " Address by Northcutt Ely to National Water Commission (Nov. 6, 1969), quoted in Alan E. Boles, Jr., and Charles M. Elliott, "*United States v New Mexico* and the Course of Federal Reserved Water Rights," *University of Colorado Law Review* 51, no. 2 (Winter 1980): 209, 210 (n. 6). The doctrine of reserved federal water rights has raised the melodramatic ire of westerners. One commentator has, for example, called the doctrine a "rhetorical, chimerical phantasmagoria," a "perversion and a prevarication" of the law. Charles Corker, "A Real Live Problem for the Waning Energies of Frank J. Trelease," *Denver Law Review* 54 (1977): 499, 500.

On a less rhetorical and more pragmatic level, the Wyoming state engineer announced to the National Water Commission in 1969 that the doctrine would " '[a]t its extreme . . . seriously damage existing water users, and at a minimum' " create " 'a cloud over future development which needs to be removed.' " *Hearings Before the National Water Commission* (Denver, 1969), quoted in Boles and Elliot, *United States*, 210 (n. 6). This statement captures some of the practical concerns that the doctrine has raised, and continues to raise, even today. The respective rights of natives and nonnatives to the use of water are essentially administered vis-à-vis conflicting doctrines of water use. That is, non–Native American water rights in most western states are based upon the prior-appropriation system, which awards a water right only when water is put to a beneficial use, and which allocates water during times of shortage according to the "first-in-time, first-in-right" principle. In other words, junior non–American Indian appropriators are required to limit or abate their water use during dry periods so as to satisfy the rights of senior non–American Indian water users with an older appropriation date to their water rights. Even those western states that follow the riparian doctrine of water use generally impose upon respective water users a sliding scale of "reasonable use," which may require a reduction of water use during times of water shortage so as to satisfy correlative rights to water among all users.

In contrast, American Indian water rights are based upon the judicially created Winters doctrine of reserved rights, which awards water rights not according to application to a beneficial use, but, rather, according to the date of establishment of a Native American reservation. That is, Native American water rights have a priority date that relates back at least to the date when the land was reserved by the federal government as an Indian reservation. Because tribal water rights are not dependent upon actual application of water to a beneficial use, the specter of unquantified tribal water rights looms as a massive uncertainty over the state law allocation of water according to the priority system. The establishment of most American Indian reservations at a time when western water law was in its infancy implies that American Indian entitlements to specific water quantities—often sizable in the context of arid, overappropriated western states where practically every last drop of water has been claimed by beneficial use—predate most senior state water rights and thus jeopardize the balance of all the established rights in state water-law systems.

These potentially large, super-senior Native American water rights have led commentators to complain that "[m]ost non-Indian water rights are [individually] . . . *de minimus*," whereas the "same is *not* true of [collective] Indian water rights," which threaten to upset the time-honored equities of the prior-appropriation system with significant claims to water quantities in arid regions (Corker, "Real Live," 504). One of the endearing qualities of the prior-appropriation system is "its protection to economies based upon existing water uses." This "stability" of the prior-appropriation doctrine "has contributed significantly to making the West an inhabitable and economically productive region." In sum, contrary to the prior-appropriation system, publicly defined beneficial use is not the basis of American Indian reserved water rights; these reserved rights are rarely stated in terms of a definite quantity, nature, or time of use; they cannot be terminated by abandonment or forfeiture as can appropriative rights; their priority date is not later than the date upon which the reservation was created, which often predates most state water rights; and American Indian water rights may be transferable (that is, by lease or sale) without state approval. See Western States Water Council, *Indian Water Rights in the West* (Denver: Western Governor's Association, 1984), 9–11.

Indian reservations encompass substantial land area in the western United States and can also be a major source of water resources in the West. As a result, reservation-related water resources are sometimes a primary source of water supply for irrigation, municipalities, industries, and other off-reservation uses. The possibility that these nonreservation water uses dependent upon reservation water will be affected negatively is significant—particularly where existing water users have sizable capital investments bound up with their state-approved beneficial uses. This issue is especially problematic because persons whose state water rights were established after the date a reservation was created have rights subordinate in priority (that is, junior) to the the reserved tribal water rights. Therefore, they would probably not be entitled to any compensation under state law for losses resulting from a tribe exercising its reserved rights. See Comptroller General, *Reserved Water Rights for Federal and Indian Reservations: A Growing Controversy in Need of Resolution,* Report to the Congress of the United States (Washington D.C.: General Accounting Office, 1978), 6–7.

Moreover, the Winters doctrine has exacerbated already heightened tensions between the federal government and western states. Due to a longstanding federal policy of deferring water-allocation issues to state law, westerners have expressed both confusion and anger over the insertion of uncertain federal reserved water rights in state-law systems based in certainty of water allocation and use. The Colorado Supreme Court has nicely expressed this frustration based in federalism: "We have a situation in which the federal sovereign claims water rights which are nowhere formally listed, which are not the subject of any decree or permit and which, therefore, are etheric in large part to the person who has reason to know and evaluate the extent of his [or her] priorities to the use of water. To have these federal rights in a state of uncorrelated mystery is frustrating and completely contrary to ordinary procedures–and this is equally true from the standpoint of the United States as well as Colorado and its citizenry." *United States v District Court in and for the County of Eagle,* 458 P.2d 760, 772 (Colo. 1969).

71. Although the watershed *Winters v United States* decision exemplifies that tribal water rights have sometimes been a matter of litigation, the current trend is toward negotiated settlements in which Native American and non–Native American water users attempt to achieve a quantification of Native American water rights that is fair to tribal interests while not unduly upsetting established nontribal water rights. As David Getches has expressed this idea: Although "[l]itigation is a starting point for sharpening the issues and articulating the positions of the parties. . . . [n]egotiation is a more promising vehicle for reaching a meaningful, practical resolution that provides the Indians with deliverable water and non-Indians with genuine certainty." Getches points out that "[p]ractical arrangements, designed by mutual agreement, can realize the benefits of Indian rights without major dislocations of non-Indian water users" (Getches, "Indian Water Rights," 7, 19–20). As an anonymous Department of the Interior official commented, "We should litigate at the same time that we negotiate; people then take you more seriously. One drives the other." Quoted in Elizabeth Checchio and Bonnie G. Colby, *Indian Water Rights: Negotiating the Future* (Tucson: Water Resources Research Center, University of Arizona College of Agriculture, 1993), 15.

General stream adjudications to determine American Indian water rights under the McCarran Amendment are expensive and protracted trials. All water users along a given river system must be joined as parties–this can mean hundreds, sometimes thousands, of parties in a large river basin–and each party is adverse to every other party. This is because each water user attempts to prove competitively his or her rights to scarce water. Each party must prove his or her priority date, quantity of historical use, and place and purpose of water use. This generally requires the use of expensive expert witnesses and attorneys. As a result, a state court general adjudication proceeding can take several years and cost in the millions of dollars. See Reid Payton Chambers and John E.

Echohawk, *Implementing Winters Doctrine Indian Reserved Water Rights: Producing Indian Water and Economic Development Without Injuring Non-Indian Water Users?*, Natural Resources Law Center Discussion Paper Series, No. 10 (Boulder, Colo.: Natural Resources Law Center, 1991), 7. In a general adjudication, every water user views every other water user with suspicion, as a potential enemy, as someone who may claim the last available water in a given river system.

In contrast, "[n]egotiations potentially offer Indian and non-Indian entities more timely clarification of water rights in a nonadversarial setting and give all parties greater control over the eventual out-come. However, negotiations are not a panacea." Benjamin Simon and Harvey Doerksen, "Conflicting Federal Roles in Indian Water Claims Negotiations," in *Indian Water in the New West*, 28–9. There is very little guarantee, at the outset, that a negotiated settlement will take less time or that the interested parties will be any less adversarial in attempting to secure their water rights. As a practical matter, it is also infeasible to allow each individual party to participate in the negotiations. Parties must therefore team up in groups and elect agents to represent them at the negotiating table.

Numerous American Indian water rights settlements have already been achieved, and others are proceeding apace at various locations. From 1962 to 1992 Congress ratified fourteen settlement agreements by statute or compact: the Southern Ute and Ute Mountain tribes of Colorado; the Assiniboine and Sioux tribes of the Fort Peck Reservation in Montana; the Ak-Chin, Tohono O'odham (Papago), Salt River, and Fort McDowell tribes in Arizona; the five Mission bands along the San Luis Rey River in southern California; the Shoshone-Bannock tribes of the Fort Hall Reservation in Idaho; and the Fallon and Pyramid Lake Paiute tribes in Nevada. See Simon and Doerksen, "Conflicting Federal Roles," 27, 29 (table 2.1); Chambers and Echohawk, *Implementing Winters*, 8.

Four common elements can be identified in all of these settlements: (1) either a federal investment in the development of water facilities or federal acquisition of sufficient water to enable the tribes to put their water to use without injuring established, non–Native American water uses; (2) sizable nonfederal cost sharing by state and local interests to cover the costs of project construction or other settlement expenditures; (3) the creation of substantial American Indian trust funds, acquired from both federal and nonfederal sources, for tribal water development purposes; and (4) the allowance of limited off-reservation water marketing, thereby allowing tribes the opportunities for viable economic gains from their water resources while simultaneously making scarce water available to non–American Indian users (see Getches, "Indian Water Rights," 21).

72. Since announcement of the doctrine of implied reserved rights, the U.S. Supreme Court has extended its application to other federal reservations of land (*Arizona v California*, 373 U.S. 546 [1963]). For example, in *Cappaert v United States* the needs of the desert pupfish for sufficient water caused the Court to find the existence of a federal reserved water right for groundwater in the Devil's Hole National Monument. In *United States v New Mexico*, 438 U.S. 696 (1978), the Court clarified that federal reserved water rights exist only for the

primary purposes for which the reservation is established and only for the minimum amount of water necessary to accomplish those purposes.

73. *United States v New Mexico,* 438 U.S. 696 (1978).

74. Although the public lands are by definition not reserved lands, some water sources on public lands are reserved. For example, on April 17, 1926, President Coolidge issued an executive order that reserved certain sources of groundwater on the public lands. "Public Water Reserve (PWR) 107" established a blanket reservation of springs and water holes from private disposition under the public lands laws of the United States. In particular, the executive order provided that: "every smallest legal subdivision of the public-land surveys which is vacant unappropriated unreserved public land and contains a *spring or water hole,* and all land within one quarter of a mile of every spring or water hole located on unsurveyed public land be, and the same is hereby, *withdrawn from settlement, location, sale, or entry, and reserved for public use* in accordance with [the Stock-Raising Homestead Act of 1916]."

Executive order of April 17, 1926, reprinted in *Decisions of the Department of the Interior in Cases Relating to the Public Lands,* vol. 51, ed. Daniel M. Greene (Washington D.C.: Government Printing Office, 1926), 457 (establishing Public Water Reserve No. 107) (emphasis added) [hereinafter PWR 107].

The origins of PWR 107 can be traced to the Pickett Act of 1910 and the Stock-Raising Homestead Act of 1916. The Pickett Act authorized the president to withdraw land for "public purposes." U.S. Statutes at Large 36 (1910): 847. (repealed by the Federal Land Policy and Management Act [FLPMA] of 1976). Section 10 of the Stock-Raising Homestead Act further clarified this withdrawal power of the executive by specifically authorizing the president to withdraw public land containing water holes or other water bodies either used or needed by the public. In particular, sec. 10 provided that "[l]ands containing water holes . . . needed or used by the public for watering purposes" may be reserved and, where reserved, shall "be kept and held open to the public use for such purposes." U.S. Statutes at Large 39 (1916): 862, 865 (also repealed by FLPMA).

The underlying congressional intent was to prevent private monopolization of public water sources under the public land disposal laws, for example, by homesteading around the only available spring in a given area for stock watering. To illustrate, a 1916 House Report explained that public water reserves were necessary "so that a person cannot *monopolize or control* a large territory by locating as a homestead the *only available water supply for stock in that vicinity.*" H.R. Report No. 35, 64th Congress, 1st Session, (1916) (emphasis added). Although the withdrawal authorizations contained in the Pickett Act and the Stock-Raising Homestead Act were repealed in 1976 by FLPMA, reservations made under this authority before the enactment of FLPMA are valid. See Federal Land Policy and Management Act of 1976, U.S. Code, vol. 43, sec. 1701 et seq. [1994]).

Therefore, PWR 107 still has import today. For example, in the ongoing Snake River Basin Adjudication (SRBA), the federal government has asserted a federal reserved water right for each parcel of land previously reserved under PWR 107 and other public water reserves provisions. This amounts to an assertion of over ten thousand federal reserved water rights claims in Idaho. However, on December 9, 1996, the state district court ruled that, though PWR 107 may have in fact withdrawn the land surrounding watering holes from the public domain, it failed to create any reserved federal water rights that need to be quantified for purposes of the SRBA. See *Memorandum Decision and Order Re: Basin-Wide Issue 9, In re SRBA*, Case No. 39576 (Idaho Dist. Ct. 1996). The United States is now considering an appeal of this ruling. See generally Mark J. Howard, "Snake River Basin Adjudication Update," *Advocate (Idaho)* 40 (February, 1997): 10, 12.

75. A majority of the public lands, including most of the 270 million acres managed by the Bureau of Land Management (BLM), do not enjoy the protection of reserved water rights. Instead, federal policy today requires the BLM and Forest Service to pursue claims for water other than reserved rights in state courts just as any other property owner. Therefore, these agencies have utilized both "defensive" and "proactive" management strategies to attempt to protect "in-place" or in-stream needs—water resources not diverted from their natural place of occurrence—on the public lands. Examples of defensive management strategies include conditioning the use of public lands for water-diversion purposes on bypass flow requirements or participating in licensing and relicensing of hydropower facilities to secure minimum flow levels through the public lands. These actions are characterized as defensive because the federal agencies involved only take such actions in response to a proposed private action, such as using the public lands for water-diversion purposes. Examples of proactive management strategies to protect in-place water needs on the public lands include asserting state water rights and working with state in-stream flow programs, entering into cooperative agreements with state water users or administrators, or segregating certain portions of the federal lands as limited use zones. See Teresa Rice, "Beyond Reserved Rights: Water Resource Protection for the Public Lands," *Idaho Law Review* 28 (1992): 715, 715–16.

First, under FLPMA, both the Forest Service and BLM are required to include terms and conditions in all FLPMA rights-of-ways in order to "minimize damage to scenic and esthetic values and fish and wildlife habitat and otherwise protect the environment." U.S. Code, vol. 43, sec. 1765(a)(ii) (1994); *see also* Code of Fed. Reg., vol. 36, sec. 251.56 (1996). And the National Forest Management Act requires the Forest Service to ensure that any new or existing authorizations for water-diversion projects are consistent with forest plans. National Forest Management Act of 1976, U.S. Code, vol. 16, sec. 1604(I) (1994). Under this authority, therefore, the Forest Service and BLM are authorized to deny or condition water-diversion, storage, and conveyance projects on federal lands—including the imposition of "bypass flows" (that is, the maintenance of minimum stream flows) to protect in-stream water needs. See Rice, "Beyond Reserved Rights," 721.

Second, the federal land management agencies have become involved in the Federal Energy and Regulatory Commission's (FERC) licensing process for hydropower projects as a means of stream-flow protection. FERC possesses the authority to condition or prohibit hydropower projects that negatively impact the federal lands because, under the Federal Power Act as amended by the Electric Consumers Protection Act of 1986, it must give "equal consideration" to nonpower values during the licensing process, including fish and wildlife, recreation, and environmental quality. In particular, when hydropower project facilities are located or planned within federal reservations–national forests, tribal lands, or other federal lands withdrawn from disposal under the public lands laws–federal land management agencies possess significant authority to recommend mandatory license terms and conditions to protect stream flows under section 4(e) of the Federal Power Act. See Rice, "Beyond Reserved Rights," at 739–40; U.S. Code, vol. 16, sec. 797(e) (1994). On BLM lands, which are not generally reserved, FLPMA authority to condition rights-of-way necessary for hydropower projects can accomplish the same results. See Rice, "Beyond Reserved Rights," 742–43.

Third, most western states today have mechanisms for recognizing in-place water uses, which provide a proactive opportunity for federal land management agencies to obtain state-recognized stream-flow rights. The various strategies used by federal agencies for acquiring or defending claims to water according to state law are: filing for new appropriations of water, filing in-place claims in general stream adjudications, engaging in state in-stream flow programs, purchasing existing water rights and converting them to stream-flow purposes, and tracking nonfederal applications for water rights to preempt any threats to bypass flows. See Rice, "Beyond Reserved Rights," 748.

Fourth, federal land management agencies have also entered into cooperative agreements with other water users or with state or federal agencies to protect in-place water resources. This strategy has the advantage of bypassing the expensive and protracted process traditionally associated with litigation, while still securing the stream flows necessary to protect in-place resources on the federal lands. See Rice, "Beyond Reserved Rights," 767.

And, finally, federal land management agencies are proactively designating certain critical areas for special management under a limited-use regime. Although both the Forest Service and BLM are generally required to manage the federal lands under the principles of multiple use and sustained yield, both agencies possess statutory authority to designate certain lands as special management areas to be administered under a limited-use regime. For both the BLM and Forest Service, this occurs primarily in the land management planning processes. For example, the BLM may, under FLPMA planning provisions, "give priority to the designation and protection of areas of critical environmental concern," requiring "special management" to prevent damage to important natural, cultural, or scenic resources. See Rice, "Beyond Water Rights," 771; U.S. Code, vol. 43, sec. 1712(c)(3) (1994); Code of Fed. Reg., vol. 43, sec. 1601.0–5 (1996). Similarly, the Forest Service is directed, in its planning process, to "provide for the establishment of Research Natural Areas (RNAs)" in the national forests, requiring the protection of important terrestrial and aquatic systems. See Rice, "Beyond Reserved Rights," 771; Code of Fed. Reg., vol. 36, sec. 219.25 (1996).

In addition to federal reserved water rights, these foregoing alternative strategies are becoming important tactical means for federal land management agencies to secure and protect in-place water needs. "Water resource protection on the public lands," according to Teresa Rice, "is assum-

ing a primary position in the land management agencies' planning and administration. Reserved rights claims are merely one of the several strategies being
used by these agencies in light of the uncertainty surrounding the doctrine."
Rice, "Beyond Reserved Rights," 778.

76. Daniel McCool, *Command of the Waters: Iron Triangles, Federal Water Development, and Indian Water* (Berkeley: University of California Press, 1987).

77. For a useful summary of such organizations in the western states as of 1996,
see Natural Resources Law Center, *The Watershed Source Book: Watershed-
Based Solutions to Natural Resource Problems* (Boulder, Colo.: Natural Resources
Law Center, 1996) (contains descriptions of current, coordinated watershed management efforts in Arizona, California, Colorado, Idaho, Montana, Nevada, New Mexico, Oregon, Utah, Washington, and Wyoming).

78. Natural Resources Law Center, *The State Role in Western Watershed Initiatives,*
Research Report RR–18 (Boulder, Colo.: Natural Resources Law Center,
1998).

79. A potentially instructive example is the controversy concerning the imposition
of bypass flow requirements by the Forest Service in the Arapaho-Roosevelt
National Forest in Colorado. This dispute prompted Congress to appoint a
special committee to consider ways in which Forest Service concerns about
maintaining stream flows in national forests might be integrated with water
users' concerns about fully utilizing their water rights. To this point this issue
has been addressed largely as a matter of legal power: Does the Forest Service
have the legal authority to use its right-of-way regulation to require owners of
dams or diversion works on national forests to maintain some level of minimum stream flows below these structures? As a practical matter, management
approaches were developed that allowed appropriators releasing water at times
when they were not using it to obtain other water instead. This resolution took
advantage of the water-management opportunities within the affected watersheds. Report of the Federal Water Rights Task Force Created Pursuant to
Section 389(d)(3) of Public Law 104–127, August 25, 1997.

80. See, for example, Michael McCloskey, "Collaboration Has Its Limits," *High
Country News,* May 15, 1996.

81. This committee, under Gardner's chairmanship, has produced a book, *A
New Era for Irrigation* (Washington, D.C.: National Academy Press, 1996).

82. Maass and Anderson effectively convey the enterprising nature of people
with this vision in establishing their irrigation systems in . . . *And the Desert
Shall Rejoice.*

83. Committee on the Future of Irrigation, *New Era for Irrigation.*

84. Charles F. Wilkinson, *Crossing the Next Meridian: Land, Water, and the Future of
the American West* (Washington, D.C.: Island Press, 1992).

85. William Cronon, *Nature's Metropolis: Chicago and the Great West* (New York:
W.W. Norton, 1991).

86. Ibid., 385.

87. Ibid., 369.

88. "Angry as one may be at what careless people have done and still do to a
noble habitat, it is hard to be pessimistic about the West. This is the native
home of hope. When it fully learns that cooperation, not rugged individual-
ism, is the pattern that most characterizes and preserves it, then it will have

achieved itself and outlived its origins. Then it has a chance to create a society to match its scenery." Wallace Stegner, *The Sound of Mountain Water*, (New York: Dutton, 1980; reprint, Lincoln: University of Nebraska Press, 1985), 38 (page citation is to the reprint edition).

Index

Acre-foot, defined, 2–3
Active Management Areas, 348–49n31
Adjudication process, 207, 270, 273; general, 360n71; water rights and, 222
Administrative process, 243, 269
Adobe Creek, reservoir at, 32
"After the Water is Gone" (Milenski), text of, 80–82
Agriculture, 1; dryland, 3, 76; irrigation and, 25; water for, 296n4. *See also* Irrigated agriculture
Ahtanum Creek, 183, 195
Alexander, Kapper: on farming, 128
Alfalfa, 24, 65, 67, 69, 149, 174; irrigating, 150 (photo); production of, 309n106; water for, 152
Allocation, 198, 223, 237, 265, 269, 270, 273; drought and, 226; full-cost pricing and, 253; states and, 359n70; transformation of, 219–20, 221
Allotments, 167, 187, 191
Alpine Decree (1980), 152, 332n56
Alva B. Adams Tunnel, 116
American Crystal Sugar Company, 53
American River, 209
Amity Mutual Irrigation Company, 45; John Martin and, 84; storage decree of, 83
Anderson, Raymond, 4
And the Desert Shall Rejoice (Maass and Anderson), 4
Angle of Repose (Stegner), 4

Anglin, Ron: water rights and, 176
Anthony, Scott, J.: Sand Creek and, 20
Appropriation, 30, 240, 270, 364n75; changing, 244; described, 70–71; diversions and, 273; minimum, 243; public interest basis for, 269; rule of, 36. *See also* Prior appropriation
Aquifers, 3, 42, 43, 266, 293, 352n56; alluvial, 40–41; development of, 4, 9
Arapaho, 16, 18; at Sand Creek, 21; water for, 27
Arch, Matt, 94
Aridity, 4, 5
Arizona Groundwater Management Act (1980), 348n31
Arizona v. California (1963), 356–57n69
Arkansas Compact Commission, 83
Arkansas River, 16, 36; alluvial aquifer and, 293; diversions from, 247, 305n63; flows in, 13; headwaters of, 13, 47; irrigation from, 26; water rights on, 259
Arkansas River Compact, 43, 44
Arkansas Valley, 12 (map), 17, 261; brochures about, 34; groundwater use in, 305n61; transmountain diversion and, 303n52; water-dependent economy in, 35; water rights in, 300n20. *See also* Lower Arkansas Valley
Arkansas Valley Ditch Company, 45

Army Corps of Engineers, 273, 343n13; dams by, 250; development and, 279; management by, 284, 294; mission of, 38–39; multiple-purpose facilities and, 275; river regulation by, 274; section 404 and, 279, 344n13; water projects by, 276

Atchison, Topeka and Santa Fe Railway Company, 29

Austin, Mary, 4

Battlement Mesa, settlement on, 117

Benchlands, bottomlands and, 172–73, 332n60

Beneficial use, 172, 207, 243, 244, 246, 266, 288; considering, 271; increasing, 237, 263, 283; reasonable, 348n30; salvaged water for, 348n29

Beneficiaries, 253, 254–55, 355n67; payment by, 252; preferred, 325n54

Benson, Ezra Taft, 51

Bent, Charles, 16

Bent, George, 16

Bent, Robert, 16

Bent, William, 16, 18, 19; ditch for, 27; Sand Creek and, 20

Bent's Fort, 15, 18, 19, 25, 299n4, 300n17; establishment of, 17

Bessemer Ditch, 14, 45

Beyond the Hundredth Meridian (Stegner), 4

Big Sandy Creek, 19, 29

Bingham, Sam, 3

Blackburn, Ed: CWS and, 63, 72; Fort Lyon Canal and, 62, 71

Black Kettle, Sand Creek and, 20

BLM. *See* Bureau of Land Management

Blue River, 321n49, 325n54; dam on, 117

Board of Control, 199, 202, 227

Boca Dam, construction of, 151, 329n21

Boldt, George, 213, 339n69

Bonneville Dam, 210

Bonneville Power Authority, 274, 340n79

Book Cliffs, 92, 92 (photo), 109

Boomtowns, energy crisis, 322n53

Boosters, 89; writings of, 296n3

Booth Orchard Grove Ditch, 51

Border irrigation, salinity control and, 319n35

Bottomlands, 200; benchlands and, 172–73, 332n60

Bremner, Faith, 176

Broadview Water District, 246

Brower, David: Echo Park Dam and, 276

Bumping Lake Dam, 155, 196

Bureau of Indian Affairs, 336n53

Bureau of Land Management (BLM), 362n75; in-stream flows and, 363n75; multiple use/sustained yield and, 364n75; reserved-water rights and, 278

Bureau of Reclamation, 65, 164, 165, 172, 173, 201, 206, 220, 240, 250, 273; Boca Reservoir and, 329n21; C-BT Project and, 116; changes in, 225; contracts by, 196–97; dams and, 38, 151, 275; development/management and, 275; endangered fish and, 271, 272; Fifteen-Mile Reach and, 125; Fryingpan-Arkansas Project and, 117; lease water and, 221–22; Newlands Project and, 150; Orchard Mesa check and, 323n54; projects by, xiii, 99, 276, 355n67; Prosser Dam and, 212; Public Law 101–618 and, 174; Recovery Implementation Program and, 326n62; Roza Diversion Dam and, 213; Ruedi Reservoir and, 326–27n66; salinity control and, 268, 320n41; SOAC and, 215; studying projects of, 251; TCID and, 150; transfers and, 354n67; TWSA and, 222; Washoe Project Act and, 160; water laws and, 274; Yakima Basin and, 338n57; Yakima Project and, 216. *See also* Reclamation Service

Busk-Ivanhoe transmountain diversion system, 51

Bypass flows, 252, 364n75, 365n79

Caddoa, proposed dam at, 38, 39

Cadillac Desert (Reisner), 4

California Department of Water Resources, 233
Canals, 247, 354n67; building, 29–30; lining, 130
Cantaloupes, 24
Canute, King, 154
Carlson, John, 54
Carson, Kit, 16
Carson Basin, 140; agriculture in, 144, 151; irrigation in, 231, 244, 253, 290; water development in, 171–72
Carson Desert, 138, 139, 146 (photo); described, 140
Carson Division, 147, 173, 330nn22, 27; canals in, 174; Truckee River and, 175
Carson Lake, 137, 153, 155, 164, 330n27; described, 140
Carson River, 138, 140, 176; canal at, 147, 148; decree for, 152; diversions from, 156, 161, 329–30n22; homesteading along, 145 (photo); irrigation uses of, 151; Newlands Project and, 153; public lands on, 145; as Superfund site, 157; water development in, 155
Carson Sink, 137; described, 155
Carvalho, Solomon Nunes, 314n5
Cascades, 185, 187; Yakima Basin and, 181
Catlin Canal, 14, 46
Catlin Canal Company, 79; Colorado Division of Wildlife and, 78
Catlin Ditch, appropriations by, 30
Cattail-eaters, 137, 140
CB-T Project. See Colorado-Big Thompson Project
Census of Agriculture, data from, 55
Central Arizona Project, 355n67
Central Utah Project, 355n67
Central Valley Project (CVP), 245, 269, 350n33, 355n67
Central Valley Project Improvement Act (CVPIA), 350n33
CF&I. See Colorado Fuel & Iron
Cheyenne, 16, 18; at Sand Creek, 21; water for, 27
Chicago, growth of, 291–92
Chinook salmon, 211; cycle of, 209, 210, 210 (fig.); monitoring of, 210; spawning by, 215. See also Salmon

Chisholm, Graham, 175, 237; Nature Conservancy and, 176
Chivington, John M.: Sand Creek and, 20
Christensen, John: on Great Basin, 143
Christensen, Joy: quote of, 135
Chub, 119
CIG. See Colorado Interstate Gas Company
Cimarron River, 17
CLADCO. See Crowley Land and Development Company
Clean Air Act, 244
Clean Water Act, 227, 234, 244, 272; section 301 of, 343n13; section 404 of, 279
Clear Creek Reservoir, 51; construction of, 306n73, 334n31
Cle Elum Dam, 196, 198 (photo), 340n81; flows at, 214; storage capacity of, 334n31
Cle Elum Reach, flows in, 215
Cline, Joe, 72
Coffin, Chris, 228
Colorado-Big Thompson Project (CB-T Project), 116, 321n49
Colorado Canal, 14, 31, 32, 33, 36, 45, 52, 59, 77; problems with, 55; Rocky Ford Ditch and, 55; water from, 54
Colorado Canal Company, 56
Colorado Coal and Iron Company, 302n40
Colorado Division of Wildlife, Catlin Canal Company and, 78
Colorado Fuel and Iron Company (CF&I), 35, 45, 301n39; growth of, 302n40; railroads and, 302n40
Colorado Interstate Gas Company (CIG), 61
Colorado Land and Water Supply, Inc., 53
Colorado Loan and Trust, Grand River Ditch and, 94, 95
Colorado National Monument, 92, 105
Colorado pikeminnow, 120 (photo), 122, 253; as endangered species, 119, 121; habitat for, 124; ladders for, 326n64; migration of, 121; spawning by, 124

Colorado Pikeminnow Recovery Team, 121

Colorado River, 98 (photo), 313–14n5; dams on, 120–21; diversions from, 115, 127, 129, 130, 132; economic use of, 115–16, 118, 288; fish in, 121; flooding experiment on, 251; name change for, 312n3; salinity in, 111, 241; water imported from, 76–77

Colorado River Basin, 114 (map); endangered fish in, 271–72; water flows in, 115; water from, x

Colorado River Basin Salinity Control Act (1974), Grand Valley Salinity Control Project of, 110–11

Colorado River Water Conservation District, 325n54, 327n70

Colorado State University Extension Service, 14, 48

Colorado Supreme Court: Catlin Canal Company and, 79; hydrology and, 43

Colorado Volunteer Cavalry, Sand Creek and, 20–21

Colorado Water Conservation Board: Fort Lyon Canal and, 78; Grand Valley Water Management Study and, 327n70

Colorado Water Supply (CWS), 65, 69, 70, 77–78; Fort Lyon Canal and, 61, 62, 64, 71, 77; offer by, 63–64

Columbia Basin, 183; commercial fishing in, 214; salmon in, 184, 211, 213, 216–17

Columbia Plateau, 183, 186

Columbia River, 182, 185; diversions from, 190

"Concepts for a Second-Generation Truckee-Carson Settlement" (Yardas and Chisholm), 175

"Condition of the Yakima Indian Reservation, The" (Reclamation Service/Indian Service), 191

Consent decree (1945), 164, 202, 336n53, 338n56

Conservation, 347n27; defined, 347–48n28; improvements in, 242; irrigation-water, 241; planning, 241;

policy objective of, 243; strategies for, 341n90; water-rights holders and, 348n28

Consumption, 9; diversion and, 246

Continuous-flow gravity systems, 129

Convention on Wetlands of International Importance (Ramsar Convention), 156

Coolidge, Calvin, 361n74

Coors Brewing Company, barley for, 103

Corps of Engineers. See Army Corps of Engineers

Coward, Walt, xi-xii

Crawford, George, 90

Crawford, Stanley, 4

Cronon, William, 287; on rural/urban relationship, 291–92

Cross, Isabelle, 316n15

Crossing the Next Meridian (Wilkinson), 4

Cross Orchards, 316n15

Crowley County: irrigated agriculture in, 57, 259, 308n93; operator debt in, 55, 56; Otero County and, 308n93; population of, 307n80

Crowley Land and Development Company (CLADCO), 51; Twin Lakes Reservoir and, 52, 53

Crystal Sugar Company, 24

Cui-ui, 159, 160, 162, 164, 175, 329n21; danger for, 249; decline of, 154; measuring, 161 (photo); spawning of, 163

Cui-ui eaters, 137, 139

Currier, Bruce, 106, 134

Currier, Carlyle, 106

Currier, Charles, 95

Currier, Ed, 316n15; GVIC and, 106

Currier, Edward Joshua, 316n15; Golden Rule Dairy and, 97; in Grand Junction, 95–96

Currier, Melinda, 96

CVP. See Central Valley Project

CVPIA. See Central Valley Project Improvement Act

CWS. See Colorado Water Supply

Dalles Dam, 210

Dams, 2, 63, 123, 153, 247, 289, 292,

293; building, 197 (photo); burden of proof for, 276; construction problems with, 242; fish migration and, 120–21; impact of, 249, 250, 254; multiple purpose, 275
Dawes Act (1887), 141, 187
DeBeque Canyon, 93, 98, 122; dam at, 99
DeBuys, William, 4, 352n46
Decision-making processes, 237, 284; geographically based, 283
Delivery systems, 201, 268; ditch/district level, 262; improvements in, 111
Denver and Rio Grande Railroad, 89
Denver Water Board, 107, 327n70; Fraser River and, 116; Green Mountain Reservoir and, 324n54
Denver Water Department, Two Forks and, 308n94
Department of Agriculture, 14; on groundwater salinity, 101; salinity reduction and, 111; on water-application rates, 347n25
Derby Dam, 147, 147 (photo), 151, 153, 165; diversion at, 249; fish migration and, 154
Desert Lands Act (1877), 353n59
Development: comprehensive, 239, 275, 276–77; economic, 3, 234, 238, 279, 292; environmental costs of, 253, 276; federal role in, 275; land management and, 279; water and, 4, 255, 266; West and, 292, 293. See also Water development; Water projects
Dillon Reservoir, 324n54; Blue River and, 325n54; construction of, 117
Direct-flow rights, 112, 198, 335n33
Ditch companies, 4, 30, 63, 95, 111; failure for, 27; Fryingpan-Arkansas and, 304n53; selling shares of, 70; transformation of, 27–28; water banks and, 261; winter irrigation and, 44
Ditch systems, 2, 19, 41, 42, 62, 112, 128, 247; hazards of, 6
Diversion, 7, 9, 239, 249, 266, 269, 293; appropriations and, 273; consumption and, 246; irrigation

and, 240; limits on, 272; maximum, 129; measuring, 223; reducing, 131, 221, 241, 244; salvaging, 242; transmountain, 39, 52, 77, 117, 254, 303n52, 304n53, 325n54
Diversion structures, 289; building, 28. See also Dams
Doctrine of federal reserved water rights, criticism of, 357–58n70
Donner Lake, dam site at, 144
Drip irrigation, 349n31
Drought, 51, 162, 289; allocation and, 226; in Arkansas Basin, 32; Great Depression and, 38; irrigators and, 258; water banks and, 260; wetlands and, 156, 157
Drylands, 3, 76
Ducks Unlimited, 236

Echo Park Dam, 276
Ecological systems, 233, 238, 255; concerns about, 267; water-based, 293, 294
Efficiency factor, 161, 174
Egan, Timothy: on West, 298n11
Electric Consumers Protection Act (1986), 363n75
Ely, Northcutt: on doctrine of federal reserved water rights, 357–58n70
Endangered species, 234; recovery for, 249, 271–72; water-dependent, 267
Endangered Species Act (1973), 7, 121, 131, 159–60, 234, 237; impact of, 250; legal obligations under, 271; sections 7 and 9 of, 344n14
Energy boom, described, 321–23n53
Environmental benefits, 235, 238
Environmental damage, 238, 249, 250; responsibility for, 255–56
Environmental Defense Fund, 222; water leasing/transfer program by, 221
Environmentalists: management and, 281; water and, 288, 293; watershed process and, 284
Environmental laws: goals of, 235; hydrologic cycle and, 345–46n20; problems with, 235
Environmental protection, 236;

federal government and, 279, 280
Environmental Protection Agency,
250, 343n13; development and,
279; Grand Valley studies by, 318–
19n35; management and, 284;
section 404 of, 344n13
Environmental values, 171, 238; water
projects and, 254
Equality of rights, 303n44
Equitable apportionment doctrine,
303n44
Espresso stand, 182 (photo)
Evans, John: Sand Creek and, 20
Evaporation, 84, 173; desert, 140, 154;
losses to, 83, 120
Evapotranspiration, 173, 295n2; salt
concentration and, 317n24

Fallon, 167, 176; water for, 175
Fallon Indian Reservation: decline
of, 141; water for, 361n71
Fallon Naval Air Station, 164; water
for, 162
Fallon Paiute-Shoshone Indian
Reservation wetlands, 164
Fallon Paiute Shoshone Tribal
Settlement Act (1980), 162
*Farmers Highline Canal and Reservoir
Co. v. City of Golden,* 337–38n56
Federal Energy Regulatory Commis-
sion (FERC), 275, 353–54n61,
363n75; hydroelectric licensing/
relicensing and, 279
Federal government: development
and, 275; water resources and,
273–80; watershed partnerships
and, 280, 282. *See also* Water rights,
federal
Federal Land Policy and Manage-
ment Act (FLPMA) (1976), 362n74,
363n75; planning provisions and,
364n75
Federal Power Act (1920), 274–75,
354n61; changes to, 234
Federal Power Commission, 275,
353–54n61
Federal Water Power Act (1920), 353n61
Fellhauer, Roger: well digging by, 42
FERC. *See* Federal Energy Regula-

tory Commission
Fernley, 167, 176; water for, 175
Fifteen-Mile Reach, 124–25, 129;
endangered fish in, 271–72;
increased flows for, 131, 132,
327n66
First Food Feasts, Yakima and, 214
First National Bank, Fort Lyon and,
30
Fishing platforms, 186 (photo)
Fish ladders/screens, 252, 326n64
Fish migration, blocking, 120–21, 154
Flaming Gorge Dam, 308n94
Flip-flop, 215, 216, 249–50
Flood control, 232, 247, 251, 274, 275
Flood Control Act, 39
Flood irrigation, 128, 349n31
Floodplains, 248, 251
Floristan Rates, 162, 163
FLPMA. *See* Federal Land Policy and
Management Act
Forest Service, 362n75; in-stream
flows and, 363n75; multiple use/
sustained yield and, 364n75; right-
of-way regulations and, 365n79
Fort Lyon, 20, 21
Fort Lyon Canal, 14, 36, 42, 66, 73,
79, 261; appropriations by, 30;
assessment for, 65; Colorado
Water Conservation Board and,
78; CWS and, 62, 77; Henry and,
29, 30; irrigation from, 65; water
bank proposal for, 310–11n113
Fort Lyon Canal Company, 62, 63,
65; CWS and, 61, 64; divisions of,
66; reservoirs by, 32
Fort Lyon shares, 63, 64, 65; selling,
70, 310–11n113
Fountain Creek, irrigation along, 25
Fox, Stephen: on Muir, 331n47
Fradkin, Philip, 4, 119
Fremont, John C., 313n5; on Great
Basin, 143, 328–29n13; at Pyramid
Lake, 139
Fruita Town and Land Company, 89
Fryingpan-Arkansas Project (1962),
40, 44, 60, 65; Bureau of Reclama-
tion and, 117; water from, 304n53
Furrow irrigation, 128; salinity

control and, 319n35

Gardner, Wilford, 287

Garrard, Lewis: on Bent's farm, 25; on Lower Arkansas Valley, 17–18

Genova, Carl, 46 (photo), 84; on farming, 45–46

Geographical and Geological Survey of the Rocky Mountain Region, Powell and, 31

Gesell, Gerhard: OCAP and, 159

Getches, David, xi, 360n71

Gila Project, Wellton-Mohawk Division of, 110

Gilpin, William, 25, 31; irrigation and, 27, 54; settlement/ development and, 300n15

Glen Canyon Dam, 121, 308n94; flooding experiment and, 251, 252

Glenwood Power Canal and Pipeline, 116

Gobbo, Allen, 133

Gobbo, Bob, 133

Gobbo, Don, 133

Gobbo, Fritz, 133

Gobbo Farms and Orchards, 132–33

Golden Rule Dairy, 97

Gold mining, 18–19, 140, 314n8

Good Fruit Growing, 227

Government Highline Canal, 99, 110, 127, 316n19; changes for, 130; irrigation from, 133

Grand Junction, 237, 316n9; agriculture in, 105; ditches at, 93; Grand Valley and, 92; settlement of, 89

Grand Mesa, 92; Curriers at, 106

Grand Mesa National Forest, 106

Grand River. *See* Colorado River

Grand River Ditch, development of, 94–95

Grand Valley, 5, 90 (map), 91 (map), 96 (photo), 97 (photo), 202, 294, 314n5; Curriers in, 106; described, 92–93; diversions in, 115, 241, 250, 320–21n45; EPA studies in, 318–19n35; fruit production in, 102; growing season in, 93, 101; irrigation in, 93, 106–7, 113, 132–33, 231, 245, 253, 289–90; orchardists in, 97–98, 100–101; reservation in,

93, 315–16n9; salinity in, 109, 111, 268; settlement of, 89, 93, 109, 316n10; urbanization of, 105; water management in, 131–32

Grand Valley Canal, 29, 98

Grand Valley Ditch, 93, 94, 99

Grand Valley Irrigation Company (GVIC), 102, 111, 112, 122, 124, 130, 132; Currier and, 106; rights in, 115; salinity control and, 268; water-right shares and, 95

Grand Valley Irrigation Company Canal, 127

Grand Valley Power Plant, 122

Grand Valley Project, 96, 99, 100 (photo), 102, 240; dam for, 100; improvements in, 130; land for, 316n19

Grand Valley Salinity Control Project, 110–11, 319n35

Grand Valley Water Management Study, phases of, 327n70

Grand Valley Water Users Association (GVWUA), 99, 110, 112, 316n19, 327n70; Highline system and, 268; salinity control program for, 130

Grasses, x, 14, 25, 58 (photo) irrigation for, 59

Great Basin: described, 143, 328–29n13; Northern Paiute and, 138

Great Plains Reservoirs, 83

Greeley, Horace, 312n2

Green Mountain Reservoir, 116, 125; Blue River and, 321n49, 325n54; preferred beneficiaries of, 325n54; transmountain diversions and, 325n54

Green River, 312n3, 313–14n5

Groundwater, 2, 9, 42, 55, 167, 173, 248, 266; allocation issues and, 352n56; alluvial, 40; in Arkansas Valley, 305n61; development of, 270, 349n31; diversions of, 78; estimated, 304n56; grandfathered rights to, 349n31; movement of, 40; nonmanagement of, 348n31; overdraft of, 348n31; pumping, 40, 41–42, 44, 68, 304n60, 305n61;

rights to, 77; salinity in, 101; shortage of, 297n7; surface water and, 43, 305n60, 352–53n56; unregulated, 349n31; withdrawal of, 296n4, 351n36

Groves, James K., 43, 44

Gundy, Vern: delivery systems and, 268

Gunnison-Arkansas Project, 39–40, 305n63

Gunnison-Beckwith expedition, 313n5

Gunnison River, 39, 89, 313–14n5

GVIC. *See* Grand Valley Irrigation Company

GVWUA. *See* Grand Valley Water Users Association

Hamill, John, 123; Orchard Mesa check case and, 122; on recovery program, 124; water development and, 237

Harold D. Roberts Tunnel, 117, 324n54

Harris, Alex, 4, 352n46

Haskell, Otis L., 28–29, 30; Arkansas River Land Town and Canal Company and, 27

Hayden, Ferdinand Vandiveer: survey by, 31, 89, 274

Heki, Lisa, 160, 237

Henry, Norman, 176

Henry, Theodore C. (T. C.), 28, 32, 33, 76; Fort Lyon Canal and, 30, 31; Grand River Ditch and, 94, 95; irrigation and, 54; irrigation canals by, 28 (map), 29, 306n73; promotions by, 29

Hess, John: Fort Lyon and, 30

Hetch Hetchy Dam, 276, 308n94

Highline Canal. *See* Government Highline Canal

Hinderlider, Michael Creed, 38; dam proposal by, 37; strategy by, 39

Holbrook Canal, 45

Homestake Project, 117

Hoover Dam, 109, 275, 288, 308n94

Horse Creek, reservoir at, 32

Howard, Philip: on rules/initiative, 344n17

Howe, Charles: on water transfers, 57

Humboldt River, 144

Hydroelectricity, 116, 149, 150, 162, 211, 251–52, 253, 254, 274, 275; revenues from, 248, 276

Hydroelectric plants, 9, 212, 247, 289; fish kills by, 233; water for, 296n4

Hydrologic cycle, 236, 238, 347n20; human participation in, 345n20; interdependencies and, 346n20

Hydrology, 40–41; stream-aquifer, 43

Hydropower projects, 234; stream-flow protection and, 363n75

Idaho Department of Fish and Wildlife v. National Marine Fisheries Service (1944), 216–17

Imperial Irrigation District (IID): MWD and, 245, 260; State Water Resources Control Board and, 348n30

Independence Tunnel, 52

Indian Appropriation Act (1914), 335n33

Indian Service, 191, 334n27; diversion claim by, 190

Inland Water Commission, river-basin development and, 274

In-place claims, filing, 364n75

In Quest of Water (Milenski), 78

In-stream flows, 326n62, 341n92, 362n75; preserving, 270, 271

Interdependence, 240

Interior Department, 99, 165; benchlands/bottomlands and, 332n60; Caddoa dam and, 38; controlled flooding experiment by, 251; Glen Canyon Dam and, 252; Native American water rights and, 277; Truckee River and, 267; Yakima Project and, 190

Irrigated agriculture, xii, 2, 3, 6, 25, 36, 85, 101, 165, 167; in Crowley County, 259; environmental impact of, 287, 291; future of, 244–45, 290–91; housing developments and, 8; large-scale development and, 287–88; in Lower Arkansas Valley, 77; in Nevada, 144; problems for, 289–90; settlement and, 5; sustainable, 263; water for, 173; water quality problems and, 290–91; West and, xii-xiii, 263, 288, 290, 291

Irrigated cropland: average value of, 297n6; production from, 297n6; retirement of, 132, 297nn6, 7

Irrigation, 4, 41, 258; changing, 130–31; development of, 35; discontinuance of, 297–98n7; diversion and, 240; improving efficiency in, 244; standards/requirements for, 245–46; surface-water, 240

Irrigation districts, 4, 111, 206, 207, 337n55; water banks and, 261

Irrigation systems, 262–63; capital for, 260; efficiency of, 127; water-short, 129–30

Irrigation water, xii, 5, 64, 247, 349n31; efficient use of, 293; improving management of, 228; sale of, 298n7

Irrigators: drought and, 258; federal water projects and, 253; inefficient use of, 241; Newlands Project and, 268; suit by, 35–36, 43; water banks and, 261; water rights and, 258, 349n31

James, Edwin: on irrigation/agriculture, 25

John Day Dam, 210

John Martin Dam and Reservoir, 15, 39 (photo), 43, 78; Amity and, 84; completion of, 39; permanent pool of, 83

Jones, James C.: Lower Arkansas Valley and, 27

Jones, Wesley: allotments and, 191

Junior rights, 29, 198, 258, 272

Kachess Lake, 196, 334n31

Kahrl, William, 4

Kansas Pacific Railroad, 15

Keechelus Dam Site, camp at, 196 (photo)

Keechelus Lake, 183, 196, 334n31

Kennewick Division, 197, 211

Kennewick Irrigation District, 336n53, 340n81

Kittitas Division, 197, 335n33; consent decree and, 336n53

Kittitas Reclamation District, 222, 336n53

Kittitas Valley, 181, 183, 197

Klocker, Marcus, 102–3

Lahontan cutthroat trout, 137, 139, 175; demise of, 154

Lahontan Reservoir, 148, 148 (photo), 149 (photo), 152, 153, 156, 161, 165, 175; Carson River and, 330n27

Lahontan Valley, 156, 176, 294

Lahontan Valley Environmental Alliance, 164, 176

Lahontan Valley Restoration Trust, 175

Lahontan Valley wetlands, 156, 163, 167, 168; water for, 162; water-quality concerns in, 241; as Western Hemispheric Shorebird Reserve, 156

Lake Henry, 32, 53, 59

Lake Lahontan, 139

Lake McConaughy, 84

Lake Meredith, 32, 53

Lake Tahoe, 138, 145, 149, 153; dam at, 144, 147; snowmelt in, 330n25

Lake Winnemucca, 137; drying of, 154; Newlands Project and, 153, 154

Land of Little Rain, The (Austin), 4

Las Animas Town Ditch, 51

Laterals, 247; lining, 130

Lavender, David: on Arkansas River, 16

Laxalt, Paul, 162

Lease Oversight Committee, 221

Limiting Agreements, 190, 335n33

Little Naches, 209

Little Truckee River, 329n21; dam on, 151, 160

Littleworth, Arthur, 43

Lode Mining Law (1866), 353n59

Long, Stephen: expedition by, 25

Louisiana Purchase, exploring, 15, 16

Lower Arkansas River Commission, 83

Lower Arkansas Valley, 5, 13, 14, 261; agriculture in, 24–25; communities of, 75–76; future of, 293; gold rush and, 19; Indian claims to, 21; irrigation in, 8, 25–26, 231, 240, 259, 268, 289; overappropriation in, 240; trading in, 17; water rights in,

57, 258. *See also* Arkansas Valley
McCarran Act Amendment, 360n71;
  enactment of, 356n69
McCurry, Gordon: groundwater
  hydrology and, 304n55
McKinley Tariff Act (1890), sugar
  and, 33, 301n37
McNary Dam, 210
Maass, Arthur, 4
Management, xiii, 175, 365n79;
  centralization of, 236; comprehen-
  sive, 275, 355n67; cooperative, 236;
  environmental groups and, 281;
  geographically based, 283; goals of,
  263; improving, 77, 263; shortages
  and, 198–99
Mancos shales, 101, 109
Marble Bluff Dam, building, 160
Markoff, Dena, 33
Marsh, Malcolm: NMFS and, 217
Marshall, John: on legal status of
  tribes, 278
Martin, John: Flood Control Act
  and, 39
Martin, Russell, 4
Matchett, Kenneth, 128 (photo);
  siphon tubes and, 128
Maximum commitment, 43, 337n56
Mayordomo (Crawford), 4
Mead, Elwood, 239
Meeker, Nathaniel Cook, 93, 315n8
Mesa County Irrigation District,
  316n19, 317n20
Metropolitan Water District of
  Southern California (MWD), IID
  and, 245, 260
Mexicali Valley, 110
Middle Rio Grande Conservancy
  District, 7
Milenski, Frank, 11, 79, 79 (photo),
  288; irrigated agriculture and, 78;
  poem by, 80–82
Miles, Don: salinity analysis by, 48
Miller, Dave: on irrigated lands, 58–59
Mineral Leasing Act (1920), 322n53
Mining, 1–2, 3, 6; water for, 331n53
Minnow. *See* Colorado pikeminnow
Missouri Pacific Railroad, 32
Mitchell, Rex, 79

Moffat Tunnel, water through, 116
Morton, Rogers, 159
Mount Adams, 182, 187
Mount Rainier, 209
Muir, John, 163; ecology and,
  331n47; on Great Basin, 143, 328–
  29n13; Hetch Hetchy Dam and, 276
MWD. *See* Metropolitan Water
  District of Southern California

Naches River, 183, 195, 209; develop-
  ment of, 190; irrigation in, 215;
  salmon in, 213
National Beet Sugar Company, 32, 33
National Environmental Policy Act
  (1969), 250; text from, 233–34
National Forest Management Act
  (NFMA), 363n75
National Marine Fisheries Service
  (NMFS), 217
National pollutant discharge
  elimination system (NPDES),
  343n13
National Research Council Commit-
  tee on the Future of Irrigation,
  Gardner and, 287
National Sugar Manufacturing
  Company, 52, 54
National Water Commission, 358n70
Natural flow regimes, human
  alteration of, 255
Natural Resources Conservation
  Service (NRCS), 14; dams and, 250
Natural Resources Law Center, xiii,
  250; grant for, xi-xii
Nature Conservancy: Chisholm and,
  176; Newlands Project and, 163
Nature's Metropolis (Cronon), 287
Navigation, 37, 274, 275
Nee Gronda Reservoir, 84
Nee Noshe Reservoir, 83, 84 (photo)
NEPA, 234
Nepesta, 14, 26
Newell, Frederick H., 31, 145;
  Reclamation Service and, 144
Newlands, Francis G.: Reclamation
  Act and, 143; Truckee-Carson
  Project and, 145
Newlands Project, 145, 152, 153, 156,

165, 171–75, 177, 240, 241, 244, 245, 249, 277; Bureau of Reclamation and, 150; capital investment in, 174; establishment of, 144; farms within, 150; impact of, 159; irrigation and, 163, 167, 173–74, 268; litigation for, 207; Nature Conservancy and, 163; OCAP and, 161, 164; Reclamation Service and, 147, 148; settlement in, 148–49; USFWS and, 168; water rights and, 151, 172

New West, 4, 309n11; irrigated agriculture and, xii-xiii

NFMA. *See* National Forest Management Act

Ninth Circuit Court of Appeals, 332n60; Northwest Power Planning Council and, 217; Yakima treaty and, 214

NMFS. *See* National Marine Fisheries Service

"No injury" rule, 273

Nonproratable rights, 335n34, 341n90; proratable rights and, 198

Norman, Bob: on diversions, 127

Northern Colorado Water Conservancy District, 327n70

Northern Pacific Railroad, Yakima Valley and, 192

Northern Paiute, 137, 140; conflicts with, 141; Fremont and, 139; Great Basin and, 138

Northwest Power Planning Council, 211; approach of, 217

Northwest Resource Information Center v. Northwest Power Planning Council, 217

NPDES. *See* National pollutant discharge elimination system

NRCS. *See* Natural Resources Conservation Service

Oakes, Thomas: Yakima Valley and, 192

Oats, irrigating, 100 (photo)

OCAP. *See* Operating Criteria and Procedures

Ogallala Aquifer, 352n56

Oil-shale deposits, 117, 321–22n53

Old Jules (Sandoz), 4

Olney Springs, 58, 308n93

OMID. *See* Orchard Mesa Irrigation District

Operating Criteria and Procedures (OCAP), 156, 165, 168, 175, 332n60; cui-ui and, 162; Newlands Project and, 161; project efficiency and, 174; suit challenging, 159

Orchardists, Grand Valley, 97–98, 100–101, 103–5

Orchard Mesa, 92 (photo), 104 (photo), 316n19; pumping plant at, 122

Orchard Mesa Check, 122, 323–25n54, 324n54 (map)

Orchard Mesa Irrigation District (OMID), 99, 323n54; Reclamation Service and, 100; taxing/bonding by, 100

Orchard Mesa Power Canal, 100

Orchard Mesa Pumping Plant, 100, 122

Ordway, 57 (photo); prison at, 57, 308n93

Oregon Water Resources Code, on conservation, 347–48n28

Orr Ditch Decree, 151

Osgood, John C.: Colorado Fuel Company and, 302n40

Otero Canal, 14, 306n73

Otero Ditch Company, 51

Overcommitment, 240; subsidies and, 8

Owens Valley, Los Angeles and, 258–59

Oxford Farmers' Canal, 14, 46

Pabor, William E., 31, 54, 87, 312n2; on cattle ranchers, 299–300n14; Fruita Town and Land Company and, 89; irrigation development by, 27; on irrigation systems, 25–26; promotion by, 24–25

Pacific Institute, on sustainability, 232

Palisade Irrigation District, 107, 316n19, 316–17n20

Palmer, William Jackson, 302n40

Patterson Hollow Water Quality Improvement Program, 46–47

Peaches, 102; packing, 103–5, 105 (photo)

Peach-mosaic virus, problems with, 102

Pelcyger, Robert, 159, 236

PIA standard, 357n69

Piceance Creek Basin, oil-shale

deposits at, 321–22n53

Pickett Act (1919), 362n74

Pike, Zebulon, 25; explorations of, 15–16

Pinchot, Gifford: natural resource management and, 274

Pitkin, Governor: White River Massacre and, 315n8

Plant growth, 295–96n2

Platte River, ix, 299n1; endangered fish in, 272; headwaters of, 259; Two Forks and, 308n94

Point source, 343n13

Pollution, 235, 238, 342nn7, 93, 343n13

Polyols, 318n24

Powell, John Wesley, 119, 145; survey by, 31, 144, 274

Power Canal, 323n54

Prairie Cattle Company, land control by, 27

Preliminary Settlement Agreement, 162, 163, 164, 331n46

Price-Stubb Ditch, 122, 316n19

Pricing: full-cost, 253; per-unit, 262; tiered, 246

Prior appropriation, 189, 358n70; altering, 242–43; perverse consequences of, 132; riparian doctrine and, 302–3n44; stability of, 359n70

"Privileges Secured to Indians" treaty (1855), 213

Procter, Vernon, 46

Productive harmony, 9, 234

Progressive Movement: natural resource management and, 236, 274; river-basin development and, 274

Proratable rights, 335n34, 341n90; nonproratable rights and, 198

Prosser Dam, 160, 199, 341n90; diversion at, 211–12; flows at, 221; Reclamation and, 212; salmon at, 210

Prowers, John Wesley: Lower Arkansas Valley and, 27

Public Law 101–618 (1990), 162; OCAP and, 164; section 206 of, 163; water-use efficiency and, 164

Public Service Company, 116, 323n54

Pueblo Board of Waterworks, transactions by, 51

Pueblo Dam, 45, 60, 310n113;

construction of, 44

Pure Food and Drug Act (1906), 102

Purgatoire River, 15, 16, 18, 25, 26

Pyramid Lake, 137, 138, 139 (photo), 160, 163, 177; Anaho Island and, 156; cui-ui at, 249, 329n21; decline of, 154; fishery at, 167, 175, 267; Fremont at, 139; historical levels for, 155 (fig.); Newlands Project and, 153, 159; Paiute at, 141; stored water in, 330n25; Truckee River and, 161–62; water for, 162

Pyramid Lake Indian Reservation, establishment of, 141

Pyramid Lake Paiute, 167, 172, 173, 176, 340n85; water for, 159, 267, 277, 361n71

Quackenbush, Justin, 214, 215

Queen Reservoir, 84

Rainfall, x, 25; inadequate, 1

Ramsar Convention. *See* Convention on Wetlands of International Importance

Ransel, Katherine, 225, 237

Rattlesnake Hills, 183, 199

Razorback suckers, 119, 122, 123

Reasonable use, 338n56, 348n30

Reclamation Act (1902), 2, 143, 274; passage of, 288; Roosevelt and, 144

Reclamation movement, 288; emergence of, 231

Reclamation projects, 168, 206; federal, 232

Reclamation Projects Authorization and Adjustment Act (1992), 350n33

Reclamation Reform Act (1982), 223

Reclamation Service, 31, 102, 334n27; alfalfa and, 149; dams by, 195, 196; Grand Valley Salinity Control Unit and, 110; irrigation laws and, 189–90; Newlands Project and, 147, 148; OMID and, 100; project by, 98, 111; report by, 191; Sunnyside Canal and, 192, 194, 199; water-supply systems by, 36; Yakima Basin and, 189. *See also* Bureau of Reclamation

Recovery Implementation Program

for Endangered Fish Species in the Upper Colorado River Basin, 122; participants in, 326n62

Recreational uses, 85, 232; concerns about, 267

Redds, 209, 210, 214, 215, 339n70; maintenance of, 216. *See also* Salmon

Redlands Diversion Dam, 123

Rehyer, Dave, 73, 85; on farming, 72

Rehyer, Kent, 85; on CWS, 69, 72; farming by, 66–67, 69; on Fort Lyon system, 62, 67, 68–69; on water issues, 70

Reid, Harry, 164, 176; water matters and, 162

Reid, Mary, 176, 176, 237

Reisner, Marc, 4, 288

"Relief to water users" acts (1922, 1923, 1924), 303n46

"Report on Agriculture by Irrigation in the Western Part of the United States" (Newell), 31

Report on the Lands of the Arid Region of the United States, With a More Detailed Account of the Lands of Utah (Powell), 31

"Report on the State of the Water Resources of the Yakima River Basin," 226

Re-regulation reservoirs, 130, 202

Research Natural Areas (RNAs), 364n75

Reservations, water for, 192, 219, 277, 278, 334n23, 357n69, 361n71

Resource Investment Group, Ltd. (RIG), 53

Resources, 232, 238; control of, 265, 266, 286; developers and, 266; federal government and, 273–80; full use of, 9; human diversions of, 239; ranching/agricultural heritage and, 292; reallocation of, 168; value/importance of, 235

Retention pond, 47 (photo)

Return flows, 47 (photo), 48, 241, 242, 266, 350n32; limits on, 272; salinity and, 319–20n35; silt-laden, 130

Rice, Teresa, xii, xiii; water resource protection and, 364n75

RIG. *See* Resource Investment

Group, Ltd.

Ringle, Allen: Colorado Canal and, 60

Rio Grande, ix, 7, 299n1

Rio Grande Western, 89

Riparian areas: flooding and, 251; loss of, 233

Riparian doctrine, 36, 358n70; prior-appropriation doctrine and, 302–3n44

River No More, A (Fradkin), 4, 119

River of Traps, A (deBuys and Harris), 4

Rivers: altering, 247, 293; development of, 4, 9, 275; impact of dams on, 249; restoring, 9; surveyed, 342n7; well-functioning, 248

Rivers of Empire (Worster), 4

RNAs. *See* Research Natural Areas

Roaring Fork, 39

Robertson, Jack: on watershed partnerships, 284

Rocky Ford Canal, 14

Rocky Ford Ditch, 23–24, 30, 36, 46, 53; building of, 25–26; Colorado Canal and, 55; irrigation appropriations by, 26

Rocky Ford Ditch Company, 24

Rocky Ford Highline Canal, 14

Rocky Ford Highline Canal Company, 46

Rocky Ford Highline Ditch, 46

Rocky Ford Highline Ditch Company, 51

Roller Dam, 98 (photo), 99, 122, 132; diversions at, 130; Orchard Mesa and, 323n54

Romer, Roy, 15; CWS deal and, 63; Lower Arkansas River Commission and, 83

Romero, Jacobo, 352n46

Roosevelt, Franklin Delano, 38; public-works projects and, 39; Winnemucca Lake and, 154

Roosevelt, Theodore: natural resource management and, 274; Reclamation Act and, 144

Rowan, A. C. and Bonnie, 62

Roza Diversion Dam, 200; fish passageway at, 212 (photo); Reclamation and, 213

Roza Division, 197, 199, 335n33;

consent decree and, 336n53; described, 200–201; improvements in, 203

Roza Irrigation District, 199, 201, 202, 216, 221, 227, 240, 268; water delivery/use systems and, 201

Roza-Sunnyside Board of Joint Control, 227

Ruedi Reservoir, 125; construction of, 326–27n66; transmountain diversions and, 325n54

Runoff, 227, 247

St. Charles Mesa, 14

St. Vrain, Ceran, 16, 17

Salinity, 68, 69, 128, 317–18n24; in Arkansas River, 47–48, 49, 59; in Colorado River, 111, 241; controlling, 110–13, 129, 319n35; damages from, 112; drinking water and, 110; in Grand Valley, 101, 109–10; in groundwater, 101; plants and, 317–18n24; resisting, 49, 318n24 ; return flows and, 319–20n35

Salmon, 184, 197, 225, 253, 339n69; commercial fishing for, 214; protecting, 216–17; spawning needs of, 249–50. See also Chinook salmon; Redds

San Acacia Diversion Dam, 7

Sand Creek Massacre (1864), 19–21, 26, 29; monument to, 21 (photo)

Sandoz, Marie, 4

Santa Fe Trail, 15, 17, 299n4

Schank, Ernie, 176, 333n66

Schiel, James, 313n5

Schroeder, Ricky, 133

Searching Out the Headwaters, xi

Section 404 program (Clean Water Act), 279

Sediments, depositing of, 120, 248, 249

Senior rights, 239; displacing, 281

Settlement Act (1990), 176

Sharon, William, 143

Shasta Dam, water-temperature control at, 252

Shelton, Phil: on frontier/culture, 227

Shepard, Bill, 176

Shortages, water management and, 198–99

Short-grass prairies, x, 14, 25

Shoshone-Bannock tribes, 16; water for, 361n71

Shoshone Power Plant, 116, 118, 321n49

Side oats, 58 (photo)

Sierra Nevada, 138–39, 151

Sierra Pacific Power Company, 162

Simpson, James H.: on Carson Lake, 140

Siphons, 128, 128 (photo), 247

Snake River, 183, 186; salmon in, 211

Snake River Basin Adjudication (SRBA), 362n74

SOAC. See Systems Operation Advisory Committee

Socorro Main Canal, 7

Soil Conservation Service (USDA), 14; gate pipes and, 129. See also Natural Resources Conservation Service

Soluskin, Delano: on irrigation system, 225; mainstream culture and, 224

Southeastern Colorado Water Conservancy District, 44, 65, 78, 268, 304n53

Southeastern Project. See Fryingpan-Arkansas Project

South Platte River. See Platte River

Special Water Districts: Challenge for the Future, xii

Spill ditches, 129

Springer, Paul: farming by, 73–74

Sprinkler irrigation, 111, 349n31; salinity control and, 319n35

SRBA. See Snake River Basin Adjudication

Stampede Reservoir, 151, 160, 249; Washoe Project and, 329n21

States: allocation issues and, 359n70; development and, 269–73; as guardians/trustees, 270–71; water banks and, 273; water rights and, 257; watershed partnerships and, 280

State Water Resources Control Board, IID and, 348n30

Stauffacher, Walter E.: adjudication and, 223, 337n56; on irrigation districts, 336–37n55; procedural "pathways" by, 205; threshold issues and, 206; water-right quantification and, 338n56; water day and, 205; water rights and, 207, 336n47; Yakima water rights and, 206, 216

Stegner, Wallace, 292, 294; on aridity, 4

Stevens, Isaac F., 185

Stillwater Area Remediation Plan, 164

Stillwater Marsh, 137, 153, 155, 330n27; wetlands of, 140

Stillwater National Wildlife Refuge, 164

Stillwater Slough, 140, 155

Stillwater Wildlife Management Area, 164

Stock-Raising Homestead Act (1916), 362n74

Storage, 334n31; capacity, 76, 249, 263; compensatory, 321n49; dead, 84

Story That Stands Like a Dam, A (Martin), 4

Strauss, Michael: on development, 303n52

Stream flows: fish and, 346n20; improvement of, 241; minimum, 365n79

Subsidies, 226; overuse and, 8

Suburbanization, ix, 112

Sugar-beet industry, 32–34, 301n37; decline of, 53–54; viability of, 34

Sugar beets, 24, 34; decline of, 103; water supply for, 54, 99

Sugar City: decline of, 57–58; processing facility at, 32, 33, 34

Sunnyside Canal, 200 (photo), 335n33; government purchase of, 192, 195; Reclamation and, 194, 199; Yakima Project and, 192

Sunnyside Dam, 212–13, 341n90; flows at, 221; salmon at, 213

Sunnyside District, 199, 202, 227, 268, 342n93

Sunnyside Division, 199, 200, 201, 202, 335n34; consent decree and, 336n53; described, 199; diversion from, 212; improvements in, 203

Surface water, 241; adjudication of, 205; groundwater and, 41–42, 43, 270, 305n60, 352–53n56; irrigation with, 240; shortage of, 297n7; withdrawals of, 351n36

Surge systems, 48 (photo), 111

Sustainability, 232, 233, 341n87; changes for, 252; irrigated agriculture and, 263; movement toward, 293; water-use, 236, 237

Swink, George Washington: cantaloupes and, 24; ditch by, 23–24; irrigation and, 27, 32; at Rocky Ford, 23; Rocky Ford Ditch and, 24, 25–26; sugar beets and, 32

Systems Operation Advisory Committee (SOAC), 215, 216, 220, 225

Taft, William Howard, 99

Talbott, Harry: on Grand Valley/agriculture, 133–34; packing plant by, 103–5, 105 (photo)

Talbott Farms, 104 (photo)

Tariff Act (1894), passage of, 301n37

TCID. *See* Truckee-Carson Irrigation District

Teanaway River, salmon in, 222

Thermoelectric generation, 240, 296n4

Third Regiment (Colorado Volunteer Cavalry), Sand Creek and, 20–21

Thomson, Charles L. (Tommy), 45, 268; winter water storage and, 44

Tieton Canal, building, 195 (photo)

Tieton Dam: building, 194 (photo); storage at, 334n31

Tieton Division, 183, 195, 196, 335nn33, 34; consent decree and, 336n53

Tomichi Creek, 314n5

Tomky, Karen: on CLADCO, 55

Tomky, Orville, 55, 56; Colorado Canal and, 60; irrigation and, 59–60

Total water supply available (TWSA), 198, 201, 336n53; Yakima and, 222

Transfers, 259, 260, 310n113; agricultural-to-urban, 262; economic impact of, 57; facilitating, 273; reviewing, 354n67

Travelers Insurance Company, 29, 94–95

Treaty of Fort Laramie (1851), South Platte/Arkansas and, 18

Treaty of Fort Wise (1861), 19
Trickle irrigation, salinity control
    and, 319n35
Trout Unlimited, 236
Truckee Canal, 146 (photo), 147, 148,
    149 (photo), 175
Truckee-Carson Basin, 5, 138 (map);
    development of, 147, 171–72; irrigation
    in, 231, 244, 253, 290; water rights
    and, 172; water-use changes in, 15
Truckee-Carson Irrigation District
    (TCID), 164, 165, 174, 175, 176, 251,
    268; Bureau of Reclamation and,
    150; Pyramid Lake fishery and, 267
Truckee-Carson Project. *See*
    Newlands Project
Truckee-Carson-Pyramid Lake
    Water Rights Settlement Act, 162
Truckee Division, 147, 173, 175
Truckee Meadows, 140, 144, 151, 329n21
Truckee River, 137, 138, 140, 144, 151;
    Carson Division and, 175; control-
    ling, 267; diversions from, 156, 161,
    162, 174, 249, 251, 268; Newlands
    Project and, 153; Paiute at, 141; public
    lands on, 145; Pyramid Lake and,
    161–62; water development in, 155
Truckee River Operating Agreement,
    164
Truckee Storage Project, 329n21
Trull, Jim, 202–3, 228
Tuck, Bob, 236; natural-resource
    development/use activities and,
    284; salmon and, 209; Watershed
    Council and, 225
*Tulare Irrigation District v. Lindsay-
    Strathmore Irrigation District* (1935),
    348n30
Twain, Mark, 145
"20/20 Vision for a Viable Future of
    the Water Resource of the Yakima
    Basin, A," 226
Twin Lakes Land and Water
    Company, advertisement for, 33
    (repro.)
Twin Lakes Reservoir, 32, 33, 54;
    CLADCO and, 53; water storage
    at, 52
Twin Lakes Reservoir and Canal

Company, 51, 52, 54
Two Forks Dam, 61, 308n94
TWSA. *See* Total water supply
    available

Udall, Stewart, 251; OCAP and, 156,
    159
Uintah Reservation, 93
Uncompahgre River, 313–14n5, 316n9
Union Colony, 312n2, 315n8
Union Gap, 182, 183, 199
U.S. Army, ditch construction by, 27
U.S. Fish and Wildlife Service
    (USFWS), 7, 339n64; Colorado Pike-
    minnow Recovery Team and, 121;
    development and, 279; endangered
    species and, 154, 271, 272; Fifteen-Mile
    Reach and, 124–25; on irrigation
    diversions, 129; management by,
    284, 294; Newlands Project and,
    164, 168; Recovery Implementation
    Program and, 326n62
U.S. Geological Survey, water
    development and, 239–40
U.S. Salinity Laboratory, 49
U.S. Supreme Court: *Arizona* and, 356–
    57n69; Arkansas River and, 43, 44;
    equitable apportionment and, 37;
    Kansas irrigators suit at, 35–36;
    Kansas and, 302–3n44; PIA standard
    and, 357n69; on reservation/water,
    277; *Winters* and, 356n68; *Wyoming*
    and, 357n69; Yakima Project and, 207
U.S. Water Resources Council, 233
Upper Colorado River Recovery
    Program, 122, 131
Urbanization, ix, 1, 3–4, 5, 112, 295n1,
    351n36; agricultural water users
    and, 289; in Grand Valley, 105;
    water for, 7, 259, 260, 351n36; on
    Western Slope, 117–18
Use standards, 76–77, 243
USFWS. *See* U.S. Fish and Wildlife
    Service
Ute Indians: Grand Valley and, 92–
    93; removal of, 93, 316n10; tensions
    with, 315n8; treaties with, 314n8

Valliant, Jim, 48 (photo)

Van de Wetering, Sarah Bates, xii, xiii
Van Gundy, Ron: Roza District and, 202

Wagner, Mel, 225, 226, 226, 237; Watershed Council and, 224
Walker Lake, Paiute at, 141
Wapato Division, 187, 197, 335n33; consent decree and, 336n53; diversion from, 212; irrigation within, 192
Wapato Project, 335n34, 336n53, 340n81
Wapatox Diversion Dam, 213
Warren Act (1921, 1936), 334n27, 336n47
Washington Department of Ecology, 221, 222, 223, 342n93; surface-water rights and, 205; Yakima River and, 227
Washington Department of Fisheries, SOAC and, 215
Washington Irrigation Company, Sunnyside Canal and, 192
Washington Supreme Court, adjudication and, 335n42
Washoe Project, 151; Marble Bluff Dam and, 160; Stampede Reservoir and, 329n21
Wastewater, 67, 94, 129
Watasheamu Reservoir, 151
Water: as amenity, 288; capturing/ transporting, x; culture/ tradition and, 257; development/use of, 4, 6, 239, 257; ecological values of, 232; economic dependence on, 267; efficient use of, 241, 272; as lifeblood, 8; public values of, 232; reallocation of, 6, 176–77, 261, 293. *See also* Irrigation water
Water and Power (Kahrl), 4
Water banks: ditch/district level, 261, 262; drought and, 260; effectiveness of, 263; renting water from, 310–11n113; states and, 273; water rights and, 261, 262
Water conflicts, 7, 288
Water development, 9, 232, 237, 246; in California, 269; federal, 280; infrastructure for, 255–56, 257, 265; large-scale, 171, 258, 287–88; loss of

public support for, 265; reduced flows from, 36; states and, 269–73. *See also* Water projects
Water duties, 152, 350n31
Water-flow modeling, 319n35
Water laws, xi, 165, 189–90; changes in, 305n61; clarifications of, 242; priority system of, 29; in South Africa, 346–47n20; structural problems with, 132
Watermelons, 24, 67, 68
Water projects: beneficiaries of, 254–55; environmental values and, 254; federal, 251–55, 276, 280, 355–56n67; irrigators and, 253; market-driven, 254–55; shortcomings of, 253; state-level ownership/ management of, 355–56n67. *See also* Development; Water development
Water quality, 343n7, 345–46n20; alternative crops and, 69; concerns about, 227, 267, 290–91; federal laws and, 235–36; managing, 47; parameters for, 227; problems with, 157, 233; protecting, 345n18; standards for, 350n32
Water Resource Code (Montana), on salvage, 348n29
Water Resources Planning Act (WRPA) (1965), 275, 354n62
Water rights, 145, 173, 174, 175, 265; appurtenant, 257; buying, 51–52, 259, 260, 269, 364n75; defining, 272–73, 335n43, 337n56; environmental perspective on, 267; establishment of, 207; federal, 277, 278, 364n75, 356n69, 359n70, 361n72; junior, 29, 198, 258, 272; Native American, 205–6, 277, 278, 356n69, 358–59n70, 360–61n71; as property rights, 266; reliance on, 267; securing, 274, 360n71; selling, 94, 168, 261, 262; senior, 42, 332n53; state, 257, 278; transfer of, 207, 332n59; uncertainty of, 222
Water-rights holders: in California, 269; conservation and, 348n28; protection for, 266–69; status quo and, 268; as stewards, 267;

watershed partnerships and, 280
Watershed partnerships, 9, 265–66;
appeal of, 285; decision making/
management and, 281; develop-
ment of, 280–86; future for, 282–
83; governmental entities and, 283
Water suppliers, xiii; urban, 269
Water supply, 274, 275; security/
reliability of, 262
Water: The Answer to a Desert's Prayer
(Milenski), 78
Water use: changing, 9, 228, 232, 240,
242, 288–89; efficiency standards
for, 269; measuring, 172; transfer
of, 258
Weber, Kenneth, 54; on Colorado
Canal, 55; on Crowley County/
operators, 55, 56
Wellton-Mohawk Division (Gila
Project), 110
Wenatchee Mountains, 183
West: development and, 292, 293,
298n9; growth of, 4, 231–32, 292,
298n9, 309–10n111; irrigated
agriculture and, 290, 291; migration
to, 309–10n111; population of,
296n4; urbanization of, 117–18,
295n1; water and, 9, 288. *See also*
New West
Western Area Power Administration,
250, 274; Recovery Implementation
Program and, 326n62
Western Water Policy Review
Advisory Commission, 232
Wetlands, 171, 175, 177, 234, 292;
described, 140; drought and, 156,
157; filling of, 346n20; habitat of,
156; loss of, 233, 236
Wheeler, George M.: survey by, 31
White River Massacre, 315n8
Wild and Scenic Rivers Act (1968),
234, 279, 343n11
Wilkinson, Charles, xi, xiii, 4, 15, 290,
292
Willamette River, salmon in, 214
Williams Fork system, 116, 325n54
Wind River Indian Reservation,
water for, 357n69
Winnemucca Lake National Wildlife
Refuge, 154
Winters Doctrine, 356n69, 358–59n70
Winters v. United States, water rights
and, 360n71
Wolford Mountain Reservoir, 325n54
Worster, Donald, 4
WRPA. *See* Water Resources
Planning Act
Wynkoop, Major: Sand Creek and, 20
Wyoming v. United States (1989), 357n69

Yakima (city), 183, 199; population of,
182
Yakima Adjudication, 277
Yakima Basin, 5, 183, 221, 270;
adjudication in, 214, 272, 277;
agriculture in, 219; allocation/use
structure in, 219–20; conservation
in, 241; development/management
of, 275, 338n57; diversion in, 240;
irrigation in, 184, 189, 226, 228; old
West in, 181; reclamation in, 219;
salmon in, 211; storage in, 226;
sustainability in, 341n87; water
rights in, 205, 258, 339n57
Yakima Basin Trustees, 221
Yakima County Courthouse: claims
filed at, 205; fire at, 189; water day
at, 205
Yakima Enhancement Act, 221
Yakima Indians, 220; fishing rights
of, 214; Lewis and Clark and, 185;
SOAC and, 215; treaties with, 186–
87, 216; water rights of, 190, 214,
216, 224, 277
Yakima Project, 190, 191, 193 (map),
197, 199, 201, 215, 220, 222; appropriation for, 206; approval of, 192;
building, 196; Bureau of Reclamation and, 216; dams in, 249; delivery
obligations of, 197; Interior Department and, 190; management of,
223; office of, 220 (photo); Sunnyside Canal and, 192; Supreme
Court and, 207; Tieton/Sunnyside
units of, 190; Wapato Division of,
187; water-management plan for,
215; Yakima Nation and, 216
Yakima Reservation, 190; allotments

on, 187; life on, 186–87; population of, 333n10; water for, 192, 219, 334n23
Yakima River, 186 (photo), 198, 199, 202; administration of, 223; anadromous fishery in, 220, 223; dams along, 196; development of, 190, 220–21; diversion from, 200; drainage area of, 182–83; flows in, 215; headwaters of, 183; irrigation from, 211, 220; overappropriation from, 221, 224; rights to, 191–92; salmon in, 184, 211, 213, 214, 222, 277; TWSA concept and, 222
Yakima River Basin Systems Operation Advisory Committee, 206

Yakima River Basin Water Enhancement Project Act (1993), 220, 339n64
Yakima River Watershed Council: business community and, 225, 228; emergence of, 224, 282
Yakima Tribal Courts, 191
Yakima Valley, 180 (map), 187, 294; agricultural production in, 183–84; Indians in, 186; irrigation in, 196, 231, 253, 289; Watershed Council and, 224
Yardas, David, 175
Yosemite National Park, 276
Young, Robert, 56, 57

Zinko, Don, 62